Injury to Insult

Injury to Insult

Unemployment, Class,
and Political Response

Kay Lehman Schlozman
and Sidney Verba

HARVARD UNIVERSITY PRESS
Cambridge, Massachusetts
and London, England 1979

Library of Congress Cataloging in Publication Data
Schlozman, Kay Lehman, 1946-
Injury to insult.

Includes index.
1. Unemployed—United States—Political activity. 2. Labor and
laboring classes—United States—Political activity. 3. Political
participation—United States.
I. Verba, Sidney, joint author. II. Title.
HD8076.S34   322'.2'0973   79-13963
ISBN 0-674-45441-3

To Elliot and Frances Lehman
and to the memory of Morris and Recci Verba,
who taught us, among other important things,
the seriousness of work

Acknowledgments

We are grateful for assistance from many people in the course of our research. For yeoperson's service in various capacities we should like to thank Shawn Lampron for general research assistance; Sarah Salter for splendid interviewing; and Walter Mebane, Stanley Reichgott, Diana Sam-Vargas, and Pamela White for perseverance at the computer. Jae-on Kim patiently and generously helped us through the complexities of our multivariate analyses. Mike Fine of George Fine Associates gave sound advice on the design of our survey and supervised the interviewing.

A number of students at Boston College and Harvard also aided us: Kevin Jackman, James Leake, Ed Reade, Charles Ridewood, and Pamela Werrbach with general research tasks; Alfredo Assad and Gail Horde with interviewing; Anthony Buono and Leon Novikas with data processing.

Mary Erbafina, Yvette Forget, Kenje Gleason, Joan Hornig, and Rachel Macurdy demonstrated the acumen of detectives as they typed and retyped a manuscript often in disarray.

We acknowledge the kind permission of Random House, Inc., to reprint an excerpt from "The Unknown Citizen," from W. H. Auden, *The Collected Poems*, edited by Edward Mendelsohn (copyright 1940, renewed 1968 by W. H. Auden).

Financial support for data gathering and analysis was provided by the Center for International Affairs of Harvard University, the Department of Political Science of Boston College, and the New Prospect Foundation.

We are blessed that a number of good colleagues double as good friends. From Kristi Andersen, Jane Hughes, Jae-on Kim, Norman Nie, and Kenneth Prewitt we received careful and constructive readings.

One person merits special mention. Stanley Schlozman provided a clipping and courier service; a sense of humor to keep us from taking ourselves as seriously as he took us; and other services, intellectual and personal, too numerous to mention.

K.L.S.
S.V.

Contents

Tables

Figures

Pericles . . . sent out sixty galleys every year, manned for eight months, with a considerable number of the citizens, who were both paid for their service, and improved themselves as mariners. He likewise sent a colony of a thousand men to the Chersonesus, five hundred to Naxos, two hundred and fifty to Andros, a thousand into the country of the Bisaltæ in Thrace, and others into Italy, who settled in Sibaris, and changed its name to Thurii. These things he did, to clear the city of an useless multitude, who were very troublesome when they had nothing to do.

—Plutarch's Lives

Was he free? Was he happy? The question is absurd: Had anything been wrong, we should certainly have heard.

—W. H. Auden

CHAPTER 1

Introduction

I N THE COURSE of their history Americans have been divided by issues as divergent as marijuana and McCarthy, as transient as Masonry, and as enduring as race. The fault lines of political conflict have at times been regional, at times ethnic, at times cultural, at times ideological. However important these social and cultural issues have been as a historical theme, the leitmotif of American politics—and, for that matter, of the politics of just about every industrial democracy— is economic conflict. In various guises (the tariff, free coinage of silver, the minimum wage, Social Security, to name a few) economic issues have never been long absent from the political agenda, and conflict between economic groups has been frequent. Since the New Deal, as a matter of fact, economic cleavages have been built into our political process by a party system that is divided more or less on economic lines.

This is a book about the links between economic strain in personal life and conduct in public life, about the process by which individual economic stress becomes—or fails to become—the stuff of politics. More specifically, it is a study of one particular group of economically strained individuals, the unemployed, and the way in which they take part in American politics. We shall have occasion to look closely at the unemployed: who they are, how they interpret their joblessness, what they do about it, how they view the American social order, how they vote or otherwise take part in politics.

This is not simply a report on the political behavior of the unemployed, however. Our purpose is much more general. We are interested in a set of intertwined themes about political life in America. One theme is micro-political: the relationship between the stresses individuals confront in

their personal lives—in this case economic stress—and their political attitudes and behavior. Out of this concern grows another. What we learn
about the circumstances under which individuals convert deeply felt
strains—in our study, economic strains—in their private lives into attitudes and actions that are relevant to politics will help us to understand
the overall shape of the American political agenda and to identify the
sorts of issues about which citizens are likely to mobilize politically.

Serving as a background for our discussion of these questions is an ongoing concern with the role of economic class in American politics. We
focus on the relation between class and politics for two reasons. First, the
economic deprivation that accompanies unemployment is really an especially acute, if usually temporary, form of the long-term economic disadvantage suffered by those of lower socioeconomic position. Thus, the
politics of unemployment is actually a case study in class politics. Furthermore, although the unemployed are a diverse group drawn from all
social categories, they come disproportionately from groups that are in
some way disadvantaged. They are drawn disproportionately from those
with low incomes, little education, and low-status jobs; from the ranks of
blacks, women, and the young. A majority of those who are out of work
suffer, then, from some kind of double jeopardy: an ongoing disadvantage associated with socioeconomic position, race, sex, or youth and a
shorter-term strain associated with joblessness. Hence our title: to insult
is added injury.

Our study of the unemployed is therefore animated by concern with
more general issues. Although we use what we learn about the unemployed to amplify larger questions, our interest in joblessness is not merely as a case study. Political scientists often look at particular examples—
revenue sharing in Tulsa, a mayoral election in Topeka—because they
shed light on more general propositions. In our concern with such general
propositions we wish not to lose sight of the intrinsic significance of our
subject. Unemployment matters, not simply because it can be used as a
key to enlarged understanding of the American political process, but because it affects the lives of so many Americans—those who are or have
been themselves out of work, who depend upon others who are jobless,
who are threatened with job loss; and as we shall see, those who are so
affected often suffer considerable hardship. Thus, in our exploration of
general issues, we hope not to neglect the importance of the particular
context in which we choose to pursue them, joblessness.

We should make one thing clear at the outset. We are not economists.
It is not our purpose to recommend economic solutions to the problem of
widespread unemployment. If we describe the unemployed as disadvantaged—and we do—we do not presume to recommend policies for the

alleviation of their distress. It is not our object either to evaluate which policy, or mix of policies, would do most to help the large number of people who are out of work or suffer from job insecurity, or to measure whether the costs of such policies—dollars diverted from other purposes, potential work disincentives, risk of inflation—justify the benefits to the unemployed. If we are partisan in diagnosing unemployment as a real problem, we are agnostic in prescribing treatments. Still, the data we present about the human costs of unemployment would presumably be relevant to the formation of employment policy. To repeat, we do not presume to be able to weigh those costs against the costs of the policies designed to alleviate the distress of those who are out of work. That we describe the unemployed as "disadvantaged" and find surprising their political quiescence does not necessarily imply that we feel the government should be doing more in their behalf.

The Unemployed: A Puzzle

Although joblessness has never again reached the staggering proportions of the nineteen thirties, unemployment in the United States has remained a gnawing problem since World War II..The rate has fluctuated in the ensuing decades, rising to disturbing levels during the late Eisenhower years, falling during the sixties, and then, during the mid-seventies, reaching levels unprecedented since the depression and remaining high for an extended period of time. Regardless of the standard that is used to measure full employment (the conventional 4 percent, or the 5 percent recommended by many economists), as Eli Ginzberg puts it, there is no question that unemployment has been a continuing problem:

> For many years American economists have assumed that if the unemployment rate is 4 percent or lower, there is a rough balance between jobs and job seekers. Recently conservatively inclined economists have argued that the "natural rate of unemployment" has risen to 5 percent or even higher, to allow for the growing number of women and young people in the labor force. Using the higher figure, we find four poor years in the 1950's (1950, 1954, 1958 and 1959), five bad years a' the beginning of the 1960's and five bad years in the 1970's. This makes a total of 14 out of 27 years in which unemployment was excessive. If we accept the more conventional figure of 4 percent as the norm for unemployment, we find that only seven of the 27 years meet the test of adequacy: three years near the beginning of the 1950's (during the Korean war) and the last four years of the 1960's (during the Vietnam war).[1]

[1]Eli Ginzberg, *Good Jobs, Bad Jobs, No Jobs* (Cambridge, Mass.: Harvard University Press, 1979), p. 35. Originally from "The Job Problem," *Scientific American*, 237 (November 1977), 47.

That unemployment has been an ongoing problem in the United States is made clear by the data in Figure 1-1, in which the unemployment rates of nine industrial democracies are compared. Although joblessness rose virtually everywhere during the mid-1970s, and although many European nations have in recent years borne rates of unemployment that might once have been considered intolerable, the rate of unemployment in the United States and Canada consistently has been significantly higher than in Western Europe or Japan. And these differences cannot be fully explained by discrepancies in the ways the unemployed are enumerated.

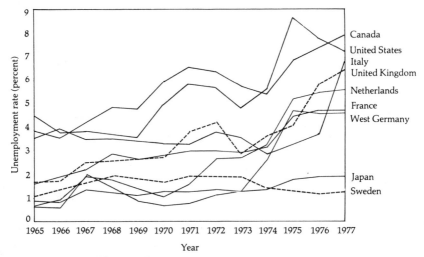

Comparison of the unemployment rates of the U.S. and Canada with those of Japan and the six largest economies among the countries of Western Europe show that with the single exception of Sweden all these countries have experienced rising unemployment rates since the recession of 1973-74. Unemployment in five of the Western European countries has now exceeded the 4 percent rate, which some economists believe is the maximum rate that can be tolerated in a healthy economy. The rate of unemployment in the U.S. exceeded that rate seven years ago. Because countries count their unemployment in different ways the data here are not strictly comparable.

Figure 1-1 Unemployment rates in the United States and elsewhere. From Eli Ginzberg, "The Job Problem," *Scientific American,* 237 (November 1977), 47. Copyright © 1977 by Scientific American, Inc. All rights reserved.

Sometimes persistent problems in American society remain invisible for long periods of time: John F. Kennedy focused attention on the poverty of the mountain folk of Appalachia during his 1960 presidential campaign; the plight of the handicapped received public attention a decade or so later, after an extended period of neglect. Unemployment has not been this sort of problem. The object of ongoing public attention and political controversy, it has been a public issue for several decades. The various policies—macroeconomic policy, manpower programs, unemployment insurance, public works, and so on—are the object of considerable, often partisan, debate about the seriousness of unemployment, its costs in social and economic terms, the appropriate strategies for reducing it, and the costs of such strategies.

Unlike many issues that engage the attention of policy makers and experts but are more or less neglected by the public, unemployment is a source of real concern to ordinary citizens. Monthly measurements of the unemployment rate by the Bureau of Labor Statistics coupled with ongoing media attention have highlighted the issue. In a recent national survey 57 percent of those contacted expressed concern about unemployment, saying that it has become a more serious problem in recent years and/or is one of the two or three most important national problems.[2] The public's concern is also reflected in the Gallup Poll's periodic reports about the national problems perceived by the public as being most serious. There is a great deal of volatility in such polls: issues appear and fade. However, throughout most of the nineteen seventies, economic issues have figured prominently in the list of issues deemed important by the public. Although unemployment often ranked lower than inflation as a source of public concern, it was clearly on the minds of ordinary citizens.

The Setting of the Mid-1970s

This then was the setting for our study. Although the political temperature of the nation was considerably lower than it had been a decade earlier, the period witnessed frequent protests by previously unorganized and unpoliticized groups—gays, Native Americans, and the handicapped, to name a few. Unemployment, a continuing problem in American economic life, stood at a level substantially higher than at any time since World War II ended the depression. In absolute terms the number of jobless workers approached that in 1931. The problem was a visible one, the object of political controversy and citizen concern. But the situation contained one puzzle. Given these twin circumstances—the politicization of previously unorganized disadvantaged groups and the high levels of joblessness—it would have been reasonable to expect to hear from the unemployed themselves. One assistant secretary of labor in the Nixon administration described watching the ascending unemployment rate in 1974 and 1975 and feeling as if he were "sitting on a powder keg." Despite pressure on behalf of the unemployed from many other quarters,

[2]Albert H. Cantril and Susan Davis Cantril, *Unemployment, Government and the American People* (Washington, D.C.: Public Research, 1978), p. 33.

the unemployed themselves were not heard from. As described by Eileen Shanahan in the *New York Times:*

> One of the major mysteries of the recession has been the lack of visible anger with which it has been endured by the American people. There has been no violent protest and even orderly, peaceful demonstrations have been few and not very large . . . Why such calm? There is no readily available answer.[3]

Superficial empirical documentation of this quiescence can be gleaned from the *New York Times Index.* For 1975, when unemployment stood at a prodigious 8.5 percent, a mere three demonstrations by unemployed workers are listed. For the preceding and following years, periods of substantial joblessness, the *Index* lists but one such demonstration in each year. Comparable data from the mid-sixties demonstrate dramatically the absence of protest. For 1964, 1965, and 1966—when the civil rights movement was at its height—the *Times Index* lists 59, 98, and 70 demonstrations by blacks.[4]

The riddle thus seemed to us a real one: other disadvantaged groups increasingly were politically involved; unemployment was widespread; it was salient; the unemployed—and those affected indirectly by joblessness—were very numerous. Why then was there not more activity and agitation on their part? The riddle seemed worth solving, not only for its own sake, but also for the light it would shed on the nature of the process by which people who have personal problems politicize those problems and seek solutions through political activity.

It is not as if there were no solutions to our puzzle; as a matter of fact, there were almost too many. Almost everyone to whom we spoke had a ready answer, and the things we read suggested even more. Some answers dealt with the situation of the unemployed in the 1970s: unlike the depression when millions of household heads were involuntarily out of work for long periods of time without benefit of government aid, the unemployed of this generation do not really suffer—because they have few

---

[3]Eileen Shanahan, "The Mystery of the Great Calm of the Unemployed," *New York Times,* 3 August 1975, sec. 4, p. 4.

[4]The absence of protest by the unemployed appeared to be a manifestation of a more general calm among American industrial workers. Citing data on satisfaction of workers and indications of discontent, John T. Dunlop concludes: "It would seem that if any events call for explanation in our times it is not so much the occasional wildcat strike at Lordstown, Ohio as the fact that the great inflation of 1973-1974 with declines in real income, and the large-scale unemployment of 1975-1977 have produced so little industrial unrest or protest." See "American Labor Organization," *Daedalus,* 107 (Winter 1978), 89.

financial responsibilities, because they are jobless by choice, because they are out of work for relatively short periods of time, because they can take advantage of government benefits. Such answers suggested that the unemployed do not *need* to be politically active. Other answers focused on the logic of their situation. It makes more sense for the unemployed to solve their problems on their own: to devote whatever resources and skills they have to seeking a new job rather than to collective action. In other words, it is not *rational* for them to be politically active. Other answers stressed attitudinal and cultural characteristics. The unemployed—and American workers generally—are committed to an individualistic Horatio Alger ethic and are not class conscious. The unemployed, according to these answers, do not *want* to seek collective political solutions to their personal problems. Still other answers dealt with characteristics of the political process. The pluralist model of American politics, these answers stressed, does not apply equally to all groups. Disadvantaged groups do not have the channels of access to the political process or the resources and skills available to the more affluent and established groups. These answers suggested that the unemployed *could* not be more politically active.

Each of these answers is persuasive. But each rests upon untested assumptions. Because accepted generalities are so often confounded by actual data, we felt it appropriate to examine them more closely in the light of relevant empirical materials. Even if we were merely to confirm what everybody already knew anyway—and we do not—the enterprise would not be a failure, for we would have given the common wisdom a solid empirical footing.

Personal Strain and Political Response

It should be clear by now that to investigate these themes is to tackle more general questions in the process. Thus, to consider the puzzle of unemployment and political tranquility is to consider the links between the problems and pressures in personal life and conduct in political life. To live is to undergo strain—at home and at work; in the head, in the heart, in the pocketbook. Most of these stresses remain personal and are interpreted by the individual as having no implications beyond himself or his private sphere. They are perceived as neither requiring intervention of political agencies nor amenable to solution through the political process. Some of these problems, however, are placed in a broader context. They are seen by the individual as problems that are shared by others and, sometimes, as requiring government activity if they are to be ameliorated. Under these circumstances the individual presumably is more likely to seek social and, in the latter case, political solutions.

Brody and Sniderman present evidence that the nature of an individual's personal problems affects his political conduct.[5] However, there is accumulating evidence of a quite different sort of a growing disjunction between specific material conditions and political attitudes or behavior. Political conduct apparently is becoming unstuck from the demographic foundations that previously anchored it. In particular, socioeconomic status seems less potent in structuring citizen politics.[6] At the same time that demographic characteristics, especially those associated with social class, are becoming less closely linked to political attitudes and behavior, political ideas are becoming linked more closely to one another and to electoral choice. Analyses of the political behavior of those who are disadvantaged economically—by their joblessness, their socioeconomic position, or both—can help us to understand how material strains affect attitudes and how the two, separately or jointly, affect political behavior.

This raises a distinction to which we shall refer periodically, the distinction between the politics of the unemployed as a group and the politics of unemployment as an issue. In the course of our study we shall frequently compare the potency of the ideas that citizens have about political issues with the potency of their actual economic circumstances in affecting their political behavior.

The Disadvantaged and the Pressure System

Our concern with the consequences for individual political conduct of strains in personal life leads directly to a concern with the processes by which groups of citizens with shared problems and needs become aware of their collective interests and act politically in order to receive favorable treatment from the government. Phrasing our concerns in this way calls to mind the issues that have divided the pluralist analysts of American politics from their critics.

Crudely put, the pluralists—or group theorists of politics—posit a political process in which governmental power is widely dispersed, with multiple channels of political access. In any political dispute opposing interests are represented more or less automatically by private interest

---

[5]Richard A. Brody and Paul M. Sniderman, "From Life Space to Polling Place: The Relevance of Personal Concerns for Voting Behavior," *British Journal of Political Science*, 7 (July 1977), 337-360.

[6]See, for example, Richard Dawson, *Public Opinion and Contemporary Disarray* (New York: Harper and Row, 1973); Gerald Pomper, *Voter's Choice* (New York: Dodd, Mead and Co., 1975), chap. 3; Norman H. Nie, Sidney Verba, and John R. Petrocik, *The Changing American Voter* (Cambridge, Mass.: Harvard University Press, 1976), chaps. 13-14; Everett Carll Ladd, Jr., with Charles D. Hadley, *Transformations of the American Party System*, 2nd ed. (New York: W. W. Norton, 1978).

groups that pressure the government for a favorable outcome. Because the political system is open, all the relevant interests in a controversy are represented in rough proportion to the intensity of their preferences. The outcome of the process of interest-group interaction is therefore a rough approximation of the public interest.

Critics of this analysis of American politics, perhaps most notably E. E. Schattschneider, have pointed out that the representation of relevant interests is by no means automatic and that the pressure system is by no means universal.[7] On the contrary, the system of private interests likely to bring pressure on the government in a political controversy is biased against the unorganized. Diffuse public interests and the interests of those who lack political resources, especially money, are less likely to be organized than their more affluent antagonists. As Schattschneider puts it so aptly, "The flaw in the pluralist heaven is that the heavenly chorus sings with a strong upper class accent."[8] In the light of this observation it is easy to understand that the pressure system might be biased against collective political action by the unemployed, a group that is neither established nor affluent.

However, class bias is insufficient as an explanation of the failure of the unemployed to mobilize politically. Paradoxically, at just the time that political scientists have come to accept as common wisdom the antipluralist observation that the pressure system is not universal, we have been in a period in which the number of organized groups pressing their arguments upon the government has multiplied. Many of those who have felt themselves aggrieved and therefore have taken their cases to the government are precisely the kinds of groups that have traditionally been articulate and effective in American politics: over-the-road truckers protesting Interstate Commerce Commission deregulation; fishermen demanding a 200-mile limit to exclude foreign fishermen; furniture manufacturers objecting to rules requiring flame-retardant fabrics; farmers seeking higher price supports. Yet the last decade and a half have witnessed the rallying of many previously unorganized interests of the sort the antipluralists would expect to be excluded from the pressure system The representation of diffuse public interests has become much more commonplace. We have heard from those who would save the whales, the children, the redwoods; from those who would ban abortions, breeder reactors, or guns; from those who would raise the drinking age or lower taxes. Even more important from our point of view, during this

[7]*The Semi-Sovereign People* (New York: Holt, Rinehart and Winston, 1960), chap. 2.
[8]Ibid., p. 35.

period many groups of disadvantaged citizens have become conscious, vocal, and active in politics on their own behalf—blacks, Chicanos, the handicapped, the elderly, gays, women, Native Americans, to name a few. In each case the politicized group has overcome some kind of deficiency in political resources: most of the members of these groups are scarcely wealthy; many lack political skills; some—especially among the elderly and the handicapped—are immobile and infirm. While the successes of such groups have hardly been uniform, the growth in recent years of political activity by the disadvantaged has been quite remarkable. We cannot attribute the absence of consciousness and organization among the unemployed simply to class bias in the pressure system.

Unemployment and the Political Agenda

We can understand more fully the nature of the puzzle with which we are dealing if we place it in the context of the general problem of how the political agenda is set[9] and, in particular, in the context of the controversy that has surrounded a concept that the antipluralists call "nondecision making." To give a rough summary of this debate: critics of the pluralist analysis of politics, particularly Bachrach and Baratz, have argued that the pluralists err in their exclusive focus on political decision making.[10] They maintain that many of the most important political decisions never get made because, for a variety of reasons, the issues are never raised in the appropriate decision-making arena. If we are to understand the uses of power we must consider the nondecision making process whereby issues are kept off the political agenda and never become the objects of decision making.

Critics of this approach rejoin that if no decision is made, nothing happens. How, then, can we verify empirically that nondecision making has taken place? At least, looking at decision making involves empirical observation. Nondecisions are nonempirical phenomena.[11]

Bachrach and Baratz point out in rebuttal that many nondecisions can indeed be observed empirically. For example, nondecision making often

[9]On the concept of agenda building see Roger W. Cobb and Charles D. Elder, *Participation in American Politics: The Dynamics of Agenda Building* (Boston: Allyn and Bacon, 1972), and Charles O. Jones, *An Introduction to the Study of Public Policy*, 2nd ed. (North Scituate, Mass.: Duxbury Press, 1977), chap. 3.

[10]Peter Bachrach and Morton S. Baratz, *Power and Poverty* (New York: Oxford University Press, 1970), chap. 3.

[11]Richard M. Merelman, "On the Neo-Elitist Critique of Community Power," *American Political Science Review*, 62 (June 1968), 451-461; and Raymond E. Wolfinger, "Nondecisions and the Study of Local Politics," *American Political Science Review*, 65 (December 1971), 1063-1080.

involves overt suppression, such as when the longshoreman who is talking to the police about dockside corruption meets with an unfortunate accident. Sometimes nondecision making involves the manipulation of procedures by elites to squelch or bury a threatening issue, such as when Emanuel Celler confines the Equal Rights Amendment to the Judiciary Committee session after session, or the President refers a volatile issue like decriminalization of marijuana to a presidential commission for extended study.

There are some kinds of nondecisions, Bachrach and Baratz concede, that cannot be studied empirically. In such cases nothing happens either because groups fear inaction or even reprisals from those more powerful and therefore opt not to make their demands, or because—most subtle of all—basic values, norms, and institutional procedures operate to keep people from converting private needs into political demands, or even from being aware of those needs.

We feel that Bachrach and Baratz yield too much. For the kinds of nondecisions in which no demand is made, institutional analysis is of little help. It does not enable us to understand why certain grievances are not expressed, why important issues are not raised. However, it is possible to use survey data to learn a great deal about those who are politically inactive and why they do not politicize their needs. Perhaps they simply do not feel needy; or they feel their problems are not appropriate material for politics; or they figure they would get nowhere if they tried the political arena; or they fear repression. Survey data can help us to understand why nothing happened.

But how does one know where to begin? In the absence of overt complaint or action, what are the clues that help us to locate the unpoliticized need? What are the criteria to guide the search for a nonissue? Frederick W. Frey has a helpful suggestion:[12] When "1) glaring inequalities occur in the distribution of things avowedly valued by actors in the system, and 2) these inequalities do not seem to occasion ameliorative influence attempts by those getting less of those values," then we have reason to suspect a nonissue.

Frey's formulation leads us to be suspicious about unemployment: millions of potential workers lack jobs, and there seems to have been no activity on their part. Thus it seems worthwhile to proceed further. Using survey data, we can investigate the roots of the failure of the unemployed to become politically articulate and active. Is it that they simply do not

[12]"Comment: On Issues and Non-issues in the Study of Power," *American Political Science Review*, 65 (December 1971), 1081-1107.

suffer? that they are not aware of their own interests? that they do not see their problems as having political implications? that they are afraid?

It is important to reiterate that, in spite of the quiescence of those who are out of work, unemployment is very much a political issue. Although its incorporation onto the political agenda was not a result of pressure by the unemployed themselves, it has been the object of public controversy and governmental policy for several decades. That an issue can be raised and debated without the direct participation of those most immediately affected is by no means uncommon in American politics. The rights of many groups—children, death-row inmates, the unborn—have been asserted and protected by surrogates, whether policy entrepreneurs within the government or committed advocates outside. Since there is political pressure on behalf of the unemployed coming, not from the jobless themselves, but from other sources—the Democratic party, labor unions, civil rights groups, and so on—it may be that the political quiescence of the unemployed, whatever its origins, makes no difference in policy terms. Whether the policy outcomes would be different if the unemployed were organized and active is a question beyond the purview of our study, albeit we consider it in the Epilogue. Nevertheless, given our concern with the mobilization of political groups, we wish to understand why the unemployed do not speak more loudly for themselves, even though others speak for them.

The Process of Political Mobilization

In Figure 1-2 we propose a schematic series of steps by which those who have interests in common become an effective political force. We present this scheme—which we consider to be neither particularly novel nor definitive—not as a model to be tested, but as a guide to the critical points at which connections are made or fail to be made. The unemployed do not provide us with a case study in political mobilization; they do not move from the condition of objective strain at the left to political mobilization on the right. However, this scheme is useful to structure the analysis that follows: the series of hypothetical steps proposed in Figure 1-2 will help us know where to look for gaps in the process. In the figure we describe both the general steps and possible specific manifestations in the mobilization of the economically deprived.

(1) We begin, not surprisingly, with the problem itself, the objective condition that creates strain. As should be clear by now, we are concerned with unemployment and low socioeconomic status.

(2) The next step is subjective: individuals must perceive the condition as stressful. In our case, unemployment or low socioeconomic position must be accompanied by feelings of dissatisfaction and deprivation.

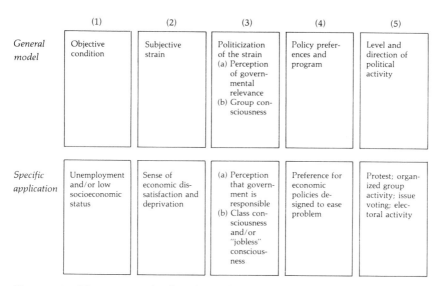

	(1)	(2)	(3)	(4)	(5)
General model	Objective condition	Subjective strain	Politicization of the strain (a) Perception of governmental relevance (b) Group consciousness	Policy preferences and program	Level and direction of political activity
Specific application	Unemployment and/or low socioeconomic status	Sense of economic dissatisfaction and deprivation	(a) Perception that government is responsible (b) Class consciousness and/or "jobless" consciousness	Preference for economic policies designed to ease problem	Protest; organized group activity; issue voting; electoral activity

Figure 1-2   The process of political mobilization.

It is clear that certain conditions an outside observer might classify as stressful are not so perceived by those who actually undergo them. For example, the women who oppose the Equal Rights Amendment so resolutely feel privileged, not disadvantaged, by society's traditional treatment of women. With reference to our case the factory worker who is able to purchase a ranch house in the suburbs might well feel satisfied economically, even though his income is a fraction of his employer's.

(3) We delineate two aspects of the process by which subjectively stressful problems are politicized and consider both to be critical links in the process of collective political mobilization. Individuals must see the problem as one for which the government is relevant, and they must perceive the problem in some meaningful way as being shared by others. With respect to the former, we can think of many problems that produce subjectively perceived strains—family tensions or marital problems, for example—which individuals would assume they must contend with privately.[13] Although they might join with others experiencing similar difficulties, say in group therapy, it would be unlikely for people to expect the government to solve the tensions with their in-laws. If strained individuals do not feel that the government can or should help them solve

[13]In this discussion we are guided by the helpful distinctions made by Brody and Sniderman in "From Life Space to Polling Place." They do not, however, attempt to confront the difficult issue of how problems come to be seen as amenable to solution through government action.

their problems, then we would not expect political mobilization. In our example, if the reaction to economic stress is to internalize the problem and deal with it privately, we would expect little of political consequence to ensue. Observers have pointed out that American culture contains a strong streak of individualism, which encourages people to internalize problems that might otherwise become political.

Presumably many factors are related to whether the government is perceived as responsible for solving a problem. Obviously, the ease with which a problem can be alleviated through individual efforts is one. Some problems—air pollution or overcrowding on mass transit, for instance—cannot be solved directly (although perhaps they can be avoided) by an individual without help from the government. While blacks of a decade or two ago could attempt to improve themselves through individual efforts, certain problems they faced—such as voting rights or legally sanctioned segregation—necessitated governmental intervention. Other problems seem more amenable to individual solution. The jobless person, for example, can solve his problem on his own by getting a new job. Again, our culture sanctions the solution of personal problems individually. However, it is characteristic of the modern nation-state that government intervention is increasingly sought in the solution of problems once thought to be private.

Furthermore, we would expect that the more intense the strain, the greater the probability of politicization. Left-handed people, for example, are the victims of systematic social discrimination. They have a difficult time with public drinking fountains; the desks in lecture halls fit them poorly. Yet the deprivation suffered by southpaws is hardly so acute that we would expect them to launch a collective rebellion. Problems that are short term, even though severe, presumably would be more limited in their political potency. For example, people with broken legs would be less likely to politicize their problem than the permanently disabled, even though for a time their disabilities are equivalent. In our own specific case, we can contrast joblessness, which is usually perceived to be temporary, with lower socioeconomic status, which is more likely to be considered long term.

It would seem that not only must the problem be viewed as within the province of governmental activity, but also it must be seen as shared if effective political mobilization is to take place. An important link in the process is group consciousness—a sense that a problem is shared and can be solved more effectively through joint action than through individual initiative. Our concern here is derived at least indirectly from Karl Marx, who emphasized that only when workers are aware of their common bonds of oppression and are ready to act together can they overcome their subjugation. It is consciousness, he claims, that converts objective class disadvantage into a collective political program. Although we do not expect revolutionary consciousness from the disadvantaged in contemporary America, the form of group consciousness that is relevant to our enterprise is, indeed, class consciousness.

Once again, it would seem that there are many factors that would predispose group members to group consciousness or, on the other hand, inhibit the development of such consciousness on the part of those who share a common problem. For example, we would expect group consciousness to be facilitated by propinquity among group members, or at least by effective networks of communications among them.[14] On this point we shall examine whether the fact that the unemployed are dispersed inhibits the development of group consciousness among the jobless. Also, we shall test whether blue-collar workers who are clustered together in factories or unions are more likely to exhibit working-class consciousness. In addition, it would seem that groups that are divided by cross-cutting cleavages would be less likely to manifest group consciousness. The racial and ethnic cleavages that divide the working class have often been held responsible for the absence of class consciousness among American workers. This, too, is a hypothesis we shall wish to evaluate.

Furthermore, we would expect the emergence of group consciousness to be facilitated to the extent that group membership is perceived to be permanent or to the extent that the costs of shedding group membership are high. On this basis blacks should be relatively likely to manifest group consciousness. By and large, racial status is permanent. Furthermore, for those blacks who would be able to deny their race, the psychological costs of so doing would probably be high: it would almost necessarily imply a rejection of those to whom one is tied by blood, friendship, or ethnic kinship and would probably be viewed as an act of betrayal. A similar point of view is expressed by a gay activist: "You cannot join the gay movement or leave it. It is your way of life. You can evade it or betray it, thereby betraying yourself, but it is not a voluntary association."[15] No such opprobrium would be attached to a handicapped person's leaving the group, but unfortunately for many the disabilities are permanent.

The situation is quite different for the unemployed. Joblessness is quite likely to be viewed as a temporary condition, and there are substantial benefits—and virtually no costs—attached to shedding group member-

[14]On this issue see Jo Freeman, *The Politics of Women's Liberation* (New York: David McKay Co. 1975), chap. 2.
[15]Laud Humphreys, *Out of the Closets* (Englewood Cliffs, N.J.: Prentice-Hall, 1972), p. 104.

ship. Surely there is no social disapproval attached to solving the problems associated with being out of work by finding a job. The only cost is the burden of jobholding. The situation is somewhat more complicated with respect to lower socioeconomic status. On the one hand, working-class status is unlikely to be a short-term condition. On the other, American culture gives powerful cues to those of lower economic status to strive to shed that condition through individual effort and initiative. This is a theme we shall pursue in some detail when we consider whether there is group consciousness among American workers.

Clearly, then, the substance of the problem faced by group members will have an influence over whether that problem will be viewed as individual or shared, as best solved through private efforts or government activity. However, we should recognize that the same problem can reasonably be considered in a variety of ways. Figure 1-3 illustrates this point by showing alternative ways in which the same problem can be conceptualized by those who confront it and the resultant forms of activity consonant with each conceptualization. The alternatives are generated according to whether the solution sought affects the individual only or others who share the problem, and whether the problem is seen as best solved privately or through government intervention. The figure illustrates the abstract case and two hypothetical problems: the educational disadvantage associated with a learning disability and the economic disadvantage associated with joblessness. In each cell we indicate the kind of strategy that might be adopted if the problem were conceptualized in that mode.

Let us consider these alternatives:

(a) We would expect individual private activity when a problem is seen as best solved for the individual alone by private activity. Such an approach seems quite reasonable in either of our illustrative cases: the parents of a learning-disabled child might help the child with his schoolwork every evening; a jobless person could look for work, draw on savings, borrow money from a friend, or otherwise attempt to alleviate the situation on his own.

(b) If a problem is seen as requiring a solution that affects others who share the problem, but still amenable to private activity, we might expect cooperative private activity. In the educational example, the reasonable solution would be to join with the parents of similarly disabled children and start a special after-school program. Analogously, for the unemployed, solution in this mode might include taking advantage of the services provided to the jobless by private agencies or benefits available as part of a union contract.

Problem should be solved through—	Problem is—	General		Learning disability		Joblessness	
		Individual	Shared	Individual	Shared	Individual	Shared
Private efforts		Individual private activity	Cooperative private activity	Help child with schoolwork every evening	Organize after-school program with other parents and hire learning disabilities specialist	Find a new job; cope on own by drawing on savings, etc.	Include SUBs from company in union contract; get services from private agency like Catholic Vocational Service
Government intervention		Seek government benefits: existing programs and patronage	Politicization: pressure for public policy	Ask teacher for special after-school tutoring for child	Politicization: pressure school board to hire learning disabilities specialist	Get patronage job from ward boss; claim unemployment benefits	Politicization: pressure government to stimulate economy, create jobs, raise unemployment benefits

Figure 1-3 Conceptualization of personal problems: four alternatives.

(c) If a problem is seen as having a solution affecting the individual only but requiring government intervention, we would expect the individual, as an individual, to seek government assistance, either by taking advantage of existing programs or by seeking special treatment. Thus, the parents of the learning-disabled child might attempt to enroll him in the appropriate special program if there were one or, in the absence of such a program, they might prevail upon the child's teacher to give him extra attention and special tutoring. The jobless worker would probably take advantage of whatever government assistance was available— unemployment benefits, job placement services, and so on; in addition, he might seek some kind of special favor such as a patronage job.

(d) Finally, we would expect political activity—through either the electoral system or the pressure system—aimed at influencing public policy when a problem is seen as requiring a solution that affects others who share the problem and as necessitating governmental intervention. In the educational case, we might expect pressure for the creation of new programs for those with learning disabilities, or the expansion of old ones, or a campaign to elect a school board more sympathetic to the problems of the learning-disabled. In the jobless case, we might expect the unemployed to pressure the government to stimulate the economy or raise unemployment benefits, or to support candidates who promise such policies.[16]

Figure 1-3 suggests that a given problem can quite appropriately be conceptualized in several ways. With reference to unemployment, each of the alternative modes of viewing the problem—and each of the corresponding strategies—is quite reasonable. Furthermore, these strategies are not mutually exclusive; it would be perfectly sensible to combine them. We would probably consider foolhardy an unemployed person

---

[16]Such political activities need not be collective. Thus, the jobless individual who contacts a congressman to demand higher jobless benefits would be engaged in behavior aimed at obtaining governmental intervention to aid others who share the problem—just as a group of unemployed persons might join together to pressure the congressman.

This observation—that appropriate activities can be either individual or collective—holds for the other modes of problem conceptualization as well. An individual might endeavor in the private sector to solve a problem for a large collectivity. Private individual philanthropy (for example, all the libraries established by Andrew Carnegie) represents individual activity of this sort. Conversely, collective activity might be applied to an individual problem. In the private sector, a group of neighbors might aid an individual in need; in the public sector, a group like the American Civil Liberties Union might champion the cause of an individual whose civil liberties have been violated before the government.

who did not supplement his participation in collective political efforts to solve his problems with private efforts as well.

Also, political mobilization would seem to be most likely when the problem is viewed as requiring government intervention in order to implement a solution affecting a collectivity. This points, in our consideration of the process of political mobilization, to a concern with the way in which a problem is conceptualized, whether it is seen as shared and whether it is seen as requiring governmental intervention.

(4) The final step facilitating joint political activity is for the group, or at least some of its members, to arrive at a program based on common policy preferences. Presumably, the effectiveness of a group in politics is enhanced by its ability to articulate a common policy position to which the government can respond. A group without a program can evoke a response from the government simply by acting so disgruntled or alienated that the government develops policies to meet its needs. However, it would seem that a common set of preferences would both facilitate group mobilization and augment political effectiveness.

(5) The final step in the process is the mobilization itself. American democracy provides many avenues for the expression of political interests and many points of access for those who wish to influence the government. Citizens can act alone or in groups; they can engage in electoral or pressure politics; they can operate through regular channels or engage in protest activities. We shall look for evidence of all these kinds of political activity on the part of those economically disadvantaged by unemployment.

Some Caveats

The scheme we have proposed is meant to be merely suggestive, to specify relationships that we shall wish to test empirically. However, before we leave the subject of political mobilization, some caveats are in order.

First, we posit these hypothetical steps as necessary but not sufficient conditions in the process of mobilization. It would seem that even if all the conditions in steps (1) through (4) were fulfilled, political mobilization might not ensue. Joint political activity, especially effective joint political activity, would not be inevitable. Other factors, in particular the level of political resources, would be relevant. It is reasonable to expect that the probability of the political mobilization of a group of individuals sharing a joint, politicized problem and a political program would depend upon a variety of political resources: not simply time, money, and political skills, although those are obviously critical; but leadership, organizational resources, links with governmental agencies and officials, communications networks, solidarity—or at least the absence of serious internal divisions. Thus, we can differentiate between the politically explosive situation in which a group is ripe for political mobilization but lacks political resources, and the situation in which the blockages occur earlier in the process. In particular, we shall be interested in learning whether those disadvantaged economically by their class position or their joblessness constitute a political powder keg or whether their political mobilization has been truncated at an earlier stage.

We should note also that there are feedback loops. We have specified that consciousness begets mobilization, but it is undoubtedly the case that mobilization begets consciousness. Political mobilization by some group members can affect the ways in which others, who are not politicized, view their problems. Strikes and protests among workers are known to foster class consciousness where there has been none before. Recognizing these possibilities, the women's movement has explicitly espoused "consciousness raising" as a political tool. Responding directly or indirectly to the themes of movement leadership, many women have come to reevaluate their situations, to recognize as shared problems they once thought purely personal, to feel a sense of kinship with other women, and, in some cases such as job discrimination, to expect the government to help them in solving their problems. We should not overlook the role of leadership in propagating consciousness and the way in which political activity among the disadvantaged has served to diffuse political consciousness.

Finally, we should reiterate a point made earlier, that the variant of politics we have been discussing, in which groups are active on their own behalf, is not the only kind that is typical of the American political process. Frequently, and perhaps increasingly, political actions are undertaken by individuals and groups whose vital interests are not at stake in the name of asserting and defending the interests of others. Political advocates, both within and outside the government, often act as surrogates. They have protected the interests of—among others—children, consumers, and the hungry. Furthermore, members of the mass public are often motivated in their political behavior by preferences on issues that do not affect them directly: the citizen whose children are grown might quite reasonably campaign or vote for a local school bond referendum. As we shall see, the unemployed as a group have less impact on the political process than does unemployment as an issue. The policy preferences that individuals have about economic matters—even if they are not directly related to their own personal experiences—are a potent political force.

The Politics of Economic Class

Our concern with the economically disadvantaged in pursuing the question of the links between strain in personal life and behavior in political life inevitably leads us to consider the special nature of class politics in America. As we have mentioned, there are two reasons why we focus on the problem of class politics. First of all, although the unemployed are a heterogeneous group, they are drawn disproportionately from the ranks of the lower socioeconomic orders. Conversely, those of lower socioeconomic status are particularly vulnerable to employment insecurity. Thus, as we pointed out before, many American workers suffer from a kind of double jeopardy: to the ongoing economic disadvantage associated with lower socioeconomic status is appended the shorter-term disadvantage associated with joblessness. If only to avoid the error of spuriousness—attributing to unemployment the effects of lower socioeconomic position—we must keep one eye on class as a variable as we proceed.

Furthermore, joblessness is a special case of class disadvantage, associated with a particularly acute form of economic deprivation. Studying the two in tandem permits us to make inferences in two directions at once. We can use what we learn about the politics of the unemployed to illumine the general nature of class politics in the United States, and we can use what is known about the special character of class politics in America to understand more fully the absence of political mobilization among the unemployed.

It is commonly observed that, among industrial democracies, the United States is exceptional in the relative unimportance of class as a basis of political contention. Although the system of party competition that has obtained since the New Deal is based on, if anything, cleavage over economic issues, there has never been an effective, cohesive, radical, working-class political movement in this country. American unions have been less political than their counterparts elsewhere, more prone than those in other nations to place primary emphasis upon the bargaining table rather than the political arena. In addition, no working-class party has ever sustained a serious electoral threat to the hegemony of the Democrats and Republicans. The largest share of votes ever polled by a working-class party was just under 6 percent—in 1912 when Eugene V. Debs headed the Socialist ticket. In the depths of national economic crisis in 1932 the Socialists under Norman Thomas polled an insignificant 2 percent of the votes.

Our microlevel investigation of the links that are made—or not made

—between economic strain and political ideas and action among the unemployed is relevant for understanding the failure of the American working class to sustain a radical political mobilization. Conversely, the solution of the puzzle of the absence of political response among the unemployed may lie in the general nature of class politics in the American context. Thus the questions "Why no working-class movement?" and "Why no mobilization of the unemployed?" illumine each other.

Why No Working-Class Radicalism—A Procession of Theories

A variety of answers have been proposed to the question of why working-class politics has not flourished in America, many of which have never been subjected to empirical test.[17] Some of the theories of American exceptionalism deal with historical development and therefore are not amenable to test with the contemporary survey data we have gathered. Some of these historical explanations focus on factors intrinsic to the working-class movement itself, for example, schisms within the Socialist Party or the decision by early craft-union leaders to eschew alliance with a single political party. Others among the well-known and traditional interpretations include the role of the frontier as an outlet for the discontent of the ambitious; the fact that two-party competition preceded industrial development, so that the working class could be absorbed into existing parties; the absence of a feudal tradition with its hierarchy of ascribed social statuses; the relative affluence of American workers relative to their counterparts in Europe; the opportunities for upward mobility offered by an expanding economy. A more recent explanation focuses on the separation of the community and the workplace as arenas of conflict, a function of constitutional structure, which results in the diminution of a single coherent conception of class in American politics; class thereby becomes a series of partial relationships rather than an all-encompassing basis for political conflict.[18]

Most of these historical explanations cannot easily be tested with contemporary survey data. However, there are interpretations of the unique character of American working-class politics for which our data are more relevant. Many of these have never been subjected to empirical examination. In the process of testing these explanations we hope both to illumi-

---

[17]In a helpful essay Seymour Martin Lipset discusses these and other theories and gives extensive bibliographic suggestions: "Why No Socialism in the United States?" in Seweryn Bialer and Sophia Sluzar, eds., *Sources of Contemporary Radicalism* (New York: Westview Press, 1977), pp. 31-149.

[18]Ira Katznelson, "Community Conflict and Capitalist Development," prepared for delivery at the Annual Meeting of the American Political Science Association, San Francisco, September 1975.

nate some of the themes that have figured importantly in the analysis of the role of class in American politics and to assess their relevance for a special case of economic disadvantage, joblessness.

CLASS CONSCIOUSNESS AND AMERICAN EXCEPTIONALISM

One of the most frequently cited interpretations of the special nature of class politics in America focuses upon the absence of class consciousness among American workers. American workers are said to show little of the kind of group consciousness we have posited as critical in the process of politicization. They are assumed not to feel a sense of kinship with other workers, to perceive themselves as having interests in common with them, or to be committed to collective action. We shall use our survey data to assess the degree to which such attitudes are indeed characteristic of American workers as a preliminary to understanding the way in which group-conscious views for workers would fit into an overall political and social ideology. Furthermore, we shall investigate whether unemployment, when added to objective class status, enhances class consciousness.

In the theories of American exceptionalism that place importance on the failure of American workers to achieve consciousness, the question thus becomes "Why no class consciousness in America?" rather than "Why no socialism in America?" The theories traditionally see the absence of consciousness as responsible for the absence of institutions committed to social change on behalf of workers. However, we might posit that at this stage of historical evolution it is difficult to differentiate dependent from independent variable, to know whether the lack of institutions results from the lack of consciousness or vice versa. This recalls a point made earlier, that political consciousness, organization, and activity are mutually reinforcing.

The absence of class consciousness among American workers has been attributed to many factors. Two of them, the effects of belief in the American Dream of success and the divisions within the working class, are of particular relevance for our concerns and will receive special attention as we proceed.

The American Dream: American culture contains a sturdy individualistic strand. According to the ideology of equality of opportunity, American society provides ample opportunities for mobility to the able and ambitious, regardless of accident of birth or previous disadvantages. It is quite understandable that such beliefs would have political effects. Presumably the emphasis upon the availability of opportunity would inhibit the understanding of problems as socially structured or shared; the emphasis upon individualistic striving would encourage the disadvantaged to satisfy their needs and ambitions on their own and dampen the possibilities for worker solidarity; the emphasis upon self-reliance would diminish the probability that the government would be held responsible for helping the individual. These themes have a parallel for the circumstances of the unemployed. The individualism implicit in the American Dream theoretically would provide an ideological context that would encourage those out of work to cope on their own—by seeking work, dipping into savings, taking out loans, having another family member go to work. Such activities would be a quite rational way of dealing with the personal consequences of joblessness. However, to the degree that such self-reliant solutions are culturally sanctioned, the political potential of the strain associated with unemployment would be reduced.

We shall not be able to examine these themes historically: to enter into the controversy over whether there has indeed been more opportunity for advancement available in the United States than in Europe; to measure whether upward mobility among the most talented and aspiring was sufficient to deprive a nascent movement among workers of more effective leadership; to assess how widespread was the perception, if not the fact, of open opportunities. Our data do, however, permit us to investigate how contemporary Americans view the opportunities available both in general and in their own lives. We shall also be able to investigate the links between individualistic belief in the American Dream and low levels of class consciousness.

Conflict among Members of the Working Class: A second factor held responsible for the absence of class consciousness in the American context is the racial and ethnic diversity of the working class. The coincidence of massive industrialization and waves of European immigration produced an urban working class that was divided by cultural heritage, language, and religion. Later the exodus of blacks from the rural South to the industrial cities provided the basis for still another cleavage, this time on the basis of race. Such divisions, so the argument goes, impeded the emergence of a sense of solidarity among workers and inhibited the growth of working-class consciousness. This theme, too, has relevance for the unemployed. As we shall see, the unemployed are a diverse group. We shall be interested in learning whether their heterogeneity acts as a barrier to their effective political mobilization.

Our pursuit of these themes will be, of necessity, partial. However, we shall look closely at the fundamental racial cleavage that divides the economically disadvantaged. We shall focus, in particular, upon the attitudes of blacks: their commitment to the individualistic ethic of the

American Dream; the degree to which their attitudes could be considered either working-class or race conscious; their willingness to join with white workers in pursuit of shared economic goals. Also, with respect to these issues, we shall consider the extent to which the experience of unemployment increases intergroup hostility.

Overview

By now it should be clear that we shall be pursuing several interlocking themes in the course of our analysis.

The most specific theme is the puzzle of the quiescent unemployed: why, given that unemployment seems to be stressful, is there little political response? Much of our analysis turns on a comparison of working and jobless members of the work force in order to isolate and explain distinctive patterns of attitude and behavior associated with joblessness.

The riddle of the quiescent unemployed is, we believe, a specific manifestation of a more general question: Why the "exceptional" pattern of class politics in America? The puzzle of American exceptionalism will take us beyond a consideration of the unemployed to a concern with the role of class and class consciousness in the political behavior of American workers.

Our concern with the role of unemployment and class in American politics leads to a consideration of the role of economic deprivation more generally and to the issues of the relation between personal economic strain and political response and the mobilization of the disadvantaged more generally. In this connection we shall look periodically at the politics of race in order to make comparisons with the politics of class.

These three themes are not easily separable; indeed, each is a different way of looking at the same phenomenon. As we move through our analysis we shall often shift our perspective—at times focusing on unemployment, at times focusing on social class, often looking at the interrelationship between them. Our model of the process of political mobilization will be a guide for dealing with these questions.

In the various sections of our book we take up sequentially the sections of the schematic diagram presented in Figure 1-2.

Part One considers the nature of the strain associated with unemployment in the 1970s. In Chapter 2 we describe the major characteristics of the unemployed. In Chapter 3 we consider the extent to which unemployment is indeed a stressful condition. And in Chapter 4 we deal with attempts by the unemployed to cope with the strain of being out of work. These chapters are a crucial first step in our argument. The main issue is whether unemployment is a strain on the individual and, if so, whether individual efforts on the part of the jobless are sufficient to alleviate that strain. We consider this issue first because, if unemployment is relatively painless, we have no puzzle to solve; there is no problem to be politicized.

Part Two deals with the relationship between objective economic strain and social and political beliefs, a major connection in our model of political mobilization. Chapter 5 presents data on the social ideology of the American work force—the extent to which one finds evidence of class consciousness and commitment to an American Dream of individual advancement. In addition, we consider how these relate to each other: whether commitment to the American Dream of individualism diminishes class consciousness. In Chapter 6 we investigate the extent to which the general social ideologies held by members of the work force relate to their own economic experience and we examine the extent to which such economic strains as unemployment affect class consciousness and other aspects of social ideology. In Chapter 7 we look more closely at the political ideology of blacks. This allows us to juxtapose race and class consciousness and to consider whether conflict between the races impedes solidarity on economic issues. In Chapter 8 we consider from two perspectives the links between economic strain and attitudes. First we probe the issue of where the jobless place responsibility for unemployment; then we look at the relationship between attitudes on economic policy questions and the economic strains of joblessness and lower socioeconomic position.

Part Three considers the political activity of work force members and its susceptibility to economic strain. In Chapter 9 we consider the level of political participation among working and unemployed respondents, and in Chapter 10 deal with the effectiveness of organization and ideology in mobilizing the economically disadvantaged. In Chapters 11 and 12 we look at the voting behavior of these two groups in 1976 in order to estimate the impact of the behavior of the unemployed on electoral outcome and compare it to the impact of unemployment as an issue.

In the Epilogue we look beyond the data on the work force to speculate on the meaning of what we have learned for policy outcomes, asking whether it would have made any difference if the unemployed had been more active.

Studying the Unemployed: Our Survey

Closer study of the unemployed would, we felt, give us an opportunity to study the political and social effects of economic strain: not only to evaluate a number of plausible, but untested, hypotheses about the political consequences of joblessness; but also to examine more general questions about American exceptionalism and the links between personal strain and political mobilization. Because we are dealing with a negative case, a group that has not made it to the institutional level, the kind of organizational analysis of group activity and the policy process that has been so helpful in understanding more successful groups would not be appropriate. To understand the links that are made, and those that are bypassed, it is necessary to look directly at affected individuals.

There are a variety of studies that deal with the role of unemployment in the political process. Some analyze the making of policies relevant to joblessness: macroeconomic policy, manpower policy, income maintenance policy. Others relate unemployment to electoral outcomes, using aggregate data to relate the rate of unemployment to election returns, or survey data to relate attitudes on unemployment to vote choice. However, we could find little about the unemployed themselves—their own interpretation of their joblessness, their attitudes, their political behavior —or their role in the political process. When we searched existing archives for data useful to study the unemployed, we soon learned why. Ordinary survey samples produce too few cases of unemployed individuals for analysis—even in times of fairly substantial unemployment like the 1970s. These samples permit the investigator to study public attitudes on unemployment but are inadequate for considering particular reactions of the unemployed.[19]

In order to examine the unemployed more closely, we conducted a survey of the American work force, weighted in such a way as to produce a sample of unemployed workers large enough for analysis, but with sufficient cases of employed respondents to permit comparison. The procedure used in our telephone survey of the urban work force involved two separate but parallel samples. In one, we interviewed members of the work force whether employed or unemployed. In the other, larger sample, we screened respondents and conducted interviews only with unemployed people. The result is a set of 1,370 interviews of which 571 are with jobless respondents. These data represent, we are fairly sure, the

[19]In the Gallup presidential polls conducted since 1944, the number of jobless respondents is impossible to ascertain because they are categorized along with those who are "not in the work force"—those who are retired, keeping house, or in school. Until 1976 the biennial election surveys conducted by the Center for Political Studies at the University of Michigan contained very few respondents who were out of work. Averaging 30 per survey, the number of jobless respondents in the Michigan studies ranged from 20 in 1964 to a high of 50 in the study conducted at the time of the congressional election of 1970. Both because the unemployment rate was at a higher level in 1976 than at any time since the inception of the Michigan presidential surveys and because the overall sample in the 1976 survey was especially large, the 1976 Michigan study contains significantly more unemployed respondents, over 150, than any of its predecessors.

largest set of interviews extant on the political and social views of the unemployed. We should repeat for the sake of emphasis that our survey
was of the metropolitan work force, a fact that we shall not reiterate over
and over. (For example, we shall refer to "blacks" rather than to "metropolitan work force blacks.") In addition to the large sample survey, we
conducted follow-up interviews of a less structured sort with a small
number—60—of the unemployed respondents in our original sample.
Most of these were lengthy interviews conducted in person, which allowed us to probe more deeply into the attitudes and beliefs of our
respondents. Although these data are not systematic, they are rich in
nuance and permit us to probe questions that would otherwise remain
unanswered. (For a more complete discussion of the sample design and
the research procedure, see Appendix A.)

Part One

Unemployment and Economic Strain

CHAPTER 2

The Unemployed: Some Preliminaries

Old imagery inhibits new ways of thought—a truth with special relevance when the issue is unemployment. Listening to the politicians describing and decrying unemployment, one would think it to be the same phenomenon that it was forty years ago: the sorrowful people in line, the long hopeless wait, the eagerness for work . . .

People hopelessly waiting, destitute, asking only for a job— these emotion-fraught phrases tell very little about most of the unemployment in the 1970's. In fact the unemployed are an ever-changing mass, on a kind of shuttle, moving between working and waiting, never fitting comfortably into any job, yet usually able soon to find another. Testimony to their restlessness is found in a startling statistic: only about half of the 7.5 million left jobs involuntarily. The other half is made up of people who quit, or who have just entered or reentered the labor force. The average duration of unemployment is not very long and the individuals involved keep changing. Although the number of unemployed in 1975 never exceeded 8,540,000, the number who experienced unemployment was much higher: about 21 million people knew some unemployment last year.

This turbulence tracks back to shifts in the composition of the civilian labor force, which now numbers 95 million. The number of adult white men, who have a low rate of unemployment, has been dwindling in relation to the total force. But teenagers, blacks, and women, who have high rates, have been joining in record numbers; surprisingly, they now make up half its total. Last year's increases illustrate the trend: the labor force expanded by 1.6 million, of whom 1.2 million were women or teenagers.[1]

WE HAVE POSED as a puzzle the question of why widespread unemployment has so few apparent political consequences. However, according to a complicated argument frequently put forth, there is no puzzle to be solved; upon closer inspection, contemporary unemployment turns out not to be such a major problem after all. In this chapter and the two that follow,

---

[1] Walter Guzzardi, Jr., "How to Deal with the New Unemployment," *Fortune* (October 1976), 132, 133-134.

we look more closely at the issue of whether joblessness in contemporary America is a problem, essentially asking, "Does the 'new' unemployment hurt?"

The quotation that opens this chapter reflects a widely held position. As the chief economist for Merrill, Lynch, Pierce, Fenner, and Smith put it, "In my judgment, the true nature of today's unemployment is not understood, the statistics are not understood, and the gravity of the problem is perceived by the vast majority of people, including politicians, to be far greater than it really is." Economist Milton Friedman argues similarly, "The report that eight million persons are unemployed conjures up the image of eight million persons fruitlessly tramping the streets looking for a job. That is a false picture. Most people recorded as unemployed are between jobs or between entering the labor force and finding a job. Most are in families that have one or more other earners. Most receive some income while unemployed. Each week more than half a million find jobs, while some half-million other people begin to look for jobs."[2] And Arthur Burns, former chairman of the Federal Reserve Bank, focused on one aspect of the new unemployment when he said, "With two-worker families, unemployment is not the horror it once was."[3]

Defining Unemployment

Because the position that elevated unemployment rates are deceptive rests so heavily on a certain characterization of the unemployed, our assessment of the dimensions of unemployment will rest first on an understanding of who the unemployed are. Simply deciding who is to be included among the unemployed turns out to be a complex matter—not just technically but politically as well. The Bureau of Labor Statistics, which uses data from a monthly Census Bureau survey of roughly 47,000 households including information about the employment status of civilian household members aged sixteen and over, considers as employed any person who had a job during the preceding week—even if that person did no work because he or she was ill, on vacation, or out on strike. On the other hand, the Bureau of Labor Statistics considers as unemployed any person who was without a job during the past week, who is currently available for work, and who has made active efforts to find work during the past four weeks.[4]

---

[2]Quoted in Alfred L. Malabre, Jr., *America's Dilemma: Jobs vs. Prices* (New York: Dodd, Mead and Co., 1978), pp. 33-34.

[3]Quoted in the *New York Times*, 24 December 1978, sec. 4, p. 4.

[4]A more detailed account of the government's sampling procedures and the definitions used to classify members of the work force can be found in the Bureau of Labor

Although there is no quarrel over the way the government collects this information, and hence over its accuracy, there is substantial political controversy over who ought to count as unemployed, a controversy that is organically related to the question at hand, whether or not unemployment is a serious problem. Conservatives argue that the government's definition of unemployment inflates the rate because it gives the same weight to the unemployment of a teenager who is making occasional, half-hearted attempts to search for a job or a housewife looking for part-time work as to the unemployment of a household head seeking full-time work. They urge that those who live with a parent or spouse who has a full-time job, those who are insufficiently skilled or educated to qualify for most jobs, and those who are not making serious efforts to find work should not be counted as unemployed. Liberals, on the other hand, argue that the government's definition, because it does not consider as unemployed part-time workers who would prefer full-time work and "discouraged workers" who want jobs but are so pessimistic about their chances of finding work that they have given up looking, actually understates the amount of unemployment.[5]

What is in essence being debated is not so much how to enumerate the jobless as how to adjust the enumeration so that it reflects the amount of stress caused by unemployment. The conservatives, not surprisingly, see that stress as being less substantial and serious than the liberals do. Thus, involved in the very definition of who is to be considered unemployed is the problem we outlined earlier, understanding whether unemployment is a serious problem. For our own purposes it is sufficient to accept the government's definition at the outset and then to specify various subtypes of unemployment, because one of our goals is to ascertain how much strain is associated with various kinds of unemployment. Thus, unless otherwise noted, we will use the government's controversial definition in our analysis.

Statistics pamphlet, *How the Government Measures Unemployment*, Report 418 (Washington, D.C.: U.S. Department of Labor, 1973). The report makes clear how ambiguous cases, such as workers who are waiting to be recalled from layoff, are handled. Complicated issues of definition, such as how to decide whether a person who is not working is actually available for work, and the government's justification for what it considers a value-free definition of unemployment, are discussed in Julius Shiskin and Robert L. Stein, "Problems in Measuring Unemployment," *Monthly Labor Review*, August 1975, pp. 3-10.

[5]For an account of this debate see Eileen Shanahan, "Study on Definitions of Jobless Is Urged," *New York Times*, 11 January 1976, p. 36.

Who Are the Unemployed?

The assertion that high rates of unemployment should be viewed more with circumspection than with alarm rests upon the premise that the number of jobless adult male heads of household has dwindled relative to the number of jobless women and teenagers, and upon the conclusion that unemployment among the latter groups causes little distress. That conclusion will be examined in detail in following chapters. At this point we wish to examine the characterization of the unemployed as a swarm of housewives whose children are sufficiently well launched that they can reenter the work force, and a gang of inner-city teenagers—utterly lacking in job skills—who hang out on street corners.

These stereotypes of certain modal kinds of unemployment are derived from the rather well-known fact that unemployment does not affect all groups equally. As shown in Table 2-1, the overall national unemployment rate of 7.5 percent, which obtained in April 1976 when our survey was taken, masks considerable variation in the rates for different groups in the population. In particular, minorities, women, the young, and those whose jobs require little skill have relatively high rates of unemployment. Membership in more than one of these unemployment-prone categories increases substantially the likelihood of being out of work: for instance, a whopping 52 percent of the black females who were sixteen or seventeen years old in April 1976 were jobless.

The data in Table 2-1 are relevant for another reason as well. We are interested in a variety of aspects of the way in which the unemployed think and behave—their satisfaction with life, their political and social attitudes, their participation in political life. We know as social scientists that these kinds of attributes are not undifferentiated across social categories. Political participation, for example, tends to be strongly related to measures of socioeconomic status. We can infer from Table 2-1 that unemployment is likely to be related to socioeconomic status as well. Therefore, in assessing the relationship between unemployment and political participation, we are going to have to be careful to be sensitive to problems of spuriousness, to be sure that any relationship we find is indeed a function of unemployment rather than of socioeconomic status. In addition, these data alert us to another complexity in assessing the political consequences of unemployment. As mentioned, the unemployed are likely to be drawn from social categories less likely to have high rates of political participation. Even if we were to ascertain that unemployment has no independent additional effect upon the level of participation, we would expect the fact that the unemployed are unlikely to have been active political participants in the first place to have consequences for the development of unemployment as a political issue.

Table 2-1 Seasonally adjusted unemployment rates as of April 1976.

Total		7.5% of the population or 7,040,000 people unemployed
Occupation		
White collar		4.8
Professional and technical	3.4	
Managers and administrators	2.8	
Sales workers	4.9	
Clerical workers	7.0	
Blue collar		9.0
Craft and kindred workers	7.0	
Operatives	9.3	
Laborers (nonfarm)	13.2	
Service workers		8.1
Farm workers		4.8
Sex		
Men		6.7
Women		8.5
Race		
White		6.4
Black and other		13.0
Age		
16-19		19.2
20-24		11.8
25-54		5.3
55 and over		4.6

SOURCE: *Employment and Earnings*, May 1976, pp. 43-44.

The data in Table 2-1 show us that, even though unemployment does not affect all social groups equally, no group is spared. While the unemployed are—as shown in Table 2-2—a diverse group, they are different in composition from the employed. In varying degrees those in upper-status occupations, men, whites, and older people are underrepresented among the unemployed, while those in lower-status occupations, women, blacks, and young people are overrepresented. Although not perfectly representative of the work force, the unemployed are a very heterogeneous group, divided along lines of race, occupation, sex, and age—

Table 2-2 Composition of the employed and unemployed populations as of April 1976.

Variable	Employed	Unemployed
Occupation		
Professional and technical	14.9%	7.3%
Managers and administrators	10.7	4.3
Sales workers	6.3	4.4
Clerical workers	17.8	19.7
Craft and kindred workers	12.8	13.4
Operatives	15.5	22.1
Laborers (nonfarm)	5.1	10.8
Service workers	13.6	16.7
Farm workers	3.3	2.3
	100 %	101 %
Sex		
Men	60.1	53.8
Women	39.9	46.2
	100 %	100 %
Race		
White	89.1	79.3
Black and other	10.9	20.1
	100 %	100 %
Age		
16-19	7.9	23.6
20-24	13.9	23.2
25-54	62.7	43.9
55 and over	15.6	9.4
	100 %	100 %

SOURCE: Calculated from *Monthly Labor Review*, June 1976, pp. 76-79 (seasonally adjusted). The age data are calculated from *Employment and Earnings*, May 1976, pp. 32, 44 (seasonally adjusted).

precisely the lines on which political conflict in America has often been based. Presumably, this diversity has implications not only for the way in which unemployment is experienced, but also for the way in which the unemployed might be brought together to act collectively.

These data suggest that we should not be overly hasty in making generalizations about the unemployed, but they are of little help in assessing whether or not unemployment is a problem. Returning for a moment to the quotation with which we opened the chapter, several aspects of unemployment are cited as being relevant for a rethinking of the problem of unemployment. The point is often made that many of the unemployed are not people who have been fired or laid off, that most unemployment is not long term, and that adult, white males—who have low rates of unemployment—are a shrinking part of the labor force. It is relatively easy to see that unemployment would not be considered a problem if most of the unemployed were people who were out of work for a short period of time after having quit their previous jobs. It is less easy to understand why the unemployment of adult, white males is the only sort of joblessness that is cause for concern. Presumably, the reason unemployment of adult males is especially problematic is that they are more likely than female and teenage members of the labor force to be chief earners for their households; their unemployment, therefore, would be potentially more disruptive. However, why *Fortune* seems to feel that the unemployment of white—as opposed to nonwhite—adult males is of special concern is not clear to us.

The data in Tables 2-3, 2-4, and 2-5 indicate that, just as it is inaccurate to stereotype the unemployed in terms of their demographic characteristics, it is erroneous to stereotype them in terms of their unemployment-related characteristics. For example, Tables 2-3 and 2-4 show that the unemployed differ from one another both in their reasons for being unemployed and in the length of their joblessness. Those who contend that high levels of unemployment are not cause for alarm find comfort in the fact that in April of 1976, over 40 percent of the 7 million unemployed had been out of work less than five weeks. However, nearly 20 percent had been out of work six months or more, and the mean length of joblessness was nearly four months. In Table 2-4 we see a summary of the reasons why the unemployed were out of work in April 1976. The Bureau of Labor Statistics discerns four kinds of unemployed persons, based on their reasons for unemployment:[6]

---

[6]These distinctions are elaborated in Kathryn Hoyle, "Job Losers, Leavers and Entrants," *Monthly Labor Review,* April 1969, pp. 24-29.

(1) Job losers—those who have lost their jobs by being dismissed or laid off and who immediately begin to look for work.
(2) Job leavers—those who leave their jobs voluntarily and immediately search for new ones.
(3) Entrants—those who have never worked at a full-time job for two weeks or more.
(4) Reentrants—those who have previous work experience, but are returning to the labor force after a hiatus.

Although, as shown in Table 2-4, only half of the unemployed in April 1976 were workers who had lost jobs and immediately began to look for new ones, the largest group among the unemployed were job losers. As a matter of fact, over 80 percent of those among the unemployed who had previously been working were workers who left their jobs involuntarily. The second largest group, over a quarter, were entrants, most of whom were relatively young.

Turning to the data from our own survey of the metropolitan work force, we can assess one of the implicit assumptions of those who would minimize the importance of unemployment as a problem—that most of the unemployed are normally dependent upon others for their support. Presumably the emphasis upon the low rates of unemployment for adult males and the diminution in their numbers relative to the rest of the work force reflects the fact that they are especially likely to be the main sources of support, rather than supplementary wage earners, for their households. As shown in Table 2-5, the composition of the unemployed in terms of their family responsibilities differs somewhat from that of the employed: they are less likely to have the substantial family responsibili-

Table 2-3   Length of unemployment, as of April 1976 (seasonally adjusted).

Mean length	15.7 weeks
Less than 5 weeks	43.2%
5-14 weeks	27.3
15-25 weeks	9.7
26 or more weeks	19.8
	100. %

SOURCE: *Employment and Earnings*, May 1976, pp. 43-44.

Table 2-4   Reason for unemployment, as of April 1976 (seasonally adjusted).

Job losers	49.6%
Job leavers	11.8
Entrants	26.0
Reentrants	12.7
	100. %

SOURCE: *Employment and Earnings*, May 1976, pp. 43-44.

ties that come from being a main earner with dependent children.[7] However, the case should not be overstated. Nearly two-thirds of the unemployed, 65 percent, are main wage earners for their households. Nearly half of these—45 percent, or 29 percent of all of those out of work—have children who are dependent upon them for support. As in so many other ways, it is incorrect to stereotype the unemployed.

What we have seen is that those hard-headed souls who wish to take an honest look at the "new unemployment" have become trapped in a new and equally unrealistic set of images. If the unemployed are not, as they once were, a huddled mass of hopeless, job-hungry individuals, they are also not an undifferentiated mass of teenagers and housewives. While the unemployed are clearly not a perfect reflection of the work force from which they are drawn, they are—like the work force—a heterogeneous group. Not only are they diverse in terms of their demographic characteristics, containing members of both sexes and all age, ethnic, and occupational categories, but they are diverse in terms of several dimensions more clearly related to the question of whether unemployment is a problem meriting serious consideration: their family responsibilities, their reasons for being out of work, and the length of their joblessness.

How New Is the New Unemployment?

Implicit in the argument that old definitions no longer suffice for the new unemployment are some assumptions about the nature of the unemployed during the thirties that warrant closer examination. The demographic composition of the unemployed at any time is a function of several factors: the relative size of the demographic subgroups within the population; the labor force participation rates of these various groups;

[7]Unless otherwise noted, all data in the tables and figures of this book are from our metropolitan work force survey.

Table 2-5 Family responsibility and employment status.

Family role	Employed	Unemployed
Main wage earner—		
With children	39%	29%
Without children	35	36
Non-main wage earner—		
With children	18	20
Without children	8	15
	100%	100%
	(799)	(571)

SOURCE: 1976 metropolitan work force survey.

the unemployment rates of these groups. A change in any of them will precipitate a change in the composition of the unemployed as a group.[8]

Because data about unemployment rates of population subgroups are available only since the late nineteen forties, we cannot construct a portrait of the unemployed of the thirties analogous to that contained in Table 2-2 for 1976. The data in Tables 2-6 and 2-7 do, however, permit us to draw some inferences. Table 2-6 shows the unemployment rates for various population groups in representative years since 1948. Although the unemployment rate has fluctuated over the period in response to economic forces, certain regularities are apparent. Whatever the overall unemployment rate, the rate for nonwhites is always roughly twice that for

[8]We can clarify this with some illustrative examples. For instance, as a large cohort of postwar babies has come of age and entered the work force in the late nineteen sixties and nineteen seventies, the work force has become younger. Setting aside for a moment the unusually high rates of unemployment sustained by the young, we recognize that as the work force has become younger, so too has the group of unemployed individuals. Changes in labor force participation rates can have similar effects. In recent years more and more women have entered the labor force; thus, the labor force has become more female—not because there are more women, but because so many more of them are working. Again, if we ignore the impact of differential rates of unemployment for the sexes, as the work force has become more female, so too has the composition of the jobless group. Finally, changes in differential rates of unemployment can affect the composition of the unemployed group. During the late 1950s unemployment rates for men and women were roughly equal. More recently, women have suffered a relative disadvantage in terms of employment. As unemployment rates for women have climbed relative to those for men, the unemployed group has become relatively more female.

Table 2-6   Unemployment rates for selected groups from 1948 to 1976.

	YEAR			
Variable	**1948**	**1960**	**1970**	**1976**
Total	3.8	5.5	4.9	7.4
White	3.5	4.9	4.5	7.0
Negro and other	5.9	10.2	8.2	13.2
Male	8.6	5.4	4.4	7.0
Female	4.1	5.9	5.9	8.6
Both sexes, 16-19 years	9.2	14.7	15.2	19.0
Men, 20 and over	3.2	4.7	3.5	5.9
Women, 20 and over	3.6	5.1	4.8	7.5

SOURCE: U.S. Department of Commerce, Bureau of Labor Statistics, *Historical Statistics of the United States*, pt. 1, p. 134. The figures for 1976 are from *Employment and Earnings*, January 1977, pp. 138-139.

whites, and the rate for teenagers is always roughly three times that for adults. The rate for women has, with the exception of a few years, always been higher than that for men; however, the size of the gap has fluctuated over time and has been relatively large in recent years.

In terms of the composition of the labor force, as shown in Table 2-7, the dramatic difference between the contemporary work force and that of the thirties is its sexual makeup. The female portion of the work force has grown in all age categories—a growth that has come at the expense of older males. This change has yielded a work force that is somewhat less old and considerably more female than it was during the depression of the thirties.

What inferences can we draw from these data about the composition of the unemployed during the thirties? Making the perhaps incorrect assumption that the generalizations about the unemployment rates of various groups that have obtained since the late forties hold also for the thirties, we can conclude that the unemployed were an imperfect reflection of the work force from which they were drawn. Most likely, they were—as today—younger, blacker, more female than the labor force. Given the changes that have taken place in work force composition, they were—compared to the contemporary unemployed—certainly less female. However, given that the labor force was then—as now—composed of

Table 2-7   Labor force composition from 1920 to 1976.

Sex and age	1920	1930	1940	1950	1960	1970	1976
				YEAR			
Male—total	79.6	78.1	75.4	72.2	67.9	62.8	60.3
16-19[a]	7.3	5.9	4.8	3.7	3.8	4.4	5.3
20-24	10.1	10.0	9.4	7.7	6.6	7.6	8.7
25-44	38.1	36.9	35.3	34.4	31.5	26.9	26.4
45-64	20.6	21.5	22.4	22.4	22.8	21.2	17.8
65 and over	3.4	3.8	3.5	4.0	3.2	2.5	1.9
Female—total	20.4	21.9	24.6	27.8	32.1	37.2	39.7
16-19[a]	4.1	3.4	2.6	2.2	2.5	3.2	4.3
20-24	4.4	4.9	5.1	4.3	3.6	5.7	6.5
25-44	8.2	9.3	11.5	12.9	13.6	14.2	16.5
45-64	3.3	3.9	4.8	7.5	11.2	12.7	11.3
65 and over	0.4	0.5	0.5	0.9	1.3	1.4	1.1

[a]Ages 14 to 19 before 1950.
SOURCE: U.S. Department of Commerce, Bureau of the Census, *Historical Statistics of the United States*, pt. 1, p. 132. The figures for 1976 are from *Employment and Earnings*, January 1977, pp. 138-139.

members drawn from all social groups, the unemployed during the depression were presumably a diverse lot in demographic terms.

We can speculate further from the data on the reasons for unemployment. The assumption seems to be made that while only half of today's unemployed are people who lost jobs, most of those out of work during the thirties were job losers. Data about reasons for unemployment have been collected only since 1967. However, certain generalizations hold for the last decade:[9] the ratio of job losers to job leavers has fluctuated with changes in the overall rate of unemployment, ranging from 2.5 to 1 in the low unemployment year of 1969 to over 4 to 1 in 1976; the relative number of entrants has remained relatively stable, about 12 to 14 percent of the unemployed over the period. If these relationships can be extrapolated back to the thirties, it would seem logical to infer that the unem-

[9]Data upon which these generalizations are based may be found in the following issues of the Bureau of Labor Statistics' journal *Employment and Earnings:* January 1968, pp. 120-121; January 1971, p. 123; January 1973, p. 130; January 1975, p. 144; January 1977, p. 147.

ployed during the thirties contained very few job leavers. Given that the relative number of teenagers in the work force is virtually unchanged—9.3 percent in 1930 and 9.6 percent in 1976—it would seem reasonable to conclude that the portion of the unemployed who are entrants has remained more or less unchanged also over the period. It seems safe to conclude that the old unemployed, like the new unemployed, were heterogeneous in terms of both their reasons for unemployment and their demographic characteristics. Clearly the composition of the unemployed has changed since the depression. However, just as it is misleading to stereotype the unemployed of the mid-seventies, it is probably a mistake to stereotype the jobless of the depression.

Who Else Is Exposed to Unemployment?

Exposure to job insecurity and unemployment is not confined simply to those who are out of work at a given moment. Those who are fearful of losing their jobs, those who have been unemployed in the past, and those whose families or friends are out of work share in the experience of joblessness and unemployment insecurity. Tables 2-8 to 2-10 report data from our metropolitan work force survey, which indicate the degree to which those who have jobs are exposed to unemployment.[10]

As shown in Table 2-8, the bulk of those with jobs feel relatively secure in them. Only about one in five indicated some fear of job loss in the near future when interviewed in April 1976.[11]

Table 2-9 shows that many workers, especially those currently unemployed, have histories of unemployment. Over a third of those with jobs

[10]The sample for our metropolitan work force study is described in Appendix A. In Appendix B we have provided a set of tables containing the number of cases in various cells of the major categorizations we use throughout the book. The reader therefore has ready access to the number of cases on which a particular percentage is based. When we use a categorization not contained in Appendix B, we present the number of cases in the specific table or figure. Furthermore, when a particular categorization is used several times in a chapter, we provide the number of cases in the first table or figure where the categorization is used, even if similar numbers may be found in Appendix B.

[11]We have analogous data for the unemployed, which are of some interest. We asked those who were looking for work about their chances of finding employment in the near future and those not currently looking for work but intending to do so about their chances when they did look. Each of these groups was fairly equally divided among those optimistic about the chances of finding a job, those somewhat uncertain, and those reporting very little chance of finding employment. Not surprisingly, among those currently looking for work, those who have been out of work longest are least optimistic about their chances of finding employment: one out of four of those out of work less than a month say they have "very little chance" of finding a job, while half of those out of work a year or more take this pessimistic position.

Table 2-8 Job insecurity among the employed.

Chance of losing job in near future:	
Very likely	5%
Somewhat likely	13
Unlikely	82
	100%

have been out of work for a month or more during the past decade—13 percent within the year preceding the study; about half of the working respondents who have been unemployed have been out of work more than once. Among the unemployed, a substantial share, 42 percent, have had previous experience with joblessness.

Finally, the impact of joblessness is not confined to those who are out of work; those with jobs are exposed to unemployment when their friends and relatives are out of work. In general, the percentage of households in which a member has been out of work during the past year is roughly twice the unemployment rate. We asked about a somewhat less direct form of exposure to unemployment, the unemployment of friends and acquaintances. It is clear from the data in Table 2-10 that the unemployed are much more likely than those with jobs to live in an environment of unemployment. A third of those out of work report that many of their friends are unemployed, and only 41 percent say that most of their friends have jobs. In contrast, only 12 percent of the employed report that many of their friends are out of work, and seven out of ten say that most of the people they know have jobs.

In this context it is interesting to note the patterns of response for demographic groups. For the most part, members of various demographic

Table 2-9 History of unemployment over the past ten years.

Unemployment history	Employed	Unemployed
Never for a month or more in past ten years	65%	—
Once	18	58%
Two or three times	10	24
More than three times	7	17
	100%	99%

Table 2-10 Proportion of friends who were without work.

Employment status of friends	Employed	Unemployed
Many out of work	12%	32%
Some out of work	17	27
Most have jobs	71	41
	100%	100%

groups are equally likely to know people who are unemployed. For example, 10 percent of working men, as opposed to 12 percent of working women, and 32 percent of unemployed men, as opposed to 31 percent of unemployed women, know many people who are out of work. The contrast between blacks and whites in this regard is striking: only 9 percent of employed whites, as opposed to 27 percent of employed blacks, report that many of their friends are out of work; the analogous figures for the unemployed are 27 percent of the whites, as opposed to 42 percent of the blacks. In view of the degree of residential segregation in our metropolitan areas and the astronomically high rates of unemployment among minority youth, this is perhaps not surprising. In the words of one black teenager whom we asked whether many of the people he knew were out of work: "Of course. This is the ghetto, isn't it?"

Summary

We have reviewed a great deal of evidence about the unemployed in the process of beginning to grapple with the seemingly simple question of whether unemployment is a problem. We have seen that the unemployed are not perfectly representative of the work force; as a group they are less male, less old, less white, and less occupationally skilled than the work force from which they are drawn. In addition, the unemployed are diverse, in terms of their demographic attributes and also in terms of the length and causes of their joblessness and the extent of their family responsibilities. Although conclusive statements are impossible, available evidence indicates that the unemployed during the depression—while different in composition from today's jobless—were also a heterogeneous group. Finally, we have seen that exposure to unemployment is not limited to those who are out of work at a particular moment.

Given this diversity of the unemployed, it seems unwise to accept any one image of contemporary unemployment as definitive. Those who make the case that high rates of unemployment are no cause for alarm cannot make that claim solely on the grounds of a more detailed under-standing of the characteristics of those included in the "new unem-ployed." If we are to understand whether elevated rates of unemploy-ment are cause for concern, we must have some more direct measure of whether unemployment causes hardship. It is the association of unem-ployment and stress to which we now turn.

CHAPTER 3

Does Unemployment Hurt?

IDESPREAD UNEMPLOYMENT during the depression of the 1930s was accompanied by suffering and deprivation of staggering proportion. Chronicled in the pages of *The Grapes of Wrath* and the photos of Walker Evans, the human degradation and misery wrought by widespread joblessness impressed itself on the consciousness of an entire generation that came of age during those painful years.

Many studies of the impact of unemployment were conducted at the time and they coincide remarkably well in the patterns of hardship they describe.[1] Clearly the most immediate and pressing consequence of unemployment was loss of income. When faced with unemployment, the first response of the family was to compensate by dipping into savings. Given that most of those who lost their jobs had hardly been paid handsomely in the first place, these reserves usually were soon exhausted. As prospects became grimmer, debts were incurred, meats and nutritious foods sacrificed, illnesses left unattended, mortgages foreclosed, cheap living quarters sought, heat forsworn. Children, fatigued by under-

---

[1]Among many such studies are the Following: Ewan Clague and Webster Powell, *Ten Thousand out of Work* (Philadelphia: University of Pennsylvania Press, 1933); Grace Adams, *Workers on Relief* (New Haven: Yale University Press, 1939); Robert Cooley Angell, *The Family Encounters the Depression* (New York: Charles Scribner's Sons, 1939); Jessie A. Bloodworth and Elizabeth J. Greenwood, *The Personal Side* (New York, Arno Press, 1971; originally published 1939); E. Wight Bakke, *Citizens without Work* (New Haven: Yale University Press, 1940) and *The Unemployed Worker* (New Haven: Yale University Press, 1940); Mirra Komarovsky, *The Unemployed Man and His Family* (New York: Dryden Press, 1940); and Eli Ginzberg, *The Unemployed* (New York: Harper and Brothers, 1943).

nourishment yet ashamed to partake of the hot lunches provided by the government for members of relief families, stayed away from school. Wives and children were sent to relatives who could provide for them more adequately, and idled breadwinners took off in search of employment. The ultimate recourse for many who could no longer provide for themselves was charity in its various available forms and, in later years, relief. For a desperate few, the final act was suicide.

The impact of unemployment was not solely economic. Idleness and loss of income had severe consequences for physical and mental health and for family relations as well. In terms of physical health, not only was there no money for the luxury of health care, but the physical symptoms often associated with psychological pressure tended to multiply. The process of making do financially sometimes entailed the breakup of families; even when the family was able to remain intact, tensions were virtually inevitable as the jobless male household head found his authority undermined by his inability to fulfill his usual role as breadwinner. Sometimes the wife or children were able to find employment—usually at ridiculously low wages—leaving a bewildered and resentful husband to do "woman's work" at home. Even when the authority of the jobless breadwinner remained unquestioned, the blow to his self-esteem was often crippling. In the words of one man who had been laid off six months previously from his job as a special mechanic in a tire factory, "I am a human being, but I have been thrown on the rubbish pile like a bundle of rags. I am a discard."[2]

The Argument for Reduced Impact in the Seventies

That unemployment implied suffering during the 1930s is undisputed; whether the unusually high rates of unemployment that have characterized the economy of the mid-1970s imply similar hardship is, as we have mentioned, a matter of some controversy. This is an issue that we must examine, for if there is no suffering, there is no reason to anticipate political mobilization.

A number of arguments are adduced in support of the position that unemployment in the 1970s is accompanied by far less hardship than it was during the depression of the 1930s. The first has to do with the length of unemployment. During the thirties, it is argued, many of the most catastrophic consequences of unemployment—loss of homes, breakups of family units, ill health, and the like—did not occur immediately. It was only after weeks of unemployment stretched into months and years, and

---

[2]*Report and Recommendations of the California State Unemployment Commission* (San Francisco: California State Printing Office, 1932), p. 93.

after savings and other available resources were exhausted, that the real impact of unemployment was felt. Today, the thesis runs, the unemployed are idled for much shorter periods of time. Therefore, the consequences of unemployment could hardly be as severe as they were during the thirties.

A second argument has to do with the reasons for unemployment. According to this position, unlike the thirties when millions of steady workers were thrown out of their jobs, only a minority of the unemployed have actually been fired or laid off; the majority are in some sense voluntarily unemployed, either because they are reentering the labor force after a hiatus, or they are entering for the first time, or they quit their last jobs. Presumably, those who have elected to be unemployed cannot be suffering to the same extent as those whose joblessness is involuntary. At the very least, as we face the potentially costly task of reducing unemployment, we should not be overly concerned with the majority of unemployed who have chosen unemployment.

A third explanation of why unemployment in the 1970s creates less strain than it did during the 1930s has to do with the changing composition of the labor force. Unlike the thirties, when most of those who were unemployed were principal wage earners for their households, many of those who are unemployed these days are secondary earners—wives and teenagers, whose earnings function as a supplement to the family budget. Presumably the consequences of loss of income under these circumstances are much less severe than when a main earner is idled. In addition, because their earnings are merely supplementary, these unemployed non-main wage earners have less incentive to find work.

A final argument made by those who feel that unemployment no longer creates extreme hardship has to do with the financial cushion provided by unemployment compensation and the supplemental unemployment benefits (SUBs) of companies and unions. During the thirties, according to this position, once the unemployed worker had depleted his savings, available additional resources—if any at all—were dependent upon the generosity of local governments and charities. Today benefits are available automatically to the worker who is laid off. Beyond shielding the unemployed worker from hardship, these benefits actually create unemployment by giving the jobless worker little incentive to endure the pain of working. In short, as one labor economist put it, "unemployment isn't what it used to be."

Although these arguments are rarely stated so baldly or systematically, it is clear from contemporary treatment of the issue in the media that they inform much of the understanding of unemployment in the 1970s. A series of vivid articles by several authors about the unemployed, which appeared in the *Wall Street Journal*, illustrates the degree to which the arguments stated above provide a basis for comprehending the real dimensions of the unemployment problem. Because they are so engagingly written, we have chosen to quote from them extensively in order to communicate their prevalent tone. The first unemployed person we meet is "Bo Grier, Aristocrat of the Streets":

ATLANTA—Raymond "Bo" Grier, 24, spends most of his afternoons and evenings shooting baskets at the Peoplestown gym in a declined inner-city neighborhood here. These are the good times, with his buddies, working off the tensions that build during the long, idle days.

The bad times are the mornings, smoking the endless chain of cigarets and watching, empty-eyed, indistinguishable television game shows at the apartment where he lives with his sister. Since it is winter, the weather is usually too bad to get out and attack the powerless power steering on his faded gold 1968 Buick Wildcat parked outside. The Buick functioning would mean a vast uplift in status—wheels instead of riding the bus.

It has been two years since Bo had any kind of steady work, and by now his ways of existing on the streets without a job may be so deeply ingrained that he may never change . . .

Categorizing Bo Grier is simple, but analyzing why he doesn't work is not. One thing that has to be considered is a slight physical handicap resulting from a landmine injury in Vietnam. It doesn't interfere with his ability to swivel and drive down the court past his opponents at the gym. But it is a definite factor in his not having a job, because the government considers him 30% disabled and sends him a $149 check every month, making his quest for a job that much less pressing.

Living with his sister is another factor. She has a job on a production line making plastic drinking cups and pays the $140 rent and $30 or so monthly utility bill . . .

The thing is that Bo, and many others in his situation, have enough going for them that economic survival is not the question, only the style in which one survives. And the truth is that Bo, by freeloading on his sister, stretching his government check and hustling on the side, has made such an admirable adjustment to not having a job that it is not hard to see why he is not out pounding the pavements.[3]

Mark Rinaldi, the next jobless worker to whom we are introduced, differs radically from Bo Grier in social background. Still, in terms of their unemployment situations the two are remarkably similar:

[3]Douglas R. Sease, "Bo Grier, Aristocrat of the Streets," *Wall Street Journal*, 31 January 1977, p. 12. Reprinted by permission, © Dow Jones & Company, Inc. All rights reserved.

WEST HARTFORD, CONN.—Last March the Konover Investment Co. decided to lease its parking lot in downtown Hartford rather than continuing to operate it itself. In the resulting management change, Mark Rinaldi, who had been an attendant at the lot for two years, was laid off.

After two months without a job, Mr. Rinaldi applied for unemployment compensation. Ever since then he has received a $54 check from the state of Connecticut every two weeks. He could go on receiving it another 39 weeks.

For the spare, bearded 23-year-old who lives with his parents in this upper-middle class suburb, the unemployment checks spell the difference between the need to keep working "at some crummy job" and his present leisurely lifestyle . . .

Contrary to much conventional wisdom about employment, Mr. Rinaldi demonstrates that being out of work doesn't automatically mean painful suffering . . .

Although his lifestyle isn't exciting, it's certainly comfortable. He's able to indulge his penchant for imported German Hofbrau beer. And he has enough friends with cars and places to go that he isn't trapped in one place. He says the most unpleasant element of unemployment is being nagged by his parents. "They say 'go to work, everybody works.' I say 'everybody's miserable.' "[4]

Unlike the preceding two, Sandy Biggest does not collect unemployment compensation. Nonetheless, her unemployment situation seems similar to theirs both in that she does not appear to be suffering unduly and in that she seems to have little incentive to find work quickly:

LEMONT, ILL.—Sandy and Ed Biggest like to fly for fun and last spring they bought their second two-seater airplane. The Biggests, both 33 years old, also own two cars and a comfortable six-room house, fully paid for, in this pleasant suburb of Chicago. Their two children, aged nine and 14, attend Catholic school.

Ed is an $18,000-a-year mechanic for Amoco Chemical Co. Sandy is a housewife. The couple currently has no outside income, but in the early days of their marriage Sandy worked and Ed put in many seven-day weeks, allowing them to build a respectable nest egg. They still consider themselves quite comfortable financially.

Yet Sandy, an attractive and energetic woman, is an unemployment statistic because she's bored with housework and has been looking for a job. And not just any job, mind you. Despite the fact that she has only a high school education, she says she won't settle for less than a position selling sophisticated business machines at a minimum salary of $15,000 a year.

[4]William M. Bulkeley, "Mark Rinaldi: Jobless by Choice," *Wall Street Journal*, 1 February 1977, p. 20. Reprinted by permission, © Dow Jones & Company, Inc. All rights reserved.

"I'd be working right now if I wasn't so fussy about the kind of work I'd take," she admits. "I'm not looking for a job because we need the money, so why shouldn't I be choosy?"[5]

Unlike Bo Grier, Mark Rinaldi, and Sandy Biggest, the final unemployed person whom we meet in the series, Harry Bernstein, is a main wage earner. Like all three of them, his recent unemployment has scarcely been accompanied by misery:

PHILADELPHIA—Harry Bernstein, a 62-year-old textile cutter, was laid off his job at a local sportswear manufacturer last March. It's been a struggle, Mr. Bernstein says, but he and his non-working wife "aren't really suffering," and he's enjoying the leisure.

One reason they're not suffering is that Mr. Bernstein is drawing $96 a week in tax-free state unemployment compensation. That's far below his weekly take-home pay of $140, but it eases the strain while he hunts for work. And there's comfort in knowing the unemployment checks will be there again in case of future layoffs.[6]

How typical are the experiences described in the *Wall Street Journal?* It is certainly possible to cull from our follow-up interviews examples of jobless workers whose experiences are reminiscent of those just described.[7] For example, we interviewed a twenty-four-year-old bank teller who was fired when she gave too much money to a customer cashing a check. She actually rather likes being unemployed. Shielded from financial hardship by unemployment compensation and the paychecks brought home by her husband, a unionized printer, she describes joblessness as something of a relief. She enjoys having spare time to cook, sew, and read. Freed from the pressures of her old job, she finds herself more relaxed. She is untroubled by the psychosomatic symptoms that haunt many of the unemployed and says that she has lost weight and is in better health since she has been unemployed.

Another case of a worker who did not suffer extraordinary hardship is an inner-city teenager from Chicago. Unlike Bo Grier, our respondent is now working—at a menial job, packing boxes—but in other respects his

---

[5]Christopher A. Evans, "Sandy Biggest: Search for Fulfillment," *Wall Street Journal*, 7 February 1977, p. 12. Reprinted by permission, © Dow Jones & Company, Inc. All rights reserved.

[6]Harry B. Anderson, "Layoffs and Jobless Benefits," *Wall Street Journal*, 11 February 1977, p. 8. Reprinted by permission, © Dow Jones & Company, Inc. All rights reserved.

[7]As mentioned, we have conducted longer follow-up interviews with sixty of the jobless workers contacted in the original telephone survey. These open-ended interviews are described in Appendix A.

experience recalls Grier's. Supported by his mother, a factory worker, he did not experience acute financial strain. Occasionally he would do odd jobs, but most of the time he would play basketball.

Another unemployed person to whom we spoke does not seem to be enduring undue stress as the result of his jobless status: a forty-nine-year-old bachelor who was formerly an oiler in the merchant marine, he admits unabashedly that the three dollars an hour he would earn if he were working simply isn't enough to justify taking a job. He is quite emphatic in stating that he does not depend upon anybody—he draws neither unemployment compensation nor welfare. Though he regrets his inability to afford luxuries like a new car, he prefers to get by on a small fixed income of uncertain origins than to undergo the agonies of job holding.

So—the case would seem to be closed. The suffering once endured by the unemployed has now, like smallpox, been relegated to history. However, for every case like the ones just summarized in which unemployment, if not an actual blessing, is at least no trauma, there are a number of cases in which joblessness has been accompanied by genuine hardship. Take, for example, one of our respondents, a cost accountant who was fired at age sixty from his job when the firm for which he was working lost a government contract. Although he has finally been hired by the Department of Health, Education, and Welfare after a job search lasting over a year, the experience of being unemployed was in his words "traumatic." While the loss of income necessitated financial sacrifices, what was much more devastating was the psychological strain. As his self-confidence ebbed, he became irritable with his wife and was so withdrawn that he reached a point where, as he describes it, he was no longer interested in anything.

For another respondent, a thirty-five-year-old widow with three children who lost her job as an assembler in an electronics plant, the pressures were quite different—but no less anxiety producing. Her fundamental problem was how to pay the rent. Although she showed considerable ingenuity in finding ways to cut down on expenses, in the final analysis her "standard of living wasn't too high in the first place so there wasn't much to cut out." Given that she had finished two years of college, she originally hoped to find a job requiring more skill. However, in view of her financial difficulties (her income in 1976 was less than $6,000, on which she had to support herself and her children) and the attendant anxieties, she found another job as soon as possible—doing precisely what she had been doing before.

Or consider yet another respondent for whom the experience of unemployment has been a devastating one. Formerly an elevator operator, he seems to have lost all sense of interior compass when, after many years of steady work, he was replaced by an automatic mechanism—and therefore laid off. With mock dignity he asserts, "I enjoyed my job as The Elevator Man. It ain't much fun going up and down all day, but I was satisfied." Entirely without family or friends, he spends almost all of his time in his shabby Harlem apartment watching television and sleeping, with only his dog for companionship. Totally disheartened, he apparently no longer has a sense that he can in any way control his own destiny.

The most poignant example in our study is from an interview never conducted. In our first round of structured interviews we talked to an unemployed man who had lost his job handling telephone orders for a steel company, a job he had held for three years. He had taken from his savings and cut back substantially on spending. Dissatisfied with his economic circumstances, he was nonetheless optimistic about finding a job. When we tried to contact him four months later for a follow-up interview, he was angry that we had found him again. Here is our interviewer's transcript of the telephone conversation: "Don't call me again. This is too painful to discuss. There is nothing you can do. I've become a has-been. I've gone from being comfortable to being hungry. I can't find my way out of a brown bag, though I've never been on welfare. I don't want to go through it again. It's too painful to discuss. Please don't call again."

Hardship and Unemployment: A More Systematic Look

This series of brief individual profiles should serve to reinforce the conclusion of the preceding chapter, that the unemployed are a heterogeneous lot. Now to the diversity in their demographic characteristics and occupational histories, we need to add the diversity in the degree of hardship endured while out of work. In view of the variety with which we are dealing, the hypothesis that unemployment no longer implies suffering cannot be tested by looking at individual cases. Obviously, a more systematic look is in order.

There is one contemporary study that takes such a systematic look, Harvey Brenner's *Estimating the Social Costs of National Economic Policy*.[8] Using regression techniques, Brenner links economic distress—as measured by rate of unemployment, rate of inflation, and real per capita income—to social pathologies—as measured by age-specific and sex-specific mortality rates, cardiovascular-renal disease mortality rates, suicide mortality rates, homicide mortality rates, mental hospital admission rates, and imprisonment rates. His most consistent set of relationships is between unemployment and his measures of social pathology. He finds a statistically significant correlation between rate of unemployment and

[8]*A Study Prepared for the Use of the Joint Economic Committee, Congress of the United States* (Washington, D.C.: Government Printing Office, 1976).

each of these indicators for virtually all age groups, for men and for women, and for whites and for nonwhites.

This is important evidence; yet because it relies on aggregate data, it cannot help us to understand the impact of unemployment as perceived by the unemployed. It is in interpreting the meaning of Brenner's significant macrolevel findings that our survey data are of special use.

UNEMPLOYMENT AND INCOME

Whether lost wages were providing groceries or movie tickets, this month's rent or this season's fashions, virtually all of the unemployed report that one thing they miss about their jobs is the money. Let us deal with the matter more systematically by considering Figure 3-1, which presents data on the relationship of occupational level and employment status to satisfaction with income. Because the data are presented in a format to be used throughout the remainder of the book, we shall explain in some detail how the figure should be interpreted. In Figure 3-1 the percentage of respondents who report being dissatisfied with their incomes is plotted for the working and unemployed members of each of four occupational groups. The solid line reports the data for those with jobs, the dotted line for those who are unemployed. The slope of each of the lines shows the relation between occupational level and income dissatisfaction; the sharper the slope, the stronger the relationship. The distance between the lines gives the impact of unemployment upon dissatisfaction; the farther apart the lines, the greater the difference between working and jobless members of a given occupational level.[9] The data make clear that the unemployed at each level are substantially more likely to report dissatisfaction with income than are those who are working. While about 80 percent of the unemployed in the three lower occupational categories and 70 percent of the unemployed from the highest occupational level

[9]We measure employment status by applying the somewhat controversial definition used by the Bureau of Labor Statistics (discussed in Chapter 2). As we have shown, the unemployed are hardly a uniform group. They are differentiated by the length of their joblessness, the seriousness of their financial responsibilities, and so on. Although in general we treat the unemployed as a group in making comparisons between employed and jobless workers, where relevant we shall differentiate among the jobless in terms of the special characteristics of their unemployment.

Our measure of occupational level was constructed by standardizing and adding three variables: occupation, occupational prestige, and occupational skill. The last was determined by asking respondents how much formal education and how much on-the-job training were needed for jobs like theirs. According to Charles R. Walker and Robert H. Guest in *The Man on the Assembly Line* (Cambridge, Mass.: Harvard University Press, 1952), p. 36, workers are quite capable of making such judgments accurately. On the basis of this additive scale, respondents were divided into four

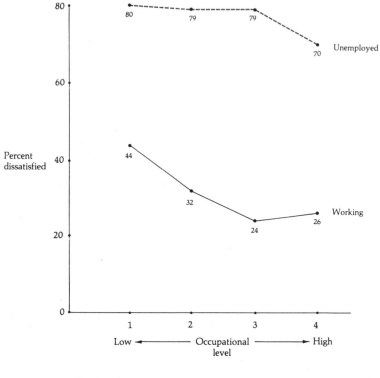

Figure 3-1   Dissatisfaction with income, by employment status and occupational level.

Number of cases:

	Occupational level			
Status	1	2	3	4
Working	(173)	(190)	(181)	(198)
Unemployed	(222)	(110)	(72)	(61)

categories of occupational level. The following examples give an idea of some actual occupations that fall into these four groupings, from low to high:

(1) Taxi driver; supermarket cashier; motel chambermaid; school custodian.

(2) Carpenter; switchboard operator; tool-and-die maker; billing clerk.

(3) Computer programmer; executive secretary; insurance salesman; draftsman.

(4) Interior designer; elementary school teacher; microbiologist; oral surgeon.

This measure (which we use frequently) is, we feel, a more accurate depiction of occupational level·in a postindustrial society than the simple dichotomous distinction between blue-collar workers and white-collar workers. From time to time, when the

indicate dissatisfaction with their incomes, much smaller proportions of those with jobs—44 percent of those at the lowest occupational level and 26 percent at the highest—say that they are dissatisfied with their incomes.

We had originally expected that those of lower occupational levels would undergo particularly acute economic strain when unemployed, and had hypothesized a negative relationship between income dissatisfaction and occupational level among the unemployed. The data in Figure 3-1 do not support this hypothesis. There is actually less variation in income satisfaction among the unemployed than among those with jobs. Among the employed, those with low-level occupations are substantially more likely than those with middle- or high-level occupations to report dissatisfaction with income. Among the unemployed, there is little difference across occupation levels. The only noticeable difference is, however, consistent with our original hypothesis, the relatively lower level of overall income dissatisfaction among the unemployed whose former occupations fell into the highest occupational category. What is most apparent is that the unemployed—regardless of occupational level—feel the impact of their unemployment in their pocketbooks.[10]

---

context dictates, we do look at these two broad occupational groups as well.

It is our substantive interests that dictate the distinction between these two measures and the adoption of these two measures instead of a standard scale of socioeconomic status. However, we should also note the results of a factor analysis that yielded three distinct job-related factors: an occupational factor, including the variables that comprise our occupational-level scale; a job-security factor, including variables like current employment status and past history of unemployment; and an income factor. Our distinction between employment status and occupational level is consistent with these results.

[10]This is one of the few cases where we have been able to check our data on the attitudes of the unemployed with another source. The National Opinion Research Center of the University of Chicago conducts a periodic General Social Survey that contains a question about satisfaction with one's financial circumstances. By combining a number of their studies we were able to obtain a sample of 334 unemployed respondents. If we divide this sample into four occupational levels, we find a pattern similar to that in Figure 3-1: the unemployed are less satisfied, and there is less variation across occupational levels among the unemployed.

Occupational status	Percent dissatisfied by occupational level—			
	Low ←————————————————————→ High			
	1	2	3	4
Working	28	25	20	16
Unemployed	47	54	51	53

Unemployment and Extra Time

Obviously unemployment not only means a loss in available income, it means an increase in available time. Such extra time can be blessing or burden. For some, extra time provides an opportunity for the pursuits—hobbies, family activities, and the like—that are preempted when working. For others, extra time brings boredom or worse. At the extreme—as reported in *Marienthal*, Jahoda, Lazarsfeld, and Zeisel's classic study of the unemployed in an Austrian community during the thirties—the sense of time is so distorted that what were once trivial chores (drawing water from the well or chopping wood) come to consume hours.[11] One of the respondents to our in-depth interview, the cost analyst whom we met earlier, reported being so psychologically disoriented that he could get nothing done. This extreme reaction seems unusual for our respondents. A number of them did complain of boredom, though, and in general the extra time appears to have been a burdensome weight on the hands of the unemployed. "I don't like the extra time. Extra time is for lazy people," one respondent put it. The following quotation illustrates the ambivalent —but probably ultimately negative—view that a number of the unemployed had about their extra time: "It [unemployment] is a lot of time, but a man needs time sometimes. If there's no job to be got then you might as well sit back. I do a lot of bowling now, but that's about it. I like going to the movies but I can't do that anymore. Most of the time, I just watch TV. I really wish I was working again."

From the interviews it is clear that there is a great deal of variation among individuals in terms of their ability to use time productively. Although it is difficult to say anything systematic, it seems that the ability to take advantage of extra time is a function of both personal idiosyncrasy and financial responsibilities. Those who are the principal earners for their families seem especially likely to spend significant amounts of time looking for a new job and also to use spare time to make extra money. The opportunity to pick up odd jobs to compensate for loss of income is clearly related to the individual's skills. Some—for example, the college music teacher who gave music lessons and the construction worker who helped a friend build an addition to his house—were able to use their occupational talents rather directly. Others—like the social worker who repaired air conditioners while unemployed—mobilized other skills in doing odd jobs. Aside from looking for work or doing odd jobs, unemployed respondents use their time in a great variety of ways. Some—such

[11]Marie Jahoda, Paul Lazarsfeld, and Hans Zeisel, *Marienthal* (Chicago: Aldine-Atherton, 1971; originally published 1933), chap. 7.

as the musician who plays in the orchestras of Broadway shows and who spends his time during periodic sieges of unemployment practicing with his friends—simply do what they would normally be paid to do. Many use the time to putter around the house—cooking, sewing, repairing—and to spend more time with their families. Some pursue hobbies, read, or visit museums. And some, especially, but not exclusively, among the teenagers, simply hang around—at home, on the streetcorner, in the local tavern.

We do have one bit of systematic data about the use of time by the unemployed. They seem to watch more television than their counterparts with jobs. Figure 3-2 shows the average number of hours spent watching television for the working and unemployed members of each of the occupational level categories. Once again, the solid line gives data for those with jobs, the dotted line for those without; the slope of each line shows the relationship of television viewing to occupational level; and the distance between the lines shows the effect of unemployment for each level. In each of the categories the unemployed report that they watch more television than do the employed, confirming the impression gleaned by reading the interviews, that many of the unemployed are bored and feel burdened by extra time.

The data in Figure 3-2 tend to lend credence to a second impression given by the follow-up interviews, that by and large those unemployed in lower occupational categories have more difficulty using the spare time generated by unemployment than those in higher categories. Not only do they watch 60 percent more television—an average of 3.7 hours per day as opposed to 2.3 hours for the upper occupational category—but the difference between the employed and unemployed is greater, both in absolute and in relative terms, for the lower occupational groups than for higher ones. At the lowest occupational level, the difference between the unemployed and the employed is more than an hour; at the highest level, about a half hour.

UNEMPLOYMENT AND FAMILY LIFE

The problems that accompany unemployment are not confined to the scarcity of income and the abundance of time. We know that at least during the thirties unemployment had consequences for family life.[12] Some-

12Virtually all of the microstudies of the unemployed conducted during the 1930s reported that unemployment had an impact on family life. See, in particular, Komarovsky, *The Unemployed Man and His Family;* the *Report of the California Unemployment Commission;* and Jessie Bloodworth, *Social Consequences of Prolonged Unemployment,* University of Minnesota Employment Stabilization Research Institute, vol. 2 (Minneapolis: University of Minnesota Press, 1933).

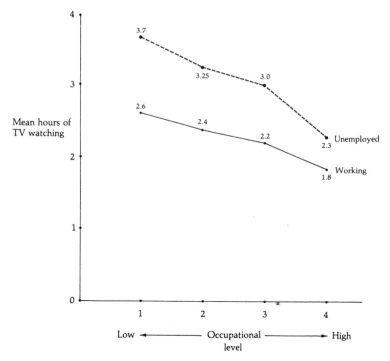

Figure 3-2   Hours spent watching TV, by employment status and occupational level.

times families were broken apart as family members either were sent away or abandoned the family unit in the name of alleviating the financial pressures; relations between couples became strained, sometimes as a function of the breakdown of traditional sex-role divisions of labor between male breadwinners and female homemakers, sometimes as a function of the simple increase in propinquity; relations between parents and children became strained as youngsters, sometimes ashamed and sometimes resentful of their fathers' failure to bring home a regular paycheck, questioned parental authority.

We find a few cases in our in-depth interviews where unemployment seems to have had this kind of severe impact on family relations. One respondent, a health administrator who was let go when the program for which he was working lost its government funds, and his wife, a college teacher who lost her job in a budget cut, almost separated as a result of the tensions surrounding this double unemployment. "My wife and I were on the verge of breaking up," he told us. Fortunately, she eventually found a teaching job in another section of the country and he planned to follow her there. Although their marriage seems to have survived, they clearly underwent severe strain during the period of their joint unemployment. Another respondent, when asked whether unemployment had affected his family, replied quite bluntly, "I wound up in divorce court," adding that he might have brought it on himself because his "disposition and temper were horrible."

Only a few of those respondents whom we contacted in our follow-up interviews described so intense a kind of marital strain, although many experienced it to some degree. In general, the tension was attributed simply to being around the house more or to financial anxieties. Typical is the comment of an unemployed construction worker, "We got on each other's nerves a lot." As another respondent put it, "My wife is just not used to having me around." Tensions with children were also evident. One respondent reported that his preschooler's "grades" suffered! Another, an unemployed chemist, said that his college freshman son changed his major from science and math to English and history. Financial restrictions placed pressure on parent-child relations in several cases: "I snapped at my children more when they asked for things. They were always asking for things they can't have like cake and ice cream. When you don't have it, they seem to ask for it more." Very few respondents spontaneously indicated that they enjoyed having increased amounts of time to spend with their families.

We attempted to document increased family tensions in our sample survey in two ways: we asked the unemployed whether there was any change in the level of tension in the family since they had become unemployed, and we asked all respondents about the level of satisfaction they felt with their family life. The data on the responses to these questions are reported on Figure 3-3. The top line on that figure presents the percentage of the unemployed at various occupational levels reporting more tension in the family since the onset of unemployment. The figures are surprisingly high, given the sensitive and personal nature of the question. In the lower two occupational groups nearly half of the respondents report more family tension. At the highest occupational level about a third of the unemployed report higher levels of family tension. Thus it seems that upper-status families are somewhat better able than lower-status families to withstand the strain of unemployment—or else that they are more reticent to report increased family tension.

The two lines at the bottom of Figure 3-3 present the proportions of the two groups who say that they are dissatisfied with family life. By and large, both the unemployed and the employed express a great deal of satisfaction with family life although, with the exception of one occupation-

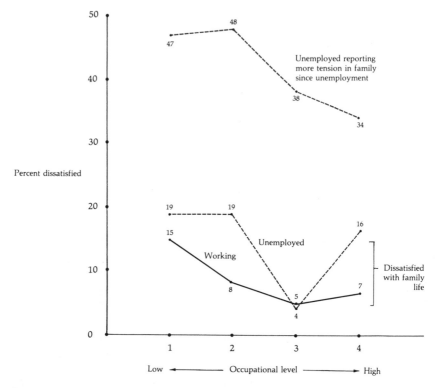

Figure 3-3 Dissatisfaction with family life, by employment status and occupational level.

al category, the unemployed seem somewhat less satisfied than those with jobs. A comparison of satisfaction with family life to satisfaction with income (shown in Figure 3-1) is instructive. First, the overall level of satisfaction with family life, for both those with and those without jobs, seems to be higher than the overall level of satisfaction with income. In addition, the unemployed are relatively less dissatisfied with family life than with income: that is, at all occupational levels, especially the higher occupational ones, we found a substantial difference between the working and the unemployed in terms of satisfaction with income; the difference between jobless and working respondents in terms of family satisfaction is consistently smaller. Furthermore, while the gap in income satisfaction grows as occupational level rises, there is no particular pattern across the occupational levels to the difference in satisfaction with family life between working and unemployed respondents.

As we have indicated, these data probably should be interpreted with caution. Family tension and family satisfaction are difficult to evaluate in structured interviews. The high level of satisfaction with family life expressed by our respondents, and those in other surveys,[13] seems out of phase with other well-known indicators of family instability such as the soaring divorce rate. Figure 3-3 may overstate the amount of satisfaction with family life. Still, it is the difference between working and unemployed that is important for our purposes. We have no reason to believe that the unemployed would be systematically more likely to reveal, or to hide, feelings of dissatisfaction with family life.

UNEMPLOYMENT AND PSYCHOLOGICAL STRAIN

It is the universal observation of past students of unemployment that the experience of being without a job has a psychological price. Summarizing a large number of studies of unemployed workers conducted in Europe and the United States during the thirties, John Garraty describes the typical response to joblessness:

> When workers lost their jobs their response, perhaps after a brief period of waiting for something to turn up, was to search for a new one. Then they became discouraged, sometimes emotionally disorganized. Finally, after months of continuous idleness, most either sank into apathy or adjusted to their condition, leading extremely circumscribed lives in apparent calm.[14]

Many of the idled workers to whom we spoke indicated that unemployment had taken a direct or indirect psychological toll. For some the evidence of increased psychological strain is indirect. A number of respondents reported an increase since the onset of unemployment in symptoms that are often associated with nervous tension—difficulty sleeping, frequent headaches, increased drinking or smoking, irritability. Respondents also discussed the nature and effects of the psychological strains induced by unemployment more directly. The thirty-five-year-old widow who lost her job as an assembler in an electronics plant was particularly articulate in expressing the anxieties she felt. "I got to be so nervous. How will I pay the rent? Then the anxiety went to depression. It's heartbreaking." Clearly her decision to take a relatively undesirable job

---

[13]In the 1974 General Social Survey conducted by the National Opinion Research Center, only 6 percent of those questioned said that they got some, a little, or no satisfaction from family life. Seventy-seven percent said that they got a great deal or a very great deal of satisfaction.

[14]John A. Garraty, *Unemployment in History* (New York: Harper and Row, 1978), pp. 177-178.

rather than to risk a delay in finding a better one was related to these psychological tensions.

The psychological strain is not, however, confined to anxieties about how to cope with loss of income and whether an acceptable job will materialize. In addition to fears about the future, a real loss of self-confidence and self-esteem is common. The degree to which work is critical to self-definition in America—far more so than in other cultures—has been remarked upon by many observers. Even when the job in question is not itself particularly demanding or fulfilling, simple job holding—the fact of being a steady and responsible worker and a consistent provider—is an important source of self-esteem, especially to a worker whose occupational advancement has been relatively limited.[15] In view of the sense of self-worth that many are able to derive from the reliable assumption of their roles as workers and breadwinners, it is not surprising that a large proportion of the unemployed to whom we spoke related joblessness to feelings of failure. Respondents referred to loss of "confidence" or "self-respect," to being "withdrawn into myself."[16]

It is, unfortunately, impossible to probe these kinds of deep feelings in the course of a closed-ended interview over the telephone. However, one question asked in our general survey can provide clues to the relationship between sense of self-worth and unemployment status. Respondents

[15]The point about the importance of work to self-definition is made by, among others, Robert Blauner, *Alienation and Freedom*, Phoenix Books (Chicago: University of Chicago Press, 1964), chap. 2; and Paul Jacobs, "A View from the Other Side: Unemployment as Part of Identity," in William G. Bowen and Frederick H. Harbison, eds., *Unemployment in a Prosperous Economy* (Princeton, N.J.: Princeton University Press, 1965), pp. 45-63. Much of the literature on the subject is summarized by Robert L. Kahn, "The Meaning of Work," in Angus Campbell and Philip E. Converse, eds., *The Human Meaning of Social Change* (New York: Russell Sage Foundation, 1972), pp. 159-203. For an elaboration of the theme of work and self-esteem see Kay Lehman Schlozman, "Coping with the American Dream: Maintaining Self-Respect in an Achieving Society," *Politics and Society*, 6 (1976), 241-263.

[16]Mirra Komarovsky describes a more extreme form of this syndrome in summarizing interviews conducted with jobless men during the depression: "The general impression that the interviews make is that in addition to sheer economic anxiety the man suffers from deep humiliation. He experiences a sense of deep frustration because in his own estimation he fails to fulfill what is the central duty of his life, the very touchstone of his manhood—the role of family provider. The man appears bewildered and humiliated. It is as if the ground had gone out from under his feet. He must have derived a profound sense of stability from having the family dependent upon him. Every purchase of the family—the radio, his wife's new hat, the children's skates, the meals set before him—all were symbols of their dependence on him" (*The Unemployed Man and His Family*, pp. 74-75). Our respondents do not seem to have undergone as severe a reaction as that described by Komarovsky.

were queried about their satisfaction with what they were "accomplishing in life." As shown in Figure 3-4 the unemployed, at each occupational level, were more likely to report dissatisfaction with their accomplishments. There is also some tendency for those in lower-status occupations to be more likely to express dissatisfaction with their accomplishments than those in higher-status occupations.

We had originally hypothesized that, while the consequences of unemployment in terms of financial strain would be particularly severe for those in lower-status occupations, the impact on psychological strain would be particularly acute among those in higher-status occupations. We reasoned that loss of a psychologically rewarding and prestigious job would be potentially more devastating psychologically than loss of one that is ill paid, dull, or belittled. The data in Figure 3-4 indicate that this is not the case. The unemployed whose former occupations fall into the highest category are less likely to report dissatisfaction with their accomplishments than those whose former jobs fall into a lower category; furthermore, the satisfaction gap between the working and the unemployed is smallest at that level. In retrospect, this finding is understandable. The unemployed professional retains a sense of his professional identity. A number of them—for example, the Broadway-show musician—actually continue to practice their professions in one way or another. The unemployed assembly-line worker or the jobless typist is less likely to have derived a sense of self-esteem from his profession in the first place; rather, he is more likely to have gained a sense of self-worth from his ability to hold a steady job and to act as a responsible breadwinner. Under these circumstances unemployment would seem to be peculiarly threatening: deprived of being a good provider, the unemployed nonprofessional has no other identity to fall back on.

Assessing the Argument for Reduced Impact

Clearly, the argument summarized above, that unemployment has few repercussions for personal life, is not upheld by our data. If we can believe the reports of our respondents—and it is difficult to imagine how anything so subjective as personal satisfaction could be gauged without resort to such reports—the unemployed are in a variety of respects less satisfied with their lives. Furthermore, the differences across the three dimensions measured—income, family life, and accomplishments—both in terms of the overall levels of satisfaction and in terms of the relative impact of unemployment lend credence to our findings. Not surprisingly, unemployment has its most noticeable effect on satisfaction with income. It also has a fairly substantial effect on sense of accomplishment in life. The data on satisfaction with family life indicate a less marked impact,

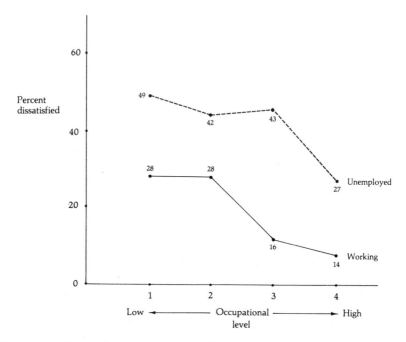

Figure 3-4   Dissatisfaction with accomplishments, by employment status and occupational level.

though there is some tendency for the unemployed to report more frequently that they are dissatisfied with that aspect of life as well. However, even in relation to family life one sees evidence of strain in the fairly substantial proportion of the unemployed who report increased family tension since losing their jobs.

Although our data lend little support to the conclusions reached by those who feel that unemployment no longer implies hardship, their arguments seem so plausible that they merit further attention. It seems perfectly reasonable to hypothesize that those who choose unemployment by leaving their jobs, those who have been unemployed for short periods of time, those who have few family responsibilities, and those who are protected by unemployment compensation would suffer less than their jobless counterparts who have been fired, who have been unemployed for long periods of time, who have family responsibilities, or who cannot collect unemployment compensation. Since we know that the unemployed are a diverse group, not simply in terms of their social characteristics but in terms of their unemployment characteristics as well, it seems worthwhile to test whether these characteristics are related to the degree to which unemployment is accompanied by dissatisfaction.

Dissatisfaction and Reasons for Unemployment

As we have discussed, many of the unemployed have in a sense chosen unemployment by quitting jobs they once held. Presumably they would suffer less than those whose unemployment is involuntary: the psychological strain would be less severe because the job leaver would know that his predicament is a result of his own actions; the financial strain would be less severe because the job leaver would have had the opportunity to anticipate and plan for the loss of income.[17] In Figure 3-5 we compare those who have quit their jobs (job leavers) with those who have been fired or laid off (job losers) in terms of their relative satisfaction with various aspects of their lives. There are slight differences in the expected direction: the job losers are a bit more dissatisfied with their incomes and very slightly more dissatisfied with their family lives than the job leavers. However, the differences are so small as to be virtually negligible. What is striking about Figure 3-5 is not that there is a very weak association between the reason for unemployment and level of dissatisfaction but that there is a strong association between joblessness and dissatisfaction.

Dissatisfaction and Length of Unemployment

It seems reasonable to hypothesize that the amount of hardship induced by unemployment is directly related to the length of the jobless period. Figure 3-6, which compares working respondents with the short-term and long-term unemployed in terms of their dissatisfaction with various aspects of their lives, confirms this expectation. In each case, the long-term unemployed (those out of work for six months or more) are most likely to express dissatisfaction. There are, however, patterns to the impact that prolonged unemployment has upon satisfaction. When it comes to satisfaction with income, unemployment seems to have a severe and relatively immediate impact. The short-term unemployed are more than twice as likely to express dissatisfaction with their income as the employed, and the increment in dissatisfaction found when one compares the short-term to the long-term unemployed is relatively small. With the other two types of dissatisfaction—with life's accomplishments and with family life—there is a steady increase in dissatisfaction as one moves from the employed group to the short-term unemployed to the long-term unemployed.

[17]It should be noted that those who argue that the impact of unemployment is less severe than it once was are less emphatic in insisting that those who leave jobs voluntarily suffer less than those who are laid off, than in asserting that the government has less responsibility for alleviating the suffering of those who have chosen to be unemployed, especially in view of the potential costs of that relief.

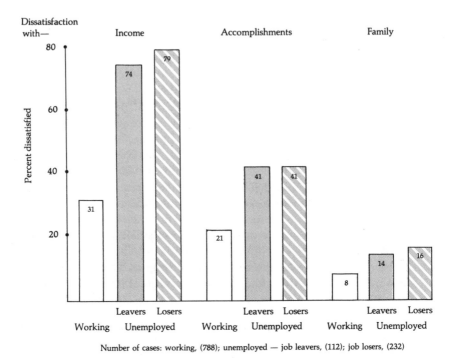

Number of cases: working, (788); unemployed — job leavers, (112); job losers, (232)

Figure 3-5 Dissatisfaction with various aspects of life, by reason for unemployment.

DISSATISFACTION AND FAMILY RESPONSIBILITIES

One of the points implicit in the series of articles from the *Wall Street Journal* is that little hardship accompanies the unemployment of workers who are not the chief earners for their households. Surely this makes intuitive sense. Mark Rinaldi, the beer-drinking former garage attendant, was hardly suffering acute financial distress. Not only was nobody else depending upon him for support, he was actually able to rely upon his parents, at least for a roof over his head. Sandy Biggest, the jobless aviatrix whose continued unemployment was a function of her selectivity about accepting a job, was not exactly in anguish either. She could rely on her husband's paychecks to maintain a comfortable life-style, and she could rely on an alternative set of identities, as housewife and mother, to relieve the psychological strain experienced by many of the unemployed. Not only is Sandy Biggest comfortable financially, she has not been haunted by feelings of uselessness. Thus, the argument that the unem-

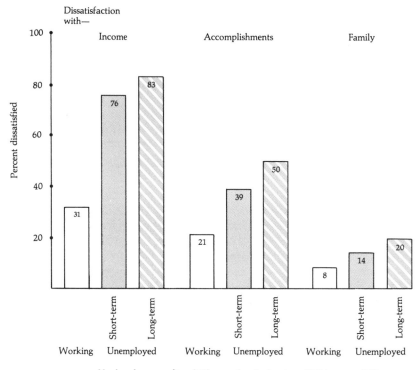

Number of cases: working, (778); unemployed—short-term, (338); long-term (196)

Figure 3-6 Dissatisfaction with various aspects of life, by length of unemployment.

ployment of those who are not chief earners implies little hardship seems a plausible one.

In Figure 3-7 we compare working and unemployed respondents who are and are not main wage earners for their households in terms of their satisfaction with various aspects of their lives. The hypothesis that non-main wage earners suffer less when unemployed receives some confirmation: in each case unemployed main wage earners are more likely to express dissatisfaction than those who are not the chief earners for their households. However, the more striking difference is between the working and the unemployed: for each type of respondent and for each type of dissatisfaction the unemployed are more likely to express dissatisfaction. Thus, unemployment is not a burden simply for those who are chief earners; those who are not main wage earners are still more dissatisfied than their working counterparts.

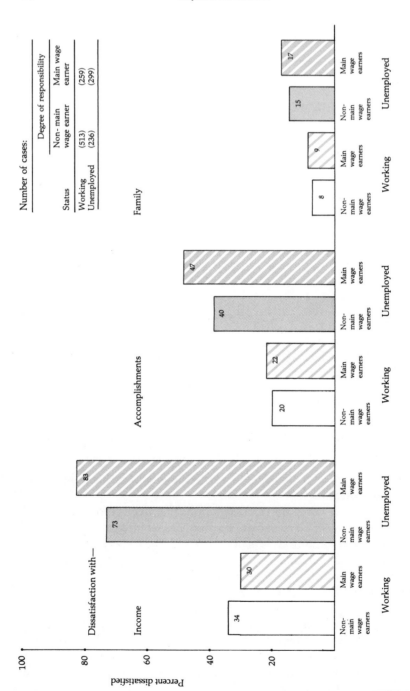

Figure 3-7 Unemployment, dissatisfaction, and family responsibilities.

The pattern of the relative impact of family responsibilities upon dissatisfaction with various aspects of life is readily understandable. Unemployed main wage earners are most dissatisfied with their incomes, least dissatisfied with their family lives, when compared with their jobless non-main earning counterparts. In view of our discussion of the ways in which unemployment creates strain, it is understandable that whether the unemployed person is a main earner or not would have relatively little to do with whether there is more tension in the family and more to do with whether unemployment creates financial hardship or feelings of uselessness and psychological strain.

It may be that it is not simply being a main earner that creates hardship, but being a main earner with dependent children. When we divided the unemployed main wage earners into two groups, those with dependent children and those without, we found that those unemployed with the greatest family responsibilities (main earners with dependent children) indeed were most likely to express dissatisfaction with various aspects of their lives. Although the differences are in the expected direction, again they are quite small. Among unemployed main wage earners, 84 percent of those with dependent children, as opposed to 82 percent without, express dissatisfaction with their incomes; 50 percent of those with dependent children, as opposed to 46 percent without, express dissatisfaction with what they are accomplishing in life; 19 percent of those with dependent children, as opposed to 15 percent without, express dissatisfaction with family life.

In general, the data on family responsibilities produce differences in the expected direction. The greater the family responsibility, the more unemployment seems to be a burden—particularly when one is dealing with income. However, the differences are not as great as one might have expected. Once again, the data show striking differences between the employed and the unemployed regardless of family responsibility.

Dissatisfaction and Unemployment Benefits

A final argument made by those who feel that unemployment no longer implies hardship is that unemployment compensation eases the burden of joblessness. Unlike the thirties, when idled workers were forced to rely upon their own resources or upon whatever charity might be available locally, many unemployed today are entitled as a matter of right to unemployment compensation and in many cases to supplementary unemployment benefits (SUBs) from a company or union as well. If the experience of Harry Bernstein, the textile cutter described in the *Wall Street Journal,* is typical, these benefits, which are not federally taxed, go a long way toward relieving the strains of unemployment.

Although it is reasonable to assume that unemployment benefits diminish the hardship associated with joblessness, there is no reason to hypothesize that they have obliterated that hardship altogether. First of all, although such benefits presumably would alleviate financial hardship, they would in no way ameliorate the psychological strains or family tensions that accompany unemployment. Furthermore, many of the unemployed do not qualify for these benefits. As is the case with many government programs that rely upon federal funding, the individual states retain a great deal of discretion over the specific provisions of unemployment insurance programs. What this means is that there are substantial—and, it turns out, growing—disparities among the states in terms of eligibility, benefit levels, and the like.[18] However, all states require previous work experience—usually between 14 and 20 weeks in the base year—in order to qualify for unemployment compensation. Entrants and reentrants therefore are not eligible. In two-thirds of the states, job leavers are not covered at all; in others, those who quit are not eligible until after a waiting period has elapsed. A substantial number of those who left jobs involuntarily—about a quarter of all who apply—are disqualified for other reasons: because they are unavailable for work, because they were fired for misconduct, and so on. Thus, not all those whom the government considers to be unemployed are eligible for unemployment benefits.[19] Furthermore, although the benefits are sizable, they do not replace lost wages. One government study estimated that on the average they replace between 50 and 60 percent of a worker's after-tax income.[20] In addition, although congressional action extended the period during which

[18]Unless otherwise noted, information in this discussion about the operation of unemployment insurance programs is taken from Raymond Munts, "Policy Development in Unemployment Insurance," in Joseph P. Goldberg et al., *Federal Policies and Worker Status since the Thirties* (Madison, Wis.: Industrial Relations Research Association, 1976), chap. 4.

[19]We did not ask our respondents directly whether they had collected unemployment benefits. However, we did ask questions about the household units. Only 43 percent of the unemployed to whom we spoke live in households in which somebody has received unemployment benefits, and only 9 percent live in households in which some member has received SUBs from a company or union. There is clear overlap between the two types of benefits, for only 45 percent of our unemployed respondents live in households in which either type of support is received.

[20]Congress of the United States, Congressional Budget Office, *Unemployment Compensation: A Background Report* (Washington, D.C.: Government Printing Office, 1976), p. xii. Because benefits are not taxable, they are a smaller percentage of the worker's gross weekly wage. These figures do not include the effects on income of fringe benefits or work-related expenses. Munts points out ("Policy Development," p. 85) that, although average weekly benefit *amounts* have risen six-fold in the period

benefits can be claimed, these programs are of limited duration and many individuals eventually exhaust their benefits. For all these reasons we should not expect the availability of unemployment benefits to dispel entirely the strain associated with unemployment.

The data in Figure 3-8, where we compare unemployed respondents who do and do not have access to unemployment compensation or SUBs in terms of their satisfaction with various aspects of life, confirm our expectations. As we hypothesized, the availability of unemployment benefits has no effect upon dissatisfaction with accomplishments or family life. Those without benefits are no more unhappy than those who receive them; as before, both unemployed groups are considerably less satisfied than those with jobs. In terms of income, those who live in households in which somebody has received such benefits are actually a bit more dissatisfied; once again, however, the major difference is between the working and the unemployed.

Types of Unemployed Workers

We have been discussing how various categories of unemployed workers—those who qualify for benefits and those who do not, those who are chief earners and those who are not, and so on—respond to the experience of being out of work. The categories we have been using are analytic ones. However, in considering the plight of the unemployed, we normally think not in terms of abstractions like degree of family responsibilities, but in terms of a variety of stereotypes, some of which were implicit in the *Wall Street Journal* series. For example, we think of the inner-city

---

between 1940 and 1975, benefits were a smaller *proportion* of average wages in 1975 than thirty-five years earlier.

It is difficult to make comparisons between unemployment compensation in the United States and in other industrial democracies. Among systems in eight industrialized nations the United States compares favorably with other countries in terms of the portion of the labor force covered and the duration of the benefits. Benefit levels seem somewhat less generous here than elsewhere. For example, in 1972 unemployment benefits would have replaced roughly 60 percent of the disposable income of a production worker with two children living in Detroit and roughly 80 percent of that of a production worker with two children living in Germany. Because estimates of replacement of disposable income must include consideration of tax rates and the taxable nature of benefits as well as benefit levels, explicit comparisons are difficult. One way in which unemployed American workers are less well protected than their counterparts elsewhere is that Americans are likely to lose their health insurance coverage when they lose their jobs. See Constance Sorrentino, "Unemployment Compensation in Eight Industrial Nations," *Monthly Labor Review*, July 1976, pp. 18-24; and Axel Mittelstädt, "Unemployment Benefits and Related Payments in Seven Major Countries," Paris OECD papers, July 1975.

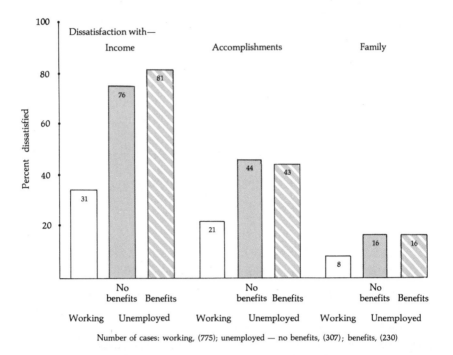

Figure 3-8 Dissatisfaction with various aspects of life, by availability of unemployment benefits (unemployment compensation or SUBs).

black teenager, utterly lacking in job skills and experience, hanging around the streets of Harlem and managing to get by from day to day courtesy of the contributions of his relatives and the welfare system; or of the down-and-outer who floats aimlessly from marginal job to marginal job; or of the poverty-bound welfare mother trapped in a tenement by her lack of skills and her brood of preschool children; or of the suburban housewife, bored and isolated by keeping house, whose children are sufficiently well launched that she can look for work once again; or of the auto assembly-line worker in a little bungalow in suburban Detroit, laid off in a period of economic slowdown; or of the graduate aerospace engineer fired when congressional defense cutbacks necessitate massive corporate reductions in expenditures for research and development.

Implicit in each of these capsule characterizations is a stereotype of a more or less readily recognizable kind of jobless person. Of course, the unemployed are not a coalition of identifiable groups; the kinds of people who are out of work and the reasons for their joblessness are myriad. Still, in order to understand responses to some of the modal circumstances under which joblessness is experienced, we have created several categories of unemployed workers, categories designed not to be either mutually exclusive or exhaustive, but to include several readily recognizable types of unemployed workers:

(1) *Urban youths:* noncollege respondents between the ages of eighteen and twenty-one.[21]

(2) *Unskilled workers with a history of joblessness:* mature workers typical of those in what is often called the secondary labor market.[22]

(3) *Women with dependent children who are main wage earners for their households.*

(4) *Housewives who are reentering the labor force.*[23]

(5) *White, male, unionized blue-collar workers.*[24]

(6) *College graduates who have lost their jobs.*[25]

[21]Because our sample was designed with measurement of political effects in mind, we included only those who were old enough to vote. The group of urban youths therefore does not include teenagers younger than eighteen, who have quite high rates of unemployment. In addition, we include only those with no education beyond high school and no family to support (dependent children or spouse). The stereotyped urban unemployed is black. We had too few cases of blacks to separate them out.

[22]In this category we included unskilled manual workers at least thirty years old who had been unemployed in the recent past and—for the unemployed—who were job losers or job leavers, as opposed to entrants or reentrants. These are basically unskilled workers with some history of employment instability.

[23]In this category we included married women who were not main wage earners for their households. Among the unemployed we included only those who were reentering the work force.

[24]Among the unemployed we included only job losers (those who had been fired or laid off).

[25]Unemployed professionals have received a considerable amount of attention from the media, especially during the white-collar recession of the early 1970s. (See, for example, Berkeley Rice, "Down and Out along Route 128," *New York Times Magazine,* 1 November 1970.) We had originally planned to do considerable analysis of the responses of this group. However, because the unemployment rate for well-educated workers is quite low, too few appeared in our sample to permit extensive analysis.

We were also interested in investigating the phenomenon of underemployment— that is, underutilization of skills—among the college educated. For this purpose we selected all respondents with college degrees who reported that their present or former jobs required no more than a high school diploma. Upon further probing we discovered that in many cases the underutilization of skills was somewhat ambiguous. For example, one of those whose formal education exceeded what he considered his job to require was a professional musician; another owned a group of movie theaters.

One of the reasons for looking at such groups separately is that we would expect there to be considerable variation in the amount of dissatisfaction felt by the members of the various groups when out of work. For example, we would expect the housewife reentrants—like Sandy Biggest in the *Wall Street Journal* series—to find joblessness relatively less burdensome than female chief earners, a large percentage of whom fall below the poverty line even when they are working, or unionized blue-collar workers. However what is perhaps most noticeable about the data in Table 3-1—in which working and jobless members of these various groups are compared in terms of their satisfaction with income and accomplishments in life—is the congruence with the general pattern we have found throughout this chapter: in each category the unemployed are considerably more dissatisfied than their working counterparts. In some cases the level of dissatisfaction reaches near unanimity within the group: nine out of ten of the unemployed youth and unemployed female heads of household are dissatisfied with their income. The differences between the working and the unemployed are not as great when it comes to life's accomplishments; nevertheless, the differences are clear within each of the groups.

As we expected, however, there is variation across the groups in terms of the level of dissatisfaction expressed. In each group those out of work are more likely to express dissatisfaction; however, the jobless members of certain of the categories are especially likely to indicate dissatisfaction. Housewives attempting to reenter the labor force are less likely to express satisfaction with their incomes than are married women who have jobs. However, relative to other unemployed groups the level of dissatisfaction with income expressed by the housewife reentrants is quite low: over half of them are actually satisfied with their incomes. Furthermore, it is for this group that the gap in satisfaction between one of our prototypical unemployed groups and their working counterparts is smallest. Among college graduates, white male unionized manual workers, and women with dependent children who are main wage earners, those who are unemployed are substantially more likely to express dissatisfaction than those who have jobs.

Class, Race, Joblessness, and Satisfaction

The unemployed are less satisfied with their incomes and with what they are accomplishing in life than are the employed. But how much less satisfied are they? It is a hard question to answer because we have no precise measure of satisfaction. Figure 3-1 gives one intuitively understandable answer. A glance back will show that it compares the percentages among the employed and the unemployed who report in response to a

Table 3-1 Dissatisfaction with various aspects of life among stereotypical groups.

Dissatisfaction	All	Urban youth	Unskilled workers, history of joblessness	Women with dependent children[a]	Married women[b]	White male blue-collar union members	College graduates
Percent dissatisfied with income							
Working	31	37	42	47	28	31	28
Unemployed	78	89	72[c]	92	44[d]	71[e]	79[e]
Percent dissatisfied with accomplishments							
Working	21	19	26	30	17	31	16
Unemployed	43	47	54[c]	63	36[d]	41[e]	32[e]
Number of cases							
Working		(31)	(43)	(48)	(176)	(67)	(266)
Unemployed		(78)	(39)	(39)	(27)	(38)	(33)

[a]Main wage earners only.
[b]Non-main wage earners only.
[c]Job losers and job leavers only.
[d]Reentrants only.
[e]Job losers only.

direct question that they are dissatisfied with their income. Another way of gauging the severity of the impact of unemployment on satisfaction is to compare unemployment with other social characteristics; two associated with satisfaction are class (as measured by occupational level) and race. Does the fact of being in a low-status rather than a high-status job or of being black rather than white contribute more to dissatisfaction than the fact of being jobless rather than employed? Since class, race, and employment status are closely related (lower-status workers are more likely to be black, and both black and lower-status workers are more likely to be jobless), we shall have to estimate the impact of each on satisfaction while controlling for the effects of the other two.

One particularly appropriate approach to categorical data is log-linear analysis. Log-linear models can be used in a variety of ways for a variety of purposes. Our purpose is to estimate the relative effect of each of the three independent variables—class, race, and employment status—on satisfaction over and above the other two.[26]

Race and occupational level will provide a benchmark for interpreting the magnitude of dissatisfaction associated with unemployment. This benchmark is particularly useful because the statistics that measure the effects of one variable on another in the log-linear model do not have any clear intuitive meaning. The comparison of race and occupational level with employment status, plus the tabular data already presented on the difference in the percentage of dissatisfied individuals among the working and the unemployed at each occupation level, should give the reader a fairly clear sense of the burden that unemployment places upon the individual.

To estimate the effect of each of our three characteristics, we proceed through several steps. First we calculate the chi square statistic for the deviation of a model containing the additive effects of each of the three independent variables on satisfaction from a "saturated" model containing all additive and interactive effects of the three variables. (The saturated model is equivalent to the actual data.) Second, we calculate the chi

[26]The log-linear models are discussed in Leo A. Goodman, "The Multivariate Analysis of Qualitative Data: Interactions among Multiple Classifications," *Journal of the American Statistical Association*, 65 (March 1970), 226-257; "A Modified Multiple Regression Approach to the Analysis of Dichotomous Variables," *American Sociological Review*, 37 (February 1972), 28-46; and "A General Model for the Analysis of Surveys," *American Journal of Sociology*, 77 (May 1972), 1035-1086.

The specific coefficients used in Table 3-2 are suggested and discussed in Jae-on Kim and Charles Mueller, "Predictive Measures of Association for Contingency Table Analysis," working paper, Department of Sociology, University of Iowa, 1977. We are indebted to Professor Kim for suggesting this approach to multivariate contingency table analysis and for advice on its application.

square statistic for the deviation from the saturated model for three other models that contain the effects of two but not the third of the three independent variables. Lastly we compare the chi square for the deviation of the three-variable model from the saturated model with the chi square for the deviation for each of the three two-variable models. For each of the three two-variable models the greater the increase in chi square over that for the model containing all three variables (that is, the greater the increased deviation from the saturated model), the greater the effect on satisfaction of the variable left out of the model.

For example, the chi square for the deviation of the model containing the additive effects on satisfaction of all three independent variables from a saturated model containing all effects is 17.4. The model that contains only the additive effects of race and of class has a chi square of 187.4. The increase in chi square of 170.0 when employment status is left out of the model is a measure of its effect on satisfaction over and above the effects of class and race.[27]

The approach is analogous to stepwise multiple regression, where one enters first the effects of several variables on a criterion variable and then calculates the increase in explained variance when an additional variable is entered—the increase being a measure of the effect of the additional variable over and above the ones previously entered into the equation. The approach as outlined above (which we shall use at various places in this book) pays too little attention to interactive relations between the independent variables and the dependent. Where interactions are significant, we shall discuss them. We shall also report the effects of interactions (statistically significant or not) where they are of particular relevance to our argument. In the case of satisfaction we report the interactive effect of class and employment status.[28]

Table 3-2 contains the result of such an analysis. The overall effect of the three variables on income satisfaction is large and statistically significant: class, race, and employment status together have a substantial ef-

[27]Since an "independence" model, which assumes no additive or interactive effects of the three variables on satisfaction, has a chi square of 309.6 from the saturated model, the much smaller deviation of 17.4 for the model with additive effects indicates that interactive effects of the three variables on satisfaction are not important, a fact that simplifies our analysis. (In log-linear analysis any lack of independence between two variables is considered to be interaction. We are, however, referring to interaction involving at least two independent variables and a dependent one.)

[28]This interactive effect is calculated by comparing the chi square for a model containing the additive effects of each of the three variables with a model containing the additive and interactive effects of class and employment status plus the additive effect of race. The larger the chi square for the model containing only additive effects, the greater is the interactive effect of class and employment status.

fect on satisfaction with income. When we consider the effect of each separately—controlling for the others—we find that employment status has by far the largest effect, followed by the effect of race, then that of class. The interaction of class and employment status has a smaller but statistically significant effect as well. The data both confirm and highlight what our tabular analysis has already told us: being without work has a significant effect on one's satisfaction with income. That effect is larger than either the effect of one's position on an occupation hierarchy or one's race.

The data on satisfaction with one's accomplishments in life are similar in that employment status has the largest effect. Class, rather than race, has the next largest effect. The three variables, however, do not predict sense of accomplishment as well as they predict income satisfaction.[29]

Job Insecurity and Dissatisfaction

While we have shown quite unambiguously that there is an association between joblessness and dissatisfaction, we should like to take the analysis one step further and probe the relationship between satisfaction and job insecurity. Both working people and unemployed people differ in the degree to which their employment histories are characterized by past instability and future insecurity. In order to measure the dimension of employment insecurity we constructed scales that included the following items: for the employed—length of employment in present job, history of unemployment, and subjective appraisal of the chances of losing their current job; for the unemployed—length of unemployment, history of past unemployment, and optimism about finding work.[30]

[29]The relative importance of unemployment in relation to dissatisfaction is consistent with the results of a recent study of the "quality of life" in America. Using a composite measure of subjective "well-being," they find that the unemployed ($n = 75$) score by far the lowest on the scale—much lower than those with limited education or blacks, to mention two groups whose level of satisfaction falls below the average for the population as a whole. The next least satisfied group is divorced people, but their score on the satisfaction scale deviates in a negative direction from the population average about half as much as the negative deviation of the unemployed. A control for income level does little to change the dissatisfaction level of the jobless. See Angus Campbell, Philip E. Converse, and Willard L. Rogers, *The Quality of American Life: Perception, Evaluation, and Satisfaction* (New York: Russell Sage, 1976), pp. 51-55 and 313-314.

[30]For working respondents, a short time on the current job, history of unemployment, and the expectation of likelihood of job loss in the near future were taken as evidence of job insecurity. For jobless respondents, long-term unemployment, history of past unemployment, and pessimism about finding a job in the near future were taken as evidence of job insecurity. As with our measure of occupational level, we standard-

Table 3-2   Effect of class, race, and employment status on satisfaction.

Variable	Satisfaction with income	Satisfaction with accomplishments
Effect of—		
Class (occupational level)	11.6*	20.9**
Race	33.7**	8.8*
Employment status	170.0**	32.2**
Class and employment status	7.7*	3.6
Overall effect	309.6**	117.4**

*Significant at .01 level.
**Significant at .001 level.

As shown in Figure 3-9, there is a relationship between this composite measure of job insecurity and satisfaction for both working and unemployed respondents, for both satisfaction with income and satisfaction with accomplishments. Furthermore, the relationship is not a spurious one, a function of the associations between high occupational status and job security and high occupational status and satisfaction. When occupational status is controlled, the relationship between job security and satisfaction tends to persist, though not always very clearly.[31] Once again, however, the most substantial difference in terms of satisfaction is between the working and unemployed. Among the unemployed, even the most secure are more likely to express dissatisfaction than the least secure among working respondents. Furthermore, when occupational level is controlled, the difference between working and jobless respondents remains unambiguous.

Summary

It turns out that those who posit that certain changes since the thirties would nullify the personal consequences of unemployment, draw a false conclusion from the changes they recognize so accurately. They are correct in asserting that over the past several decades the relative number of

---

ized these items and added them. We then divided the working and the unemployed into three subgroups based on their scores. The items included on these scales were those that loaded together in the factor analysis to which we referred earlier in the chapter.

[31]The following tables show the relationship between job security and satisfaction within occupational levels (for numbers of cases see Appendix B):

(note continued on page 82)

unemployed who are job losers has diminished; the length of the average bout of unemployment has decreased; the relative number of jobless who are chief earners has been reduced; and unemployment benefits are available on an unprecedented scale. Yet from these correct premises an incorrect conclusion is drawn. In spite of these changes, unemployment hurts. Why? One way to answer the question is to point out that there are still many unemployed who have been fired, who have been jobless for long periods of time, who are main wage earners for their households, or who do not receive benefits. What is more to the point, however, is to reiterate that the links between these changes and reduction in hardship are much more tenuous than many observers have assumed. Job leavers are not less dissatisfied than job losers. Those who receive unemployment benefits express as much dissatisfaction as those who do not. Those with fewer family responsibilities and those who are unemployed for short periods of time are somewhat less dissatisfied than those with greater family responsibilities and the long-term unemployed. But these differences ought not obscure what is probably the most important finding of our data: namely, that all types of unemployed are considerably more likely to express dissatisfaction than their counterparts among the working.

In concluding, we should indicate that it has not been our purpose to give a comprehensive view of the consequences of unemployment for society. We did not attempt to measure the kind of aggregate effects that Brenner found—significant increases in rates of suicide, homicide mortality, or mental hospital admissions with rising levels of unemployment. Nor did we try to document systematically the kinds of impacts often

Occupa-tional level	Working, job security is—			Unemployed, job security is—		
	Low	Medium	High	Low	Medium	High
	Percent dissatisfied with income					
1	44	56	36	83	80	76
2	46	31	31	90	78	69
3	46	31	14	90	75	75
4	33	37	22	83	60	65
				Second-order partial gamma = .22		
	Percent dissatisfied with accomplishments in life					
1	31	30	22	55	47	44
2	38	38	24	54	46	31
3	17	20	14	67	26	33
4	14	24	10	30	14	35
				Second-order partial gamma = .16		

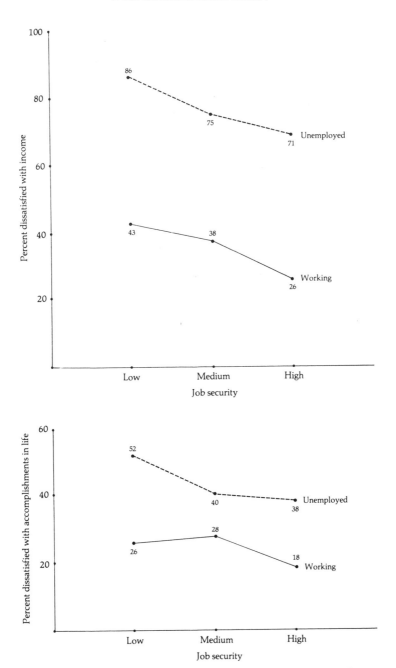

Figure 3-9   Dissatisfaction with income and accomplishments, by job security. and employment status.

reported in the media—that child beating, marital instability, and violent crime are the side effects of high rates of joblessness. Our questions attempted to measure several somewhat less sensational aspects of the human costs of joblessness, in terms of loss of income, psychological stress, and family strain. However, we know quite well that our questions hardly exhaust the multiple ways in which unemployment has costs both to the unemployed themselves and to society.

Skeptics might argue that we have leaped too quickly from dissatisfaction to the inference of hardship. Although there are consistent and substantial differences between working and unemployed respondents in terms of the satisfactions they express, the unemployed might simply be a whiny lot, responding with complaints to circumstances in which there is little objective deprivation and hardship. However, we must bear in mind the replies to the open-ended follow-up interviews as well. When single-item, forced-choice questions were posed, the pattern of responses was indeed striking: the unemployed expressed a great deal less satisfaction. It is from the less systematic follow-up interviews that we cull evidence that the jobless suffer. When given an opportunity to express their feelings, most of those with whom we talked discussed at some length and with considerable intensity the difficulties they had endured: the struggle to make ends meet, the self-doubt, the family tension, the anxiety, the sleeplessness. What we learned from these more spontaneous utterances amplifies our understanding of the consistent pattern in the survey responses and makes clear that the dissatisfaction expressed by the unemployed is evidence of hardship, not petulance.

CHAPTER 4

Coping with Unemployment

W E ARE BEGINNING to see that what we originally posed as a puzzle—the question of why widespread unemployment in the 1970s seems to have so few apparent political consequences—is indeed a puzzle. We have seen quite clearly that unemployment does produce dissatisfaction, and presumably such dissatisfaction is the stuff from which political pressure arises. However, it may well be that the rational unemployed person would not squander his limited resources of time or skills in political action designed to elicit aid from the government. Rather, the rational actor might devote those precious resources to activities that would have a greater probability of diminishing his dissatisfaction—looking for a job and searching for supplementary income. Especially since Americans are supposed to be characteristically inventive and self-reliant, it seems reasonable to inquire into what the unemployed are doing on their own to moderate the hardships they experience and to assess whether any efforts they make are successful in reducing their dissatisfaction.

Our conversations with jobless workers made it clear that they expend a great deal of effort in attempting to deal with the difficulties attendant to unemployment. Almost by definition, since the government counts among the unemployed only those who are available for work, one of the most important activities of the unemployed is looking for work. The mode of job search is a function of the specific kind of work being sought. Different occupations have characteristic patterns of job search: the unionized construction worker will keep in touch with his union about the availability of work; the aerospace engineer will prepare a résumé and contact an executive recruiter; the telephone operator will watch the want ads. Practically everybody talks to friends. The intensity of the job search is apt to be a function of many factors—work history, family responsibilities, available resources, and the like. However, virtually all the unemployed to whom we spoke were making some concerted effort to find work.

It is almost tautological to assert that the way to reduce the difficulties associated with unemployment is to find work. In the meantime, however, most of the unemployed to whom we spoke were trying in other ways to cope with their situations. Particularly obvious were their struggles to deal with financial pressure. In our follow-up interviews the unemployed workers to whom we spoke went into some detail about what they had been doing to manage financially. One way in which most of our respondents—both working and unemployed—coped with financial pressure was to reduce spending. There seemed to be as many ways to cut back on expenses as there were respondents. A number of those we interviewed eliminated luxuries such as bowling, movies, or magazine subscriptions, but many found that they had to curtail expenditures on necessities as well—for example, by eating less meat or moving in with other family members. One unemployed woman, whose wardrobe budget had evaporated, exchanged clothes with a friend so as not to have to wear the same outfit every day. An unemployed man had sold his car and begun to ride the bus. The natural complement to reducing expenditures is raising income, and our respondents were quite ingenious in the ways they found to generate resources. Once again, the methods of increasing income were nearly as numerous as our respondents. Some sold possessions, in particular their homes or cars; some found odd jobs, baby-sitting or doing construction for a friend. One way in which some unemployed people raised money is through illegal activities—especially stealing and selling drugs.[1]

Managing Financially

In our survey we asked both working and unemployed respondents what the members of their households have been doing in the recent past to deal with the financial pinch, both by cutting back on expenditures and by making efforts to generate additional resources. In terms of resource generation, we asked about several methods of managing self-

[1]Most of our information about the extent of illegal activity came from the responses to the question, "Are there any other things that people you know do to make ends meet—even though you don't do these things yourself?" One respondent, however, when asked what he had been doing to make ends meet, answered quite unabashedly, "Stealing."

reliantly: dipping into savings; having someone who was not previously employed take a job; having someone in the household take a second job. We also asked about receiving help from others, either by getting financial help from family or friends or by taking out loans. In addition, we asked about the receipt of government welfare benefits or food stamps.

Given the high level of economic strain among the unemployed, we expected this group to be substantially more likely than those with jobs both to cut back expenditures and to raise resources. The data in Figure 4-1 lend general confirmation to our hypothesis. The unemployed are considerably more likely to have cut back: 79 percent of the unemployed, as opposed to 51 percent of the employed, say they have cut back in recent months; furthermore, the unemployed are more than three times as likely as the employed to say that they have cut back substantially—37 percent as opposed to 12 percent. In terms of generating resources, both the employed and the unemployed report having undertaken in various ways to increase resources but, in general, the unemployed are even more apt to have done so. For example, with respect to the most frequent way of generating resources—dipping into savings—the unemployed are somewhat more likely to report having done so. Fewer of the unemployed presumably have resources to tap, a fact that probably depresses the relationship. Furthermore, the unemployed report more frequently that someone in the household not previously working has taken a job, that they have gotten financial help from family or friends, or that they have received food stamps or welfare payments. It is with respect to the latter two activities that the unemployed differ most substantially from the employed. There is no difference between the two groups in the frequency with which they report that someone in the household has taken on a second job to supplement income. Furthermore, the employed are more likely to report that they have taken out loans to deal with the financial pinch. This, we assume, is more a reflection of the greater credit worthiness of the employed than a reflection of the relative need for such loans.[2]

Only 21 percent of the unemployed, as opposed to 41 percent of the working, report having done nothing in the recent past to increase family resources. It is true that, as compared to working respondents, five times

[2]A study of the unemployed during the recession of the late 1950s reports similar results. Large percentages of unemployed families indicated that they had tapped savings, postponed expenditures, gone into debt, or gotten help from family (an average of two of these activities per family). See Eva Mueller and Jay Schmiedeskamp, *Persistent Unemployment, 1957-1961* (Kalamazoo, Mich.: Upjohn Institute for Employment Research, 1962).

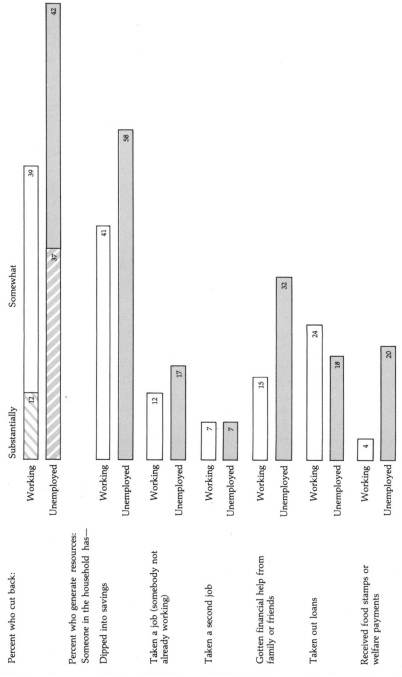

Figure 4-1 Methods of coping with the financial pinch.

as many of the unemployed live in households receiving welfare or food stamps. However, the bulk of those on welfare have also engaged in some other activity to generate resources. Of the 20 percent of the unemployed who have received welfare, two out of three report other activities. In other words, only about 7 percent of the unemployed have limited their resource-generating activities to obtaining welfare benefits from the government. Among our unemployed respondents the number who have made no efforts on their own, but have simply been content to accept government benefits, is very, very small.[3]

Occupational Level and Coping with Unemployment

Obviously there is a substantial difference between the working and the jobless in terms of their efforts to manage financially. However, the relationship may be a spurious one. Given that those from lower occupational categories—who, we would assume, have the greatest need to find additional resources—are overrepresented among the unemployed, it could well be that the difference between the employed and the unemployed is actually a function of occupational level rather than joblessness.

The data in Figure 4-2, in which the employed and unemployed members of various occupational-level categories are compared in terms of their efforts to make ends meet financially, confirm that the difference between the employed and the unemployed cannot be explained by differences in occupational level. As before, working respondents are represented by a solid line, unemployed ones by a dotted line; the slope of each line indicates the degree to which the employment groups differ according to occupational level; the distance between the lines indicates the degree to which unemployment has an impact for each of the categories. At each occupational level the unemployed are considerably more likely to report having made efforts to cope financially both by cutting back substantially and by engaging in at least one of the activities listed in Figure 4-1 to generate new resources. As a matter of fact, the expected negative relation between occupational level and efforts to cope financially appears in only one case: among respondents with jobs, the likelihood of having generated resources decreases as occupational level rises. Among the unemployed, occupational level seems to have no impact at all upon the likelihood of having generated resources. With respect to curtailing expenditures, there is no consistent relationship between occupational

---

[3]Among the employed, we find also that most—three out of four—of those who have been on welfare or received food stamps have engaged in other resource-generating activities.

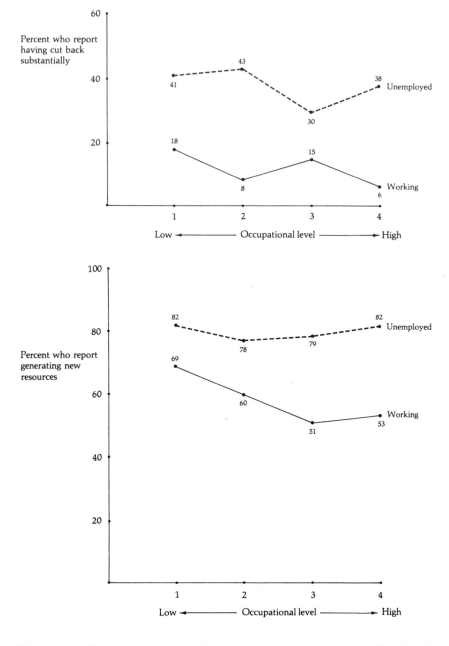

Figure 4-2   Methods of coping with unemployment, by occupational level and employment status.

level and efforts to manage financially—for either the employed or the unemployed. It seems clear that the unemployed make special efforts to make ends meet, efforts that cannot be explained by differences in occupational level.

Unemployment and Coping

In Chapter 3 we hypothesized that certain kinds of unemployment— long term, among chief earners, and among those ineligible for unemployment benefits—would create special hardship. It turned out that there were some differences among the various unemployed groups in terms of the amount of dissatisfaction; however, the obvious difference in terms of dissatisfaction was between the working and unemployed. It now seems worthwhile to examine whether these unemployed groups, whom we expect to have special needs, are making special efforts to cope with financial hardship.

Length of Unemployment and Coping

As we discussed in Chapter 3, the studies conducted during the thirties indicate that the consequences of unemployment were multiplied as the period of unemployment grew longer. We saw that the long-term unemployed did report more strain than those whose unemployment had been of shorter duration. However, the difference associated with length of unemployment was perhaps less dramatic than one might have expected, and members of both unemployed groups were substantially more likely to report dissatisfaction than those with jobs.

We expected to find length of unemployment to be related to efforts to manage financially, either by cutting back or by generating resources. As shown in Figure 4-3, no matter what the length of their joblessness, the unemployed are considerably more likely to report substantial cutbacks than are those with jobs. Only 12 percent of the working respondents, as opposed to 25 percent of even the short-term unemployed (those out of work one month or less) have cut back substantially. Not surprisingly, the proportion of unemployed who report having cut back substantially rises sharply with length of unemployment. Among those who have been unemployed one year or more, over half report substantial cutbacks. Taking a looser criterion, we find that most of the long-term unemployed —87 percent—reported having cut back at least somewhat.

The pattern is quite different for the relationship between length of unemployment and attempts to generate additional resources. As we have seen, there is considerable difference between the employed and the unemployed in terms of the likelihood that they have undertaken one or more of the resource-generating activities listed in Figure 4-1. Contrary

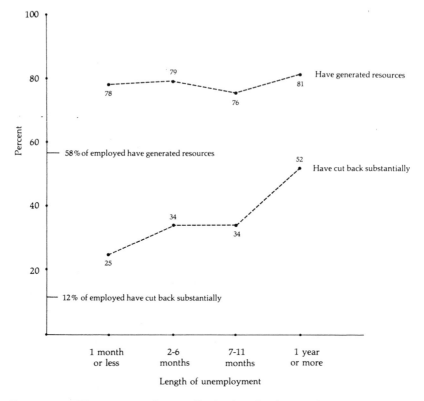

Figure 4-3 Efforts to cope financially, by length of unemployment.

to our expectations, the likelihood of having done something to supplement income does not seem to rise as length of unemployment increases. Apparently, moves to generate new resources are made by most of the unemployed at the onset of joblessness, and lengthened unemployment does not induce those who have not generated additional resources to begin to do so.[4] Thus, the data indicate that the unemployed begin very quickly to seek new resources to compensate for lost income. A smaller number reduce spending substantially at the onset of unemployment.

[4] Finding this result somewhat puzzling, we then hypothesized that perhaps most of the unemployed do something to generate resources right away, but that the long-term unemployed undertake more activities in the attempt to make ends meet. This hypothesis, too, was disconfirmed. There was no consistent relationship between length of unemployment and the number of methods used to generate resources. Mueller and Schmiedeskamp do report an increase with prolonged unemployment in the average number of measures taken to cope with unemployment. But their measure

However, as unemployment continues, more and more of the unemployed find it necessary to reduce family spending—even though the proportion seeking other resources does not increase.

FAMILY RESPONSIBILITY AND COPING

The data in Figure 4-4, in which we compare working and unemployed respondents who are and are not main wage earners for their households in terms of efforts to cope financially, confirm our expectation that those with family responsibilities would be forced to make special efforts to make ends meet. Once again, we see that the unemployed, regardless of their family responsibilities, do more than their employed counterparts in terms of both cutting back expenditures and generating resources. However, the data also indicate that, among the unemployed, main wage earners are more likely both to have cut back and to have generated resources. In addition, jobless main wage earners with dependent children are particularly likely to have cut back expenditures: 55 percent of the unemployed main wage earners with dependent children, as opposed to 45 percent of those without, report having cut back substantially.[5] Thus, as with the data on income dissatisfaction, the data on financial coping offer support to both sides of the argument about whether the composition of the contemporary unemployed population has reduced the strain of unemployment. If we compare the short-term and long-term unemployed or those with major family responsibilities and those without, we find that unemployment has a greater impact upon both those who have been out of work a long time and those who have responsibility for the support of others. On the other hand, we find that even the less burdened groups appear to be more likely than the employed to have sought to manage financially by cutting back and increasing resources.

UNEMPLOYMENT BENEFITS AND COPING

We saw in Chapter 3 that those who receive either public or private forms of unemployment benefits are not less likely to express dissatisfac-

---

mixes our two categories of acts—those involving a cutback in expenditures and those involving the generating of resources. Their measure of cutting back spending shows a pattern similar to ours, with a substantial increase in the proportion reporting such a cutback among the long-term unemployed. See *Persistent Unemployment*, p. 29, table 23.

[5]Dependent children seem to have relatively less impact on efforts to generate resources. Virtually all unemployed main wage earners have engaged in at least one of the resource-generating activities: 91 percent of unemployed main wage earners with dependent children, and 88 percent of those without, have generated resources.

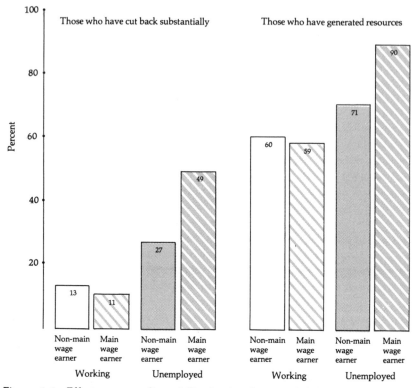

Figure 4-4   Efforts to cope financially, by family responsibilities and employment status.

tion with income. Now we wish to inquire whether receipt of these benefits obviates the need to make efforts to manage financially. As shown in Figure 4-5, in which we compare those unemployed respondents who live in households receiving benefits with those who do not, these benefits do not seem to relieve the need to make efforts to get by economically. Once again, the striking difference is between the employed and unemployed groups, whether or not benefits are available: the unemployed are considerably more likely than those with jobs both to have cut back and to have generated resources. In terms of the difference between the unemployed groups, those who have access to unemployment compensation or SUBs are actually somewhat more likely to have made additional efforts to manage financially: among the unemployed, 84 percent of those living in households with these benefits, as opposed to 74 percent without, have curtailed spending; 82 percent of those in households with such benefits, as opposed to 76 percent without, have done something to in-

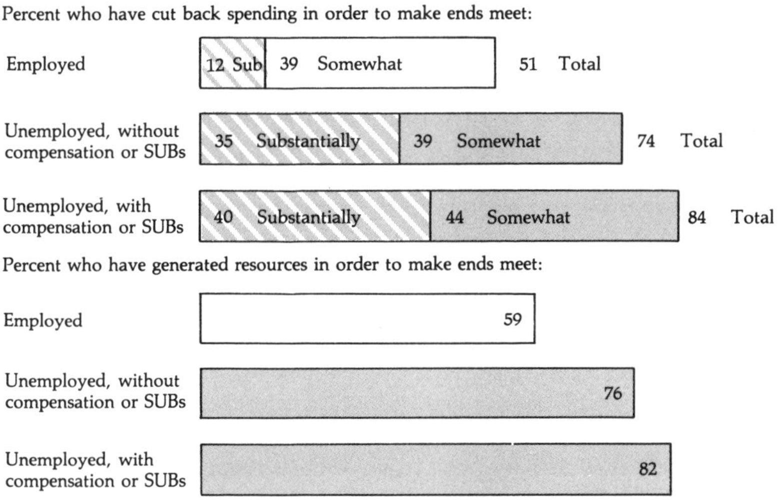

Percent who have cut back spending in order to make ends meet:

Percent who have generated resources in order to make ends meet:

Figure 4-5 Availability of unemployment benefits and efforts to cope financially.

crease other resources. These data make clear that the availability of unemployment compensation or SUBs does not create a class of leisured jobless persons. The recipients of such benefits are somewhat more likely to report that they have also tightened their belts by cutting back on spending; furthermore, they are more likely to have sought other means of supplementing their income in time of need.[6]

At the start of Chapter 3 we set forth a line of reasoning concerning the degree to which unemployment in the mid-1970s causes hardship. This thesis holds that contemporary unemployment, unlike that of the 1930s, does not cause great strain: many of the unemployed are entrants, reentrants, or job losers who have in some sense chosen unemployment; many are out of work for relatively short periods of time; many are secondary wage earners for their households; many are able to use unemployment compensation or SUBs to replace lost income. We saw that unemployment under all circumstances is associated with dissatisfaction. In the beginning of this chapter we queried whether the rational way to deal with such dissatisfaction was not through individual efforts to ameliorate one's own personal situation, rather than through political activity. We have seen clearly that such efforts are made. We must now ask whether they do in fact reduce dissatisfaction.

[6]See Mueller and Schmeideskamp, *Persistent Unemployment*, p. 32, table 27, for data proving the same point.

In Figure 4-6 we see the relationship between the number of methods used to generate additional resources and dissatisfaction with income. The data do not confirm the argument that the hardship accompanying unemployment is reduced for those who make efforts to manage on their own financially. As a matter of fact, the relationship runs in precisely the opposite direction: those who are doing the most to generate additional resources on their own are actually the least satisfied. The gap in income satisfaction between working and jobless respondents is sufficiently large that we never would have predicted that the unemployed who were doing most to cope on their own would approach the employed in terms of satisfaction with income. However, as shown in Figure 4-6, not only are the unemployed who are doing the most to manage on their own substantially more likely to express dissatisfaction with income than the employed, they are considerably more likely to express such dissatisfaction than their jobless counterparts who have done nothing to generate additional resources.[7] It is not our contention that the generation of new resources within the household makes people less satisfied with their income. The data most probably reflect the opposite process: within those families where there is dissatisfaction with income, more attempts are made to supplement family income. The important point from our perspective is that making efforts to generate additional income does not relieve the financial strain of unemployment.

Thus, we have seen that unemployment is associated with dissatisfaction with income and that neither the benefits automatically available to many of the unemployed (unemployment compensation and SUBs) nor the resources generated by individual efforts are sufficient to moderate

[7]The relationship between income dissatisfaction and efforts to generate resources is similar for the employed, although, of course, working respondents at all levels of individual coping express less income dissatisfaction than jobless respondents. For the employed, the figures are as follows:

Number of methods of resource generation	Percent expressing dissatisfaction with income
0	18
1	38
2	39
3 or more	52

Thus, for working respondents as well, efforts to generate resources do not produce greater satisfaction with income.

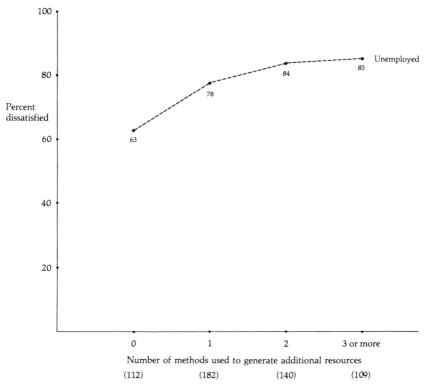

Figure 4-6 Dissatisfaction of the unemployed with their income, by efforts to cope financially.

that dissatisfaction. As a matter of fact, 84 percent of the unemployed who live in households in which these automatic benefits have been received and additional efforts to manage financially have been made express dissatisfaction with income, a figure substantially higher than the 32 percent of the employed who express such dissatisfaction.

Summary

The data discussed so far suggest that we are dealing with a real puzzle when we ask why it is that the substantial rates of unemployment found in the United States in the mid-1970s produced relatively little political response on the part of the unemployed. We have examined several aspects of the argument that widespread unemployment in the 1970s is not a real problem to be taken seriously because, unlike the depression of the thirties, unemployment is no longer accompanied by hardship, and we have found that argument to be wanting.

The first contention of those who argue that unemployment today has limited effects has to do with the demographic character of the unemployed. Unlike the 1930s, the claim runs, contemporary unemployment has its principal impact upon women and teenagers, who are not main wage earners for their households. Only a minority of the unemployed are involuntarily unemployed, having been fired or laid off from their jobs. And most present-day unemployment is not of the long duration that it was in the thirties.

Although the proponents of this point of view are correct in assessing certain changes in the character of the unemployed population, the unemployed are a very diverse group. Whereas they are younger and more female than in previous decades, many of the unemployed—including many young and female workers—are main wage earners for their families. The number of unemployed who are not chief earners has undoubtedly increased, yet the largest group among them, just a trifle under half, are job losers. Finally, although the average period of unemployment is undoubtedly shorter than it was during the 1930s, the mean length of unemployment at the time our data were collected was nearly four months, and many of the unemployed were out of work for considerably longer periods of time. The unemployed are a heterogeneous group: it is unfair to stereotype them and then to draw inferences from the stereotype.

Not only is it erroneous to characterize the contemporary unemployed as uniformly secondary earners who have been voluntarily out of work for a short time, it is incorrect to assume that any of these characteristics is associated with strain-free unemployment. We have seen that joblessness is associated with high levels of dissatisfaction with various aspects of life—especially income—for all kinds of unemployed: those who quit their jobs as well as those who were fired; those who have been out of work a short time as well as those who have been jobless for a long period; those with substantial family responsibilities as well as those without. Although there is variation among the unemployed in terms of the degree of dissatisfaction, all of them—regardless of reason for joblessness, duration of unemployment, or family responsibilities—are substantially less satisfied than those with jobs.

A final contention of those who hold that unemployment no longer causes hardship was also refuted by our data. It is argued that the availability of resources—either those provided to the unemployed more or less automatically by the government, or private programs, or those which the unemployed generate themselves by dipping into savings, taking loans, going on welfare, and so on—alleviates the strain caused by lost income. We have seen that although many of the unemployed are the beneficiaries of these programs and many more engage in activities on their own to generate additional resources, the income dissatisfaction associated with unemployment is not reduced.

We cannot make explicit comparisons between the suffering caused by unemployment during the depression of the thirties and the hardship caused by joblessness in the mid-1970s. The anecdotes that emerge from the literature of the earlier period indicate that the contemporary strain is less severe. Nevertheless, even if the pain is less acute than it was four decades ago, it is clear that unemployment hurts. It is strongly associated with dissatisfaction, and the best efforts by those out of work to manage on their own do not reduce that dissatisfaction.

The puzzle remains: if unemployment causes hardship and unhappiness, why is it that such suffering and dissatisfaction have so few political consequences? It is to that puzzle which we now turn.

Part Two

Unemployment, Economic Strain, and Ideology

CHAPTER 5

American Social Ideology:
Class Consciousness and the
American Dream

A T LEAST SINCE the days of Alexis de Tocqueville, observers of American politics and society have commented on the special nature of the democratic order in America and sought to explain it. These analysts have contrasted the United States with societies on the opposite side of the Atlantic and noted many ways in which this country was distinctive—the absence of a feudal past, the abundance of land and resources, the relative equality of economic and social conditions. Furthermore, they described a distinctive culture that complemented these conditions, based on a deep-rooted belief in the equality of all men and a strong sense of individualism. The American was born into no bounded or defined place in the social hierarchy; the opportunities for the able and ambitious to succeed were seen as virtually unlimited.

Individualistic pursuit of success received a sort of cultural codification in works penned by the self-help writers and success novelists of the Gilded Age before the turn of the century. These came at precisely the time when the United States was undergoing a massive social metamorphosis, a change that many observers—especially those following Marx—expected to have profound implications for such individualistic beliefs. The second half of the nineteenth century witnessed the beginnings of the transformation of American society from an agrarian to an industrial order and the corresponding diminution of the number of yeoman farmers and growth of an urban, often immigrant, working class. According to Marx, such a development should be accompanied by the emergence of working-class consciousness—the perception on the part of workers that they are part of a clearly identifiable group, whose members are not only aware of the interests they share but also willing to organize in opposition to the owners of capital in order to change a system that oppresses them.

Presumably diffusion of such views, with their collectivist overtones, would have been fatal to American individualistic beliefs. In spite of the fact that the history of this country has been characterized by frequent, sometimes bloody, industrial conflict, observers of American politics tend to agree that the kind of class consciousness described by Marx never emerged here. Many interpretations have been advanced to account for the absence of class consciousness in America; they range from the absence of a tradition of feudalism, with its hierarchy of ascribed social statuses, to the role of the frontier, which is said to have acted as an escape valve for the discontent of a restive yeomanry, to the significance of ethnic diversity and racial conflict, which are said to have divided working-class people from one another.[1] Among the explanations cited most frequently is the belief in individual opportunity for success—what is called the American Dream.[2] By focusing on the opportunities for the man of industry and character to get ahead on his own, the American Dream is said to have inhibited the emergence of a collective working-class consciousness.

These two perhaps competing sets of beliefs—individualistic beliefs in opportunity and collectivist views of class conflict and solidarity—are relevant for our overall project, the understanding of the process by which individuals who share a problem become an effective collective force in politics. In Chapter 1 we posited that the degree to which a subjectively stressful problem is politicized—viewed as best solved through governmental activity and viewed as, in some meaningful way, shared with others—affects the likelihood of its becoming the basis for political mobilization. If those who are disadvantaged economically, either by their long-term social class position or by their joblessness, espouse the individualistic beliefs associated with the American Dream, they would be more likely to view self-help, rather than government intervention, as the appropriate mode for dealing with their economic problems. On the other hand, it would seem reasonable that those who have a class-con-

---

[1]These and other hypotheses are explored in John M. Laslett and Seymour Martin Lipset, eds., *Failure of a Dream* (Garden City, N.Y.: Anchor Books, Doubleday and Co., 1974). The essays therein contain, in addition, extensive bibliographic suggestions. In his essay, "Why No Socialism in the United States?" (in Seweryn Bialer and Sophia Sluzar, eds., *Sources of Contemporary Radicalism* [New York: Westview Press, 1977], chap. 2), Lipset reviews these theories in some detail.

[2]One of the earliest and most provocative versions of this theory is found in Leon Samson's *Toward a United Front* (New York: Farrar and Rinehart, 1935), chap. 1.

scious view of the workings of the social order would be predisposed to make collective demands upon the government. Thus, an understanding of how citizens view the social order—in terms of individualism, opportunity, and class—is clearly relevant to the solution to our puzzle: why so few consequences of unemployment?

The understanding of these underlying beliefs will concern us at various points in the remainder of the book. In this chapter we shall delineate their contours as revealed by our data and examine their roots in demographic groups. Furthermore, we shall investigate the relationships among these beliefs, looking at the usually untested assumption that individualistic tenets undermine class consciousness. In the next chapter we look directly at one of the sets of links in the hypothetical process of political mobilization by investigating the relationship between these principles and personal circumstances. We shall seek the roots of social ideology in personal experience by considering both the specific issue of the link between joblessness and social beliefs and the general issue of the link between an individual's understanding of his personal circumstances and his understanding of the operation of the social order. Later on we shall return to these themes, examining the link between social ideology and political attitudes in Chapter 8 and the link between ideology and political participation in Chapter 10.

The American Dream

Let those who would leave their mark in the world pull off their coats, roll up their sleeves and set manfully to work . . . Hosts of successful men have risen from the humbler walks of life, brushing away, by industry and force of character, the social impediments to their upward flight, with which the peculiarity of their birth essayed to tether them.

Simms, Secrets of Success, 1873[3]

The American Dream of success undoubtedly has undergone significant alteration in the last century. A modern Ragged Dick might be encouraged to get himself a scholarship to Yale rather than a job as a bootblack; in an age of installment consumption and massive consumer indebtedness, frugality no longer retains the status in the hierarchy of virtues it once enjoyed. Still, there seems to be a considerable commit-

---

[3]Quoted in Irvin G. Wyllie, *The Self-Made Man in America* (New Brunswick, N.J.: Rutgers University Press, 1954), p. 42. This book is a valuable exposition of the components of the belief in opportunity in late nineteenth-century America. Wyllie's description of the American Dream as embodied in the works of writers like Horatio Alger and his contemporaries makes clear the ways in which these beliefs have changed.

ment at least in public rhetoric to equality of opportunity and to the notion that any talented and hard-working person, no matter how humble his origins, can become successful.[4] However, the past decade has witnessed growing alienation on the part of the American public.[5] This cynicism has been documented by those who study public opinion in terms of a growing distrust of the major institutions, public and private, of American society. Given these attitudes, it would not be surprising to find an erosion of belief in the availability of opportunities for success in contemporary America. Unfortunately, there is little, if any, precise information about belief in the American Dream, now or in the past.

In our metropolitan work force survey we asked several questions about the existence and distribution of opportunities to get ahead. First we inquired which of the following—luck, hard work, or family background—is most important in determining who gets ahead in this country. In the ideology of the American Dream, industriousness rather than accident of fortune or birth should be the basic element in determining success. Then we asked about the opportunities for upward mobility, the chances that the child of a factory worker can become a professional or a business executive. Next we asked about the comparative chances for success of the child of a factory worker and the child of a business executive. Finally, we asked those who found the opportunities for the two children to be different whether such differences are fair.

Table 5-1 summarizes the answers to these questions. The data show that the members of our work force sample have considerable faith in the efficacy of hard work and in the availability of opportunities: nearly 70 percent feel that hard work is the key to success, and a similar proportion feel that the child of a factory worker has at least some chance to get ahead. When it comes to the distribution of chances for success, 31 percent say that the child of a factory worker has about the same chance for success as the child of a business executive, while 40 percent say the worker's child has somewhat less chance and the remaining 28 percent say the worker's child has much less chance. We can add the 11 percent who saw a difference between the life chances of these two children, but who deemed such differences to be fair, to the 31 percent who saw no difference. This yields 42 percent of the respondents who consider the distri-

---

[4]We should emphasize that until very recently the American Dream was meant to apply to males, especially white males, only.

[5]This trend has been documented by many researchers. See especially Philip E. Converse, "Change in the American Electorate," in Angus Campbell and Philip E. Converse, eds., *The Human Meaning of Social Change* (New York: Russell Sage, 1972); and Arthur Miller, "Political Issues and Trust in Government: 1964-1970," *American Political Science Review*, 68 (December 1974), 951-972.

Table 5-1   Beliefs about the opportunities for success.

Most important factor in determining who gets ahead:		
	Luck	8%
	Hard work	68
	Family background	24
Chances for the child of a factory worker to become a business executive or a professional:		
	A good chance	41%
	Some chance	30
	A slight chance	25
	No chance at all	4
Chances for the child of a factory worker to get ahead relative to those for the child of a business executive:		
	About the same	31%
	Somewhat less	40
	Much less	28
Fairness of opportunities:		
	Fair	42%
	Unfair	58

bution of opportunities to be just—either because they saw opportunities as being equally distributed or because they judged the differences to be fair. Conversely, 58 percent of our respondents saw the opportunities as being differentially distributed by class and considered the differences to be unfair.

It is difficult to know how to interpret these figures, to assess whether in absolute terms they reflect faith or skepticism insofar as opportunities for success are concerned.[6] We can, however, gain greater understanding

[6]It is perhaps even more difficult to make a judgment on whether Americans' views on these subjects are naive or realistic. The issue of how much mobility actually exists is an extraordinarily complicated one. See the classic study conducted by Peter M. Blau and Otis Dudley Duncan, *The American Occupational Structure* (New York: John Wiley and Sons, 1967). David L. Featherman and Robert M. Hauser, in "Changes in the Socioeconomic Stratification of the Races, 1962-1973," *American Journal of Sociology*, 82 (November 1976), 621-651, report on a replication of the Blau-Duncan study and give extensive bibliographic suggestions.

of the meaning of these responses by looking at the way they relate to other social and economic characteristics.

OCCUPATIONAL LEVEL AND BELIEF IN THE AMERICAN DREAM

We have referred to the argument made by observers of U.S. politics that belief in the American Dream has inhibited the development of class consciousness. One perhaps somewhat ideological version of this argument holds that belief in the American Dream of success is a bourgeois ideology devised, at least implicitly, to co-opt working-class dissatisfaction and divert it into individual striving. The only empirical test of this formulation is Joan Huber and William H. Form's study of a sample of 354 residents of Muskegon, Michigan, stratified on the basis of income. From their data they conclude that this formulation is correct: the poor are less likely to believe in the existence of equality of opportunity than the rich.[7]

Our data, presented in Table 5-2, do not support this conclusion: belief in opportunity is not confined to those who have been most successful. In terms of both believing that hard work is the key to success and feeling that opportunities for success are fairly distributed, there is no progressive increase in faith in the American Dream as we go up the occupational ladder. Only on the question about whether the worker's child has a good chance to get ahead are there consistent differences across occupational levels, with those in lower-status occupations more likely to express skepticism than those in higher-level occupations; even here, the differences among occupational levels are not large and there is considerable confidence in the lowest occupational group.[8]

CYNICISM AND THE DECLINE OF THE AMERICAN DREAM

What we know about increasing political alienation and distrust would lead us to expect a diminution of belief in the American Dream in recent years. Unfortunately, we do not have the kind of longitudinal data that would permit us to test this proposition. The best we can do with the data we have is to see whether various age groups have different views on the subject. Any relationship we find, however, might be a function of

[7] *Income and Ideology* (New York: Free Press, 1973), pp. 78-89. Their data are not quite as unambiguous as their attendant prose would suggest. On some measures the poor are more cynical about equality of opportunity than the rich; on other measures the income groups are equally likely to see opportunities for success as unequally apportioned.

[8] Presumably the divergence between our findings and those of Huber and Form derive from the differences between our samples.

Table 5-2   Belief in the American Dream, by occupational level.

	OCCUPATIONAL LEVEL			
Belief	Low ←————————————→ High			
	1	2	3	4
Percent agreeing that:				
Hard work is the most important factor in getting ahead	67	66	69	70
A worker's child has at least some chance to get ahead	62	65	73	77
The chances for success are distributed fairly	40	38	46	43

changes that occur during the life cycle rather than a function of long-term secular change.

The data in Table 5-3 indicate that younger Americans are definitely more skeptical about the American Dream than their elders, especially when it comes to the fairness of the distribution of opportunities. It may well be that this relationship does not signal a long-term decline in faith in the American Dream but indicates that, as the more cynical generation matures, their attitudes will become progressively less skeptical. Since other studies of attitude changes over the life cycle indicate that people tend to become more pessimistic with age, we do not find this explanation compelling.[9]

Table 5-4, in which we examine the relationship between age and belief in the American Dream within occupational levels, permits us to explore further. The table contains a confusing amount of data, but several decisive relationships show up. First of all, the generation gap is most pronounced among those at the highest occupational levels. Only on the item about fairness of opportunities is there a clear generational pattern within all four occupational levels. However, such a pattern is evident on each item in the highest occupation-level group.

Looking at the data from another perspective, we discern an additional pattern that amplifies our foregoing discussion of the relationship between social class and belief in the American Dream. Reading the columns instead of the rows and comparing, in each case, the first three columns with the final one, we see that while there is no consistent relationship between occupational level and belief in the American Dream for

[9]See, for instance, George Katona et al., *Aspirations and Affluence* (New York: McGraw-Hill, 1971).

Table 5-3   Belief in the American Dream, by age.

Belief	AGE			
	Under 30	30-39	40-54	55 and over
Percent agreeing that:				
Hard work is the most important factor in getting ahead	64	68	73	76
A worker's child has at least some chance to get ahead	63	72	76	79
The chances for success are distributed fairly	30	38	53	63

any of the first three age groups, a pattern does emerge for those age fifty-five and over. For this group, those who came of age before or during the depression, there is a consistent relationship between social class and belief in the American Dream. It is shown more clearly in Figure 5-1, which plots belief in the American Dream against occupational level for two age groups, those below and those above fifty-five years of age. For the older group, those in higher occupational groups are more likely to be committed to the American Dream of opportunity than those at the low end of the occupational scale. This relationship does not hold for the younger group.[10]

Although, as we have mentioned, we cannot distinguish generational from life-cycle effects using cross-sectional data only, it would seem unlikely that the relationship we have found between belief in the American Dream and occupational level would emerge as an adjunct to the process of aging. It seems more plausible to us that, in the past, belief in the American Dream was more prevalent among the middle than the working classes, but that this relationship has become attenuated over the past several decades. We realize that we are basing this inference on somewhat slender evidence. However, the theme of increasing homogeneity across social classes is one to which we shall return again and again in the course of our investigation. Because our findings on the decreasing class relatedness of attitudes toward opportunity accord so clearly with other

[10]We should note that Figure 5-1 masks the random variations within the younger subgroups that emerged in Table 5-4. Still, what is interesting is the relationship between class and belief in the American Dream among those over fifty-five.

Table 5-4   Belief in the American Dream, by occupational level and age.

Hard work is the most important factor in getting ahead (percent agreeing)

Occupational level	Age			
	Under 30	30-39	40-54	55 and over
Low 1	62	71	74	65
2	66	58	71	71
3	59	76	74	73
High 4	66	66	72	86

A worker's child has at least some chance to get ahead (percent agreeing)

Occupational level	Age			
	Under 30	30-39	40-54	55 and over
Low 1	59	64	70	63
2	59	69	70	78
3	70	80	66	81
High 4	63	72	90	86

The chances for success are distributed fairly (percent agreeing)

Occupational level	Age			
	Under 30	30-39	40-54	55 and over
Low 1	34	40	41	58
2	26	33	56	63
3	34	44	55	71
High 4	26	35	55	64

(see Appendix B for number of cases.)

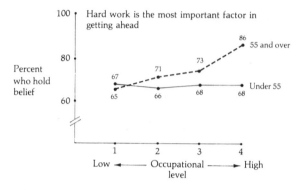

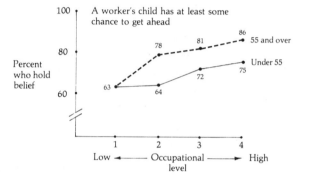

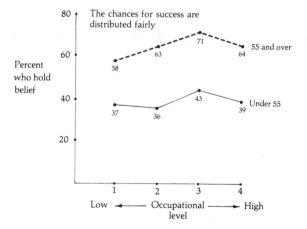

Figure 5-1   Belief in the American Dream, by occupational level and age.

findings that will be examined later, we feel it appropriate to present them.

Thus we have found a considerable, though probably diminishing, commitment to the American Dream of success. It is not confined to the upper occupational levels; on the contrary, we find no relationship between occupational level and belief in opportunities for success. However, our speculative interpretation of our cross-sectional data is that such a relationship probably did obtain more strongly in the past.

Class Consciousness

In spite of Engels' enthusiastic predictions about how hospitable the "more favored soil of America, where no medieval ruins bar the way,"[11] would be to class struggle, and in spite of a long and sometimes violent history of labor disputes, radical politics on the left has enjoyed little success in this country. Observers of American society, including Engels himself, have advanced a large number of theories, ranging from internal disputes of the socialist party to general prosperity and affluence, to explain the failure of socialist politics in the American context. According to the most commonly cited of these explanations, this failure is a function of the absence of class consciousness among American workers.

Class consciousness figures importantly in Marx's understanding of how revolutionary change takes place. According to Marx, class consciousness—collective awareness of commonly held interests—is the lever that converts the deprivations associated with the conditions of working-class oppression into revolutionary activity to change those conditions.[12] C. Wright Mills's oft cited definition gives a succinct summary of the various elements that make up class consciousness:

[11]"The Labor Movement in the United States," in Lewis S. Feuer, ed., *Marx and Engels: Basic Writings on Politics and Philosophy* (New York: Anchor Books, Doubleday and Co., 1959), p. 491.

[12]Marx's views on class consciousness are contained in a variety of his major writings as well as in his correspondence. Among the works in which he discusses class consciousness are Karl Marx and Friedrich Engels, *Manifesto of the Communist Party* (New York: International Publishers, 1932); Marx and Engels, *The German Ideology* (New York: International Publishers, 1939); Marx, *The Poverty of Philosophy* (New York: International Publishers, 1939). Two articles that analyze the multiple dimensions of class consciousness are relevant here: Richard T. Morris and Raymond J. Murphy, "A Paradigm for the Study of Class Consciousness," *Sociology and Social Research*, 50 (April 1966), 297-313; and Bertell Ollman, "Toward Class Consciousness Next Time: Marx and the Working Class," *Politics and Society*, 3 (Fall 1972), 1-24.

Class consciousness has always been understood as a political consciousness of one's own rational class interests and their opposition to the interests of other classes. Economic potentiality becomes politically realized: a "class in itself" becomes a "class for itself." Thus for class consciousness, there must be (1) a rational awareness and identification with one's own class interests; (2) an awareness of and rejection of other class interests as illegitimate; and (3) an awareness of and a readiness to use collective political means to the collective political end of realizing one's interests.[13]

There is considerable disagreement among social scientists about how actually to identify class consciousness. The most frequent method is to ask a blue-collar worker to what class he belongs and to consider as class conscious those who identify with the working class.[14] However, as the quotation from Mills should make clear, identification with the working class would clearly seem necessary for class consciousness; but it hardly seems sufficient. Many who identify with the working class mean by that identification simply that they work for a living. It would seem that only when that identification is coupled with a sense that the members of the working class are the victims of economic injustice because they do not receive their fair share of the fruits of their labor; that the source of this injustice is the fundamental conflict of interests between the working class and the bourgeoisie; and that the means to correct the injustice is through activity with other members of the working class, would that identity assume a clearly political potential. Such attitudes would be meaningless for political action if not linked to a sense of personal identification with the working class; on the other hand, such identification would likewise be without political potency unless coupled with a sense of the interests of the working class and a willingness to act on behalf of those interests.

What Mills's description makes clear is that full class consciousness has multiple dimensions. In recognition of the various aspects of the concept, we measured class consciousness in several ways: respondents were asked not only about their class identification but also about their sense of the fairness of the economic reward system in America, their sense of conflict between the classes, and their sense of the wisdom of collective action by the working class. It should be made clear that, although these measures do tap several of the dimensions of class consciousness, they in

[13]In *White Collar* (New York: Oxford University Press, 1936), p. 325.

[14]Even this widely used measure is not without controversy. For a discussion of some of the difficulties involved in using class self-identification as a measure, see the methodological note appended to this chapter.

no way measure the kind of revolutionary class consciousness that Marx predicted would emerge within the ranks of the working class. Even if, on the basis of our measures, we were to find a great deal of class consciousness among American workers—and we do not—it would be unwise to predict explosive class rebellion. These questions measure general beliefs about how the world works in class terms, not the commitment to act on behalf of those beliefs—much less the commitment to act aggressively or violently.

CLASS SELF-IDENTIFICATION

We presented our respondents with an open-ended question about the class to which they thought they belonged. Those who could not answer and those who gave answers that were either ambiguous—for example, "the lower middle class"—or not grounded in class as it is usually construed—for example, "the average class" or "the liberal class"—in short, all those who did not answer "middle" or "working" were asked a closed-ended follow-up question in which those two alternatives were offered.

As shown in Figure 5-2, which reports the responses to these questions for three occupational groups—executives and professionals, lower white-collar workers, and blue-collar workers—we find relatively few work force members who spontaneously identify with the working class.[15] The unshaded portion of each bar in the figure gives the proportion who responded "middle" or "working" to the open-ended question on class; the upper shaded portion shows the additional increment provided by answers to the forced-choice closed-ended question; the figure at the top of the bar is the total percentage of the group which chose that class designation in response to either the open or the closed-ended question. In each of the groups, identifiers with the middle class far outnumber working-class identifiers. Indeed, blue-collar workers are somewhat more likely than the other two categories to identify with the working class. Still, only 8 percent made this spontaneous choice, while 50 percent chose the middle class. If we consider only responses to the closed-ended follow-up question, the pattern changes somewhat: executives and professionals identify with the middle class by a margin of 2 to 1; lower

[15]In discussing measures of class consciousness, we divide our respondents into specific occupational groups rather than into our occupational-level categories. We do so because of the clear reference in several of our questions to "workers," and because of the importance that the working class as so defined assumes in the work of Marx. The distinction we use allows us to compare manual workers and members of the lower white-collar "proletariat." On this issue see Richard F. Hamilton, *Class and Politics in the United States* (New York: John Wiley and Sons, 1972), and Harry Braverman, *Labor and Monopoly Capital* (New York: Monthly Review Press, 1974).

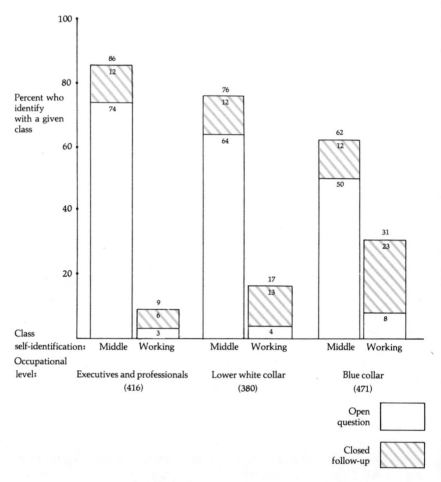

Figure 5-2   Class self-identification in response to open-ended question and closed-ended follow-up question.

white-collar workers split their responses almost equally; and blue-collar workers choose the working-class option by a ratio of nearly 2 to 1. Taking the responses to the two questions together, we find an overwhelming preference among upper and lower white-collar workers, and a 2-to-1 preference among blue-collar workers, for middle-class identification.

Even without a standard of comparison it is obvious that this represents a low level of working-class identification; just how low, however, becomes obvious when analogous data from other societies are considered. Figure 5-3 presents the results when similar open and closed questions are posed to blue-collar workers in France and Britain. It is quite

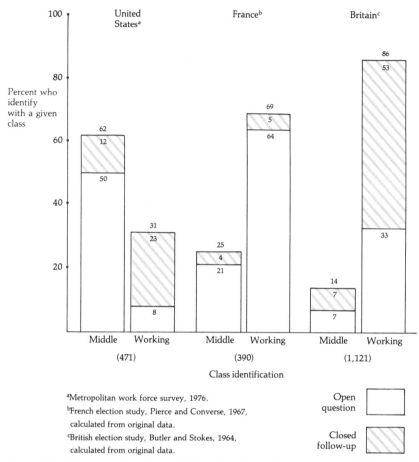

Figure 5-3 Comparative class self-identification in three countries (blue-collar workers only).

clear that the level of class consciousness, as measured by class self-identification, is much higher in these two societies. While only 8 percent of American blue-collar workers indicate a working-class identification in response to an open-ended question, 64 percent of French and 33 percent of British blue-collar workers identify spontaneously with the working class.[16]

[16]The British open-ended question of class self-identification was preceded by a screening question that asked people if they "think in class terms." The percentage given in Figure 5-3 is of all respondents—those who think in class terms and those who do not. If we consider the responses to the open question of only those who said they thought in class terms, we find that 66 percent of blue-collar workers identify with the working class.

Other Measures of Class Consciousness

We asked several other questions in order to tap additional dimensions of class consciousness. We asked about the fairness of economic rewards —whether first factory workers and then business executives are paid too much, too little, or about the right amount; we asked about class conflict —whether the interests of workers and management are fundamentally in opposition or fundamentally the same; and about solidarity among workers—whether workers in America would be better off if they stuck together or if they worked as individuals to get ahead on their own.

Figure 5-4 gives the proportions of each of the three groups who gave class-conscious replies. On each of these dimensions—fairness, conflict, and solidarity—we find blue-collar workers most likely to give a class-conscious response: to say that workers are paid too little and executives too much; that the interests of workers and management are in opposition; and that workers should stick together. The item about working-class solidarity elicits the most class-conscious replies from all occupational groups, followed by those about conflict and fairness respectively. It is interesting to note that the sharpest difference between the occupational groups appears on the question about fairness, the smallest on the question about conflict. The data suggest—and we shall return to this theme later—that the politics of economic position in America, while it involves disagreement over the equitable division of economic rewards, is not a matter of fundamental conflict among cohesive social groups.

It is hardly surprising that blue-collar workers manifest greater class consciousness than white-collar workers. Even though there is nothing inappropriate about a white-collar worker's responding that workers are paid too little and executives too much, that there is fundamental conflict between the classes, or that workers should stick together, it is difficult to suggest an interpretation of what it means for a white-collar worker to identify with the working class or, for that matter, what we would mean by a working-class consciousness on the part of white-collar workers.

So far, we have located whatever class consciousness exists where one would expect to find it—among blue-collar workers—but we have not found very much of it. In order to understand more fully why there is so little, it seems germane to probe further the circumstances that are commonly thought to nurture—or to inhibit—its development.

Unionization, Factories, and Class Consciousness

Marx made clear that individual workers in isolation from one another would be unlikely to achieve "true" consciousness; however, when concentrated together in factories they would have the opportunity to communicate with one another and to combine into associations. Thus, class

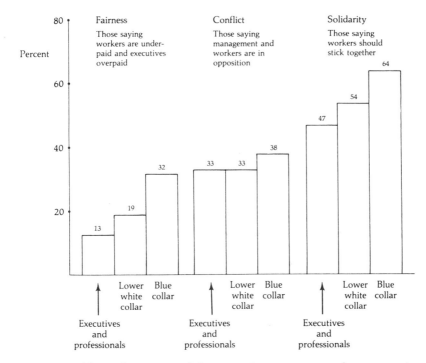

Figure 5-4 Additional measures of class consciousness among three categories of workers.

consciousness would be fostered where workers have an opportunity to interact. On this basis we would expect both factory workers—as opposed to those who perform manual work in nonfactory settings like beauty shops, restaurants, or laundries—and union members to be especially likely to be class conscious. We emphasize unionization as a consciousness-raising mechanism because, in the absence of a socialist or social democratic party, there are few institutions in American society that are as explicitly concerned with representing workers' needs as unions are.

The data in Figure 5-5 show the effects upon class consciousness of associating with other workers in unions and in factory settings. In each case we compare all blue-collar workers with all blue-collar union members, and then these two groups with blue-collar union members who work in factories, the group we would expect to exhibit the highest level of consciousness. In each case, union members are more class conscious than blue-collar workers as a whole. Interestingly, it is the difference in terms of solidarity—believing that workers should stick together if they wish to get ahead—that is largest. On other dimensions the differences

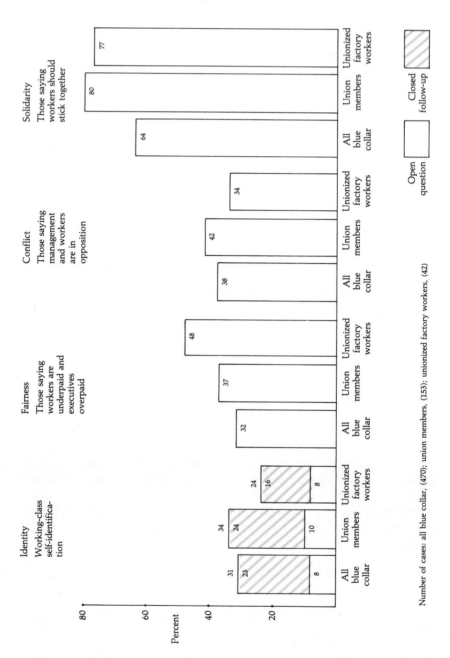

Figure 5-5 Measures of class consciousness, by union membership and factory work setting (blue-collar workers only).

are relatively small and are of consistent magnitude. It is noteworthy that unionization seems to increase the understanding of the efficacy of collective activity, but to be less effective in creating the sense of the class system against which such collective activity would be taken. In particular, we should note that, even though union members are relatively more likely to give a spontaneous working-class identification, the number of such identifiers among union members is a mere 10 percent.[17]

If the differences associated with union membership are consistent, although not overwhelmingly large, the effects of working in a factory setting are not even consistent. Unionized blue-collar factory workers, whom we would predict to be the most class-conscious group, are more likely to see the existing distribution of rewards as unfair and to believe that workers should stick together, but less likely to identify with the working class and to see conflict between the classes. Thus, we cannot confirm the hypothesis that factory settings are conducive to the development of class consciousness—at least in the contemporary United States.

CLASS CONSCIOUSNESS IN A POSTINDUSTRIAL AGE

An often heard—and as frequently disputed—generalization about contemporary American politics is that class politics is of diminished salience in a postindustrial society. In an era of technological development, a service-oriented economy, and pervasive affluence, class lines supposedly have become less distinct and class conflicts are said to have been

[17]We were interested, in addition, to consider the effect of unionization within that segment of the work force in which unions have made their most substantial recent inroads, white-collar workers. As shown by the figures below, unionized white-collar workers are, on each of the measures, more class conscious than their nonunionized counterparts. Nonetheless, they are still less class conscious than nonunion, blue-collar workers. It is interesting that unionization among white-collar workers does not enhance the commitment to collective activity, as it seems to do among blue-collar workers.

Percent class conscious	Blue collar		White collar	
	Union	Nonunion	Union	Nonunion
Class self-identification				
Open	10	7	7	3
Closed	34	29	20	11
Fairness	37	28	23	14
Conflict	42	35	35	32
Solidarity	80	57	53	50
	(153)	(317)	(88)	(699)

eclipsed by disputes over matters of style, morals, and way of life. As an abstract interpretation of the current direction of American society, this analysis is not without its critics. At a more concrete level, the evidence is somewhat mixed; however, those who study public opinion and voting have found, by and large, a weakening over time of the relation between social class and expressed political preferences.[18] At various points in our analysis we shall be interested in learning whether class has become less important as an axis about which American politics is structured.

Although the data are exceedingly sparse, we can make some instructive inferences about changes in level of class consciousness over time. Our cross-sectional data do not permit us to distinguish generational from life-cycle effects, but we can begin by looking at the relationship between age and class consciousness. We would expect the small group of people in our sample who came of age politically during the depression of the thirties to have a relatively stronger sense of class consciousness. As shown in Figure 5-6, which gives the percentage of blue-collar workers in various age groups who identified with the working class in response to our open and closed questions, there is a fairly clear relationship between age and the propensity to identify with the working class. Virtually none of the younger blue-collar workers identify spontaneously with the working class. Although the proportion spontaneously identifying with the working class reaches only 19 percent in the oldest group, this is still a substantially higher proportion than in any of the other age groups. Figure 5-7, however, shows that this pattern does not hold for our other measures of class consciousness. In no case is there anything resembling a linear relationship, and in no case is the oldest group relatively the most class conscious.

We do have some data from a study conducted in 1939 by the Roper poll for *Fortune* magazine about two of our measures, class self-identification and perception of conflict between the classes, which allows us to engage in some informed speculation about how the level of class consciousness has changed since the depression.[19]

[18]See, for example, Richard E. Dawson, *Public Opinion and Contemporary Disarray* (New York: Harper and Row, 1973), chap. 4; Gerald Pomper, *Voters' Choice* (New York: Dodd, Mead and Co., 1975), chap. 3; Norman H. Nie, Sidney Verba, and John R. Petrocik, *The Changing American Voter* (Cambridge, Mass.: Harvard University Press, 1976), chaps. 13-14; Everett Carll Ladd, Jr., with Charles D. Hadley, *Transformations of the American Party System*, 2nd ed. (New York: W. W. Norton, 1978).

[19]For a fuller analysis of these data, including an explanation of the difficulties involved in using them and the rationale for dropping the few blacks and looking at whites only, see Sidney Verba and Kay Lehman Schlozman, "Unemployment, Class Consciousness and Radical Politics," *Journal of Politics*, 39 (May 1977), 291-323.

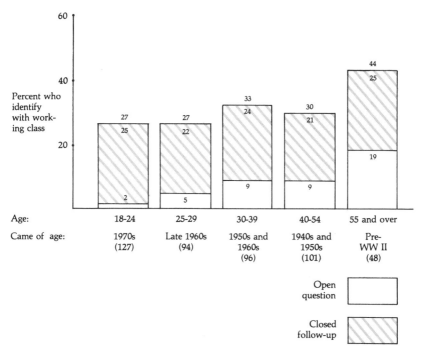

Figure 5-6 Working-class self-identification, by age (blue-collar workers only).

Recently a certain amount of debate has taken place among social scientists about whether there has been an actual decrease in the number of working-class identifiers or whether the alleged decline is a function of differences in sampling and question wording.[20] The debate centers around responses to closed-ended class self-identification items. Although it is impossible to settle this issue definitively, the responses to the open-ended question asked in 1976—a replication of the question used by Roper in 1939—can be used to supplement available figures. Table 5-5, which gives the responses of the white nonfarm work force in 1939 and 1976, shows some significant changes over the past several decades.

[20]See Richard F. Hamilton, "The Marginal Middle Class: A Reconsideration," *American Sociological Review,* 31 (April 1966), 192-199; Charles W. Tucker, "On Working Class Identification," and Hamilton's "Reply to Tucker," *American Sociological Review,* 31 (December 1966), 855-856. E. M. Schreiber and G. T. Nygrun, in "Subjective Social Class in America," *Social Forces,* 48 (March 1970), 348-356, attempt to reconcile the various positions of these and other authors. See also Richard T. Morris and Vincent Jeffries, "Class Consciousness: Forget It!" *Sociology and Social Research,* 54 (April 1970), 192-199.

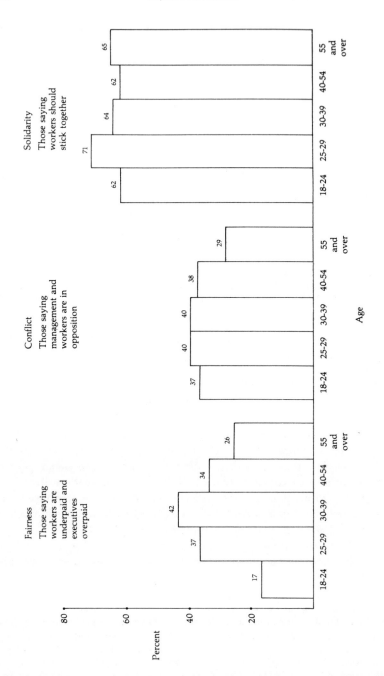

Figure 5-7 Measures of class consciousness, by age (blue-collar workers only).

Compared with 1976, there were more working-class identifiers and more people who did not answer at all, and fewer middle-class and miscellaneous replies in 1939. It is important to note that, even then, a majority of the respondents were spontaneous middle-class identifiers and only 16 percent were spontaneous working-class identifiers.

Because the white nonfarm work force has changed substantially in composition in the years since 1939, it seems appropriate to examine class self-identification within various occupational levels. In Figure 5-8, upper white-collar, lower white-collar, and wage workers are compared in terms of their class self-identifications.[21] There was less difference among the occupational groups in 1976 than 1939. Virtually no one, regardless of occupational level, identified with the working class in 1976. Although there is some relationship between occupational level and the likelihood of identifying as middle class in 1976, the relationship is not as strong as it was in 1939, when the number of middle-class identifiers rose more rapidly—and the number of working-class identifiers fell correspondingly—with movement up the occupational ladder. It is interesting to note, furthermore, that in 1976 the beliefs of all occupational groups more or less approximated those of the upper white-collar group in 1939: at that time in the highest occupational group, 3 percent spontaneously identified with the working class and 67 percent with the middle class, figures that approximate the results across all class levels in 1976.

In contrast to the change in the number of working-class identifiers since 1939, there is very little variation over the period in the overall perception of conflict between the classes. That within itself is notable, in that the thirties were a period of considerable conflict between labor and management and a time when the rhetoric of class conflict was more frequently heard than in the seventies. However, as shown in Figure 5-9, there has been a change in the relationship between occupational level and perception of class conflict, a change analogous to that found for the relationship between class self-identification and occupational level. In 1939 twice as many wage workers as upper white-collar workers gave class-conscious responses to the item about class conflict; in 1976 the figures for the two groups were virtually the same. In the case of class self-identification the lower occupational groups had come to resemble the upper white-collar group of 1939. The convergence is in the opposite direction, however: the white-collar groups have moved toward the position taken by the wage workers in 1939. Most significant of all is that

[21]The 1939 data are somewhat crude and do not permit us to construct sophisticated occupational categories. We have therefore regrouped the 1976 data to conform to the occupational categories of the Roper study.

Table 5-5   Open-ended class self-identification (whites only), 1939 and 1976.

Class identification	1939	1976
Upper or middle class	51%	67%
Working class	16	4
Miscellaneous	12	20
No answer	21	9
	100%	100%
	(2,048)	(1,370)

with reference both to class self-identification and to perception of conflict between the classes, what has occurred is not so much an absolute diminution of the level of class consciousness as a homogenization across class in this regard.

With respect to class self-identification, though not perception of class conflict, this brief look at the thirties has lent credence to the hypothesis that our contemporary affluent society is a less class-conscious one. Furthermore, with respect to both class self-identification and perception of conflict, there has been a reduction in the degree to which these attitudes are differentiated along class lines; the attitudes of white-collar and blue-collar workers resemble each other more closely today than they did a generation ago. Still, what is perhaps most striking about the data from the thirties is that, even then, the level of class consciousness—especially as measured by class self-identification—was quite low. So, even though our data indicate that class consciousness has diminished in recent decades, there was not very much of it around before.

Class Consciousness and the American Dream

So far we have found the stereotyped version of the American social ideology—that it is characterized by relative commitment to individualistic equality of opportunity and relatively limited class consciousness—to be rather accurate. But observers of American politics have often suggested that these beliefs are related. It seems quite sensible to posit links between commitment to individualistic equality of opportunity and limited class consciousness, for the two suggest very different versions of how American society works and how one ought to cope with it. According to the American Dream, American society is essentially fair: the unequal distribution of rewards is a function of the fact that some people

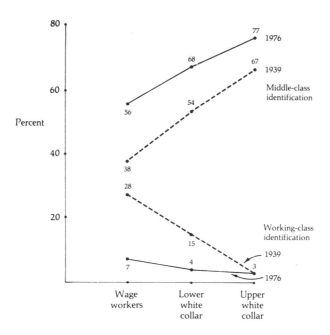

Figure 5-8 Open-ended class self-identification, by occupational level (whites only), 1939 and 1976.

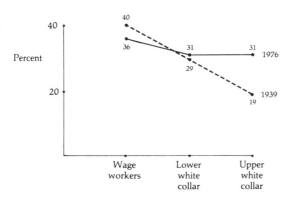

Figure 5-9 Perception of class conflict, by occupational level: those saying management and workers are in opposition (whites only), 1939 and 1976.

work harder and are more talented than others and are therefore able to advance; accordingly, the worker who wishes to improve his lot should work hard on his own. According to a class-conscious view, on the other hand, the division of social rewards is unfair, based on position in the economic order rather than any measure of merit or industry; thus, the worker who wishes to increase his share of those rewards should join with other workers and act collectively to change an unjust system. Although this relationship between belief in the American Dream and the absence of class consciousness has been often hypothesized, and sometimes taken for granted, it has rarely if ever been submitted to empirical test.

The American Dream and Class Self-Identification

Considering this logic—that an individualistic vision of advancement is incompatible with a class-conscious view of the way society divides its rewards—we would have no specific expectations about class self-identification. There would seem to be no particular conflict between identifying with the working class and believing in the American Dream. One could easily call himself a worker and believe that there are plenty of opportunities for success and that those opportunities are fairly distributed; on the other hand, there is no reason why someone who thinks of himself as middle class must be optimistic about those opportunities. Thus, there is no special reason to expect that those who believe in the American Dream would be unlikely to identify with the working class.

The data presented in Figure 5-10 indicate that, indeed, there is no relationship between cynicism about the American Dream and working-class identity. Among blue-collar workers there is relatively little difference in frequency of working-class identification between those who believe there is little openness for advancement on the part of the child of a factory worker or who believe the opportunities are unfair, and those who take a more sanguine view of the opportunity structure in America. Those who believe that the chances for the child of a factory worker are good, or that the allocation of chances between a factory worker's child and an executive's child is fair, are actually very slightly more likely to consider themselves working class than are those who believe that a working-class child has no chance or that the distribution of chances across classes is unfair.

The American Dream and Other Measures of Class Consciousness

It is on the other measures of class consciousness that a relationship would be expected between belief in the American Dream and the absence of class consciousness, for it is the other measures that tap the re-

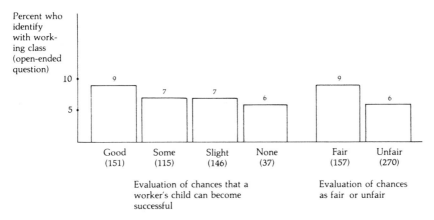

Figure 5-10   Belief in the American Dream and class consciousness (blue-collar workers only).

spondent's sense of how the world works, as opposed to his sense of himself. As shown in Figure 5-11, there is such a relationship. The first set of graphs shows the relation between views on how much opportunity for advancement a factory worker's child has and the likelihood of choosing the "class-conscious" answer to the several measures of class consciousness: belief that workers are unfairly rewarded; belief in conflict between the interests of management and workers; and belief that workers must stick together. The second set of graphs shows the relationship between belief in the fairness of opportunities in America and the choice of a class-conscious response. Almost all the relationships are positive for both white-collar and blue-collar workers. Though belief in the American Dream is unrelated to class self-identification, it clearly does have relevance to other measures of class consciousness. Interestingly enough, the relationships are positive for both blue-collar and white-collar workers and, despite variation from question to question, they are of similar magnitude for the two groups. The argument that belief in the American Dream would dampen down class consciousness is, of course, pitched in terms of the impact of this belief on consciousness among those who objectively would fall within the working class—presumably blue-collar workers. In fact, however, the relationship holds for both groups.

Thus we have given empirical verification to several components of the common wisdom about the beliefs of Americans. On the whole, Americans' beliefs about the social order seem to be characterized by a relatively high level of commitment to the American Dream of success and a very low level of class consciousness. Furthermore, the attitudes seem to be fairly uniform across classes: with respect to commitment to

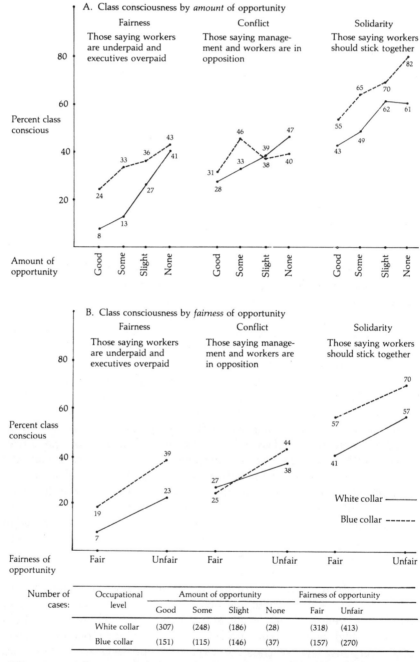

Figure 5-11   Measures of class consciousness, by amount and fairness of opportunity.

individualistic notions of success, the Horatio Alger ethic is not a middle-class ideology rejected by lower socioeconomic groups; with respect to class consciousness, although class-conscious attitudes are least characteristic of professionals and executives, they are not altogether common among blue-collar workers. Finally, the two sets of beliefs seem to be interrelated. Commitment to the individualistic success ethic seems to be related to the circumscribed degree of class consciousness.

Measuring Class Self-Identification: A Methodological Note

There seems to be no disagreement among social scientists on the importance of class consciousness, but there is considerable dispute over how it should be identified and measured. Although several authors have attempted multidimensional measurement of class consciousness,[22] the measure most frequently used in this country is class self-identification.

Measures of class self-identification have been the subject of controversy since they were introduced by social scientists in the late thirties. The basic notion is that the class-conscious worker is the one who responds "working class" when asked the class to which he belongs. However, there is considerable skepticism about the meaningfulness of such an answer. One reason for these suspicions is that replies to these questions are notoriously sensitive to changes of wording. In his classic book, *The Psychology of Social Class*, Richard Centers challenged the finding of earlier studies that most Americans think of themselves as being middle class.[23] When offered the choice among three classes—upper, middle, and lower—the overwhelming majority of Americans, between 79 and 88 percent depending upon the particular survey in question, identified with the middle class. When Centers added a fourth choice, "working class," the number of middle-class identifiers dropped sharply; a majority of those questioned, 52 percent, indicated an identification with the working class. Centers' work was important not only in demonstrating the sensitivity of class self-identification to changes in the wording of questions, but also in questioning the conclusion of an earlier study that Americans think of themselves as belonging to the middle class.[24]

---

[22]See, for example, Jerome G. Manis and Bernard Meltzer, "Attitudes of Textile Workers to Class Structure," *American Journal of Sociology*, 60 (July 1954), 30-35; Oscar Glantz, "Class Consciousness and Political Solidarity," *American Sociological Review*, 23 (August 1958), 375-385; John C. Leggett, "Uprootedness and Working Class Consciousness," *American Journal of Sociology*, 68 (May 1963), 682-692.

[23]Princeton, N.J.: Princeton University Press, 1949, pp. 30-31, 77.

[24]"The People of the United States—A Self-Portrait," *Fortune*, February 1940, p. 21.

Centers' study may have been definitive in showing that the inclusion of a "working-class" alternative changes the results in terms of class self-identification, but his methodology is vulnerable to criticism on other grounds. A number of authors have pointed out that if class consciousness as measured by class self-identification implies something real about a person's sense of himself, then at the very least a person should be able to name the thing to which he feels a sense of belonging without being prompted.[25] This argues for the use of open-ended questions wherein the respondent is asked to name the social class to which he feels he belongs without having any suggestions made to him about what the names of these classes might be, as opposed to the closed-ended questions adopted by Centers and many investigators before and after him. The open-ended approach has costs both in terms of the additional effort required to code the answers and in terms of the number of responses ("I belong to the average class"; "I belong to the American class"; "I am in a class by myself") that fall into categories not analytically useful to social scientists. In spite of these costs, it seems that the minimal demand exercised upon the respondent by the open-ended question makes it a more appropriate measure of the person's sense of identity in class terms.

When this approach is taken, the number of working-class identifiers declines precipitously. The results we report are not idiosyncratic. While closed-ended questions have consistently elicited substantial numbers of working-class identifiers, open-ended questions have evoked very few such responses: 56 percent of the respondents to the University of Michigan 1964 election survey identified with the working class in response to a closed-ended question offering "working" and "middle" as alternatives; but only 6 percent mentioned the working class when asked an open-ended question in a National Opinion Research Center survey conducted in the same year;[26] 51 percent of those questioned by the SRC in 1976 chose the working-class alternative, while only 6 percent of those contacted in our metropolitan work force survey identified with the working class in response to an open-ended question.

[25]The point is made by several authors, among them H. J. Eysenck, "Social Attitude and Social Class," British Journal of Sociology, 1 (March 1950), 56-66; and Neal Gross, "Social Class Identification in the Urban Community," American Sociological Review, 18 (August 1953), 398-404.

[26]The figure from the University of Michigan 1964 election survey is taken from John P. Robinson, Robert Athanasiou, and Kendra B. Head, Measures of Occupational Attitudes and Occupational Characteristics (Ann Arbor, Mich.: University of Michigan, Institute for Social Research, 1969), p. 371. The 1964 NORC figure is cited by Robert W. Hodge and Donald J. Treiman, "Class Identification in the United States," American Journal of Sociology, 73 (March 1968), p. 535. An additional 5 percent of the NORC respondents spontaneously identified with the lower or upper-lower classes.

How can these discrepant findings be explained? What is going on that explains the tendency for respondents to identify with the middle class in response to open-ended questions? It is impossible to be certain, but one plausible conjecture is that what may be involved is a change in the criteria by which individuals identify themselves, from identification in terms of productive role to identification in terms of life-style. Students of social stratification have generally followed Max Weber in distinguishing multiple hierarchies of stratification in advanced societies.[27] The following example, quoted by Hodge and Treiman, illustrates that it is not only social scientists who perceive this ambiguity:

> A merchant marine seaman, who was buying an apartment house for investment purposes, owned a tan-colored Cadillac, which he had purchased in a used-car lot the year before because he thought it was a good buy. Since this four-year-old Cadillac was a large gasoline consumer, he was thinking of buying a Plymouth the next time he purchased a car. This 38-year-old business-minded seaman thought that he was "about middle class as an apartment house owner, and working class as a merchant marine."[28]

It seems reasonable to surmise that when manual workers are confronted with a dichotomous choice between working-class and middle-class identification they are more likely to think in terms of economic position (occupation and income) as opposed to social status (consumption, life-style, and aspirations) than when they are asked an open-ended question. No evidence can be adduced in support of this conjecture, for few investigators have inquired what criteria people use to assign membership in various class groups.[29] But the speculation gains a certain amount of credibility in view of the finding of Joseph A. Kahl that definitions of classes are sensitive to the context in which the interview takes

[27]"Class, Status and Party," in H. H. Gerth and C. W. Mills, eds. and trans., From Max Weber: Essays in Sociology (New York: Oxford University Press, 1966), chap. 7.

[28]"Class Identification in the United States," p. 535, quoting I. Roger Yoshino, "The Stereotype of the Negro and His High-Priced Car," Sociology and Social Research, 44 (November-December 1959), 114.

[29]Centers did ask his respondents what puts a person into various classes. Unfortunately, the way he phrased the question renders the responses virtually useless for solving the riddle we have posed. First he asked his respondents into what class they would place various occupations such as factory workers or salesmen; then he inquired what criteria other than occupation define the various classes. Thus we cannot ascertain the importance of occupation as a defining criterion relative to other factors such as education, way of life, or income.

Manis and Meltzer, who asked questions about bases of class placement in a more helpful format, found that wealth was cited as the defining criterion of class member-

place as well as to the precise nature of the questions asked: thus, when interviewed at home about neighbors, respondents discuss class in terms of life-style and consumption; a quite different pattern of responses emerges from interviews conducted at work.[30] Summarizing Kahl's findings, Harold L. Wilensky puts the matter succinctly: "The average American is a Veblenian at home, a modified Marxist at work."[31]

Given the sensitivity of class self-identification to changes in the wording of questions and the ambiguity of what Americans have in mind when they think in class terms, should we not, then, conclude that the measure is meaningless? There is at least one body of evidence which suggests that we should not subscribe to this conclusion too hastily. Responses to three successive questions asked in a 1956-1960 Michigan panel study would indicate that class self-identification may have greater personal meaning than the foregoing suggests. In spite of the instability shown by responses to different questions about class self-identification, individual responses to identical closed-ended questions show remarkable stability over time. As shown in Table 5-6, about three-fourths of those who identified with either the working class or the middle class in response to a forced choice identified with the same class when asked in a successive survey. This finding takes on added meaning when the comparison with the stability of partisan political identification over time is made. Partisan identification shows somewhat greater stability over time than class identification: about 85 percent of those who identified themselves as Democrats or Republicans identified with the same party in a successive survey; however, the figures are somewhat lower when independents are included in the tabulation.[32] The rough similarity in terms

---

ship three times more often than any other standard; occupation was the runner-up ("Attitudes of Textile Workers," p. 32). These findings, however relevant, unfortunately are marred by the special nature of the sample—ninety unionized textile workers in Paterson, New Jersey—and by the low response rate—less than half.

In the British context, David Butler and Donald Stokes found that occupation is by far the most frequently cited criterion in characterizing the classes. See *Political Change in Britain*, 2nd ed. (New York: St. Martin's Press, 1974), p. 70.

[30] *The American Class Structure* (New York: Holt, Rinehart and Winston, 1956), p. 86.

[31] "Class, Class Consciousness and American Workers," in William Haber, ed., *Labor in a Changing America* (New York: Basic Books, 1966), p. 19.

[32] When those who called themselves Independents are included in the analysis, the percentages identifying with the same party are as follows:

1956 and 1958	78
1958 and 1960	81
1956 and 1960	76

Table 5-6   Stability of class and party identifications over time.

| | PERCENT GIVING SAME IDENTIFICATION IN SURVEYS OF— | | |
Affiliation	1956 and 1958	1958 and 1960	1956 and 1960
Class	74	75	74
Party	86	86	83

SOURCE: Center for Political Studies, University of Michigan, Election Panel Study.

of stability over time between party and class identification is reassuring. Although the meaningfulness of partisan identification has been questioned recently, it has had sufficient acceptance as a concept that a whole literature in political science has been built around it. Since class self-identification seems to behave similarly to party identification, it may be an identification that indicates something about a person's sense of himself.

When the data in Table 5-7—which compares middle-class and working-class identifiers in terms of their responses to the three other class-consciousness items—are considered, our confidence in class self-identification as a measure is further increased. Those who identify with the working class in response to our open-ended question are more likely to see workers as underpaid and executives as overpaid, more likely to see conflict between the classes, and more likely to think that the working class should stick together. The additional data in Table 5-7 help us to understand the relationship between class self-identification and other class-related attitudes. We present the data separately for blue-collar and white-collar workers and find that, no matter what the measure of class consciousness, blue-collar workers who spontaneously identify with the working class are more class conscious than blue-collar workers who identify with the middle class. For white-collar workers, the pattern is mixed: when it comes to seeing opposition or perceiving fairness in the distribution of rewards, the working-class identifiers are more "class conscious"; when it comes to feeling that workers should stick together, they are less likely to take a class-conscious position. That the results should be consistent for blue-collar workers but mixed for white-collar workers is perhaps not surprising, for the meaning of a working-class identity for

Table 5-7 Class-conscious beliefs, by class and open-ended class self-identification (percent).

Percent who believe	ALL WORKERS		WHITE-COLLAR WORKERS		BLUE-COLLAR WORKERS	
			Self-identification with—			
	Middle class	Working class	Middle class	Working class	Middle class	Working class
System of rewards is not fair	17	38	14	25	27	53
			Gamma = .36		Gamma = .51	
Classes are in opposition	31	49	30	52	34	47
			Gamma = .45		Gamma = .27	
Workers should stick together	53	57	50	36	61	77
			Gamma = -.27		Gamma = .37	

a white-collar worker is less intuitively clear than the meaning of a middle-class identity for a blue-collar worker. We also indicate the gammas for these relationships in order to give a sense of the degree of association. Because of the skewed nature of the distributions—there are very few working-class identifiers in any group—these coefficients should be interpreted with caution.[33]

This discussion of the relationship between class self-identification and other measures of class consciousness suggests a final problem in the measurement of class consciousness. We have argued that class consciousness, as defined by Marx and those after him, is not unidimensional and that several separate measures are needed to measure it. Although it seems appropriate to conceptualize class consciousness in terms of analytically separate dimensions, we had expected that these attitudes would form a coherent belief system. As shown in Table 5-8, this is not the

[33]This methodological caveat suggests a substantive point worthy of note. If we were to transform the data in Table 5-6 and give the percentage of members in each attitude group who identify with the working class, we would find that even among blue-collar workers who express class-conscious views there are very few working-class identifiers, in no case more than 11 percent.

Table 5-8   Measures of association (gammas) between items on class consciousness and between items on belief in the American Dream.

Items associated	All workers	White-collar workers	Blue-collar workers
Class-consciousness items			
Solidarity and conflict	.11	.09	.14
Solidarity and fairness	.35	.44	.10
Conflict and fairness	.26	.30	.15
American Dream items			
Success and chances	.34	.30	.43
Success and fairness	.36	.34	.33
Chances and fairness	.62	.63	.59

case.[34] Although the relationships among the various aspects of class consciousness are all in the predicted direction, they are quite unimpressive in their strength, especially for blue-collar workers.[35] The relative weakness of the relationships among class-consciousness measures becomes even clearer when the coefficients are compared with those in the second portion of Table 5-8, which give analogous information for various aspects of belief in the American Dream. The relationships among these substantively related items are clearly more robust than those among the class-consciousness measures. Both because the consciousness measures are substantively related and because the belief systems of ordinary citizens have been characterized by considerable structural coher-

[34]Two other authors use multidimensional measures of class consciousness and report different results on the degree to which class-consciousness attitudes cohere. Glantz finds little coherence among his measures in a sample of white, Protestant, and Catholic males in Philadelphia ("Class Consciousness and Political Solidarity," pp. 378-379). Leggett, on the other hand, studying blue-collar males in Detroit, finds that his measures form a Guttmann scale ("Uprootedness and Working Class Consciousness," p. 686).

[35]We had conflicting expectations about whether these attitudes should be more coherent for blue-collar or white-collar workers. On the one hand, because the referent in each case is "workers," we might expect that the questions would have an immediate personal relevance for blue-collar workers, which they would lack for white-collar workers. On the other hand, the findings in the literature on belief systems are unambiguous in terms of the relationship between high levels of education and attitude consistency. On this basis we would expect the relationships to be stronger for white-collar respondents.

ence in recent years,[36] we are puzzled about why the relationships among various measures of class consciousness exhibit so little coherence.

Our conclusion to this note must, therefore, be both methodological and substantive. Class consciousness is elusive, and social scientists have not reached a consensus on how to measure it. Furthermore, responses to questions about class self-identification tend to be sensitive to the way in which the question is posed, and the relationships among items that attempt to measure other dimensions of class consciousness are not too substantial. These considerations, taken together with the fact that, as we have seen, open-ended questions (and we believe that such questions are appropriate in measuring class self-identification) produce very few working-class identifiers, undoubtedly have implications for the development of working-class politics in the United States.

[36]On this point see Norman H. Nie with Kristi Andersen, "Mass Belief Systems Revisited," *Journal of Politics*, 36 (August 1974), 540-587.

CHAPTER 6

Social Ideology and
Personal Experience

O UR ODYSSEY into the realm of the American social ideology now brings us squarely back to the concerns set forth in Chapter 1. There we presented a series of hypothetical steps linking personal strain to political mobilization. One step involved the effects of strain in personal life on social ideology, more specifically the effects of economic strain in personal life on both class consciousness and belief in individualistic opportunity structures. We have examined personal economic strain and social ideology separately. In this chapter we attempt to relate the two.

We shall undertake our exploration first by considering the effects of the economic strain associated with unemployment upon social ideology, beliefs about the opportunity structure in American society, and relationships between the classes. Then we shall investigate the personal experiences of our respondents in terms of their evaluations of the opportunities that they—and their children—have enjoyed. We shall also consider the relationship between these measures of personal experience and views of the social and economic system. Finally, we examine personal experiences in terms of our respondents' desire to get ahead in the prescribed Horatio Alger manner, by going into business for themselves. In so doing, we shall in essence be taking shots at a complicated problem from several points of view rather than dispensing with it straightforwardly. However, the various parts of the presentation all point so unambiguously to the same interpretation that we feel confident in drawing conclusions from somewhat disjointed pieces of data.

Unemployment and Ideology

As we saw in Chapter 3, unemployment hurts. The strain associated with joblessness might be expected to affect the way in which individuals interpret social reality. For example, their personal experiences might lead the unemployed to be more cynical about the American Dream. After all, hard work has not yielded success for them; in spite of their previous diligence, they are jobless. Why then should they believe in the efficacy of hard work? Similarly, their own experiences might lead them to question just how much opportunity for advancement there is these days. In addition, the experience of being unemployed might enhance class consciousness—at least among blue-collar workers. It seems reasonable to expect the jobless worker to be more likely to find the reward system unfair or to consider his interests to conflict with management, and less likely to believe that the best way to make it is on his own.

These expectations are not borne out by the data. As shown in Figure 6-1, at least in terms of commitment to the American Dream, there is little difference between working and unemployed members of the same occupational category. For example, with reference to the contribution of hard work to success, there is a slight difference between working and unemployed occupational cohorts. Given the cynicism we might expect the unemployed to show regarding the rewards attendant upon hard work, what is surprising is not that this difference exists, but that it is not much larger. At least 60 percent of the unemployed in each occupational category take the position that hard work is the key to success. When it comes to our other questions on the chances open to the child of a factory worker or on the fairness of the opportunity system in America, the results are similar: the unemployed do not differ from the employed in any consistent way. An unhappy experience with the economic system—and the unemployed can clearly be said to have had such an experience—does not appear to reduce belief in the extent or fairness of opportunities in America. In this sense, social ideology as embodied in the beliefs about mobility does not appear sensitive to the individual's personal experience.

Although the personal stress that accompanies unemployment does not seem to be associated with cynicism about opportunities for advancement, it may be that (at least for blue-collar workers) it affects class consciousness. Our expectations about the effects of joblessness on consciousness might be conflicting. On the one hand, we might expect the material deprivation and occupational insecurity associated with enhanced class consciousness. We would expect both that unemployed blue-collar workers would be more likely to think of themselves in economic terms and therefore to place themselves in the working rather than the middle class, and that personal economic stress would color the way the system is perceived—that the unemployed would be more likely to believe that workers should stick together, that classes are in opposition,

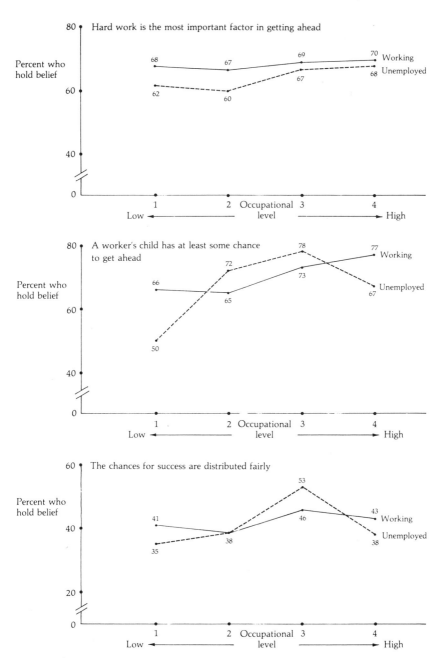

Figure 6-1 Belief in the American Dream, by occupational level and employment status.

and that the distribution of rewards in America is inequitable. On the other hand, there are studies which show that the insecurity associated with widespread unemployment "disciplines" a work force, making workers more reluctant to make wage demands or go on strike.[1] According to this logic, the unemployed might react by abandoning attitudes of class solidarity and adopting more individualistic views of the polity and economy.

With reference to the relationship between class self-identification and unemployment, we would have different expectations depending upon whether we see unemployment as an experience that raises consciousness or one that induces caution. If unemployment is associated with enhanced class consciousness, then we would expect the experience of being out of work—with its obvious meaning for personal life—to have a relatively greater effect upon class self-identification than upon other attitudes related to class consciousness. We make this deduction because class self-identification is clearly the most distinctly personal and least abstractly ideological of the measures. On the other hand, if the effect of unemployment is to discipline workers, we would expect the consciousness-dampening effect of unemployment to be greatest upon the abstract ideological measures and least upon class self-identification. In Figure 6-2 we consider the relationship between class self-identification and unemployment for blue-collar workers, once again in terms of both spontaneous responses to the open-ended question and replies to the closed-ended follow-up question. The effect of unemployment seems to be confined to responses to the open-ended question. Among blue-collar workers, the unemployed are less likely to call themselves "middle class": 54 percent of those with jobs—as opposed to 35 percent without—spontaneously gave a middle-class identification. However, there is no corresponding increase in the number of working-class identifiers. Our tentative interpretation of this finding hearkens back to a theme we have discussed before, that class self-designations have a multiplicity of meanings. In this case it seems logical to reason that unemployed manual workers would be less likely to think of themselves as middle class because they no longer have the financial wherewithal to support a middle-class life-style and not more likely to consider themselves working class because, quite simply, they are not working.

Figure 6-3 presents similar comparisons between the employed and the unemployed in relation to the other measures of class consciousness introduced in the previous chapter. The data show some slight differences

[1]Douglas A. Hibbs, Jr., "Political Parties and Macro-economic Policy," *American Political Science Review*, 71 (December 1977), 1467-1487.

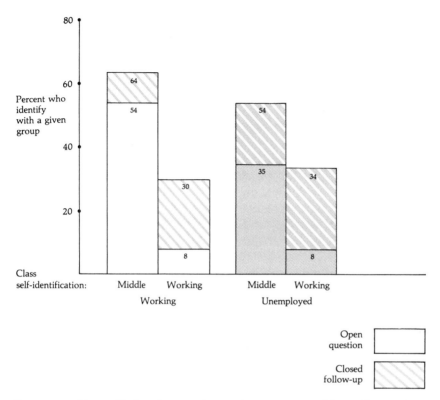

Figure 6-2 Class self-identification, by employment status (blue-collar workers only).

between working and unemployed blue-collar workers. The unemployed consistently are more likely to give what one would consider the class-conscious response, but the differences in all cases are quite slender. Thus, it seems that unemployment is not associated with a heightened sense of class consciousness among blue-collar workers.

The weakness of the relationship between employment status and social ideology can be seen more clearly if one compares the effect of employment status with the effect of other social characteristics on our measures of social ideology. We use the same log-linear technique as described in Chapter 3. Employment status is compared with class (that is, occupational level) and race. We compare the effects of each characteristic when the other is controlled. The results are quite clear. None of the three variables has a significant effect on our measure of the extent to which the system provides fair chances to succeed. Consider next the

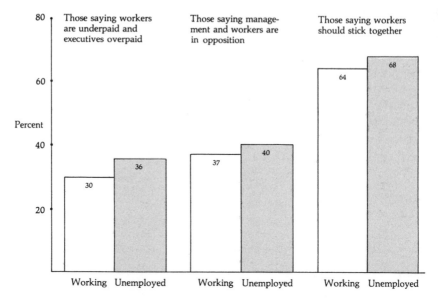

Figure 6-3 Measures of class consciousness, by employment status (blue-collar workers only).

measures of class consciousness. Class and race each have a significant effect on working-class identification, on the belief that workers should stick together, and on the belief that the allocation of pay is fair. Employment status has no effect on either. When it comes to a belief that the interests of workers and management are in conflict, none of the three social characteristics has a significant effect on its own. The only noticeable effect is the interaction of class and employment status, but even that is not very great.

In sum, we find no clear connection between the personal strain of unemployment and social ideology. The unemployed do not differ from the employed either in their beliefs about the opportunity system in America, or in the extent to which they are class conscious. A comparison of the effects measured in Table 6-1 with the effects of the same variables on satisfaction (Table 3-2) highlights this point. In terms of satisfaction with one's own life, we found unemployment to have a big impact; when it comes to more general social ideology, we find none. Thus, we seem to have found a gap in our series of proposed links. The experience of unemployment does not seem to influence general concepts of the operation of the social world.

Table 6-1   Effect of class, race, and employment status on social ideology.

Variable	Belief that chances are fair	Identification with working class	Belief that workers are underpaid and executives overpaid	Belief that management and workers are in conflict	Belief that workers should stick together
Effects of —					
Class (occupational level)	6.4	8.9*	22.3**	2.2	19.5**
Race	2.8	7.2*	8.7	1.8	33.5**
Employment status	0.0	0.2	2.9	0.2	0.0
Class and employment status	1.5	1.6	1.6	8.4*	2.0
Overall effect	21.7	23.1	66.6**	22.3	79.5**

*Significant at the .01 level.
**Significant at the .001 level.

Personal Opportunities for Advancement

Unemployment usually involves a strain which, while severe, is of limited duration. Viewed from this perspective, it is perhaps not surprising that the effects of such short-term tremors upon underlying social ideology would be quite contained. It seems sensible, then, to inquire whether an individual's long-term ongoing encounters with the American economic and social system affect his views of the social order. In the previous chapter we investigated the relationship between long-term objective economic position and social ideology and found it to be weak. Now we turn to a more subjective measure of ongoing personal experience, the individual's assessment of the opportunities he and the generations before and after have enjoyed, and how that assessment relates to a more general understanding of the social order.

Let us first look in some detail at how Americans perceive and evaluate the opportunities they have enjoyed personally. To get at these perceptions we asked our respondents to compare their own opportunities to succeed with those in both their parents' and their childrens' lives.[2] Figure 6-4, which reports the answers to these questions, shows that Americans are quite sanguine about the opportunities in their personal lives: reading the marginals we see that very few perceive their own and their children's opportunities to have shrunk, and most perceive these opportunities to be better than those experienced by the previous generation. The largest single group—43 percent—sees their own opportunities as better than those of their parents and expects those of their children to be better yet. If we combine the four groups in the upper right of the table, we find 22 percent who see no improvement either for themselves or for their children—although only one in ten in this group, a bare 4 percent of the total, are actually downright pessimistic, seeing their opportunities as worse than their parents' and their children's as worse than their own. Finally, there are two groups of approximately equal size: the 20 percent of the sample who believe that their opportunities have exceeded their parents' but that their children's will not; and the 16 percent who have the opposite perception, that their opportunities were no better than their parents' but that their children's opportunities will surpass their own. Americans seem relatively positive about the opportunities available to them and to their children.

We can carry this one step further by considering whether the perception of the availability of opportunity varies with occupational level.

---

[2]For those without children, we asked about hypothetical expectations for success if they did have children. We must caution, of course, that our data are not on actual mobility, only on subjective evaluations.

Children's opportunities compared to respondents'

Respondents' opportunities compared to parents'	Better	Same	Worse	
Worse	7	4	4	15
Same	9	12	2	23
Better	43	16	4	63
	59	32	10	101

Figure 6-4 Evaluation by respondents of their own opportunities relative to those of their children and their parents (percent).

Presumably, those in higher occupational levels would be more likely to report having had better opportunities than their parents, but it is unclear what we would expect in terms of the relationship between occupational level and perception of opportunities for children. On the one hand, those in higher occupational levels have the wherewithal to provide for their children the kind of educational and cultural advantages that are helpful in getting ahead. On the other hand, the offspring of those in the lowest occupational category have nowhere to go but up, while their more fortunate counterparts may have much more difficulty outdistancing the accomplishments of their parents.

The data presented in Figure 6-5 both confirm and disconfirm our expectations. As shown by the slope of the bottom line—which shows the proportion of the various occupational levels who take the most optimistic view, that opportunities have expanded in the past and will continue to expand in the future—those in lower occupational categories are somewhat more likely to take a consistently sanguine view. However, as shown by the upper two lines, the difference between the occupational categories is entirely in terms of expectations for children's opportunities. Those in upper-status occupations are somewhat more pessimistic about their children's future opportunities, a response that could be interpreted either as a self-servingly naive refusal to acknowledge the degree to which privilege can be passed on to successive generations or as a realis-

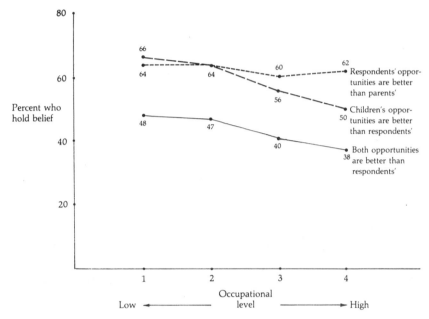

Figure 6-5 Perception of opportunities for success, by occupational level.

tic comprehension that their children may have difficulty surpassing their own success.

The figure shows no consistent difference across the occupational groups in terms of their evaluation of their own opportunities vis-à-vis those of their parents. This is a striking finding, especially in view of our discussion in Chapter 5 of the social class basis of belief in the American Dream. At that time we considered the hypothesis that belief in the availability of opportunity—that is, belief in the American Dream—is a bit of bourgeois ideology that has not been bought by those it is designed to keep in place. We found, however, that belief in the American Dream was not differentiated along lines of occupational category. What was true of acceptance of opportunities for mobility in the abstract is true of evaluation of opportunities in personal terms. The relative confidence— both concrete and abstract—which those of lower occupational groups seem to have in the opportunities for advancement would seem to be potent for politics in America, taking the edge off discontent and diverting energies into individualistic competition for success.

Perceptions of Opportunities in the Past

These relationships gain additional meaning when viewed in the light of data from the 1939 Roper poll to which we referred in the last chapter.

Table 6-2   Opportunities for success of parents relative to opportunities of respondents, and those of children relative to respondents (whites only), 1939 and 1976.

Class	PERCENT WHO BELIEVE OWN BETTER THAN PARENTS'		PERCENT WHO BELIEVE CHILDREN'S BETTER THAN OWN	
	1939	1976	1939	1976
Upper white collar	67	57	62	49
Lower white collar	69	66	71	62
Blue collar	60	63	76	58
Unemployed	45	53	64	57

Number of cases:

Year	Upper white collar	Lower white collar	Blue collar	Unemployed
1939	(504)	(772)	(486)	(176)
1976	(274)	(218)	(206)	(394)

Once again, we have transformed our data to correspond to the Roper sample. The similarities and differences between the two sets of data, presented in Table 6-2, are instructive. In terms of confidence in opportunities, respondents in 1976 are fairly close to respondents in 1939 in the proportion who report that their chances have been better than those of their parents; however, in 1976 respondents are in general less sanguine about the opportunities for their children than were respondents at the end of the depression. In each case it is the respondents in the highest occupational category, the upper white-collar workers, who are least optimistic about the chances available to their children. Perhaps it is simply a function of the precise timing of the earlier study: at that time things had been so bad for a decade that there was probably reason to assume that they would improve. In any case, the overall confidence in children's opportunities has declined among white work force members from 70 percent in 1939 to 55 percent in 1976.

UNEMPLOYMENT AND PERCEPTIONS OF OPPORTUNITIES FOR ADVANCEMENT

We have seen, so far, that unemployment is an experience that alters people's lives and affects the satisfaction they express. However inescapable these personal effects, unemployment does not seem to distort the more general perception of opportunities for advancement in America. It may be, however, that while abstract commitments are unaffected by the experience of joblessness, unemployment has an impact upon the more personal dimension of the way in which opportunities are evaluated. Presumably, if there is such an effect, it would render the unemployed less positive about their own opportunities relative to their parents' and, according to the foregoing logic, more positive about the opportunities available to their children, who would be expected to surpass their parents.

In fact, the data presented in Figure 6-6 do not confirm these expectations. Differences between working and unemployed respondents of various occupational categories are quite small and are not consistent in direction. With minor variations the unemployed are as sanguine about opportunities for advancement as their working counterparts. In other words, the effects of unemployment upon attitudes are quite circumscribed: while unemployment is associated with low levels of satisfaction with personal life, it does not seem to be accompanied by disenchantment with the class system, with opportunities offered by the system, or with the opportunities available to the jobless and to their offspring.

Personal Experience and Ideology

We have outlined in some detail the way in which personal opportunities for success are evaluated. We can consider the connection between personal experience and social ideology more directly with our parallel questions about the respondent's understanding of the American system and of his own life. A question about the fairness of the respondent's wages deals with the same issue within the respondent's own life-space as does our more general question about the fairness of economic rewards to workers and executives. A similar parallel exists between our questions on the personal opportunities enjoyed by the respondent and his children and questions on the respondent's beliefs about general opportunities offered by the American system. These parallel questions allow us to test somewhat more directly the proposition that seems to have emerged from the foregoing analysis, that there is a barrier between the two.

First we consider belief in opportunities offered by the system and perception of opportunities in personal life. We might expect a strong association between the two: those who feel that their own opportunities have been better than their parents' and that their children's opportunities will exceed their own would be more likely to feel that opportunities to succeed in general are more sufficient and fairly distributed. As shown in Table 6-3, again this is not the case. There is virtually no relationship

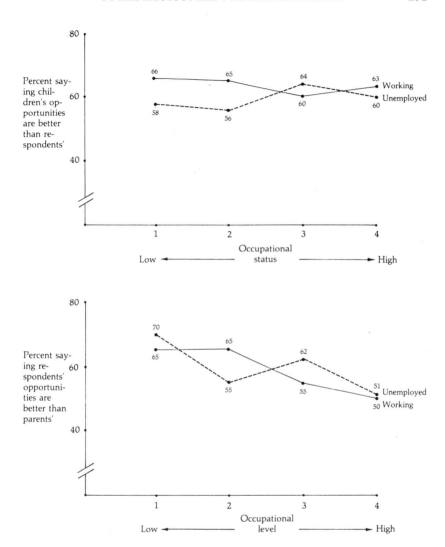

Figure 6-6 Perception of personal opportunities, by occupational level and employment status.

between beliefs about opportunities in general and evaluation of personal opportunities. On the one hand, this finding is surprising. Given that people have no way of verifying the tenets of the American Dream empirically—after all, students of the issues have reached no consensus— we would expect them to look to their personal experience for guideposts to understanding how the opportunity structures of the society operate. On the other, the absence of any association between beliefs about

Table 6-3 Association between belief in the American Dream and perception of personal opportunities.

Belief	RESPONDENTS' OPPORTUNITIES AS OPPOSED TO PARENTS'			CHILDREN'S OPPORTUNITIES AS OPPOSED TO RESPONDENTS'		
	Better	Same	Worse	Better	Same	Worse
Percent saying:						
Hard work is the most important factor in getting ahead	70	69	63	73	67	57
		Gamma = .08				Gamma = .19
A worker's child has at least some chance to get ahead	70	72	68	70	74	62
		Gamma = .02				Gamma = .04
The chances for success are distributed fairly	41	47	37	42	46	31
		Gamma = −.01				Gamma = .02
	(771)	(291)	(195)	(733)	(364)	(127)

personal and system opportunities is further evidence of an invisible barrier between personal experience and abstract ideology.[3]

The data in Table 6-4, in which we compare the relationship between class consciousness and belief in the opportunities offered by the system with that between class consciousness and perception of opportunities in personal life, confirm the disjunction between personal life and social ideology. We differentiate blue-collar from white-collar workers because of the ambiguities in the meaning of class consciousness for white-collar workers. However, the relationships we find hold for both manual and nonmanual workers. The top two rows repeat the moderately strong relationship between belief in the American opportunity structure and the absence of class consciousness that we found in Chapter 5: as we saw then, those who believe the opportunity structure is open and fair are less likely to believe workers are in conflict with management, that workers should stick together rather than trying to make it on their own, or that workers are rewarded unfairly. As shown in the bottom two lines of the table, there is very little relationship between perceptions of personal opportunities—or belief in the American Dream in a personal sense—and understanding of how the class system operates. Indeed, almost all the coefficients of association are near zero.

These data provide an important amplification of our analysis. As so often posited by students of American politics, belief in opportunities for advancement and class consciousness are related: those who believe in the existence of an open opportunity system are less likely to be class conscious. It is, however, the generalized belief about the American system that is related to class consciousness, not perception of advancement in personal terms. Those aspects of personal life—advancement opportunities as one has experienced them, or hopes for one's children—have no bearing on views of the relations between social classes.

The data presented in Figure 6-7 amplify further the disconnection between personal experiences and general views of the system. At the top of the figure is repeated the graph of a relationship we have discussed sever-

[3]This finding is compatible with the conclusions drawn in several studies of the beliefs of American workers, which are based on in-depth interviewing of a limited sample. Put generally, these studies find that, although individuals do not necessarily believe in the existence of complete equality of opportunity, most subscribe to the view that there is sufficient opportunity to get ahead and that they must therefore take responsibility for their own situations. See, for example, Eli Chinoy, *Automobile Workers and the American Dream* (Boston: Beacon Press, 1955), p. 124; Robert Lane, *Political Ideology* (New York: Free Press, 1962), pp. 61-62; Richard Sennett and Jonathan Cobb, *The Hidden Injuries of Class* (New York: Vintage Books, Random House, 1972), p. 92.

Table 6-4   Perception of personal and system opportunities related to class-consciousness measures for blue-collar and white-collar workers (gammas).

	CLASS-CONSCIOUSNESS MEASURES					
	CONFLICT		SOLIDARITY		FAIRNESS	
Perception	White collar	Blue collar	White collar	Blue collar	White collar	Blue collar
System opportunities:						
Chances for worker's child	.14	.06	.19	.23	.48	.21
Fairness of chances	.23	.32	.30	.27	.58	.46
Opportunities in personal life:						
Respondent compared with child	−.09	.20	−.05	.06	−.08	−.16
Respondent compared with parents	−.02	.05	.12	.12	−.02	.00

Summary of relationships:

System opportunities and class consciousness: mean = .29

Personal opportunities and class consciousness: mean = −.01

al times already, the fairly strong relationship between belief that opportunities for success are distributed fairly and belief that rewards in terms of compensation for work *of the system* are distributed fairly. Below it, we show for comparative purposes the relationship between belief in the fairness of opportunities in America and belief that *one's own* economic rewards are fair. The fairly strong relationship in the first comparison is not found in the second. The measures of association between beliefs about the equality of opportunity and the equality of economic reward within the American system—the wages of workers and executives in the abstract—are .58 and .48 for white-collar and blue-collar workers respectively. In contrast, the measure of association between beliefs about opportunities for advancement in America and the fairness of one's own wages are .10 and .09 for white-collar and blue-collar workers. Once

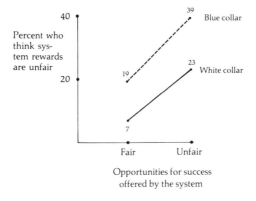

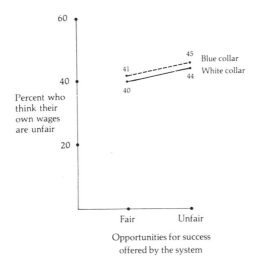

Figure 6-7 Perception of systemic opportunities in relation to fairness of system rewards and personal rewards.

again, there seems to be disjunction between general views of the American economic system and specific experiences with that system.[4]

Conclusion

In a variety of ways our data suggest the existence of a significant disjunction between the experiences individuals have with the American

[4]We can compare the relationship between belief that the opportunities for advancement in America are fair and belief in the fairness of system rewards, with the relationship between the former and belief in the fairness of one's own rewards more

economy and their more general views of American society. Beliefs about social reality—about either opportunities for advancement or the class structure—seem relatively impermeable to the effects of personal experience. We found this gap both when we considered the relationship between social ideology and unemployment, an experience we know to be accompanied by severe short-term stress, and when we examined the relationship between social ideology and various measures of personal perceptions of opportunity and the fairness of compensation.

When we weigh these findings in conjunction with those of the preceding chapter, it seems that the prospects for political mobilization are relatively limited. Americans' views are characterized by an individualistic belief in opportunity and a low level of class consciousness, and furthermore, there seems to be no link between personal experience and more abstract understanding of society. Both factors lead us to be dubious about the possibilities for mobilization along lines generated by personal economic strain.

A Note on Going into Business for Oneself

In a society in which some of the major cultural heroes—or villains—are the men whose entrepreneurial ventures rendered them fantastically wealthy and powerful in the late nineteenth century, going into business on one's own has enjoyed a special stature as a means of getting ahead. We were interested in investigating whether people have aspirations to self-employment, both because going into business might be one strategy for dealing with economic stress or unemployment, and because faith in entrepreneurship is another of the components of American individualism.

Scholars may debate whether opportunities for social mobility have

---

directly by using the log-linear models discussed in Chapter 3. The following figures compare the effects on belief in the fairness of the opportunities structure in America of four variables: belief in the fairness of system rewards, belief in the fairness of personal rewards, class, and employment status.

Effect of—

Belief that system rewards are fair	28.4**
Belief that personal rewards are fair	.0
Class (occupational level)	3.3
Employment status	.3
Overall effects	53.6*

*Significant at .01 level.
**Significant at .001 level.

As can be clearly seen, when all four variables are considered simultaneously, belief in the fairness of system rewards has the only statistically significant effect on beliefs about the opportunity structure.

become constricted in recent times, but there is no disagreement about self-employment. We know that one of the unmistakable changes of recent decades is the decline in the number of Americans who are in business for themselves: the nation of yeoman farmers and small shopkeepers and tradesmen has become the nation of agribusiness and conglomerates. In short, Americans no longer work for themselves; they work for large organizations.

It was in view of this change that we were especially interested in learning whether Americans still harbor aspirations of going into business for themselves. Once again, the data from the 1939 Roper study make possible comparisons with the past; as usual, we have transformed our own data to conform to the earlier sample by eliminating nonwhites and redefining the occupational groups. The data presented in Figure 6-8, in which we show the proportion of those not already self-employed who indicated a desire to go into business for themselves (three occupational groups and the unemployed in the two time periods), suggest that the meaning of self-employment has changed over the past generation. Two differences are immediately apparent. First, a much higher proportion of respondents wanted to go into business for themselves in 1939—71 percent overall as compared with 34 percent in 1976. In addition, the relationship between occupational level and desire for self-employment has reversed: in 1939 it was the upper white-collar workers who were most likely to report such a preference, the unemployed least likely; in 1976 it was just the opposite. The data suggest that self-employment no longer is the mode of advancement preferred by those in upper-status positions. In 1939 four out of five of the group had considered going into business for themselves, in 1976 only one out of three. On the other hand, the unemployed in 1976 were only slightly less likely than their counterparts in 1939, but much more likely than their upper white-collar contemporaries, to aspire to self-employment. With the 1976 data, we can divide the unemployed into occupational levels. When we do so, we find that the jobless at each level are more likely to prefer self-employment, the difference being especially pronounced among respondents in upper-status occupations.[5]

[5]The data are as follows:

	Percent wanting to go into business for themselves			
	Low ←	Occupational level		→ High
Employment status	1	2	3	4
Working	49	50	62	58
Unemployed	40	29	40	28

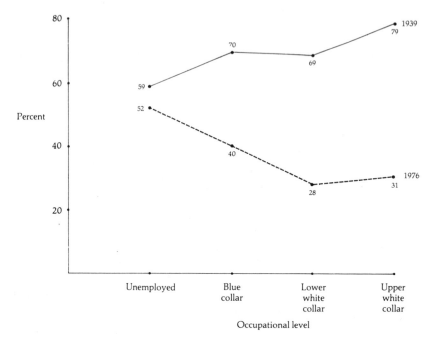

Figure 6-8 Proportion who desire to go into business for themselves, by occupational level (whites only), 1939 and 1976.

These data suggest that the meaning of entrepreneurship has been transformed. Once the preferred strategy of upper-status groups, it is now relatively most favored by the economically strained. Presumably, it is seen as a means to financial security and personal autonomy rather than an avenue to individual advancement, a method of dealing with a severe economic problem rather than part of a master plan for occupational achievement.[6] Thus, we see the preference for self-employment more as a means of coping individually with economic hardship, analogous to all the activities designed to raise resources that we discussed in Chapter 4, rather than as a manifestation of belief in an American Dream of success through entrepreneurship. These data on preferences for self-employment further confirm our understanding of the personal impact of

[6]This is consistent with Chinoy's finding that 50 percent of the 62 factory workers he interviewed wanted to go into business for themselves. Their main reason was not desire for wealth but desire for security—to avoid being laid off or given menial work when they grew older. They also believed self-employment conferred autonomy and dignity (*Automobile Workers and the American Dream*, p. 82).

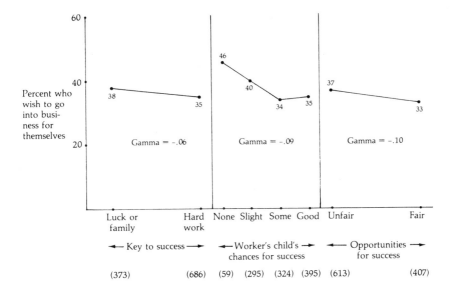

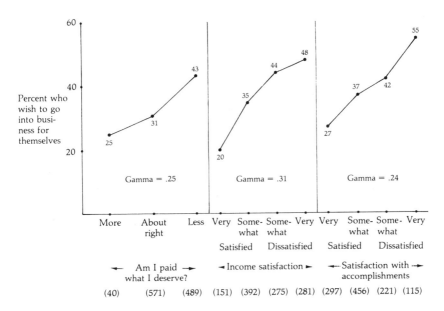

Figure 6-9   Proportion who desire to go into business for themselves, by belief in the American Dream and personal satisfaction.

unemployment, an impact that can be described as severe but contained. Unemployment makes people unhappy; it forces them to generate resources and cut back expenditures; it leads them to contemplate entering business for themselves. But it does not seem to affect their beliefs—either their evaluations of the class system and opportunity structures in America or their perceptions of the opportunities available to them and to their children.

Given our interpretation of the desire to go into business for oneself as a specific response to experiences of economic insecurity rather than a part of a general ideology, we would expect preference for self-employment to be closely related to the respondent's personal economic experiences, but unrelated to his more general view of the world. That this is the case is clearly indicated by the data in Figure 6-9, in which we compare the association between the aspiration to going into business on one's own and beliefs about the opportunity structure in America with the association between desire for self-employment and the individual's perception of his own economic situation. As one can see, those who believe in the American Dream—who think that hard work is the key to success, that a worker's child has a good chance to get ahead, and that chances for success are fairly apportioned—are not more likely to think about going into business for themselves. On the contrary, they are actually slightly less likely to have such aspirations. What is perhaps most interesting is the slight negative relationship between belief in hard work and the desire for self-employment. Presumably, those who have faith in the efficacy of industry would have a special incentive to go off on their own because they would be more certain that their efforts would be rewarded with success. In contrast, we find that there are moderately strong relationships between personal unhappiness and the desire to go into business. Those who feel that their wages are unfair or are dissatisfied with their incomes or accomplishments are more likely to indicate aspirations to self-employment. Thus, these data seem to confirm our interpretation of the desire to go into business on one's own as a preference emanating from personal difficulties and unhappiness rather than as a part of a general ideology of the nature of advancement in America.

CHAPTER 7

The Social Ideology of Black Americans

S OME OF THE issues we have been considering have special relevance for black Americans, to whom equality of opportunity has been denied and to whom the promises of the American Dream have been foreclosed. Both because of the unique deprivations that blacks have suffered in American history and because of the emergence more recently of an awareness on the part of blacks of their collective interests and a concomitant predisposition to act on behalf of those interests, we wish to examine their beliefs more closely.

One reason for us to take a more careful look at the attitudes of blacks has to do with our principal project, to understand the meaning of unemployment for political and social life. As we indicated in Chapter 2, blacks have traditionally had rates of unemployment substantially higher than whites. In April 1976, for example, when our metropolitan survey was conducted, the unemployment rate for whites was 6.7 percent; for nonwhites it was 12.6 percent. For some groups, especially teenagers, the rates were still more alarming: in April 1976, 38.9 percent of nonwhite teenagers were out of work.[1] Given the high rate of unemployment of blacks, there is a risk that the relationships we have found—and some that we have failed to find—are a function of race rather than unemployment. Nearly 30 percent of the unemployed respondents in our metropolitan work force survey were black;[2] thus, in delineating the social re-

[1]*Employment and Earnings*, May 1976, p. 25. Monthly statistics show rates of unemployment to be even higher when blacks are considered apart from other nonwhites.

[2]Because blacks are the most urban group in the population, our metropolitan work force survey netted more black respondents than a national work force survey would have. At the time, in April 1976, 17.5 percent of the unemployed were black.

sponses of the unemployed, we run the risk of spuriousness. It makes sense to focus briefly on blacks to learn if the effects we have attributed to unemployment should in fact be attributed to race—or to the interactive combination of unemployment and race.

It is not merely our desire to avoid committing the methodological error of confusing the effects of race with the effects of unemployment that leads us to investigate the attitudes of blacks more thoroughly; for in several ways aspects of the black experience have relevance to the larger questions we have been asking. For example, behind our analysis of the consequences of unemployment has been a concern with the way in which the disaffection concomitant to strain in personal life is politicized, translated into political preferences and public action aimed at the alleviation of that strain. Obviously, to be black in American society is to undergo personal strain—though a different sort of strain from the strain of unemployment. As a matter of fact, there are several aspects of the black experience that contrast with unemployment and would lead us to expect that personal strain for blacks would be more readily transformed into politically relevant attitudes and actions. For example, while most of the unemployed are out of work for only relatively short periods of time, blacks are black permanently. This point and its expected consequences perhaps require some elaboration. As we have seen, the mean length of unemployment in April 1976 was just under four months. In terms of the disruption that can be caused to a personal life, four months is a long time, but in terms of the kinds of attitudes we have been discussing— general orientations toward the operations of the social world—four months is perhaps too short a time in which to alter such basic beliefs. It is not simply that such a fundamental reorientation may take a longer period of time to effect, but that the unemployed can quite reasonably conceive of their predicament as temporary, a perception that would tend to limit the effects of joblessness. Blacks, on the other hand, presumably are aware from a very early age that their racial status is permanent.

Furthermore, unlike the unemployed, blacks are more or less readily identifiable. To a degree unmatched by any politically relevant group— except, perhaps, women—blacks can be physically differentiated. Thus, unlike class, unemployment, or, in many cases, ethnicity, racial status is worn externally. Also, compared to the unemployed—who are scattered, though not necessarily uniformly—across virtually every community and neighborhood in the nation, blacks are much more concentrated residentially and institutionally. Once again, to a degree unmatched by members of other politically relevant groups, especially the unemployed, blacks are likely to live, work, worship, and go to school with members

of their own group. In addition to all of the foregoing, and in part because of the foregoing, blacks draw upon a larger context of commonal-
ity than the members of most politically relevant groups. Once again,
unlike the unemployed, who have in common only their joblessness and
who differ from one another in virtually every other way, blacks share a
common history and culture.

In some ways, then, we can equate the experience of being out of work
with the experience of being black. Both are accompanied by personal
hardship and the hardship is potentially political. Blacks and jobless
workers both can be thought of as having mutual interests amenable to
government action and might reasonably be expected to act collectively
in pursuit of those interests. Yet we might expect greater community of
belief and action on the part of blacks than the unemployed.

There is still another reason why we are especially interested in taking
a more careful look at the social ideologies of blacks. At least since
Engels, observers of American society have remarked upon the degree to
which ethnic diversity divides the working class and renders more difficult the emergence of the politics of economic conflict:

> American conditions involve very great and peculiar difficulties for a steady
> development of a workers' party . . . immigration, which divides the workers
> into two groups: the native-born and the foreigners, and the latter in turn into
> (1) the Irish, (2) the Germans, (3) the many small groups, each of which under-
> stands only itself: Czechs, Poles, Italians, Scandinavians, etc. And then the
> Negroes. To form a single party out of these requires unusually powerful in-
> centives.[3]

Such a view seems to make intuitive sense given the prominence of racial
conflict in American history and contemporary politics. The point is frequently made that those most directly threatened by thrusts for equality
on the part of blacks are the whites who are closest to them in economic
status: whites whose craft-union training programs have been targeted
for inclusion of minority trainees, whose neighborhoods have been selected for public housing sites, or whose inner-city schools have been in-
corporated into busing plans. Those who would be expected to be allies
in a politics of economics continue to be, as they have often been in the
past, frequent antagonists in a politics of social and cultural issues. Clearly our data cannot begin to speak to the overall issue of the degree to
which racial conflict dampens worker solidarity. Still, we can inquire

[3]Letter to Friedrich A. Sorge in Lewis S. Feuer, ed., *Marx and Engels: Basic Writings on Politics and Philosophy* (New York: Anchor Books, Doubleday and Co.,
1959), p. 458.

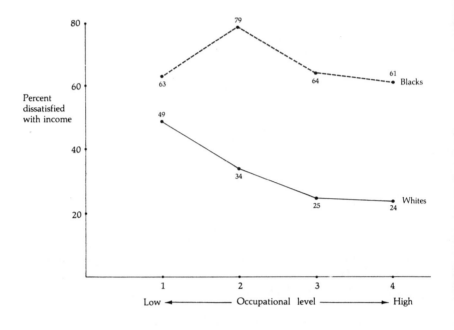

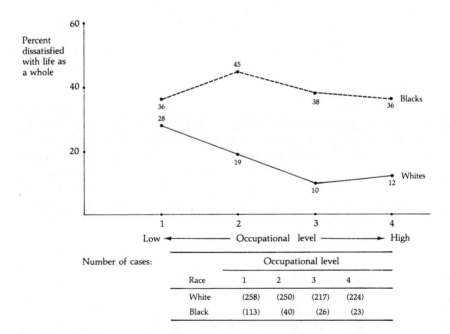

Figure 7-1 Level of satisfaction, by race and occupational level.

whether race consciousness on the part of blacks undermines class consciousness. Furthermore, we can examine what is perhaps a reciprocal question, the degree to which the economic stress that accompanies unemployment exacerbates hostility between the races.

If the foregoing intellectual reasons are not sufficiently compelling to justify a closer look at the social ideologies of blacks, we feel that such probing is appropriate simply to fill a gap in our understanding of the beliefs of a significant group in the American public. Recent investigations by social scientists have shown black Americans to be distinctive in their political attitudes and cohesive in their political actions, to have become in the past decade and a half the demographic group most loyally Democratic in party identification, most cohesive in casting ballots, most liberal in policy preferences, and most alienated from government.[4] Although we know quite a bit about the commitment of blacks to policies of change and their feelings of disaffection toward government, we know very little about the fundamental orientations to American society that underlie these attitudes. It is in this respect that our data can be used to fill a gap in the understanding of the beliefs of the blacks.

Race and Personal Dissatisfaction

Earlier we asserted, almost glibly, that to be black in American society is to experience personal strain. Everywhere there is abundant evidence for such a conclusion. If there are those who remain unconvinced, we can give evidence of a systematic sort. Figure 7-1, which presents data broken down by race on satisfaction both with income and with life in general, shows that at each occupational level blacks are substantially more likely to express dissatisfaction than whites. Thus our data support the conclusion that would naturally be drawn from many other sources: the experience of being black, like the experience of being out of work, induces personal strain and dissatisfaction.

We compare the relative effects on personal life of being black and being out of work in Table 7-1. Both experiences are sources of personal distress: blacks, regardless of employment status, express more dissatisfaction than their white counterparts; those who are out of work, regardless of race, express more dissatisfaction than their working counterparts.[5] What is striking in Table 7-1 is the enormity of the gap in

[4]See, among others, Joel D. Aberbach and Jack L. Walker, *Race in the City* (Boston: Little, Brown, and Co., 1973), chaps. 2 and 6; and Norman H. Nie, Sidney Verba, and John R. Petrocik, *The Changing American Voter* (Cambridge, Mass.: Harvard University Press, 1976), chaps. 13-14.

[5]Lest we seem by omission to give the impression that the way blacks deal with the personal strain that accompanies their racial status is simply to complain, we

satisfaction between whites with jobs and blacks without: 28 percent of the employed whites, as opposed to an overwhelming 90 percent of the jobless blacks, express dissatisfaction with income; 15 percent of the working whites, as compared to 57 percent of the unemployed blacks, indicate dissatisfaction with their lives in general.

Blacks and the American Dream

It is perhaps only since Title VII of the Civil Rights Act of 1964, if since then, that serious attempts have been made to extend the promise of the American Dream to black Americans. With their long history of exclusion and the alienation and distrust that blacks express with reference to so many issues,[6] we were interested to know whether this cynicism extended to the promise of equality of opportunity. As shown in Table 7-2, blacks are less credulous when it comes to beliefs about opportunities: they are less likely than whites to believe that hard work is the key component of success, that a worker's child has at least some chance to get ahead, and that opportunities for success are fairly distributed. What is puzzling about the interpretation of Table 7-2, however, is deciding whether it is the greater cynicism of blacks relative to whites or the absolute degree to which they seem to accept the postulates of the American Dream that deserves comment. It is perhaps less noteworthy that blacks are somewhat more skeptical than whites on these issues than that the gap is as small as it is and that blacks are as believing as they are in the existence of opportunities.

The picture becomes even more complex when we consider Figure 7-2, which presents data for blacks and whites broken down into occupational levels. When we consider the occupational groups separately, we find that the differences between the races are not uniform. There is no consistent difference, for instance, between blacks and whites of various

---

should make clear that both working and jobless blacks are even more likely than whites to make efforts to cope on their own. As shown in the following table, both working and jobless blacks are more likely than their white counterparts to have cut back substantially on spending and to have made independent efforts to generate additional resources.

Employment status	Have cut back substantially		Have generated resources	
	Whites	Blacks	Whites	Blacks
Working	10%	29%	56%	78%
Unemployed	32%	47%	76%	83%

[6]Aberbach and Walker, *Race in the City*, chaps. 2 and 6.

Table 7-1 Proportion of respondents expressing personal dissatisfaction, by race and employment status.

| | PERCENT DISSATISFIED WITH — | | | |
| | INCOME | | LIFE AS A WHOLE | |
Employ-ment status	Whites	Blacks	Whites	Blacks
Working	28	57	15	31
Unemployed	71	90	36	57

Number of cases: working—whites, (670), blacks, (82); unemployed—whites, (365), blacks, (159)

occupational levels on the importance of hard work in getting ahead: the largest difference between the races is in the lowest occupational level, a category that accounts for half the black respondents but little more than one-fifth of the whites; therefore, the overall difference between blacks and whites shown in Table 7-2 is a function of the relative skepticism of the blacks in the lowest occupational category. On the two items about the opportunities available to the child of a factory worker, there are substantial differences between the races only among members of the highest occupational category. Among members of lower occupational categories the differences are relatively small and inconsistent in magnitude. It is among those in the highest occupational group—who presumably have experienced upward mobility in their own lives or those of their parents—who are more cynical. Thus, it is the members of the black bourgeoisie, who have sometimes been accused of ignoring their fellow

Table 7-2 Belief in the American Dream, by race (percent).

| | RACE | |
Belief	Whites	Blacks
Hard work is the most important factor in getting ahead	70	63
A worker's child has at least some chance to get ahead	73	59
The chances for success are distributed fairly	44	35

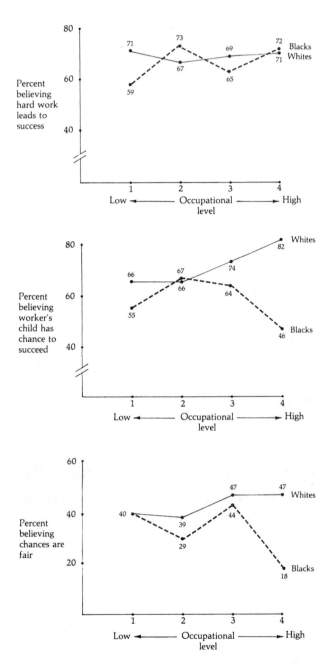

Figure 7-2   Belief in the American Dream, by race and occupational level.

blacks in favor of identification with the white majority, who are most skeptical about the openness and fairness of opportunity structures.

Blacks are somewhat less sanguine about the fairness of opportunities when it is a matter of relative opportunities for blacks and whites rather than for workers and executives. We asked our respondents whether blacks or whites had a better chance to get the good jobs; if the respondent saw a difference between the opportunities available to the races, he was asked if that difference was fair. The condensed replies to these questions in Table 7-3 show that blacks and whites feel similarly in two respects: in both cases a plurality sees whites as having an unfair advantage, and only a few respondents of either race consider a relative group advantage to be fair. However, while 21 percent of the white respondents see unfair black advantage, not a single black respondent expressed this point of view. Furthermore, a large majority of the blacks, 75 percent, but only 42 percent of the whites, indicated that whites had an unfair advantage. Thus, while there was considerable similarity between whites and blacks in terms of their views of the opportunities available to class groups, there is a substantial difference between the races when it comes to views of opportunities available to racial groups.

In Figure 7-3 we make a variety of comparisons that permit us to refine our understanding of how blacks and whites perceive the opportunities available to race and class groups. For blacks and whites within each occupational category we give the percentage who see executives' children as unfairly advantaged and the percentage who see whites as unfairly

Table 7-3   Belief in fairness of opportunity for blacks and whites, by race (percent).

Comparing blacks and whites, who has a better chance to get the good jobs—blacks, whites, or is there no difference? If respondent sees a difference: Do you think that's fair?

Response	Whites	Blacks
Whites have a better chance; it's fair	3	0[a]
Blacks have a better chance; it's unfair	21	0
No difference	32	24
Whites have a better chance; it's unfair	42	75
Blacks have a better chance; it's fair	2	0

[a]Less than 1 percent.

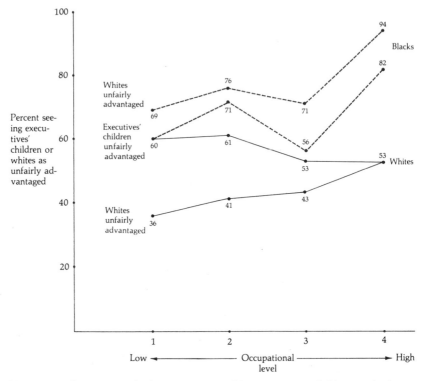

Figure 7-3 Perception of advantage enjoyed by executives' children and whites, by race and occupational level.

advantaged: the solid lines represent responses of whites, the dotted lines responses of blacks. It is clear that at all occupational levels blacks see more race and class discrimination than do their white counterparts. As we have already noted, however, with the exception of respondents in the highest occupational category, blacks and whites of the same occupational level do not differ from one another substantially in the degree to which they perceive executives' children to be unfairly advantaged. On the other hand, this is hardly the case when it comes to perception of injustice in the opportunities open to blacks and whites: in each occupational category, blacks are substantially more likely than whites to see whites as unfairly advantaged; the gap between the races is virtually uniform across occupational categories.

Figure 7-3 permits us to make further inferences about the beliefs of blacks and whites about opportunities. From the top pair of lines it is evident that blacks, regardless of occupational level, are more likely to see racial than class injustice. Furthermore, the relative perception of race as opposed to class disadvantage is more or less constant across occupational categories for blacks: the two lines form a more or less parallel zigzag. With reference to neither race nor class opportunities is there a clear monotonic relationship across occupational categories; in both cases it is upper-status blacks who are unambiguously most cynical about equality of opportunity—an extraordinary 94 percent of blacks in the highest occupational category feel that whites enjoy unfair advantages. The pattern is quite different for white respondents. Considering the bottom two lines, we see that—with the exception of whites in the highest occupational category, who are equally likely to see racial or class injustice—white respondents of all occupational categories are more likely to see unfair advantages accruing to executives' children than to whites. It is interesting that, in contrast to the pattern that obtained for black respondents, while perception of class injustice declines somewhat across occupational categories for whites, perception of racial injustice increases markedly as one moves up the occupational hierarchy: white respondents in the lowest occupational category are nearly twice as likely to see unfairness in opportunities available to class groups as to see unfairness in opportunities available to racial groups; as we have mentioned, whites in the highest occupational category are equally likely to see either kind of injustice.

Given the cynicism about equality of opportunity for the races that we have found among blacks, we were anxious to learn how black respondents viewed the opportunities in their own lives. We were especially interested in the perceptions of upper-status blacks—who, as we have seen, are very skeptical about the fairness of the opportunity structures and who, presumably, have been blessed with more expansive opportunities than most of their fellow blacks.

As shown in Figure 7-4, however skeptical blacks may be about opportunities in general, this cynicism does not extend to their evaluations of their own lives. At each occupational level blacks are more likely than whites both to report that their opportunities have been better than those in their parents' lives and to predict that their children's chances will be better than their own. With reference to the respondents' evaluations of their own opportunities relative to their parents', it is interesting that the group that is most positive about its own opportunities is precisely the group that was least sanguine about equality of opportunity, upper-status blacks: 86 percent of the blacks in the highest occupational category, as opposed to only 59 percent of their white occupational counterparts, believe they have had better opportunities than their parents. With

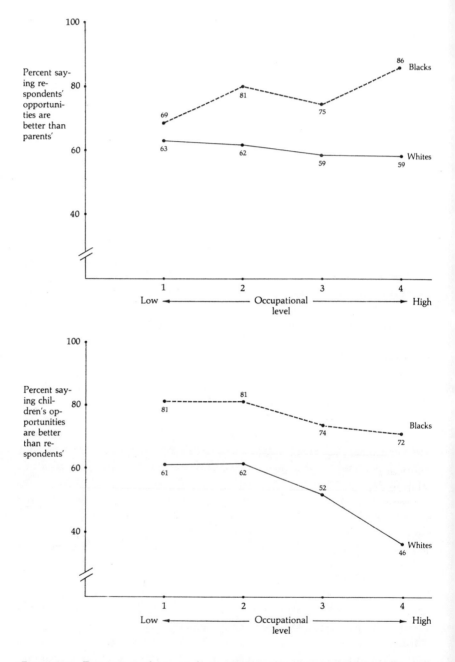

Figure 7-4 Perception of personal opportunities for success, by race and occupational level.

reference to children's opportunities, the largest gap between the races is once again found in the highest occupational category although, in this case, both upper-status whites and upper-status blacks are somewhat less optimistic than their racial counterparts in lower occupational categories.

Thus, the data indicate a good deal of optimism among blacks in general, and upper-status blacks in particular, about the opportunities available to them and to their offspring. This might seem to be out of phase with our findings that virtually all upper-status blacks are skeptical about equality of opportunity in general and that over two-thirds of blacks at all occupational levels are cynical about equality of opportunity for blacks. However, there is no real contradiction. In terms of equality of opportunity, things presumably have been getting better for blacks in the past decade; there would be every reason to expect that many of our black respondents, especially those who have prestigious, skilled occupations, would report having had better opportunities than their parents. While their situations may well have improved, according to their perception, blacks still have a very long way to go before full equality of opportunity is achieved. Even those who have been the beneficiaries of the broader opportunities for blacks see residual inequalities as persisting. The parents of most of our black respondents undoubtedly confronted a world of very circumscribed options. There is no apparent contradiction between the perception that personal opportunities have improved and will continue to do so and the belief that equality of opportunity for the races has not yet been achieved.

Race and Class Consciousness

The situation we have described is one that would seem replete with political potential: personal dissatisfaction coupled with a sense of group-relative deprivation. Although we have ascertained that blacks see improvement in the opportunities open to them and their offspring, we have no indication that those opportunities are considered sufficient; furthermore, we have convincing evidence that blacks see whites as unjustly advantaged in general. Such attitudes form the natural underpinnings for the political mobilization of blacks we know to have taken place in the past two decades.

In view of the sense of personal dissatisfaction and group deprivation we unearthed, we were eager to learn whether blacks' attitudes are characterized by the kind of group consciousness that would facilitate the politicization of such underlying beliefs. We have seen that the personal strain accompanying unemployment does not create class consciousness among workers; we were interested to ask analogous questions about blacks. In particular we wished to learn the extent to which blacks show consciousness of their economic status; to understand whether that consciousness solidifies around racial or economic class identity; and to gain further insight on an issue often discussed by those who ponder the absence of socialism in America, the degree to which race solidarity undercuts class solidarity.

We can begin by inquiring whether blacks manifest the kind of limited class consciousness we have found so rare within the American working class as a whole. Figure 7-5 gives data on the class self-identifications of black and white blue-collar and white-collar workers. In each of the occupational categories blacks are less likely than their white counterparts to assign themselves spontaneously to a social class. In addition, blacks are somewhat less likely than their white counterparts to place themselves in the middle class and slightly more likely than the parallel white group to assign themselves to the working class in response to the open-ended question. What is striking about the pattern of responses, however, is not the differences between whites and blacks, but the similarities. Even among blue-collar blacks only a few respondents spontaneously identify with the working class.

Clear differences between the races do appear in the responses to the closed-ended follow-up question on class identification. Blacks were more likely than whites to have chosen a working-class identification when presented with a forced choice between middle-class and working-class identification. Among blue-collar workers of both races, a majority identified with the working class when confronted with the dual alternatives. However, blue-collar blacks were relatively more likely to have chosen working-class identification than blue-collar whites. It is interesting that even white-collar blacks chose a working-class identification on the follow-up question by a 2-to-1 majority, while white-collar workers among whites, not surprisingly, chose a middle-class identification by the same ratio. Still, the obvious interpretation of the combined responses is that Americans identify with the middle class. In only one group, blue-collar blacks, is there a plurality of working-class identifiers. Even then, those who choose working-class identification—still not quite a majority—do so largely in response to the forced-choice follow-up question.

As shown in Figure 7-6, there are clear differences between blacks and whites in terms of their responses to our other class-consciousness measures. Each of the black occupational groups is more likely to give a class-conscious response than is either of the white occupational groups: to believe that the distribution of economic rewards in America is unfair, to see conflict between the interests of workers and management, and to

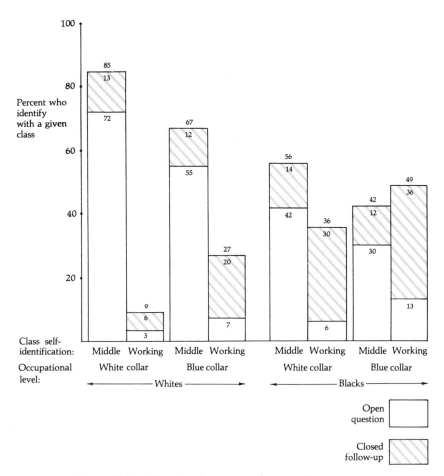

Figure 7-5 Class self-identification, by race and occupation.

believe that workers should stick together. It is interesting to note that in each case there is less difference in attitude between the occupational groups among blacks than among whites.

Table 6-1 in the previous chapter presented a multivariate analysis of the effect of race, class, and employment status on class-consciousness attitudes and indicated that the relations between race and the questions on working-class identification and worker solidarity are statistically significant. Class is significantly related to those as well. There is no statistically significant relation between class or race and the question on class conflict.

According to our measures, blacks manifest more class consciousness

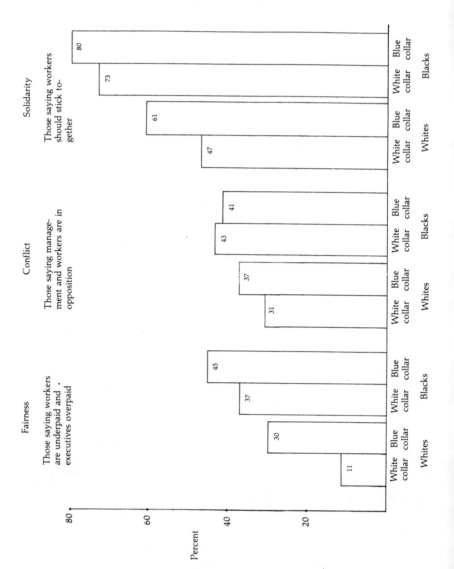

Figure 7-6 Measures of class consciousness, by race and occupation.

than do whites. How does this relate to their consciousness as members of a racially distinct group? We were interested to learn if blacks—who perceive more class conflict and subscribe to more class solidarity than whites—are more likely to perceive race than class conflict, and more likely to subscribe to race than class solidarity. Figure 7-7, in which we compare blacks' responses to our questions about class conflict and class solidarity with their responses to analogous questions about race conflict and solidarity, shows that blacks are more likely to give class-conscious than race-conscious responses: 35 percent indicate that the interests of blacks and whites are in opposition, while 41 percent said that the interests of workers and management are in opposition; 69 percent indicated that blacks should stick together, while 77 percent said that workers should stick together.

Furthermore, race consciousness does not seem to dampen class consciousness among blacks. In fact, it seems to enhance it slightly. As shown in Table 7-4, 47 percent of blacks who see conflict between the interests of blacks and whites, but only 40 percent of those who do not, also see opposition between the classes. Eighty-six percent of blacks who say that blacks should stick together, as opposed to 58 percent of those who feel that blacks should struggle on their own, feel that workers should stick together. Thus, class-conscious views are more common among the race conscious—not less.

Although these data suggest that blacks are both race and class conscious, we do not take them as evidence that blacks are more class than race conscious. It is our suspicion that when blacks respond to separate questions about race and class, they have both in mind, for the analytical distinction between race and class that informs our questions does not reflect the realities of a world in which the two are confounded. It stands to reason that in tapping the consciousness of one, we are simultaneously tapping the other.

Furthermore, our understanding of race consciousness among blacks is vitiated by the absence of any measure of racial self-identification. It is significant in itself that we consider a person's description of the class he belongs to as a measure of subjective class self-identification, whereas we would consider the response to an analogous question about race as a measure of objective racial status. The data on group identification in the 1976 election survey conducted by the Center for Political Studies at the University of Michigan permit us to probe this question further.[7] Respon-

---

[7]For a discussion of these data see Arthur H. Miller, Patricia Gurin, and Gerald Gurin, "Electoral Implications of Group Identification and Consciousness: Reintroduction of a Concept," paper presented at the Annual Meeting of the American Political Science Association, New York, September 1978.

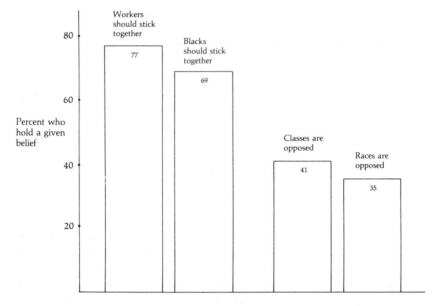

Figure 7-7   Measures of black consciousness and class consciousness (black respondents only).

dents were asked questions about a number of social groups—groups identified by race and by economic status, as well as age, region, sex, political ideology, and religion. For each, they were asked whether they felt close to the members of that group; then, from the groups to which they felt close, they were asked to select the one to which they felt closest. Although this measure differs from ours in that it is closed-ended and all respondents express some kind of group identification, it does permit us to make further comparisons.

Table 7-5 presents data on the degree to which members of various groups—blacks, whites, poor people, blue-collar workers—feel close to those groups. It is clear that blacks are more likely to say that they feel close to other blacks than are whites, poor people, or blue-collar workers to indicate feelings of closeness to their respective groups. Furthermore, as shown in Table 7-6, black blue-collar workers are more likely to indicate that they feel close to other blacks than to poor people or to workingmen. The data indicate that racial identification is more frequent than class identification for blacks. However, we should not underestimate the class consciousness of blue-collar blacks, a majority of whom feel close to poor people and to workingmen.[8] These data confirm our suspi-

[8]It is interesting to compare the group identifications of blue-collar whites and blue-collar blacks in this context:

Table 7-4   Race consciousness by class consciousness among blacks.

Percent seeing opposition between the classes among those who see:	
Opposition between races	47
No opposition between races	40
Percent saying workers should stick together among those who think:	
Blacks should stick together	86
Blacks should get ahead on their own	58

cion that racial identification is important for blacks, but that such an identification goes along with, rather than being an alternative to, identification with others in a similar economic situation.

Race Consciousness and Class Cooperation

On the basis of these data we cannot assess the extent to which race consciousness impedes cooperative activity on the basis of class between the races. That blacks identify both as blacks and as members of an economically deprived stratum does not tell us how they feel about whites from that deprived economic stratum. We have some relevant information in our follow-up interviews with the unemployed. Although we must caution that we are making generalizations on the basis of only sixty cases, two themes emerge. The first confirms what our structured interviews told us: blacks are on the whole more oriented to group solidarity than are whites. The second, and more evocative, theme is that blacks on the whole do not eschew cooperation with whites in pursuit of class-related economic goals. In our follow-up interviews we asked whether black workers should form their own separate organizations to

Degree of closeness to workingmen	Blue-collar whites	Blue-collar blacks
Closest to	27%	4%
Close to	42	52
Not close to	31	44

Although these data might seem to indicate that whites are more likely to identify with workers than blacks, we should bear in mind the results (shown in Figure 7-5) of our open-ended class identification question, which showed blacks to be more likely than whites to identify with workers.

Table 7-5   Respondents' feelings of closeness to various groups, by social group (percent).

Degree of feeling	Blacks to blacks	Whites to whites	Poor people to poor people[a]	Blue-collar workers to workingmen
Closest to	34	5	15	23
Close to, but not closest to	54	45	40	35
Not close to	12	50	45	42
	100	100	100	100
	(192)	(1,934)	(440)	(740)

[a]Respondents with annual family income less than $6,000.

SOURCE: Arthur H. Miller, Patricia Gurin, and Gerald Gurin, "Electoral Implications of Group Identification and Consciousness: Reintroduction of a Concept," paper presented at the Annual Meeting of the American Political Science Association, New York, September 1978, p. 15. The data on identification of blue-collar workers with workingmen come directly from the Center for Political Studies, University of Michigan, 1976 election survey.

solve their common problems or whether they should join with workers of other races. Only one of the sixteen jobless black respondents who answered the question said that blacks should not work with whites. The separatist approach of this twenty-year-old black factory worker was unambiguous. "You're marching against the 'man,' so why should you march with them?" The rest of the black respondents opposed demonstrations or marches on economic issues that were organized for blacks only. "We all need the same things, so we should all work together," a black plumber put it.

Several respondents were quite canny in differentiating the sorts of collective goals shared by those with common economic interests, whether those interests appear by virtue of class or unemployment status, from the civil rights goals that unite blacks—and for which many of the blacks indicated that black workers must fight alone, without the aid of sympathetic whites. "If you are fighting for equal rights or equal employment for blacks," a black telephone operator told us, "you should march on your own. But for rights for workers in general, you should march with everyone else."

Blacks' willingness to cooperate with whites in pursuit of economic goals was often expressed in terms of collective goals for blacks; that is, many blacks expressed the view that, because whites hold all the power, the only way for blacks to get ahead is to work with whites who share

Table 7-6 Closeness of black blue-collar workers to various groups.

| | PERCENTAGE OF BLACK BLUE-COLLAR WORKERS WHO FEEL CLOSE TO — | | |
Degree of feeling	Blacks	Poor people	Workingmen
Closest to	32	17	4
Close to but not closest to	52	40	52
Not close to	16	43	44
	100	100	100

Number of cases: 122

SOURCE: Center for Political Studies, Univeristy of Michigan, 1976 election survey.

their economic interests. "If we tried it by ourselves, they wouldn't listen." In a sense, class solidarity is embraced as the instrumentality for achieving racial goals.

The apparent willingness of blacks to engage in cooperative activity with whites in pursuit of commonly held economic goals led us to query them about the relative effects upon race and class consciousness of membership in perhaps the only formal organizations that encompass blacks and whites, unions.[9] In Figure 7-8 we consider the relationship between union membership and class self-identification for white and black blue-collar workers. Union membership appears to play a different role for the two races. For white workers, membership in a union is associated with an increase in the likelihood of identification as a worker. However, even among unionized whites there are few working-class identifiers—only 12 percent among those who answered spontaneously and only 35 percent if one includes those who responded to the more structured follow-up question. For blacks, unionization works in the opposite direction. Not one of the black blue-collar union members in our sample spontaneously identified with the working class; however, 17 percent of their nonunionized counterparts did so. In response to the closed-ended follow-up question, there were, once again, more working-class identifiers among nonunionized blacks than among union members. We presume that the considerable difference in class identification among blue-collar blacks reflects the degree to which the union members among blacks are able to achieve a middle-class life-style.

Figure 7-9, in which we present the relationship for black and white

[9]Thirty-five percent of the white blue-collar workers in our sample, but only 24 percent of the black blue-collar workers, are union members.

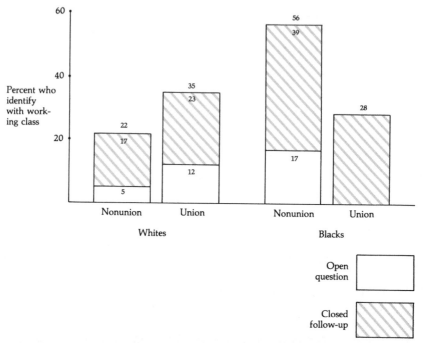

Figure 7-8 Working-class self-identification, by union membership and race (blue-collar workers only).

blue-collar workers of union membership to class consciousness—and, in the case of blacks, to race consciousness as well—indicates that union membership is associated with an increase in class consciousness for whites and with a slight increase in class consciousness and a slight decrease in race consciousness for blacks. Considering first the relation between unionization and class consciousness, we see that among both whites and blacks, union members are somewhat more likely to support class-conscious positions, to believe that the interests of workers and management are in conflict, and to think that workers should stick together. In both cases the differences between union members and nonunion members are greater for whites than for blacks. Particularly noticeable is the sharp distinction among whites between unionized and nonunionized workers who exhibit a sense of solidarity. Among whites, union membership appears to be associated with an enhanced sense of worker solidarity, but not to engender to nearly the same degree a sense of identification as a worker or a sense of conflict between workers and management. Comparing the data on race consciousness (the shaded

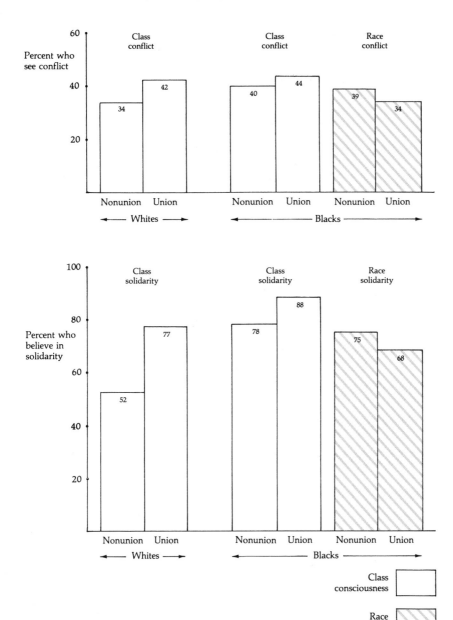

Figure 7-9 Measures of class and race consciousness, by race and union membership (blue-collar workers only).

columns) with those on class consciousness for blacks, we see that union members differ only slightly from their nonunionized counterparts. However, the differences are consistent and quite striking: among black blue-collar workers, union members are a bit more class conscious and a bit less race conscious than nonmembers.

Job Scarcity and Racial Hostility

One of the subthemes that has emerged from our discussion of the social ideologies of black Americans is the degree to which racial tensions divide the working class and therefore inhibit the emergence of class politics in America. Although our data set was not intended to contribute to the vast literature on tensions between the races, we were interested in testing a hypothesis suggested by studies of the unemployed during the thirties—that joblessness, an experience we know to be accompanied by personal and financial hardship, is associated with an increase in intergroup hostility. For example, E. Wight Bakke describes the hostility of unemployed English workers toward "foreign" workers from Ireland and Wales who were allegedly usurping all the available work at scandalously low wages.[10] In the contemporary United States we might expect some hostility to foreign workers; indeed, one of the respondents in our follow-up interviews complained about illegal aliens. However, if economic insecurity is associated with an increase in tension between groups, the principal manifestation of that increase might be in the area of black-white relations. The most obvious fault line within the American working class is a racial one. Whatever the multiple sources of racial antagonism, it is logical to hypothesize that such antagonisms would be exacerbated by the experience of unemployment, when competition for scarce jobs could be interpreted in terms of competition between racial groups.

The data presented in Figure 7-10 do not confirm the hypothesis that joblessness fosters resentment between the races. In the first part of the figure we consider whether members of the other racial group are thought to have an unfair advantage in getting good jobs; in the second we consider whether the interests of the races are thought to be basically the same or basically opposed. Several conclusions are immediately apparent from these data. With one exception, which runs counter to our expectations, the differences on these issues between working and unemployed members of the racial groups are absolutely minimal. Contrary to what we anticipated, unemployed blacks are somewhat less likely than their working counterparts to see whites as having an unfair ad-

[10]*The Unemployed Man* (London: Nisbet and Co., 1933), p. 8.

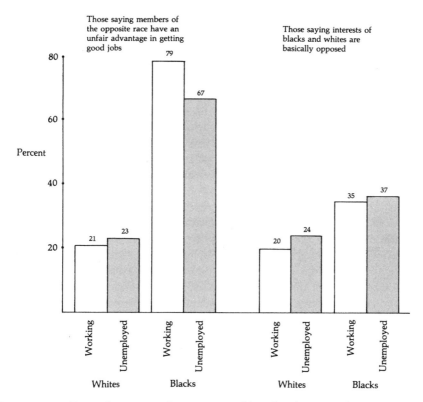

Figure 7-10 Unemployment and perception of hostility between the races.

vantage in getting good jobs; otherwise, there is little difference between the jobless and working groups. Once again we confirm the conclusion of the preceding chapter, that the experience of being out of work does not alter substantially a person's understanding of social reality.[11] What

[11]It could be that job scarcity begets racial tension, but that the effects of macro-economic changes upon racial tensions are not confined to those who have themselves been out of work. Economic downturn instead might yield generalized feelings of in-security and deprivation—among those with jobs as well as those without—and lead to the enhancement of racial antagonisms, feelings that the races are in competition or that members of another racial group command more than their fair share of scarce, and much sought, employment. A plausible alternative hypothesis would be that racial antagonisms subside during periods of economic downturn. At least one strand of analysis of American politics emphasizes that during periods of economic difficulty our politics are characterized by a pragmatic and programmatic concern about economic issues, while during periods of prosperity status anxieties and frus-trations and "the search for scapegoats" enter the political arena. See, for example, Richard Hofstadter, "The Pseudo-Conservative Revolt," in Daniel Bell, ed., *The New*

emerges clearly from the data in Figure 7-10 is that, insofar as these issues are concerned, differences between blacks and whites outweigh differences between working and jobless.[12] Blacks, regardless of their employment status, are somewhat more likely than whites to see conflict between the races and considerably more likely than whites to see their own group as unfairly disadvantaged in getting good jobs. With respect to the latter issue, it is interesting to note the absolute amount of unfairness perceived. Not only do about three-quarters of all blacks see whites as benefiting from an unfair advantage, but a not insignificant minority of whites—a bit over one-fifth—see such an advantage accruing to blacks.

The responses to our open-ended interviews, which contained questions designed to probe whether the personal experiences of the unemployed engendered feelings of intergroup resentment, amplify the fairly unambiguous conclusion we have drawn from the analysis of our survey data. We asked the follow-up subsample about their own experiences getting and keeping jobs: for those who had left their jobs involuntarily, was there any unfairness in choosing whom to lay off? Did they experience any kind of discrimination in looking for a new job?

The pattern of response to these questions confirms our earlier conclusion. Of the forty-four job losers in our follow-up subsample, somewhat over half reported some kind of unfairness when it came to their job loss and about half reported discrimination in their search for jobs. Thus, a substantial proportion perceive some unfairness connected with their own unemployment. However, when we look more closely, there is almost no mention of discrimination on the grounds of race. In describing their job loss, none of the white respondents who perceived unfairness saw favoritism to blacks; even among the blacks, only a minority of those who thought the criteria used to select workers for layoff to be unfair mentioned favoritism to whites. In terms of discrimination in hiring, none of the blacks who saw unfairness in hiring claimed that whites had been favored, and only two of the twenty whites who saw discrimination in hiring mentioned favoritism toward blacks. In sum, many of our re-

---

American Right (New York: Criterion Books, 1955). According to this logic, we might expect prosperous times to yield politically relevant racial tensions as expectations are raised and disadvantaged minorities make demands for a greater share of the abundance. Unfortunately, we do not have the kind of longitudinal data that permit us to test these alternative hypotheses.

[12] A log-linear multivariate analysis confirms that race has a statistically significant relationship to the attitudes reported in Figure 7-10, whereas class and employment status do not.

spondents report unfairness connected with their job loss or their job search, but little of it is perceived as explicitly racial.[13]

In discussing our survey data, we noted that a substantial majority of blacks and a surprisingly large minority of whites saw an unfair advantage in jobs accruing to members of the opposite race. In addition to the questions about personal experiences with discrimination in employment, we included items of a more abstract sort in our follow-up questionnaire: Are there any kinds of people who seem to be favored when they look for jobs? Are there any kinds of people who are treated unfairly? The pattern of responses again confirms what we have already learned from the survey data.

When asked about discrimination in hiring in the abstract, more of our unemployed respondents—over three-quarters of the fifty-three who replied to the question—perceived unfairness than had experienced it in their own lives. In this context race is frequently cited as a factor in hiring decisions. Of those who perceived that certain kinds of people are the beneficiaries of discrimination, two-thirds of the blacks and about half the whites made spontaneous references to members of the opposite race.[14] Although we are generalizing on the basis of a small and unsystematic sample, it seems clear that more of the unemployed perceive discrimination on the basis of race than actually undergo it. Once again we see a disjunction between personal experience and general views of the social world. If a large number of our jobless respondents believe that bias exists against their own racial group when it comes to hiring and firing, they do not do so on the basis of their own job history.

Conclusion

We have reviewed considerable data in this chapter, data that present a somewhat mixed picture but that suggest a kind of latent political ener-

[13]In terms of who is the beneficiary of favored treatment, the responses are varied. A few female respondents mentioned the opposite sex when it came to job search, and one male said that women were favored for some jobs he sought. No one, however, mentioned sex as a criterion for unfair selection in job loss. Other answers reflect the immense variety of job situations: in some cases, relatives of the boss were favored unfairly; in others, young workers who could be paid less; in still other cases, older workers with seniority. Some complained of favoritism to workers with higher skill levels or higher education, while others made the opposite complaint—that they were not hired because they were overqualified.

[14]The remainder of the respondents who perceived discrimination referred to a variety of bases for that discrimination. A few mentioned sex. However, in contrast to the perceptions with reference to race discrimination, there is little disjunction between the numbers mentioning sex discrimination as something experienced personally and the numbers perceiving it as a general social problem. Other respondents mentioned age, or skill, or education as the basis for unfair treatment.

gy on the part of blacks. We have seen that the general orientations of blacks to the social world are of a piece with the alienation, cohesiveness, and mobilization that have characterized their recent political attitudes and behavior. We have seen that, on the one hand, blacks are nearly as convinced of the reality of the American Dream as whites and are even more sanguine than whites about the opportunities they have enjoyed in their personal lives; on the other hand, they are quite cynical about the existence of equal opportunities for blacks. Furthermore, they are considerably more class conscious than are white workers, a class consciousness that does not seem to enter into competition with their sense of race consciousness. These underlying commitments would seem to establish the foundations for continued political mobilization of blacks, either on their own or in concert with whites of common economic interest.

In the course of our exploration of the social ideologies of black Americans we have considered data that shed light from two different directions on the century-old question of how the working class is divided. With reference to the degree to which race consciousness dampens class consciousness, we have seen that blacks are not only more likely to embrace the positions that we have labeled class conscious than their white occupational counterparts, but that they are also more likely to express class-conscious views than race-conscious ones. Furthermore, in our open-ended follow-up interviews they indicated a willingness to work with whites in pursuit of commonly held economic goals—albeit this willingness was often framed in terms of a desire to maximize the economic progress of blacks as a group, not of the working class. In addition, we have seen that the experience of being out of work does not intensify racial antagonisms for either whites or blacks, a conclusion that is entirely consistent with our previous findings about the effects of unemployment on social ideology.

Although we consider these findings to be striking, we do not wish to interpret them as contradicting a hypothesis as apparently congruent with the American experience from the Know-Nothings through George Wallace as is the hypothesis that working-class politics has been impeded by ethnic divisions among those who share economic interests. First of all, in our questions about group advantages in job seeking we found clear evidence of tension between the races. Furthermore, survey data can go only so far in helping to understand the unfolding of political events. The chasm dividing the opinions expressed in a survey like ours and the actions of people on a picket line outside a high school in South Boston or a housing project in Forest Hills is a deep one. Finally, even though blacks express willingness to unite with working-class whites, and race consciousness and class consciousness are both characteristic of the ideologies of working-class blacks, we do not know whether white workers are receptive to such cooperation or convinced of its necessity. We have considered only the attitudes of blacks. Obviously, the attitudes of whites are relevant to the question of whether conflict between the races will undermine cooperation within the working class.

CHAPTER 8

Economic Strain and Political Attitudes

I N OUR QUEST for an understanding of how economic strain in personal life affects the way in which individuals confront the social and political world, some of our original expectations have been confounded. We began with a notion something like the following: unemployment would produce severe economic stress; this economic pressure would influence political attitudes; however, this effect would be mediated by an individual's general orientation to the social world. Our analysis so far casts doubt upon the strength of the central link in this chain. Those who are out of work do report personal hardship, and they do take action to ameliorate that stress. However, joblessness and concomitant personal strain do not seem to have an impact on overall views of the American social and economic order. So far, it seems that such views form an encapsulated social ideology that is relatively resistant to the tremors of personal economic life.

In Chapter 1 we hypothesized that an individual problem would be more likely to become the basis for joint political action when fully politicized: seen as shared rather than private, and understood as requiring government assistance as opposed simply to private efforts for its solution. In addition, we posited that the probability of collective political action would be further enhanced if the perception of government responsibility were coupled with a political program of desired governmental intervention. In this chapter we return to these concerns in order to consider several aspects of the relationship between joblessness and political attitudes. First we examine the problem of how the unemployed assign responsibility for unemployment—in terms of where unemployment, theirs and others', comes from, and in terms of who should be responsible for dealing with it. Then we look at the effect of unemployment on attitudes toward the economic system, with special attention to how the context of unemployment intervenes between joblessness and economic policy preferences. Finally, we consider briefly whether being out of work enhances political alienation.

Unemployment: Cause and Cure

If we are to comprehend the degree to which the unemployed politicize their problems, we must understand who is held responsible for unemployment—blamed for its origins and expected to counteract its effects. Clearly, in terms of the chain of hypothetical steps to political mobilization presented in Chapter 1, what is central is the perception that the government should help to alleviate the distress that accompanies unemployment. Regardless of where the blame for the causes of unemployment is assigned, only if the government is deemed responsible for solving the problem would we expect the problem to affect political attitudes and behavior. However, perception of where the problem comes from would certainly bear on the understanding of how it should be solved: those who see the problem as a function of system rather than personal failure would be more likely to look to the government for help.[1] Thus, in attempting to understand whether those who are out of work politicize their distress, we consider both whether the individual is seen as the source of his joblessness and whether he is expected to deal with its effects individually without public assistance.

The prevailing historical stereotype holds that during the depression of the 1930s the typical response to unemployment was individualistic. According to this stereotype, the jobless American worker—in contrast to his European counterpart—was likely to blame himself for his unemployed state and to expect no help from the government in coping with it.[2] Contemporary scholarship indicates that the reality was probably more complex even then: attitudes of self-blame and exoneration of

[1]Richard A. Brody and Paul M. Sniderman provide a useful distinction among the personal concerns that individuals face in their daily lives based on what they call "locus of concern." They show that whether a problem is "self-located" or "socially located" does have some impact on political behavior. They do not, however, discuss how a problem is perceived as self-located or socially located. See "From Life Space to Polling Place: The Relevance of Personal Concerns for Voting Behavior," *British Journal of Political Science*, 7 (July 1977), 337-360.

[2]E. Wight Bakke contrasts the responses of the unemployed in Britain, who blamed the system and sought political solutions to their problems, with the reactions of jobless Americans. See *The Unemployed Man* (London: Nisbet and Co., 1933), p. 9; and *The Unemployed Worker* (New Haven: Yale University Press, 1940), p. 25.

government seem not to have been universal.[3] Whatever the reality of the thirties, however, this stereotype gives us an important baseline from which to depart in examining these issues among the contemporary unemployed.

The format of our national telephone survey precluded the kind of in-depth discussion that would have allowed us to understand how the contemporary unemployed interpret their own joblessness and that of others. With reference to the issue of who is responsible for unemployment, we did include one item about whether most of the unemployed could find jobs if they wished to. We had expected working respondents to be considerably more likely than jobless ones to agree with this statement. In fact, although there is some difference between employed and jobless respondents, it is less than might have been expected: 46 percent of working respondents, as opposed to 36 percent of the unemployed, indicated that most of the unemployed could find work if they looked hard enough.

The open-ended follow-up interviews gave us an opportunity to probe this issue more fully. We self-consciously tried to pose questions that would help us understand both whether respondents saw their joblessness as the result of the operation of the system or as the result of their own actions, errors, and miscalculations and whether they expected others, especially the government, to rescue them. Although the pattern of responses to these questions was often amorphous, it sheds light on the intermingling of individualistic and collective themes in the interpretation of who is responsible for unemployment.

We have often cautioned that we cannot aggregate the responses to our follow-up interviews and generalize from them because of the small number of cases and the unsystematic nature of the sample. It is appropriate in this context to underline these caveats. Furthermore, the pat-

---

[3]Authors who have summarized the literature of the 1930s come to somewhat different conclusions about the degree to which American workers blamed themselves for their unemployment. John A. Garraty describes in some detail the sense of hopelessness, resignation, and lack of self-worth typical of the unemployed everywhere during the thirties—in Europe as well as the United States. In the words of a British worker, "Whenever I am out of work, I feel like a dog." While such feelings imply a clear sense of the assumption of personal responsibility by unemployed individuals, they do not necessarily imply a sense of mea culpa. See *Unemployment in History* (New York: Harper and Row, 1978), pp. 177-187.

The conclusion drawn by Bernard Sternsher in his review of the studies conducted during the thirties is somewhat more equivocal. From these analyses he extrapolates evidence both for self-blame and for system-blame. See "Victims of the Great Depression, Self-Blame/Non-Self-Blame, Radicalism, and Pre-1929 Experiences," *Social Science History*, 1 (Winter 1977), 137-177.

terns of response are richly varied and—at times—downright confusing. We cannot, therefore, present concise data summaries to support our interpretation of how the unemployed affix responsibility for their jobless predicament. Yet we believe that anyone who were to spend the requisite number of hours wallowing in the 1,700 or so pages of those interviews would read them in the same way that we do.

CAUSE: WHO IS TO BLAME?

Although the unemployed could politicize their difficulties—expect government aid to bail them out and perceive their problems as shared with others who are out of work—while blaming themselves for their joblessness, we can assume that demands for government assistance would be more likely when the unemployed do not see themselves as responsible for their jobless condition. We approached causes of unemployment both in personal and in more general terms. We asked people about their own experiences: what had happened at the time they left their last jobs; whether they would choose the same occupation again— or something with more security; whether they regretted the time and money spent on their education. We also asked for explanations of unemployment more generally: is it the result of business's desire for profits? union insensitivity to workers' needs? governmental neglect? the lack of skills of those seeking jobs? the aversion to hard work of the jobless?

Explaining One's Own Job Loss: There is little evidence that people blame themselves for their unemployed state. Their descriptions of the circumstances of job loss are quite matter-of-fact: the plant closed; business was slow; I didn't get along with my boss; I wanted to try something else; we lost a government contract. Sometimes the reports are tinged with bitterness, especially when there is some perception of unfairness in the choice of who lost the job, but the unemployed do not appear to hold themselves at fault. Yet these feelings frequently coexist with a diminished sense of self. As we saw in Chapter 3, the unemployed are more likely to feel unhappy with their accomplishments in life; to feel, as one respondent put it, like a "has-been." However, such feelings of personal insecurity do not necessarily imply a sense of personal responsibility for the fact that one is out of work. We probed this theme further by asking whether the respondent regretted past occupational or educational choices; in short, was the respondent's jobless predicament the result of a miscalculation about school or career? A number of our respondents did say that they might make other choices if they had it to do over again— more education, a different specialty, another career line. This theme recurred with special frequency among unemployed professionals, who

—because they perhaps have made such choices more self-consciously than those whose jobs require less formal training—often expressed real regret. But there is little evidence of actual self-blame. Frequently, the mistake is an erroneous guess about the direction of the economy; if there is blame to be assigned, it belongs to the economy for failing to act as predicted. What may be most significant is that the explanations of one's own loss of work tend to be narrow and contingent. Our respondents do not see themselves as victims of broad social forces or governmental ineptitude but of specific events connected with their particular employment circumstances.

Explaining Unemployment in General: When it comes to the factors perceived as causes of unemployment in general, answers refer to broader social circumstances. It is, however, difficult to discern an overall pattern to these responses. Some respondents blame a number of institutions; others say that no one is at fault; still others give mixed answers. Not only is the overall pattern of responses obscure, but many of the individual respondents seemed confused. This is hardly surprising; after all, the etiology of unemployment is a subject on which Nobel laureate economists joust with one another. What is important from our perspective is that relatively few of the respondents have the kind of coherent views that would imply a political program of demands to be made upon the government. Those few who have an ax to grind—who can identify the guilty and innocent, and who can specify appropriate accompanying policies—do hold views with seeming political potential. However, such respondents are rare. In this regard, we are not concerned with the internal coherence of views as evidence of the ability or the failure of ordinary citizens to conceptualize politics in logically consistent ways. Unemployment is a complicated problem: the simple and logically consistent explanation may not be the most intellectually compelling. What is important from our point of view is whether the explanations of the origins of unemployment lend themselves to political action.

Among our respondents some seem to be generalized blamers. The unemployed, the private sector, the government, all are at fault. One senses a good deal of anger in these people. Consider an unemployed young painter: the unemployed are themselves to blame because they will not accept available positions—"People won't settle for factory jobs." Business is at fault for being unconcerned about workers whom they consider "a dime a dozen." Unions don't care about protecting workers; their leaders are corrupt. And government is interested "in itself and not the people." A graphic designer took the same general view: business, unions, the government, all are out for their own benefit. The main theme in many of these interviews is that people and institutions are selfish.

Some of our respondents took the opposite tack; rather than blaming all, they exonerated all. A commercial artist said that there are jobs for many of the unemployed, but they could not be blamed for resisting work well below their skill level. Businesses and unions should not be held responsible because they are doing their best. Nor is the government at fault—"There isn't much the government directly can do to stop unemployment." Some of those who felt that no one was to blame for unemployment felt that the government could do more. But this does not reflect failure on the part of the government. As a machinist put it, unemployment is a "reflection of the general economy . . . There will always be a certain amount out of work, but the government could improve the situation."

Most of our respondents had more mixed views: business is to blame but not unions; unions but not business; the government but not the private sector; and so forth. The number of combinations is large. Some felt that unions were not doing enough for their members and that caused unemployment; others that they were making too great demands and that caused unemployment. Some felt that the government was spending too much, others that it was not spending enough; some that the government was interfering too much in the economy, some that it was not interfering enough. Many respondents supplemented views on the specific institutions about which we had asked with a pet theory—usually quite reasonable—on the source of unemployment: imports from Japan, returning veterans, the end of the war in Vietnam, automation, high taxes, and so on.

What is important about these various patterns—that some people blame everybody, others blame nobody, others are confused, and still others have individual theories—is not that they show that Americans conceptualize politics in ways that are muddled or inconsistent. It is not the intellectual rigor, or lack thereof, of their attitudes that command our attention. Rather, what is noteworthy from our perspective is how difficult it would be for such views to become the basis for political action. Taken collectively, so many themes are cited that there would seem to be no single anchor for joint political activity. Even taken singly, these attitudes do not seem to be readily politicized. If everyone is accused, or everyone absolved, then there are no villains at whom political action can be directed and no victims on whose behalf it can be taken.

The few respondents who expressed the kinds of attitudes that would seem to have political potential were ideologues of the left and right. In intellectual terms their views might be considered simplistic. In political terms, however, the coherence of their views lends them political potential: the guilty and innocent are specified, and a political program is posed. One respondent who had such a politically relevant set of views is a jobless construction worker. A college graduate, he is a union member and a supporter of the Socialist Labor Party. He places his understanding of unemployment in a radical ideological framework. He denies that the unemployed bear the responsibility for their plight. In contrast, all the institutions of the United States are at fault because of the nature of the system: "Businesses are in business to make profit. They have absolutely no concern for the welfare of the workers." Unions do not care either. He complains that his construction union staged a demonstration against a hiring program for minority workers, but they "don't stage a demonstration to put pressure for construction of schools, hospitals . . . etc. The unions are too closely tied to the Democratic Party." Nor is the government any better. He specifies a series of programs the government should pursue—public works, shortened workweek, day-care centers, and so forth—but he believes that the government will not do so. Government leaders are committed to "reduce inflation and increase unemployment . . . They put profit above human need." This interpretation of unemployment is not a sophisticated bit of economic analysis; but it is part of a more general and consistent view of the nature of American society.

At the opposite end of the political spectrum from our lone leftist radical are several ideologues of the right. According to one, an unemployed salesman who supported Ronald Reagan as well as the American Independent Party, the blame for unemployment belongs to the unemployed themselves: "those living on welfare, on the labor of other people. They definitely, I've found, don't want to work. That's why we have welfare. They keep voting for politicians with projects." However, the main problem lies elsewhere: "I think the government is the main cause of unemployment. They've got a welfare program, a food stamp program; they're in too many businesses that they have no business being in. I'm all for the free enterprise system." Unions, he argues, do not help either because of their "impossible demands." Business, on the other hand, is helpful; businesses worry about the welfare of their workers. Once again, the coherence of this explanation might render it intellectually less than compelling. However, its very simplicity lends it political drive.

The Contribution of the Unemployed to Joblessness: One theme of discussions of the sources of unemployment for at least a millenium is that the unemployed themselves are responsible for their idleness because they do not really wish to work. John A. Garraty reports the following incident, which illustrates the point dramatically:

An English doctor, writing in 1555 recalled that when he had offered "for Goddes sake" to cure beggars with the marks of certain horrible diseases they refused his help, saying that they preferred being sick and idle to being healthy and having "with great payne and labour" to earn a living.[4]

A more modern version of this theme is that, because government benefits reduce the opportunity cost of lost wages and because many of the available jobs are unattractive ones, a substantial portion of those who are out of work prefer joblessness to the rigors of jobholding.[5]

Many of our respondents articulate a variant of this theme. On the question of the availability of jobs for those seeking them and the fit between the skills possessed by the job seekers and the skills required for the jobs available, there was less disagreement among the respondents than might have been expected. Of course, some respondents replied that there were simply no jobs for those out of work. However, the majority indicated that most of the unemployed could find work if they would be willing to accept the work available. It is sometimes difficult to interpret what is implied by the comments surrounding such responses. However, it seems that the valuation placed on the refusal to accept what jobs are available varies widely. To a few—very few—such refusal is evidence of unambiguous laziness and dependence. To many more it is evidence of selectivity, an assertion that workers, especially highly skilled or trained ones, are simply unwilling to work for low pay in jobs that do not utilize their talents. When we asked whether unemployment is high because jobless workers do not have the skills and training for the available work, we had assumed that it was *lack* of skills that kept the unemployed from finding work. Interestingly, most respondents replied that yes, indeed, it was difficult for idled workers to find jobs that would *utilize* their skills and training. Contrary to what we expected, most of our follow-up interview respondents seemed to feel that the problem is that the unemployed are overqualified rather than underqualified.

For the most part respondents seem sympathetic to the refusal of a highly skilled worker who is jobless to accept menial work, somewhat less so to the refusal of low-paying work. To be able to do work that is the equal of one's skills seems to be accepted as a legitimate need. Many

---

[4]*Unemployment in History*, pp. 27-28.

[5]See Martin Feldstein, "The Economics of the New Unemployment," *The Public Interest* (Fall 1973), pp. 3-42; and his "Unemployment Compensation: Adverse Incentives and Distributional Anomalies," *National Tax Journal*, 27 (June 1974); and Stephen T. Marsten, "The Impact of Unemployment Insurance on Job Search," *Brookings Papers on Economic Activity*, 1 (1975), for estimates of the effect of unemployment compensation on the rate of unemployment.

of the unemployed make connections between these views and the conduct of their own job searches, understanding that if they are willing to give up the trade for which they were trained—whether engineering, teaching, carpentry, or plumbing—they are likely to find work. In addition, some—though relatively few, it seems—lend credence to the economists' argument referred to before, that unemployment compensation raises unemployment rates by reducing the need to find work quickly; these respondents admit that they could find work at three dollars an hour, but that such menial wages hardly justify the effort.

To summarize, most of the respondents with whom we spoke in our follow-up interviews see the unemployment problem as the result of a variety of factors, including both the actions of jobless individuals and the operations of a complex and baffling economic system. Many of our respondents acknowledge that their own actions—either choices made in school or career or selectivity in accepting work—caused or prolonged their unemployment. In this sense, there is an unmistakable fiber of individualism embedded in the systemic interpretation of the causes of unemployment. However, this individualism is quite different in tone from the individualism that is alleged to have characterized responses to unemployment during the depression. In considering how past decisions may have had a bearing upon present distress, there is sometimes resignation —who could have known better at the time?—and occasionally bitterness, especially among recent college graduates who feel that promises have not been delivered upon and that the sacrifices made in the name of these promises have therefore been in vain. Although, as we discussed in Chapter 3, the psychological pressures are often great and sometimes unbearable, the pressures are not borne with the self-accusation said to have been common during the thirties. However acute the strain on sense of self created by contemporary joblessness, there has been sufficient change in the general understanding of the workings of the world that the burden is not borne with the sense of shame and self-blame that it once may have been. In terms of the way the cause of unemployment is interpreted, the individualism intrinsic to American culture continues to have a substantial, if transformed, effect.

Cure: Who Should Do Something About It?

When we turn from the causes of unemployment to the crucial issue for politicization, the responsibility for containing its effects, the pattern of attitudes is no less complex. In our follow-up interviews we asked both personal and general questions about sources of aid in times of economic stress: where the respondents personally prefer to turn for help in times of need; whether they had indeed received help from the government or from family and friends; and who, in general, should bear the main responsibility for dealing with economic need.

What Should the Individual Do? What is noteworthy about the pattern of answers to these questions is the degree to which most respondents seem to have assumed responsibility for dealing with the problems of joblessness. As we have seen, the tendency was not to blame themselves for the fact of their unemployment. However, once out of work, they do seem to have accepted that it is their individual problem to solve —by cutting down on what they spend, taking odd jobs, and looking for work.

Although there seems to be a consensus that the primary responsibility for managing when out of work lies with the individual, there is less agreement about whether to turn to others for assistance in time of need and, if so, where to turn. Many respondents stressed the importance of self-reliance and autonomy and the potential loss of independence that comes from outside help. However, even those who seemed most reluctant to receive aid from others indicated that the government should step in when the need is so great that individual efforts are insufficient:

> There should be government programs for those who don't have the means to help themselves.
> At times when there's not heavy unemployment, I believe it is our own responsibility. But when many lose their jobs there is no way we can help ourselves . . . When your family and friends are unemployed there is no place to go.
> In extreme cases the government has to do something. We have to get our taxes back.
> The individual should have the main responsibility unless things get really bad. Then the government would have to step in.

For others, government aid is a matter of right to which those who pay taxes are entitled:

> I paid for it. I needed it [unemployment compensation] then so I went to get it. They're my rights.
> I took care of them. Let them take care of me.

Still others, less concerned about self-reliance, view the acceptance of government benefits in more routine terms, simply as a fact of life.

It is interesting that the rugged individualists, those hesitant to accept help regardless of the source, often indicated a preference for government aid over assistance from family or friends. Concerned about the compromise to personal autonomy that comes from dependence on others, they reasoned that aid from the government, being impersonal, has fewer strings attached to it than help from those to whom one is close. According to them, it is relying on the people one knows that presents the real threat to independence. Others, equally concerned to maintain personal autonomy, expressed the view we had expected to be typical of the rugged individualists: that reliance on government assistance is to be avoided unless absolutely necessary; only when personal resources and those available from family and friends had been exhausted, would this group turn to the government.

Most of what we have learned about who is perceived to be responsible for unemployment, in terms of both causes and consequences, leads to the conclusion that these are not opinions that would lead inevitably to political action. In personal terms there is, on the one hand, none of the sense of intense self-blame said to have been characteristic of the thirties and to have been responsible for the political quiescence of the unemployed of that era. On the other, many are quite aware that if they were willing to accept employment at reduced levels of skill or compensation they could find work. Thus, while eschewing blame for the fact of their joblessness, they often accept responsibility for its continuance. In all likelihood this would dampen the potential for political protest. When it comes to the issue of who should take responsibility for coping with the effects of unemployment, we find partial politicization. The prevailing theme is self-reliance. Most of our respondents do take for granted the accessibility of government assistance—as a matter of right, routine, or last resort. Very few, however, consider it as a means of avoiding their responsibility to take care of themselves. This, too, suggests that the political effects of the economic strain of joblessness would be contained.

Is the Government Doing Enough? We should perhaps push our analysis one step further. That our respondents are not so thoroughly individualistic that they would refuse available government aid is ambiguous evidence in terms of political mobilization. After all, this is not the thirties, and many forms of government assistance are available. An unemployed worker who is eligible need only swallow his individualistic scruples in order to take advantage of government policies designed to reduce joblessness or aid the unemployed. Since he can alleviate his distress by marching to the local unemployment office, there is little reason for him to march on the White House. Only if existing government actions are deemed insufficient would we expect joint political action. If, on the other hand, existing policies are considered adequate, there is no reason to make further demands.

We did ask whether respondents felt that the government was doing enough about unemployment and, by and large, they indicated that they felt that the government should be doing more. Of course, there were a few respondents who felt that the government could not or should not do more than it was. Some of these were cynics who considered the problem beyond the capabilities of the government to solve. Others were more ideological, arguing that the government was doing, in the words of one construction worker, "too damn much already"—whether because there is no real need for such activity, because the task of creating jobs is best left to the private sector, because government programs are too costly and inefficient, or because individuals should take care of employment problems on their own.

Those who felt the government was already doing too much were heavily outnumbered (by a margin of more than four to one) by those who took the opposite point of view. Most of the respondents in our follow-up interviews seemed to agree with the jobless machinist who said, "The government can do more. Whether it wants to spend the money or not I don't know. But it should." If there was consensus that the government should be doing more, there was less agreement on *what* precisely it should be doing. The only respondent who had anything like a program of recommended government actions was our sole ideologue of the left, the construction worker whom we quoted before: "They should have a massive public works program, a shorter workweek legislated nationally. Open day-care centers so women can afford to go to work; utilize teachers more; beef up educational programs. They can improve hospitals, bridges, housing, roads. And that's just a start." Such a laundry list of suggestions may not provide the foundation for rational, or affordable, policy. But it certainly does provide a potential basis for political action. In contrast, consider the response of a jobless telephone operator, an answer that is much more typical: "The government should do more. The government is not doing anything. They think things will take care of themselves. But I don't know what they could do."

In terms of what we have posited as an important link between economic distress and joint political action—the perception that the government should be doing more—the evidence is mixed. The pattern seems to be a generalized one of latent support for government activity but with little specific programmatic content.

Unemployment and Attitudes toward Economic Policy

We can use the data from our national telephone survey in order to probe more fully the issue of whether the unemployed support a program of government intervention in the economy. Figure 8-1 indicates the

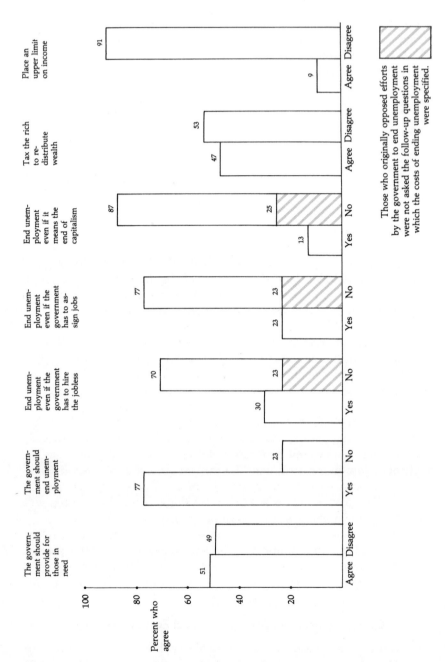

Figure 8-1 Proportion of respondents who share certain attitudes relative to economic policy.

answers to a series of items on economic policy alternatives. We asked a general question, used in many public opinion studies, about whether the government should take the responsibility for providing a decent standard of living for all Americans. As shown in Figure 8-1, members of the metropolitan work force divide evenly on the issue. On another question, whether the government should make a substantial effort to end unemployment, 77 percent—approximately the same majority as in the follow-up sample—favor such efforts. However, that majority evaporates when conditions are placed on the government's attempt to end unemployment. Only 30 percent would still favor ending unemployment if, in order to do so, the government had to hire all those without jobs. Only 23 percent would favor ending unemployment if the price were that the government would assign people to jobs; and only 13 percent would favor ending unemployment if it were necessary to end the capitalist system to do so. Thus, although most respondents support government efforts to end unemployment, few are prepared to pay the price of substantial change to realize the goal of full employment. The more radical the proposed change, the smaller the number who continue to advocate government policies to achieve full employment. We also asked two questions about governmental policy on redistribution of income. Slightly under half of the work force members polled support a government policy that would use the tax system to redistribute wealth. Since this is one of the stated goals of the progressive income tax, the lack of majority support for the proposition is further evidence of the weakness of the commitment of the American public to redistributive policies. When it comes to the more radical redistributive option of placing an upper limit on incomes, there is very little support for that proposition. Nine out of ten reject such a limit.

Figure 8-2 presents data more directly relevant to our concern with the impact of economic position on political attitudes. It shows the proportion who favor government intervention in each of these matters by occupational level and employment status. As usual, the slope of the various lines tells us how much differentiation there is in political attitudes on the basis of occupational level; and the distance between the solid line for the employed and the dotted line for the unemployed tells us how much the two categories differ within the various occupational levels. Several points emerge. For one thing, the relationship between occupational level and economic policy preferences is surprisingly weak. We might think that those in lower-status occupations would be more kindly disposed toward government intervention in the economy than those in higher occupational groups. In fact, however, this relationship obtains in only a limited number of instances; and even in those instances the associations

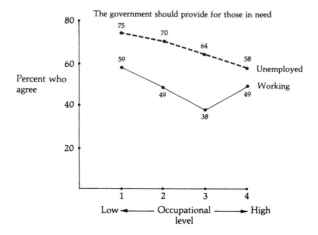

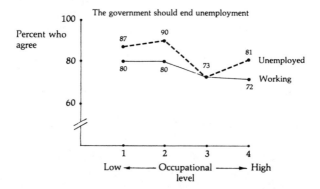

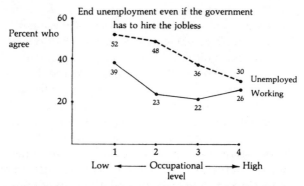

Figure 8-2 Attitudes on economic policy, by occupational level and employment status.

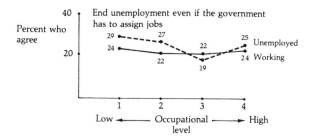

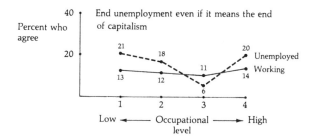

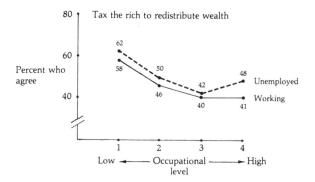

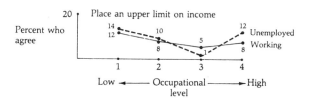

are hardly robust. With reference to government employment of those who are out of work or redistributive taxation of the rich, there is evidence of a relationship between occupational level and opinion, with those in lower occupational groups taking a more liberal position. This relationship holds for both working and jobless work force members. For the unemployed there is, in addition, an association between occupational level and belief that the government ought to provide a decent standard of living for all Americans. On the other hand, when it comes to government efforts to end unemployment or to more radical changes in the economic system, there is little differentiation in attitude across occupational levels.

What is more important from our point of view is the comparison between the employed and the unemployed. On the items in which no substantial economic change is advocated, the unemployed are more likely to espouse a liberal position. The difference between working and jobless respondents is particularly noteworthy on the questions of whether the government should act as the employer of last resort. Here the unemployed in each occupational group are more likely to favor government intervention than their working counterparts. In both cases, the difference between working and unemployed respondents is greatest at the lower end of the occupational scale. When it comes to an issue that would seem to have special relevance for those who are out of work, whether the government should make substantial efforts to end unemployment, the difference is somewhat smaller and less uniform across occupational groups. But given the high level of commitment to this proposition among the employed, a tremendous difference between the working and the unemployed would be impossible.

The pattern is different for the items suggesting more radical changes as the price of ending unemployment and for those advocating redistribution. With reference to these four items, the difference between working and jobless groups are much smaller and sometimes not consistent across occupational groups.

Thus, although unemployment seems to be related to views on economic policy, the relationship varies with the proximity of the issue in question to the specific needs and interests of the unemployed. On three items that have direct relevance to their jobless predicament, the unemployed have distinctive views. They are more likely than their working occupational counterparts to favor substantial efforts to end unemployment, to feel that the government should provide for those in need, and to accept a program of public employment for those out of work. When it comes to policies that are less immediately relevant to the special problems of the unemployed, such as redistribution of wealth by taxing the rich or limiting income, or to policies that advocate radical change as the price of reducing unemployment, ending capitalism or assigning jobs, the unemployed are less distinctive in their attitudes and the differences across occupational categories are considerably smaller.

The link between unemployment and preference for governmental policies directly related to the needs of the respondent is made even clearer by responses to a question we asked about whether the government does enough for "people like you." Figure 8-3 presents the proportion who said the government "does too little for people like me" by occupational level and employment status. It is quite clear that the unemployed are substantially more likely to feel neglected by the government than are the employed.

Table 8-1, in which we present the results of a multivariate analysis using log-linear models, permits us to consider the relation between unemployment and economic policy preferences more systematically. The analysis includes the following predictors of attitudes on economic policies: employment status, class (occupational level), and race. Since race is related to both employment status and political attitudes, its addition increases the precision of our estimate. The data in Table 8-1 confirm our previous discussion. Employment status has a statistically significant relationship to only four of the attitudes: belief that the government has responsibility to provide a decent standard of living, belief that the government should do more to end unemployment, belief that the government is obligated to hire the unemployed, and the respondent's belief that

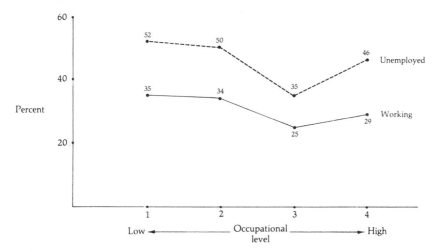

Figure 8-3 Proportion of respondents saying the government does not do enough for them.

Table 8-1 The effects of employment status, class, and race on political attitudes.

| | ATTITUDE | | | | | | | |
Variable	Provide decent living	Government end unem- ployment	Hire the unemployed	Assign jobs	End capitalism	Tax rich to redistribute wealth	Limit income	Government does not do enough for me
Effect of—								
Class (occupa- tional level)	10.9*	11.7**	8.8*	0.5	2.7	16.6**	9.0*	5.1
Race	38.1**	7.1*	61.7*	10.0**	27.5**	20.5**	14.0**	33.1**
Employment status	20.2**	3.8*	9.2**	0.2	0.0	0.1	0.0	16.2**
Class and employment status	3.0	2.3	4.5	0.9	2.8	0.7	2.2	1.1
Overall effect	116.0**	41.6**	128.3**	16.1	46.2**	56.7**	41.5**	91.3**

*Significant at the .01 level.
**Significant at the .001 level.

the government does not do enough for him. (The association of employment status with the "government end unemployment" measure is weaker than the other three for reasons noted above.) With reference to redistribution of wealth and radical changes in the economy, employment status makes no difference. The data also confirm a commonly observed pattern: race is a powerful predictor of political attitudes—more powerful, generally, than class.

These findings are quite consistent with what we learned earlier from the follow-up interviews. When asked, the unemployed do indicate support for government measures designed to curb the effects of unemployment. In several senses, however, this support is shallow. First, the unemployed respond positively when the alternatives are specified for them but cannot themselves supply the alternatives spontaneously. This would imply that there is latent support for government action among the unemployed that could be activated by a political leader who would frame the issue, but that that support is quite amorphous. Furthermore, support for government programs is confined to objects proximate to the problem of joblessness, not generalized into support for a more comprehensive program of economic change. Finally, the unemployed are not willing to countenance substantial change if that were the price of ending joblessness.

Economic Insecurity and Attitudes toward Economic Policy: A Further Probe

It is clear that the impact on beliefs of the experience of being out of work is quite contained. Still, we have been too simplistic; there may be relationships of a more complex sort that we have been missing. A variety of circumstances might enhance the impact of joblessness on attitudes or predispose those with jobs to advocate policies of economic change. Along these lines the following hypotheses seem reasonable: that those who have been out of work for long periods of time would be more likely to favor interventionist policies than those who are recently unemployed; that jobless workers who are pessimistic about the chances of finding work would be more likely to favor such policies; that employed workers who suffer from job insecurity would be distinctive in their attitudes; and that those who live in economically depressed areas would be more likely to favor policies of government intervention.

LENGTH OF UNEMPLOYMENT

It seems quite logical to expect that if joblessness has an effect on attitudes that effect would not be felt right away. Only as the siege of unemployment stretches from days to weeks and months would its impact on political ideology be felt. Table 8-2, which gives data on the relationship between attitudes and length of joblessness, discredits this hypothesis. All the relationships are negligible. The long-term unemployed are not more likely than those who have been out of work for only a short period to favor activist economic policies. Thus, the weakness of the original relationship does not mask a more complicated one in which the impact of unemployment is felt only after some time.

PROSPECTS FOR THE FUTURE

An analogous supposition is that unemployed who are pessimistic about their chances of finding jobs in the near future would be more likely to espouse proposals for economic change. As shown in Table 8-3, the data once again confound our expectation. There is no consistent association whatever between attitudes toward economic policies and the jobless worker's appraisal of his chances of finding work.

JOB INSECURITY AMONG THE WORKING

We have mentioned many times that it is not only those who are out of work at a particular time who are touched by job insecurity. Many employed workers experience job insecurity: for example, because they have been out of work in the past or because they are fearful of losing their jobs. For this reason we were led to query whether the attitudes of those with jobs are differentiated according to job security.

Using our composite measure of employment security, we distinguish in Table 8-4 among working respondents in terms of attitudes. We designate as high in employment security those who have been in their present jobs for an extended period of time, have no history of joblessness, and have no apprehensions about losing their jobs in the near future.[6] As shown in Table 8-4, working people with a low level of job security are somewhat more likely than those with high security to believe that the government should provide for those in need and should act as the employer of last resort in order to end unemployment. With reference to the issues of government assignment of jobs or the end of capitalism, the differences between secure and insecure job holders are even smaller. Attitudes toward taxing the rich and setting a limit on incomes vary somewhat with level of job security. In general, then, job insecurity among the employed is related to political attitudes in a manner not dissimilar from unemployment. We found systematic differences between respondents at various levels of job insecurity, just as we found differences between the working and unemployed. However, these differences are quite small.[7]

[6]Chapter 3, note 30 describes this measure more precisely.

[7]We attempted to test for an association between attitudes and assessments of

Table 8-2 Percent of jobless who hold specific attitudes toward economic policies, by length of unemployment.

| | LENGTH OF UNEMPLOYMENT | | | | |
Policy	1 month or less	2-6 months	7-11 months	1 year or more	Gamma
Government should provide for those in need	72	74	70	67	− .07
Government should end unemployment	84	82	84	86	.06
End unemployment even if government has to hire jobless	35	46	54	48	.10
End unemployment even if government has to assign jobs	27	26	31	27	.02
End unemployment even if it means the end of capitalism	12	17	23	20	.08
Tax rich to redistribute wealth	48	54	58	54	.07
Limit income	7	13	16	10	.09
	(112)	(235)	(73)	(125)	

future economic prospects in still another way. We considered whether respondents thought that their personal financial situation would improve, stay the same, or get worse in the near future. Because of the relationship between optimism and occupational level we introduced this factor as an additional control. However, so few of the unemployed think that things will get worse—an important fact in itself—that it is impossible to draw conclusions. As for the employed, there is some evidence that those who are pessimistic are somewhat more likely to favor government intervention in the economy, but the relationships are not consistent across occupational groups.

Table 8-3 Percent of jobless who hold specific attitudes toward economic policies, by their evaluation of their chances of finding a job in the near future.

| | CHANCE OF FINDING A JOB | | | |
Policy	Good	Some	Very little	Gamma
Government should provide for those in need	70	73	69	−.03
Government should end unemployment	83	81	88	.13
End unemployment even if government has to hire jobless	38	41	53	.17
End unemployment even if government has to assign jobs	26	26	29	.07
End unemployment even if it means the end of capitalism	19	15	17	−.03
Tax rich to redistribute wealth	52	53	54	.02
Limit income	10	10	10	−.01

EXPOSURE TO UNEMPLOYMENT IN THE COMMUNITY

Another possibility, which seemed worthy of consideration, is that these attitudes may be mediated by conditions in the surrounding economy. Unemployment may be interpreted differently depending upon whether it occurs in a context of prosperity or depression. The relevant context in fact might be national: presumably unemployment was understood one way during the prosperous sixties, another way during the constricted seventies.[8] It is also possible that the understanding of joblessness varies systematically with local conditions: that it is perceived as one thing in booming Sun Belt communities, as quite another in depressed New England mill towns or Appalachia.[9] Furthermore, the eco-

[8]Douglas A. Hibbs presents data which show that attitudes toward economic matters change in response to fluctuations in the national rate of unemployment. See "The Mass Public and Macroeconomic Policy: The Dynamics of Public Opinion towards Unemployment and Inflation," unpublished manuscript, March 1978, pp. 34-35.

[9]Using data from the late 1940s, Campbell and others found that with the exception of professionals and managers those living in areas of high unemployment are

Table 8-4 Percent who hold specific attitudes toward economic policies, by degree of job security (working respondents).

| Policy | JOB SECURITY | | | |
	Low	Medium	High	Gamma
Government should provide for those in need	62	51	43	.24
Government should end unemployment	79	80	74	.14
End unemployment even if government has to hire jobless	35	28	24	.14
End unemployment even if government has to assign jobs	26	25	22	.10
End unemployment even if it means the end of capitalism	16	13	11	.11
Tax rich to redistribute wealth	52	53	41	.20
Limit income	12	7	6	.22

nomic environment might influence the attitudes of working and jobless alike. Those living in depressed areas, where the unemployment rate is chronically high and bouts of joblessness are frequent, might reasonably favor more activist governmental policies whether or not they were themselves out of work. However, we might expect the attitudes of the unemployed to be especially responsive to surrounding conditions. Those out of work in a context of prosperity presumably would be more likely to consider the problem individual and therefore would not expect or desire the government to do much about it, while those unemployed in a context of slowdown would relate their personal circumstances to systemic conditions and be especially likely to prefer government intervention to reduce unemployment or assist the unemployed.

---

quite a bit more likely to favor government guarantees of full employment. The relationship they found between attitudes and unemployment rate in the country is substantially stronger than what we report. See Angus Campbell, Philip E. Converse, Warren E. Miller, and Donald E. Stokes, *The American Voter* (New York: John Wiley and Sons, 1960), pp. 383-384.

Table 8-5   Percent who hold specific attitudes toward economic policies, by employment status and community unemployment rate.

| | Community rate of unemployment, spring 1976 | | | | |
Policy	Under 7%	7-7.9%	8-9.9%	10% and over	Gamma
Government should pro- vide for those in need					
Working	40	48	47	58	.16
Unemployed	79	76	65	71	−.11
Government should end unemployment					
Working	76	74	75	79	.05
Unemployed	83	83	84	84	.02
End unemployment even if government has to hire jobless					
Working	26	29	22	32	.03
Unemployed	45	56	44	40	−.08
End unemployment even if government has to assign jobs					
Working	20	21	25	25	.06
Unemployed	28	27	23	31	.03
End unemployment even if it means the end of capitalism					
Working	13	14	10	14	.02
Unemployed	23	24	9	20	−.02
Tax rich to redistribute wealth					
Working	41	40	44	58	.18
Unemployed	61	54	49	52	−.08

(continued)

Table 8-5 (continued)

| Policy | COMMUNITY RATE OF UNEMPLOYMENT, SPRING 1976 | | | | |
	Under 7%	7-7.9%	8-9.9%	10% and over	Gamma
Limit income					
Working	4	8	8	12	.21
Unemployed	17	12	9	10	−.16

Number of cases:

| | UNEMPLOYMENT RATE | | | |
	Under 7%	7-7.9%	8-8.9%	10% and over
Working	(163)	(205)	(240)	(180)
Unemployed	(90)	(118)	(186)	(159)

These kinds of hypotheses are very difficult to test. Ideally what are needed are, if not panel data, at least longitudinal data. But there are none in a form that permits comparisons between working and jobless.[10] The best we can do is to distinguish our respondents in terms of the communities from which they come—for the urban areas sampled in our metropolitan work force survey differ rather substantially in terms of economic conditions.[11]

In Table 8-5 we examine the relationship between attitudes and employment status, controlling for community economic performance (using as our measure the local unemployment rate at the time of the survey). It is clear that there is little regular relationship between the amount of unemployment in the community and attitudes toward government

[10]There are studies of the relationship between the unemployment rate and voting as well as between the unemployment rate and presidential popularity. These analyses will be discussed in Chapter 10; however, they do not compare working and unemployed citizens.

[11]There is, furthermore, a problem of which specific measure of unemployment to use in assessing local conditions: absolute level of unemployment or change in the level of unemployment, contemporary unemployment data, figures for a somewhat earlier period, or averages across an extended period.

Previous studies offer no clear answer to whether it is the level of economic performance or change in that level that makes a difference, or the appropriate time lag. Hibbs finds that the impact of economic conditions on attitudes toward inflation and unemployment occurs with little time lag: he estimates that 45 percent of the total impact of economic conditions occurs contemporaneously and that 93 percent of the impact is felt after two years ("The Mass Public and Macroeconomic Policy," pp. 34-

policy on economic matters. One of our hypotheses had been that the unemployed would be particularly sensitive to the rate of unemployment within their communities, that those out of work in a context of high unemployment would be especially likely to seek government intervention. If anything, the data show just the opposite. Although the relationships are very weak, it seems that it is for the working, rather than the unemployed, that living in a high unemployment area seems to be associated with preference for interventionist policies. We are not sure why, but our original hypotheses do not seem to be borne out by the data.[12]

A Note on Unemployment and Political Alienation

It may be that in searching for politicization of the problem of unemployment and for support for general programs of governmental intervention in the economy, we have been barking up the wrong tree. While unemployment has significant effects upon attitudes toward the political world, perhaps those effects are to increase alienation rather than to foster commitment to policies of economic change. It is commonly observed that one of the most significant trends in American politics in the early 1970s was the increasing alienation of American citizens. Whatever its source—popular disillusionment at the failure of American policies to solve domestic problems, the Vietnam quagmire, Watergate—study after study has documented the erosion of trust and confidence in political leaders and institutions. It seems quite plausible that the experience of joblessness might predispose the unemployed to be especially alienated.

Figure 8-4 presents data on two measures of political alienation: whether respondents feel that the government is run by a few big interests or for the benefit of all the people and how frequently government leaders can be believed. In both cases, unemployed respondents are somewhat more alienated.[13] However, the association between jobless-

---

35). We experimented with a variety of measures of the unemployment rate: the actual rate at the time of our survey and for each of the preceding several years; the average rate over the previous three and the previous five years; the rate of change in the preceding several years; and the deviation at the time of the survey from the average for the area over several preceding years. Each time the result was the same—no relationship. For simplicity we have selected the most straightforward data to present, but the message would be the same if we had chosen one of our more complicated measures.

[12]We should reiterate that our findings about the differential effects of local economic conditions upon the attitudes of working and jobless respondents do not necessarily imply anything about the responses of the employment status groups to the national economic picture: either to the rate of unemployment or to changes in the level of joblessness.

[13]A log-linear analysis confirms the relationship between employment status and

ness and alienation is not so powerful that we can conclude that our focus on political attitudes rather than political alienation has been misguided. Once again we find unemployment associated with a relatively limited difference in attitudes.

Social Class and Political Attitudes:
What Happened to the Relationship?

In this chapter we have detected very little variation across social classes on attitudes one might expect to find differentiated by class. The absence of such a relationship, however, is consistent with a general tendency in American politics—a tendency (noted by us and by others) toward a diminution in the class basis of attitudes.[14]

Our data confirm a tendency noted by others—that political positions once characteristic of lower socioeconomic groups are frequently espoused by upper-status individuals, especially by the young. Figure 8-5 shows the relationship of attitudes on two representative economic issues —the belief that the government ought to provide a decent standard of living and the belief that the government ought to tax the rich in order to redistribute wealth—to age and education. Although the data cannot be used to demonstrate a change over time, it is clear that there is a differ-

---

belief that the government is run for the big interests, but shows that joblessness has no correlation with the view that government leaders can be believed:

Variables	Belief that government is run for the big interests	Leaders cannot be believed
Effects of —		
Class (occupational level)	25.7**	14.4**
Race	7.5*	7.8*
Employment status	15.5**	1.0
Class and employment status	0.3	0.6
Overall effect	70.9**	36.5**

*Significant at the .01 level.
**Significant at the .001 level.

[14]See, for example, Norman H. Nie, Sidney Verba, and John R. Petrocik, *The Changing American Voter* (Cambridge, Mass.: Harvard University Press, 1976), chap. 14; Everett Carll Ladd, Jr., with Charles D. Hadley, *Transformations of the American Party System*, 2nd ed. (New York: W. W. Norton, 1978), chap. 5.

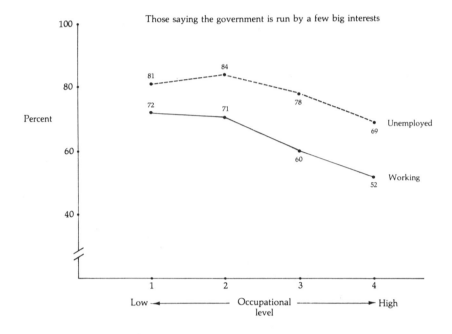

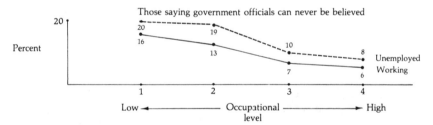

Figure 8-4   Feelings of alienation, by occupational level and employment status.

ence between the generations: among older respondents we find the expected relationship between conservatism on economic matters and high levels of education; in the younger group we find no such relationship.

We can probe this question further by comparing our data with the data from the 1939 Roper survey to which we have referred earlier. As before, we transform our 1976 data into the somewhat crude categories that correspond to those of the 1939 study and consider whites only. Figure 8-6 contains information on five political propositions posed in the late depression years and our parallel proposals in 1976: action by the government to end unemployment; taxing the rich to help the poor;

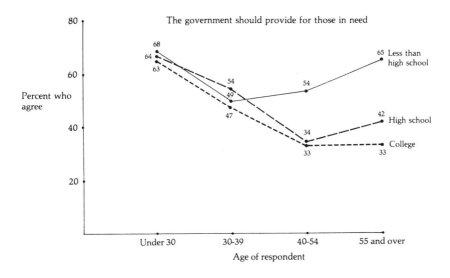

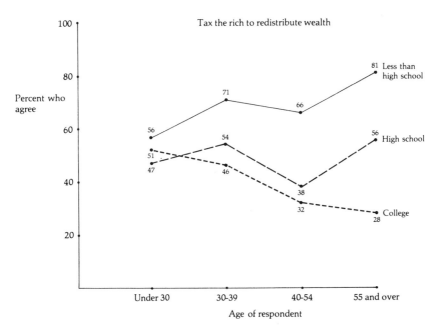

Figure 8-5 Attitudes toward economic change, by age and education.

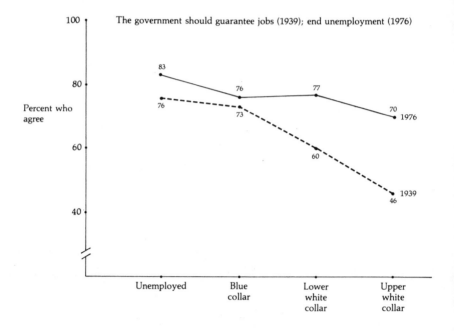

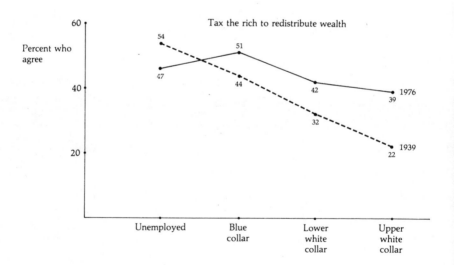

Figure 8-6 Economic attitudes by class, 1939 and 1976.

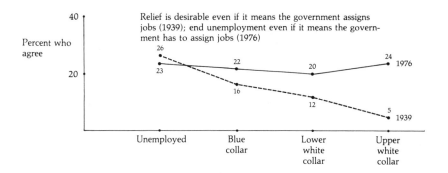

Relief is desirable even if it means the government assigns jobs (1939); end unemployment even if it means the government has to assign jobs (1976)

Percent who agree

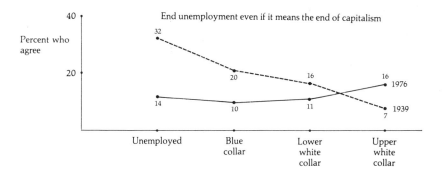

End unemployment even if it means the end of capitalism

Percent who agree

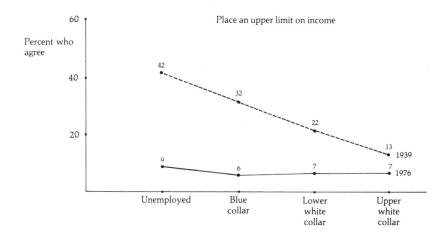

Place an upper limit on income

Percent who agree

ending unemployment even if it means that the government will assign jobs; ending unemployment even if it means the end of the capitalist system; and a government program to limit income.

The most striking aspect of Figure 8-6 is the strength of the association between occupational level and economic attitudes in 1939 as compared with 1976. There has been a marked change in the extent to which attitudes in favor of governmental commitment to economic reform are structured by class. In the late 1930s the beliefs of those who were at the top of the occupational category—the upper white-collar workers—were quite different from those of the blue-collar workers or the unemployed. This relationship holds for each of the five measures. In 1976 there is little class differentiation.

If we consider the absolute level of commitment to these various political positions, we find an interesting change since the 1930s. When it comes to the two widely accepted goals of government policy—commitment by the government to end unemployment and the use of the tax system for redistribution—we find greater average agreement in 1976 than in 1939, agreement that varies little across social groups. Americans at all social levels agree with these policies to a degree found only among the lowest occupational groups in 1939—the blue-collar workers and the unemployed. It is as if the entire nation has adopted the more liberal position held in the 1930s by the more disadvantaged groups in American society.

The pattern in relation to the two more drastic changes in the economic system—the limitation on income and the end of the capitalist system—is quite different. There was, on average, more receptivity to these radical changes in 1939 than today. In relation to the economic reform measures, the views of the upper-status groups in 1976 have come to resemble the more liberal views that were held by the lower-status groups in 1939. In relation to the more radical changes, the views of the lower-status groups in 1976 have come to resemble the more conservative positions of the upper white-collar workers in 1939.[15]

[15]For reasons we do not understand, the pattern for the question about ending unemployment even if it means government assignment of jobs resembles that for the more moderate policies; that is, the position taken by all social class groupings in 1976 is roughly that of the disadvantaged groups in 1939. Government assignment of jobs would seem a fairly radical change. In 1939, members of each of the economic groups were more likely to countenance the end of capitalism than the government assignment of jobs. In 1976, the pattern was exactly reversed: for each group the end of capitalism was the least preferred policy. These patterns perhaps reflect the increasing institutionalization and bureaucratization of American life since 1939. In an era when very few work for themselves, and most work for large organizations, the notion of government assignment of jobs may have become relatively less threatening.

These data recall an earlier finding about the declining salience of class. As we saw in Chapter 5, not only do fewer and fewer Americans identify themselves as working class, but the association between that subjective identification and actual position in the occupational structure has diminished. Thus, in two ways the significance of class has shrunk: individuals think less in explicit class terms, and class is a less adequate predictor of political attitudes. At the same time, there has been a tendency across classes toward the acceptance of moderate social programs once rejected by upper-status groups. Consider Figure 8-7, which compares data just presented on the changing nature of the class relationship to attitudes on ending unemployment with similar data on the changing nature of the relationship of class to subjective class identification. At the top of the figure we see the pattern whereby the more conservative attitude position of the upper-status group in 1939 swings up by 1976 to the more liberal position held by lower-status citizens in both years. Consensus across classes is reached at a more liberal level. At the bottom of the graph we see the opposite pattern in relation to subjective identifica-

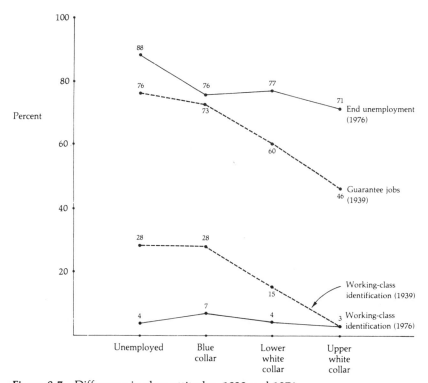

Figure 8-7   Difference in class attitudes, 1939 and 1976.

tion with the working class. In 1939, there was a clear relationship between occupational level and working-class identification: blue-collar
workers and the unemployed were substantially more likely to have a
working-class identification than were white-collar workers. In 1976,
there is an across-the-board low level of such identification. The lower-
status groups—blue-collar workers and the unemployed—swing down to
match the position held by the upper-status groups in 1939 and in 1976.
Just as the nation is becoming more homogeneous in subjective class
terms, with the lower-status groups coming to resemble the upper-status
groups in their rejection of working-class identification, the nation is becoming more homogeneously liberal in relation to moderate government
economic policy with the upper-status groups coming to adopt the more
liberal position long held by those less well off in the American economy.

Economic Position, Class Consciousness, and Political Attitudes

When we discussed political mobilization in Chapter 1 we posited that
beliefs, both general understandings of the operation of the social world
and specific policy preferences, were a critical intervening link between
objective strain and political response. We outlined a series of steps
whereby those experiencing strain would develop some kind of common
awareness of their position, which would be accompanied by a common
set of preferences for relevant government policies. Thus mobilized by
group consciousness and armed with a set of policy preferences, the disadvantaged group could become an active political force.

So far, this proposed series of steps does not seem to hold for the economically disadvantaged in America—regardless of whether the measure
of disadvantage is joblessness or lower occupational status. Neither joblessness nor social class is related to a sense of class consciousness. Neither has a strong relation to policy preferences. The objective situation of
the disadvantaged apparently is not matched by jointly held views.

We can carry our inquiry one step further by investigating the links
between class consciousness, where it does exist, and policy preferences.
Class consciousness has often been found to be associated with distinctive political attitudes and behaviors.[16] Even if neither class consciousness nor attitudes are linked directly to objective economic circumstances, among the disadvantaged there may be a relationship between
class consciousness and preference for economic change—albeit there are
very few who are class conscious.

[16]Some of the works that have related class consciousness to political attitudes and
behavior in the American context include: Richard Centers, *The Psychology of Social
Class* (Princeton, N.J.: Princeton University Press, 1949); Oscar Glantz, "Class Consciousness and Political Solidarity," *American Sociological Review*, 33 (August

In Tables 8-6 and 8-7 we use the log-linear technique we have applied to previous analyses in an attempt to separate the impact on political attitudes of class consciousness from the impact of objective economic strain, as measured by employment status, and to test for interactions between objective strain and class consciousness. We use two measures of class consciousness: belief in class solidarity and sense of class conflict.[17]

In Table 8-6 we show effects of employment status, class-consciousness measures, and the interactions among them on attitudes toward moderate economic policies specifically aimed at easing the condition of those who feel an economic pinch—government responsibility to provide a decent standard of living for citizens, government efforts to end unemployment, government programs to hire the unemployed if necessary. The results indicate that—as we already knew—the objective strain of joblessness plays a role. More importantly, the class solidarity measure is significantly related to preference for governmental policies that would directly ease the situation of those economically disadvantaged by unemployment. Seeing conflict between the classes has less effect on these attitudes and in fact is significant only on the issue of the government doing more to end unemployment, where its effect is much smaller than that of class solidarity.

Table 8-7 contains parallel data on the effects of employment status

---

1958), 375-385; Philip Converse, "The Shifting Role of Class in Political Attitudes and Behavior," in Eleanor E. Maccoby, Theodore M. Newcomb, and Eugene L. Harlet, eds., *Readings in Social Psychology* (New York: Holt, Rinehart and Winston, 1958), pp. 388-399; Angus Campbell, Philip E. Converse, Warren E. Miller, and Donald E. Stokes, *The American Voter* (New York: John Wiley and Sons, 1960), chap. 13; Avery M. Guest, "Class Consciousness and American Political Attitudes," *Social Forces*, 54 (June 1974), 496-510; Sidney Verba and Kay Lehman Schlozman, "Unemployment, Class Consciousness and Radical Politics," *Journal of Politics*, 39 (May 1977), 291-323.

[17]Unfortunately, we were forced to omit a measure of class self-identification. Because of the skewed marginals on that question and the large number of other variables in this analysis, the inclusion of the class self-identification measure created too many empty cells to allow reliable estimates. This is a regrettable omission, especially in view of the contention of Arthur H. Miller, Patricia Gurin, and Gerald Gurin that it is the interaction of group identification and evaluation of the place of the group in the world that has political potency. See their "Electoral Implications of Group Identification and Consciousness," paper delivered at the Annual Meeting of the American Political Science Association, New York, September 1978. We shall return to this theme in Chapter 10.

As usual when dealing with consciousness measures, we include blue-collar respondents only; we would not know what interpretation to put on working-class consciousness on the part of white-collar workers.

Table 8-6   Effects of employment status and class consciousness on attitudes toward policies designed to relieve economic strain (blue-collar workers only).

| | BELIEF THAT GOVERNMENT SHOULD — | | |
Variables	Provide decent living	End unemployment	Hire the unemployed
Bivariate effects of:			
Employment status	11.7**	6.8*	18.0**
Class solidarity	15.8**	26.4**	16.8**
Class conflict	0.6	7.4*	0.9
Interactive effects of:			
Employment status and class solidarity	0.6	0.7	1.6
Employment status and class conflict	0.5	0.4	3.5
Overall effect	30.1**	48.1**	43.2**

*Significant at the .01 level.
**Significant at the .001 level.

and class consciousness on two attitudes involving fundamental changes in the nature of the economic system—favoring government assignment of jobs, and favoring the end of capitalism if it were necessary to end unemployment—and two attitudes involving redistribution of wealth—favoring redistributive taxation of the rich, and favoring an upper limit on incomes. The data in Table 8-7 are easy to summarize: neither employment status nor the class consciousness measures have an effect on these political attitudes.[18]

Thus, class consciousness—at least as measured by commitment to class solidarity or perception of conflict between the classes—seems to have a rather limited association with economic policy preferences. Believing that workers should stick together is significantly related to preferences for moderate policies designed to alleviate economic strain. Otherwise, class consciousness seems to have no significant effect.[19]

[18]The two significant effects are those of employment status on a desire to end capitalism if needed to end unemployment, and of class solidarity on taxing the rich, but the effect in each case is weak and barely significant statistically.

[19]It is interesting to compare this pattern of relationships with the pattern that emerges from the following table, where we consider the effect of unemployment sta-

Table 8-7   Effects of employment status and class consciousness on attitudes toward economic policies (blue-collar workers only).

	BELIEF THAT GOVERNMENT SHOULD—			
Variables	Assign jobs	End capitalism	Tax rich to redistribute wealth	Limit income
Bivariate effects of:				
Employment status	2.6	4.1*	1.5	2.8
Class solidarity	0.2	0.5	4.9*	1.9
Class conflict	0.0	0.0	0.0	0.4
Interactive effects of:				
Employment status and class solidarity	1.7	1.2	1.1	3.1
Employment status and class conflict	3.1	1.3	0.4	2.7
Overall effect	7.5	7.8	9.7	12.7

*Significant at the .01 level.
**Significant at the .001 level.

tus and class-consciousness measures on political alienation of blue-collar workers: whether they feel the government is run for big interests and whether or not political leaders can be believed.   (note continued on page 228)

Variables	Belief that government is run for big interests	Leaders cannot be believed
Bivariate effects of —		
Employment status	1.7	5.9
Class solidarity	0.9	0.9
Class conflict	8.8**	13.0**
Interactive effects of —		
Employment status and class solidarity	4.0*	0.2
Employment status and class conflict	0.4	0.0
Overall effect	22.7*	21.5

*Significant at the .01 level.
**Significant at the .001 level.

At several points in our analysis we have noted that links which we expected to find for the 1970s, but did not, did indeed hold in the 1930s. In view of this, it seems reasonable to investigate the triangular relationship among objective position, class consciousness, and policies for that earlier period. In Table 8-8 we report the results of a log-linear analysis of the relationship among employment status, class consciousness, and policy positions in 1939 and 1976.[20] The four issues are belief that the government ought to provide relief for those in need, that the government should assign jobs if needed to end unemployment, that it should end unemployment even if it means the end of the capitalist system, and that it should put a limit on income. The first issue represents a moderate reform; the others refer to more drastic changes in the political system.

There is a distinct contrast between the data of the two periods. In 1939, both class consciousness variables have a statistically significant relationship to the three measures involving more radical change in the economic system. In 1976, as we have seen, the class consciousness variables are unrelated to these more profound changes. Belief in worker solidarity does have a significant relation to government provision of welfare; strangely, in 1939, the class consciousness measures are unrelated to this item.

Of particular interest is the difference in the role played in 1939 and 1976 by the perception of class conflict. In 1976, it is related neither to social class nor to political attitudes. In 1939, however, perception of class conflict is related both to objective social class and to preferences for radical change in the American economic system.[21] Class, class consciousness, and political positions appear to have been more closely knit in 1939 than in the America of 1976.

In contrast to what we saw before, belief in class conflict does seem to have an effect on measures of political alienation: it has a statistically significant bivariate effect on belief that the government is run for a few vested interests and on the view that government leaders cannot be believed. Thus, seeing conflict between the classes seems to be an expression of alienation related to other measures of alienation but not to other positions.

[20]Unfortunately, our measures of class consciousness for the two years are not completely comparable. For 1939 we use class self-identification and belief in the existence of conflict between management and workers, the only two measures on that survey. As mentioned earlier, we are forced to omit a measure of class self-identification for 1976 because of the skewed nature of the marginals. Thus for 1976 we use the measure of class conflict as well as belief in class solidarity.

[21]As we noted before, perceiving class conflict is related to political alienation in our 1976 study. Since there are no measures of political alienation in the 1939 survey, we cannot replicate this analysis for the earlier period.

Table 8-8 Effects of employment status and class consciousness on political attitudes (blue-collar workers only), 1939 and 1976.

| Variables | 1939: BELIEF THAT GOVERNMENT SHOULD— | | | |
	Provide decent living	Assign jobs	End capitalism	Limit income
Bivariate effects of:				
Employment status	8.7*	14.6**	8.6*	12.3**
Class self-identification	2.9	17.0**	7.1*	7.8*
Class conflict	0.4	11.3**	6.9*	10.1**
Interactive effects of:				
Employment status and class self-identification	0.2	1.5	0.0	0.9
Employment status and class conflict	0.2	0.1	4.2	0.7
Overall effect	17.5*	57.9**	34.3**	41.1**

| Variables | 1976: BELIEF THAT GOVERNMENT SHOULD— | | | |
	Provide decent living	Assign jobs	End capitalism	Limit income
Bivariate effects of:				
Employment status	11.7**	2.6	4.1*	2.8
Class solidarity	15.8**	0.2	0.5	1.9
Class conflict	0.6	0.0	0.0	0.4
Interactive effects of:				
Employment status and class solidarity	0.6	1.7	1.2	3.1
Employment status and class conflict	0.5	3.1	1.3	2.7
Overall effect	30.1**	7.5	7.8	12.7

*Significant at the .01 level.
**Significant at the .001 level.

The change is, we believe, a major one in the nature of American politics. Compared with the situation in the 1930s, political conflict in 1976 appears to be less clearly structured by a division between opposing economic groups, each with a distinctive objective economic position, a differing sense of class consciousness, and different policy preferences. We do not wish to overstate the case and argue that America was totally polarized along these lines and only these lines in the thirties. Class and class consciousness probably played a weaker role than in Europe even then. But compared with the situation today, class and the attendant sense of class consciousness were more potent political forces a generation ago.

We do not mean to imply by the foregoing that the economic matters that have traditionally divided class groups are no longer central to American politics. On the contrary, controversies about the division of economic benefits continue to be crucial. However, what we have found about the weakening of the links among class, class consciousness, and political attitudes implies that such controversies rarely take the form of conflict along a clearly defined class cleavage.

This leads us to consider again a tendency upon which we have already remarked at several junctures and to note that our findings about the decline in the relationships between class, class consciousness, and attitudes complement those of others who have been concerned about the changing behavior of citizens in American democracy. Political beliefs seem to have been uprooted from their previous grounding in objective social circumstances and appear to be autonomous from the traditional demographic bases that structured them in the past. It is not that beliefs have become irrelevant for politics. On the contrary, in recent years, citizens' political attitudes have assumed greater internal coherence and have become more closely linked to political behavior.[22] Furthermore, Ronald Ingelhardt discusses what he calls the "class inversion" in political views found among younger age cohorts in the United States and in other industrial democracies. It is often the college-educated, higher-occupation members of the younger age cohorts who hold the most liberal or radical political views, while those with more limited education who are in blue-

[22]These issues have been discussed by a variety of authors. See, for example, the analysis and additional references in Richard G. Niemi and Herbert F. Weisberg, eds., *Controversies in American Voting Behavior* (San Francisco: W. H. Freeman and Co., 1976), pts. 2 and 3; Nie, Verba, and Petrocik, *The Changing American Voter;* and Herbert Asher, *Presidential Elections and American Politics* (Homewood, Ill.: Dorsey Press, 1976), chap. 4.

collar occupations hold more conservative positions.[23] It is not that political preferences no longer matter. If anything, they seem to matter more, not less, than in previous decades; however, they do not cleave to class divisions.

If this is so, it raises important questions about the political behavior of the American electorate. In the last several chapters we have noted over and over that expected links have not emerged. We have found the stress that accompanies economic disadvantage to be contained in terms of its effects upon beliefs—whether the disadvantage is associated with joblessness or with low social class. What we have uncovered is obviously not sheer randomness: the evidence in Chapter 3 makes clear the relationship between economic position and level of individual satisfaction; the evidence in Chapter 5 indicates that beliefs about the workings of the social system, about opportunities and relations between classes, have a certain coherence. However, there seems to be a gap between the two realms. Personal experiences—subjective evaluations of wages and opportunities—seem to be unrelated to general social ideology. Furthermore, there seems to be a very limited association between personal economic circumstances and policy preferences. Finally, the links between social ideology and policy preferences seem tenuous or nonexistent. What is more, these relationships, so weak in our data, were considerably more robust during the 1930s.

Since objective position and beliefs seem not to be securely linked, we are led to inquire what, if anything, structures actual political behavior, or citizen input to politics. In the next four chapters we shall examine citizen political acts—through the pressure system and the electoral system —in terms of their bases in objective economic position, political beliefs, or neither.

---

[23] *The Silent Revolution* (Princeton, N.J.: Princeton University Press, 1977), chap. 3 and passim.

PART THREE

UNEMPLOYMENT AND POLITICAL BEHAVIOR

CHAPTER 9

Political Participation and Unemployment

I N THE TRADITION of American pluralism citizens with politically relevant concerns can be expected to communicate those concerns
to government officials and to use all available resources to coax or
compel favorable action from them; in particular, they can be expected to cooperate with others with whom they share interests and concerns in collective activity designed to secure sympathetic governmental
treatment.

We have found quite unambiguously that the unemployed, including
those who receive benefits from the government, do have problems that
are politically relevant: the overwhelming majority express the view not
only that government intervention could ameliorate their distress, but
that the government is not doing enough on their behalf. Thus, they
would seem to have ample justification for enhanced activity aimed at
acquainting political leaders with their needs and pressuring them into
responsive action. In this chapter we explore political participation—
both to understand what impact, if any, the experience of unemployment
has upon it and to assess the likelihood that the unemployed as a group,
acting either in concert or on their own, will have an impact on public
policy. We consider the activity of the unemployed as individuals both
outside and within the electoral arena. In Chapter 10 we shall consider
two ways—organization and group consciousness—in which the unemployed *as a group* might increase their political activity.

In our analysis we shall consider two possible sources of the difference
in overall activity level between those with jobs and those without—the
experience of unemployment itself and selective recruitment:

(1) Unemployment itself may have an impact on the political partici-

pation of individuals, either mobilizing those out of work to unusually high levels of activity or causing them to withdraw from political life.

(2) The unemployed may be disproportionately recruited from segments of the population that have especially high or especially low rates of political participation. In this case the experience of unemployment is not responsible for changes in the level of activity; however, there are overall differences in participation between the employed and the unemployed. That the unemployed in the aggregate have an enhanced or depressed rate of participation relative to the employed has potential consequences for politics and public policy—even though unemployment per se is not responsible for those differences.

To clarify the logical possibilities, we have mapped four alternatives in Figure 9-1: that the unemployed are on the whole more active or less active than those with jobs; and that the source of any difference is the direct effect of the experience of unemployment or the effect of selective recruitment. In each box we give some hypothetical examples of the outcome that alternative would produce. For example, in the upper left-hand box we suggest that the experience of unemployment might have the direct effect of raising participation by giving the unemployed an incentive for activity and the extra time in which to be active. In the upper right-hand box we give some examples in which the experience of unemployment would have the precise opposite effect of reducing participation, perhaps because the pressures of looking for work and generating resources preclude other commitments, or because the unemployed are so debilitated psychologically that they withdraw from social and political life. In the bottom two boxes we posit circumstances under which selective recruitment of the unemployed would have the effects of either diminishing or increasing participation: if unemployment were to hit highly skilled professionals (such as aerospace engineers) with disproportionate force, we would expect the process of selective recruitment to result in high activity rates; however, if unemployment were to fall more heavily on groups with traditionally low rates of political activity (for example, those with little education or low-status jobs), the unemployed would be a relatively inactive group.

Of course, we should not exclude the possibility that the experience of unemployment and patterns of selective recruitment affect the overall rate of participation for the unemployed simultaneously—in ways that are either mutually reinforcing or contradictory. For example, the experience of joblessness might galvanize the unemployed to unusual rates of political activity; on the other hand, the unemployed could be selected disproportionately from nonparticipant groups within the work force. In this instance the two effects would cancel each other out, and the unem-

	Unemployed more active than employed	Unemployed less active than employed
Impact of unemployment	The unemployed become more active than formerly; unemployment as an issue gives them an incentive to be active; they have more time for participation	The unemployed become less active than formerly; they withdraw socially and lose self-confidence; they need to spend time seeking work or other income
Selective recruitment	Unemployment is greater among "participant" groups: for instance, recession in high-technology industries puts highly skilled professionals out of work	Unemployment is greater among "nonparticipant" groups, such as the poor or those with little formal education

(Left axis label: Reason for difference in activity rate)

Figure 9-1 Activity of the unemployed: hypothetical outcomes.

ployed would show overall rates of activity little different from the employed. Or both effects might operate in ways that are cumulative. For example, the response of the unemployed may be to withdraw from political life; if the unemployed were selected from groups with low rates of unemployment, then the effects would reinforce each other.

Joblessness and Political Activity: Some Preliminary Hypotheses

The schematic diagram of Figure 9-1 was constructed for the purpose of clarifying our analytic project. The careful reader knows already that the hypothesized outcomes are not equally likely. Before we embark upon extensive data analysis, it seems appropriate to review somewhat more thoroughly the expectations we might have about the political activity of the unemployed.

If processes of selective recruitment affect the rate of political activity of the unemployed, then the evidence we have reviewed so far would lead us to expect the unemployed to have lower rates of activity. Those who study political participation have found with convincing consistency that women, those under thirty, and those of low socioeconomic status—low income, low-status occupation, and low educational attainment—have low rates of activity.[1] Since we know from Chapter 2 that these are precisely the groups that have high rates of unemployment, we

[1]See especially Sidney Verba and Norman Nie, *Participation in America* (New York: Harper and Row, 1972), chaps. 8-10. Extensive bibliographic suggestions are contained in Lester W. Milbrath and M. L. Goel, *Political Participation*, 2d ed. (Chicago: Rand McNally, 1977), chap. 4.

would not expect the processes of selective recruitment to result in enhanced participation by the unemployed.

If we are reasonably certain what hypothesis to make about the effects of selective recruitment upon political participation, we have no such certainty about the effects of the unemployment experience itself. Pluralist theory would predict augmented rates of activity on the part of the unemployed. According to pluralist analysis, those who have collective interests that are politically relevant—and it is clear both that the unemployed are subject to real distress and that they perceive that distress as being amenable to government action—will, quite rationally, organize to act in concert on behalf of those interests. In recent years this latent assumption of pluralist theory, that shared interests are automatically converted into shared activity, has been attacked from a variety of quarters. Particularly relevant to the predicament of the unemployed is Mancur Olson's *The Logic of Collective Action* (Cambridge, Mass.: Harvard University Press, 1965). Using the language and the logic of the economist, Olson seeks to demonstrate that in a variety of circumstances it is not rational for the actor who would benefit from some government action to join with others in its pursuit. If the benefit being sought is a public good that the interested actor would enjoy regardless of whether he personally worked to receive it, the rational actor would sit back and allow others to do the collective dirty work, knowing that if the group is large, the effort he expended would make only a negligible contribution to the acquisition of the benefit, and he would be able to reap the results in any case. Thus, because each of the rational maximizers refuses to expend effort on behalf of a public good, nobody is active in its pursuit.

This argument has particular relevance to the unemployed. Surely there is a large group—several million workers—whose lives would be less painful if the government were to raise unemployment benefits or create massive numbers of new jobs. However, these same people might quite rationally decide that the most effective expenditure of their limited resources of time and skills would be in redoubling their efforts to find work or to raise financial resources. Although the jobless worker has an interest in government benefits and programs, by any rational calculus he has a better chance of improving his personal situation if he directs his efforts toward job seeking rather than political pressure.

Our unemployed respondents—who, presumably, have not read Olson—seem to make precisely this calculation. In response to a series of questions in our follow-up interviews about whether the government would listen if the unemployed were to stage a massive political demonstration, even those who favored such collective action were unanimous in declaring that the unemployed would do better to spend the time looking for work. About a third of the respondents to our follow-up interviews (sixteen out of fifty who answered the question) said that a march on Washington such as that carried out by unemployed in the 1930s would do some good. When, however, they were asked what it was best for an unemployed person to do—look for a job or organize such a march—no respondent thought the course of collective action was better, though two respondents said that both approaches ought to be pursued. A typical response was, "It is better if you want to eat to look for a job." The extent to which our respondents accepted the subordination of collective to individual activity is reflected in the answers of one of the few respondents in our sample with relatively radical ideas. After discussing the need for greater collective consciousness and collective activity on the part of American workers, this respondent, a graphic designer, was asked about taking part in a march on Washington: "Yes, I think I would [march]. But it depends on where you're at. If things were hopeless, then I'd go. But if I was waiting for an answer to a résumé, I wouldn't." Even though the unemployed do have politically relevant collective interests to act as a spur to political activity, we find we cannot assume that their rational response would be to increase activity.

Unemployment and Participation: Evidence from the Thirties

We do not need to resort to such theoretical speculation to justify the hypothesis that the experience of unemployment does not lead to enhanced participation, for empirical observations have led to the same conclusion. Past studies of the unemployed commonly describe a pattern of withdrawal and isolation as accompaniment to the erosion of self-confidence that the unemployed so often suffer.[2] Although these studies focus primarily upon social life—participation in church or community groups and the like—the withdrawal from political life is analogous. E. Wight Bakke found that few of the unemployed belonged to organizations that represented their interests as unemployed. Those who belonged tended to be inactive, leaving main responsibility to the leaders.[3] John A. Garraty summarizes a number of the studies of the thirties, most of which found unemployment to have a numbing effect on participation. As he puts it, the unemployed "nowhere became an effective pressure group or an independent political force. Political activism was incompatible with

---

[2]See, for example, Marie Jahoda, Paul Lazarsfeld, and Hans Zeisel, *Marienthal* (Chicago: Aldine-Atherton, 1933); Eli Ginzberg, *The Unemployed* (New York: Harper and Brothers, 1943), pp. 93 ff.; Richard Wilcock and Walter H. Franke, *Unwanted Workers* (New York: Free Press of Glencoe, 1963), p. 86.

[3]*Citizens without Work* (New Haven: Yale University Press, 1940), p. 46.

joblessness. Insecurity caused the unemployed to be fearful and dependent. Fear and dependence eroded their confidence and destroyed hope. Lack of confidence and hopelessness undermined their expectations."[4]

Bakke's description of the political involvements of jobless workers is particularly interesting in this context, not only because he deals with political life more self-consciously than do most of the other chroniclers of the depression, but also because his comments demonstrate the relevance of Mancur Olson's argument to the unemployed. Bakke observes that "political action does not rank high among the tactics adopted by the unemployed as a means for solving their problems."[5] He continues to note that what political activity there was among the unemployed was viewed in the tradition of machine-style patronage politics—primarily as a means of trading individual favors, as a means of attaining particularistic benefits rather than public policy goals. Thus, not only do past studies of the unemployed document a decline in participation, but one such study characterizes political activity on the part of the unemployed as an alternative form of individual coping.

Frances Fox Piven and Richard A. Cloward draw on more recent scholarship to call into question this widely disseminated account of the unemployed in the thirties.[6] They describe extensive protests by the organized unemployed and argue that such protests led to increased relief. Piven and Cloward have, in turn, been criticized for focusing on incidents in a few cities that may have been atypical and for overestimating the amount of mass support among the unemployed given to activities organized and manned by political groups like the Communist Party and the League for Industrial Democracy.[7]

Political Activity and Involvement: Working and Jobless Citizens

Our data can help us understand the political activity of the unemployed in comparison with the employed. In our metropolitan work

[4]*Unemployment in History* (New York: Harper and Row, 1978), p. 187.

[5]*Citizens without Work*, p. 46.

[6]*Poor People's Movements* (New York: Pantheon Books, 1977), chap. 2. Some of the newer works on the organized unemployed on which Piven and Cloward draw are Roy Rosenzweig, "Radicals and the Jobless: The Musteites and the Unemployed Leagues, 1932-1936," *Labor History*, 16 (Winter 1975), 52-77; "Organizing the Unemployed: The Early Years of the Great Depression, 1929-1933," *Radical America*, 10 (July-August 1976), 37-60; " 'Socialism in Our Time': The Socialist Party and the Unemployed, 1929-1936," *Labor History* (in press); Daniel Leab, " 'United We Eat': The Creation and Organization of the Unemployed Councils in 1930," *Labor History*, 8 (Fall 1967), 300-315. These works, however, do not point unequivocally to high levels of political protest by the unemployed.

[7]Timothy G. Massad, "Disruption, Organization and Reform: A Critique of Piven and Cloward," honors thesis, Harvard College, 1978.

force survey we asked about general political interest; about exposure to political news on television and in the papers; about several participatory acts (writing a letter to a public official, contributing to a political candidate's campaign, and taking part in a political demonstration); and about membership and activity in organizations. In addition, we have data from a 1972 Census Bureau study of voting turnout in that year's presidential election.

Table 9-1 summarizes the results of these questions. In terms of general political involvement and exposure to the media, on two of three measures the unemployed show less political involvement; they report less interest in politics and are less likely to read a daily paper. They are similar to the employed, however, in the likelihood of watching the news on television. In terms of participatory acts rather than general involvement, it is obvious from the table that the unemployed are in general a less active group. They are less likely to report that they voted in 1972, or have written to an official, or contributed to a campaign. Only on the measure of participation in a political demonstration do we find the unemployed more active (by a very small amount) than the employed. To

Table 9-1 Participation and involvement profiles: the working and the unemployed.

Type of participation	Percent who are politically active or involved	
	Working	Unemployed
Political activities		
Voted in 1972 election[a]	69	53
Have written a letter to a public official	52	39
Have contributed to a political campaign	37	29
Have taken part in a political demonstration	12	14
Score "high" on political activity	29	20
Political involvement		
Very interested in politics	28	24
Read newspaper every day	77	69
Watch news on TV every day	69	73

[a]Data from Census Bureau's November 1972 Current Population Survey.

summarize the three measures of political activity that come from our own study, we created an additive scale of political participation based on the number and frequency of the respondent's participatory acts. The employed are about one and a half times as likely to fall in the "high" category of that scale as the unemployed.

Clearly, then, the unemployed are a less active group than the employed. However, the data tell us nothing about the sources of the difference in participation between the two groups, whether it is the result of the experience of unemployment itself or the result of biases in the demographic character of the unemployed or both. It is to that question that we now turn.

POLITICAL INVOLVEMENT

We begin by considering overall political involvement. If the experience of being out of work has a direct effect on political life—whether by increasing or decreasing political activity—we would find traces of that effect most immediately in terms of overall interest and attentiveness to politics, not in terms of participatory acts, which are sporadic. After all, even the most dedicated activist does not write daily letters to public officials; and it is impossible to go to the polls if there is no election. Political concern and attention to politics, on the other hand, are more or less continuous. Thus, if unemployment does have an effect, we should be able to measure that effect. Furthermore, if the effect of unemployment is to cause the kind of psychological withdrawal observed during the thirties (characterized by erosion of self-esteem and loss of purpose), we would expect that effect to be felt most directly on general political interest.

As we have seen, although the unemployed are as likely to watch the news on television as our working respondents, they are less likely than the employed to say that they are very interested in politics or to say that they read a newspaper every day. Figure 9-2 shows, however, that once we control for occupational level, the difference between the employed and the unemployed in their political involvement or exposure more or less disappears. At each occupational level the unemployed are, in fact, slightly more—not less—likely to report that they are very interested in politics and that they listen to television news every day. Only when it comes to reading a daily newspaper do we find some trace of a lower level of attentiveness among the unemployed—among those at the lowest and the highest occupational levels, though not in the two middle ones. In general, the data indicate little difference between the employed and the unemployed in involvement or attention to politics. The largest

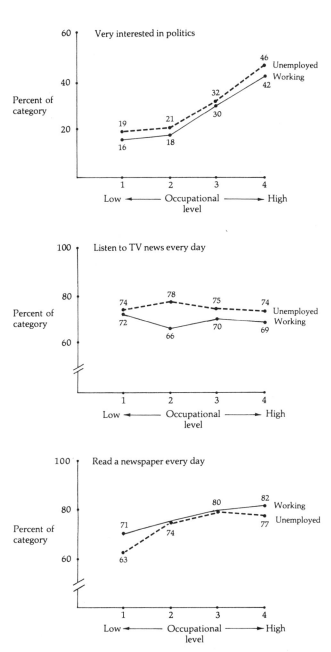

Figure 9-2   Interest in politics, by occupational level and employment status.

difference is relative to television news, with the unemployed somewhat more likely to be regular watchers. This is likely less to be a function of enhanced political interest than of the fact that the unemployed have much more time—and, as we saw in Chapter 3, watch more television—than the employed.

We can test further for the direct effects of the experience of unemployment on political interest by observing the relationship between interest and length of unemployment. We can imagine several plausible patterns: a steady decline in political interest with length of unemployment; an initial mobilization followed by a leveling off or a decline in political interest; no immediate reaction followed by an ultimate decline. As it is, however, with the exception of a slight increase in interest among the long-term unemployed (for which we have no explanation), the curve shown in Figure 9-3 is quite flat, another indication that differences between working and jobless respondents result from their sociological characteristics rather than from the experience of being out of work.

POLITICAL PARTICIPATION

We turn next to the political activity scale. The interpretation of any differences between the employed and the unemployed on the activities included in the scale—writing a letter to a public official, giving money to a political campaign, and taking part in a demonstration—is somewhat ambiguous. Unlike questions about political interest or reading the newspaper, which have a clear referent in the present, questions about the other activities have a rather broad time frame. Since these activities are intermittent, it would have made no sense to inquire whether respondents had made any campaign contributions in the past week. Presumably, then, some unemployed respondents, in reporting on past activities, are discussing acts undertaken while employed; conversely, at least some of the working respondents are probably reporting on activities performed while out of work.[8]

The data in Figure 9-4 suggest that the lower activity rate of the unemployed is in large part a function of their sociological characteristics. If we compare the employed with the unemployed within the various categories of our occupational-level scale, we find that there is relatively little difference between the two groups in the proportion who fall in the high category of our participation scale. In the lowest category of the occupational-level scale, the unemployed are slightly more active than the em-

[8]The voter turnout measure, discussed later in the chapter, is relatively unambiguous in this respect. Since the census survey was made within weeks of the 1972 election, the behaviors reported are likely to have occurred during the period of unemployment.

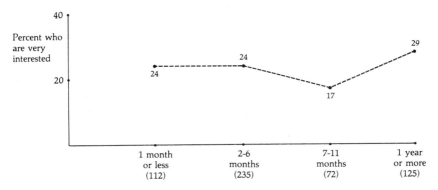

Figure 9-3 Interest in politics, by length of unemployment.

ployed, in the other three upper occupational categories, slightly less active. On the other hand, occupational level is closely related to participation for both the employed and the unemployed. It is clear from Figure 9-4 that it is occupational level, not unemployment per se, that is more closely related to political participation.

In order to isolate the impact of unemployment per se on activity, we turned to multiple regression analysis. Into an equation predicting political activity we entered employment status along with other demographic characteristics known to be related to measures of political activity: education, occupation, race, age, and sex.[9] The results of that analysis are shown in Table 9-2. With other variables controlled, the unemployed are very slightly more active than the employed; however, the difference is statistically insignificant. Thus we have further evidence that any difference between the employed and the unemployed in their amount of polit-

[9]The equation was constructed to reflect our understanding from the literature on political participation that those of advanced educational level, those in high-status occupations, whites, males, and the middle-aged have more substantial rates of political activity. We set up the regression so that a positive beta for employment status would indicate that the employed participate more than those out of work, a negative beta that the unemployed participate more than the employed. We do not include income, another variable known to be related to participation, because—unlike the other variables that we believe to be antecedent to the individual's employment status —family income is clearly influenced by whether or not the respondent is working.

We were interested in looking at the simultaneous effect of a larger number of demographic variables than could be encompassed using the log-linear techniques we have employed elsewhere. For this reason we have relied on multiple regression. We have also applied log-linear models to the participation data, with a more truncated list of variables. The results in all cases have been consistent with those reported using multiple regression.

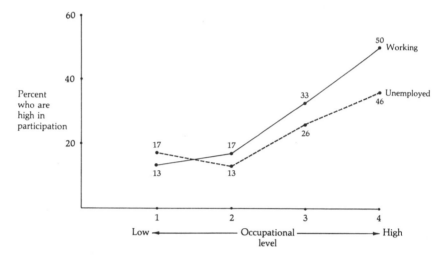

Figure 9-4   Political participation, by occupational level and employment status.

ical activity is a function of the sociological characteristics of the unemployed rather than a result of the experience of unemployment.

We can look further for direct effects of the experience of unemployment by relating political activity to length of joblessness. Whereas many patterns are plausible, a flat curve would seem to be evidence that unemployment itself has no direct impact on participation. The curve in Figure 9-5 is indeed quite flat. Political participation neither increases nor diminishes with length of unemployment. The evidence so far has been consistent: differences between working and jobless respondents in political activity and involvement are a function of selective recruitment of the unemployed from nonparticipant groups in the population rather than the experience of being out of work.

Voter Turnout

Perhaps the single most important means by which citizens affect political leaders is their vote. In the remainder of this chapter we shall replicate the logic of the foregoing analysis in order to assess the impact of joblessness upon individual electoral turnout. Once again we shall seek to ascertain whether differences between working and jobless respondents are a function of the effects of the experience of being out of work or of the disproportionate selection of the unemployed from certain demographic groups. Of course, the electoral effect of unemployment might be felt, not in terms of the degree to which the jobless are more or less likely to go to the polls, but in terms of how they cast their ballots

Table 9-2   Multivariate analysis of participation scale.

Variable	Beta	F ratio
Education	0.23	80.9
Occupational level	.18	48.0
Race	.08	24.7
Age	.05	10.7
Sex	.04	6.5
Employment status	−.03	0.7

Multiple $r = .43$
$r^2 = .18$
Simple r, employment status and participation $= .05$

when they get there. In Chapters 11 and 12, we shall focus both on the direction of the vote and on the degree to which partisan commitments are undermined or reaffirmed by joblessness. Here we consider turnout.

Even if we find that unemployment has a substantial effect upon electoral behavior at the individual level—if we find, for example, that those out of work are especially likely to go to the polls, or that jobless Republicans overwhelmingly vote Democratic—the aggregate electoral impact of unemployment will depend, of course, upon the number and geographic dispersion of unemployed voters. Obviously, the size of the bloc of jobless voters varies with the unemployment rate. In November 1968, when the unemployment rate was 3.3 percent, approximately 1.5 percent of the electorate was out of work; four years later, 4.9 percent of the work force—and about 2.6 percent of the electorate—was unemployed; and in November 1976, 7.4 percent of the labor force—about 4.3 percent of the electorate—was jobless.[10] Thus, even in the high unemployment year of 1976, the unemployed were a small minority of voters. Furthermore, the unemployed are dispersed geographically, not concentrated in jobless ghettos, which would presumably diminish their potential electoral impact.

However, we should not be too hasty in dismissing the unemployed as a voting bloc. In 1976 the electorate contained substantially more people who were out of work than it did Jews, farmers, residents of the eight

[10]Calculated from unadjusted figures given in *Employment and Earnings*, December 1968, pp. 11, 13, 14, 19; December 1972, pp. 19, 21, 22, 27; December 1976, pp. 22, 24, 25, 31. With the inclusion in 1972 of those aged eighteen to twenty-one, the ratio of the rate of unemployment in the electorate to the rate of unemployment in the work force increased.

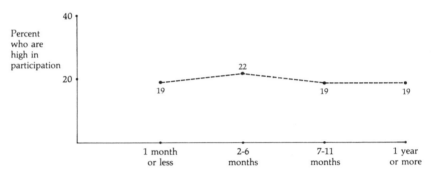

Figure 9-5   Political participation, by length of unemployment.

Rocky Mountain States, or members of the three largest trade unions (United Auto Workers, Teamsters, and Steelworkers).[11] Certainly, no presidential candidate would ignore these blocs of voters and their special problems. Looked at from another point of view, in each of half the states (including the nine most populous) with a combined electoral vote of 359, the majority sustained by the winning presidential candidate in 1976 was smaller than the number of unemployed workers in that state's electorate.[12] Furthermore, the effects of unemployment are not confined to those currently out of work. If we include, in addition, those whose family members were unemployed and those who were out of work at some point during the preceding year, the size of the potential unemployment voting bloc swells substantially. Thus it seems fair to conclude that —at least in 1976—there was a sufficient number of strategically placed unemployed voters that, as a group, the unemployed had potential electoral clout.

Our metropolitan work force survey is inappropriate for the task of investigating the relationship between unemployment and voting turnout. As it was conducted in April 1976, questions about vote intentions for the following November would have been premature and questions about behavior in previous elections would not have been meaningful in terms of the respondents' employment status in 1976. We are fortunate, however, in having access to a study conducted by the Bureau of the Census in November 1972, which contains valuable data. Under con-

[11]Based on data in U.S. Department of Commerce, Bureau of the Census, *Statistical Abstract of the United States* (Washington, D.C.: Government Printing Office, 1976).

[12]Based on data in *Employment and Earnings*, January 1977, pp. 130-134, and *Current American Government—Spring, 1977* (Washington, D.C.: Congressional Quarterly, 1976), p. 4.

gressional mandate, a number of questions about voter registration and turnout were added to Current Population Survey (CPS). Because the sample was so big, about 40,000 cases, there are a large number of unemployed respondents, even though the unemployment rate at the time was only 4.9 percent. Because the study was conducted very shortly after the election, we can be reasonably sure of the respondents' employment status at the time of the election. Although this study provides a larger, more reliable sample than our 1976 work force study, there are limitations on the usefulness of the data. Respondents were asked about registration and turnout only, not about party identification or electoral choice.

We should mention also that 1972 and 1976 may not be entirely comparable. The relationship between unemployment and voter turnout may vary with aggregate level of unemployment, because both the composition of the unemployed and the salience of unemployment as an issue change with the jobless rate. In 1972 the unemployment rate was considerably lower than in 1976, and economic concerns—especially unemployment—were overshadowed by issues like the war in Vietnam. Analogously, our 1976 data presumably are affected by the specific events of that year. But if the results of the analysis of the 1972 data are consistent with those of the 1976 data, we would be encouraged about the generalizability of our findings.

As we saw in Table 9-1, 69 percent of the working, but only 53 percent of the jobless, members of the work force voted in 1972. The difference is substantial. The question is, once again, whether the difference is a function of demographic selection or the experience of unemployment. Table 9-3 gives the results of a multiple regression in which a variety of social characteristics, along with employment status, were used to explain voter turnout.[13] Clearly voter turnout is much more a function of such social characteristics as education, age, income, and occupational level than it is a function of unemployment per se. Nonetheless, there is a small but statistically significant beta associated with employment status after other social characteristics are controlled. If we convert this into an estimate of turnout by using the unstandardized rather than the standardized

[13]We included income among the demographic predictors of turnout because the Current Population Survey asked about 1971 family income. By and large, 1971 income would not have been affected by unemployment in November of 1972. In any case the results of the analysis do not differ substantially when income is omitted. "Region" refers to a North-South dichotomy in which residence in the North is associated with higher turnout. For a more general analysis of the census data on turnout, see Raymond Wolfinger and Steven Rosenstone, "Who Votes," paper presented at the Annual Meeting of the American Political Science Association, September 1977.

Table 9-3   Multivariate analysis of voter turnout in 1972.

Variable	Beta	F ratio
Education	0.19	247.6
Age	.19	332.2
Income	.10	69.2
Occupation	.10	65.2
Region	.08	54.4
Race	−.02	2.2
Sex	.00	0.0
Employment status	.05	24.4

Multiple $r = .37$
$r^2 = .14$
Simple r, employment status and turnout $= .14$

regression coefficients, the 15-percentage-point difference between the employed and the unemployed is reduced to approximately a 6-percent difference when other demographic characteristics are controlled. The data thus support a selective recruitment interpretation of the difference in voter turnout between the employed and the unemployed. The remaining impact of unemployment itself is not difficult to understand. Although the 1972 election was characterized by a high level of issue voting, the issues that divided Nixon and McGovern most sharply in the perceptions of voters were the war in Vietnam and social concerns.[14] The unemployed voter thus had no special incentive to go to the polls.

We can use the 1972 census data to refine further our understanding of the sources of lower voter turnout among the unemployed. Some of those who failed to vote in 1972 were not even registered; others were registered but did not actually get to the polls. If the difference in voting rate between the employed and the unemployed is a function of long-term social characteristics, we would expect an equally sharp difference in terms of registration; if it is the experience of unemployment that is responsible for the difference in voter turnout, we would expect similar rates of registration for the two groups and different rates of actual voting. The rationale behind this hypothesis is relatively straightforward. In most cases registration precedes actual vote by at least a period of weeks —in many cases, years. Presumably, most of those who were out of

[14]See Nie et al., *The Changing American Voter* (Cambridge, Mass.: Harvard University Press, 1976), chap. 18; and Arthur Miller et al., "A Majority Party in Disarray," *American Political Science Review*, 68 (September 1976), 761 ff.

work at the time of the 1972 CPS were not unemployed when they registered. Thus if unemployment has a direct effect on citizen behavior—in particular, if being unemployed makes one withdraw from voting—we should see this impact, not on rates of registration, but on voter turnout among the registered electorate.[15]

In Table 9-4 we decompose the voter turnout of the employed and the unemployed, reporting not only the fraction of each group that voted, but the portion of those registered who also voted. Clearly, the difference between the two groups is much greater in terms of rate of registration than in terms of rate of turnout among those registered to vote. Given that jobless citizens who are registered on election day vote at nearly the same rate as their working counterparts, the fact that far fewer of the unemployed are registered must be responsible for their overall lower turnout rates.

In Table 9-5 we report the results of multiple regressions predicting voter registration among all members of the electorate, and electoral turnout among registered voters. The data underline the importance of registration in distinguishing the employed from the unemployed. Even after other social characteristics have been controlled, there is a positive relationship between employment and registration for all members of the electorate; among those who are registered there is no relationship at all between employment and actual turnout. Thus we find no evidence of a direct impact of unemployment on turnout.

We are puzzled over how to interpret the relationship between unemployment and registration. Because most of the unemployed are out of work for relatively short periods of time, we assume that registration precedes unemployment in time—or at least that most of the unemployed were working at the time they registered and that some of the employed were out of work at the time they registered. Given this time sequence,

---

[15]In addition, registration is a relatively "difficult" political act compared to voting. It requires somewhat more initiative than does the vote. One must register before the fever pitch of the last days of the campaign. The voter must take the initiative to register without all the accumulated stimuli of the campaign and without the anticipation of some fairly rapid feedback from his act. Difficult political acts are more likely to be affected by such long-term social characteristics as education and income, while easier acts like voting are much more susceptible to immediate personal or political circumstances surrounding the election. Thus if the variation between the two groups results from the direct impact of unemployment, we would expect differences in voting between the employed and the unemployed to be manifested in unlike turnout rates among the registered on election day. For an extended discussion of the difference among political acts from this perspective, see Sidney Verba, Norman Nie, and Jae-on Kim, *Participation and Political Equality* (Cambridge: Cambridge University Press, 1978), chap. 3.

Table 9-4   Voter turnout in 1972, by employment status.

Turnout	Employed	Unemployed
Percent who voted	68.8	53.1
Percent who registered	76.9	61.3
Percent of registered who voted	89.5	86.6

we are reluctant to interpret the small positive relationship between unemployment and registration as evidence of any direct effects of unemployment. Given that the residual relationship between employment
status and registration does not obtain for voter turnout among the registered, we are inclined to interpret that relationship as evidence of further
processes of social selection, which are not accounted for by the controls
for region, occupation, age, and the like.

In the census survey those who were not registered and those who, although registered, did not vote were asked why. Comparing the employed and the unemployed in the frequency of responses that would indicate disaffection or withdrawal—for example, "I wasn't interested," or
"I didn't think it would make any difference," as opposed to "I was sick
in bed"—there is no difference between the two groups. This would seem
to be additional evidence for the absence of a withdrawal syndrome
among the unemployed.

Data about voting in 1968 permit us to probe further the relationship
between unemployment and voter turnout. In Table 9-6 we compare the
1972 voting behavior of the working and jobless among three voter
types: those who voted in 1968; those who, although eligible, did not
vote in 1968; and those who entered the electorate between 1968 and
1972.[16] As expected, the unemployed in all three categories were less likely to report having voted in 1972. However, in each case the difference
between the employment status groups is almost entirely a function of
differences in registration rather than in turnout on election day. Among
those who voted in 1968, there is a difference between the employed and
the unemployed in turnout rate of registered voters, but it is less than half
the size of the difference in registration. For those who did not vote in
1968, there is a particularly striking difference between the employed and
the unemployed in registration. However, among those 1968 nonvoters
who were registered at the time of the 1972 election, the turnout was ac-

[16]For almost all those out of work in November 1972, the onset of the current siege
of unemployment had begun well after the 1968 election.

Table 9-5   Multivariate analysis of registration and voting in 1972.

Variable	REGISTERED IN 1972		VOTE IF REGISTERED	
	Beta	F ratio	Beta	F ratio
Education	0.16	163.8	0.13	68.9
Age	.18	276.4	.09	42.8
Region	.05	18.6	.08	39.4
Income	.08	40.6	.08	29.5
Occupation	.09	53.9	.04	6.5
Race	−.03	6.7	.01	0.5
Sex	.00	0.0	.00	0.0
Employment status	.07	37.9	.01	0.4

Multiple r .32   .22
r^2 .11   .05
Simple r, employment status and registered = .14;
and vote of registered = .05

tually *higher* among the unemployed. Most interesting, perhaps, are the voters who entered the electorate in the four-year period between 1968 and 1972. With the entrance of eighteen- to twenty-year-olds into the electorate in 1972 and the particularly large age cohort involved, this group formed a sizable part of the electorate. Its political participation was relatively low. It is interesting to note how little of that low participation rate can be directly traced to unemployment. As shown in Table 9-6, the unemployed new entrants were less likely to become registered. But once registered, they were as likely as their working counterparts actually to get to the polls. Once again, we have evidence that unemployment per se has little direct effect on turnout. If the unemployed vote less, it is a function of their membership in social groups that are unlikely to register to vote.

If we consider the data in Table 9-6 from another perspective, it is clear that whether or not one voted in 1968 is a far better predictor than employment status of turning out in 1972. For example, of those who did not vote in 1968, 23.5 percent of those employed in 1972 voted compared with 18.6 percent of those who were unemployed, a difference of 4.9 percent. In contrast, of those who voted in 1968 but were unemployed in 1972, 78.9 percent voted in 1972 compared with a voting rate of 18.6 percent among the 1968 nonvoters who were unemployed in 1972, a difference of 60.3 percent in turnout rate. These data simply illustrate once

Table 9-6   Voter turnout in 1972, by employment status and 1968 vote (percent).

| | Voting status in 1968 | | | | | |
| | Voted | | Eligible but did not vote | | Too young to vote | |
Voting status in 1972	Employed	Unemployed	Employed	Unemployed	Employed	Unemployed
Voted	86.2	78.9	23.5	18.6	53.4	48.9
Registered	93.4	88.4	33.7	24.1	62.5	57.3
Registered who voted	92.3	89.0	69.9	78.6	85.6	85.5

again our general proposition that differences in participation between the employed and the unemployed are a function of selective recruitment rather than the direct impact of being unemployed.

Summary

Our data on the differences between the employed and the unemployed in terms of various participatory acts are remarkably consistent. Several points are clear. First, the jobless are unambiguously a less active group than the employed: they are less likely to vote, less likely to take part in other political activities, less likely to be interested in politics, and less likely to be active participants in voluntary associations. Regardless of which specific form of participation is being considered, this lower involvement in social and political life appears to be the result not of unemployment as such but of the social characteristics of the unemployed. The incidence of unemployment is greater among social groups that are ordinarily not active. The difference between working and jobless in terms of political activity is therefore a spurious effect of other social attributes. Whatever the source of the discrepancy in participation between those who have jobs and those who do not, however, the general conclusion that must be underlined is that the unemployed are a relatively inactive group. From the point of view of their potential impact on the political system, what matters is that they are in fact inactive, even though that inactivity does not derive from their jobless condition.

CHAPTER 10

Resources for Participation: Organization and Consciousness

I T IS WELL KNOWN that, all else being equal, those who are disadvantaged in terms of income, education, or occupation tend to participate less politically because they lack crucial individually based resources for politics. They are less likely to have extra money or time to devote to political activity, or to have the political skills and contacts that facilitate activity. Furthermore, they are less likely to have the attitudes that motivate participation in politics—a sense of political efficacy, intense political interest, or adherence to civic norms supportive of political activity.

But all else is not always equal. Sometimes members of disadvantaged groups participate beyond what would have been predicted on the basis of their social and economic characteristics alone. When this happens, it may indicate the presence of group-based organizational or ideological resources that can serve to compensate for socioeconomic disadvantage.[1] In this chapter we assess the situation of those who are economically disadvantaged by their joblessness or their class position, in terms of two such group-based resources, organization and consciousness. The importance of organizational membership for the disadvantaged derives from two sources. The first is quite direct: a substantial portion of citizen input in American political life is the result of group activity; it is through collective participation in political parties and voluntary associations that

---

[1]For a general discussion of the alternative resources that can be utilized by the disadvantaged, see Sidney Verba, Norman Nie, and Jae-on Kim, *Participation and Political Equality* (Cambridge: Cambridge University Press, 1978), chaps. 1, 5; and Sidney Verba and Norman Nie, *Participation in America* (New York: Harper and Row, 1972), chaps. 10-11.

the individual interests of the disadvantaged are aggregated and represented in politics. The second is less direct: organizational membership seems to spur political activity even when the specific organization is not an explicitly political one; thus, organization members tend to be politically active in other ways—beyond what would be expected on the basis of their socioeconomic status. Clearly, this is potentially significant to the disadvantaged who are in need of government assistance and who require a boost to overcome the effects of their social and economic characteristics.

Not only can organization act as a group-based resource, but group-based beliefs and ideologies can help the disadvantaged to narrow the disparity in participation. Group-based beliefs can be differentiated from a general sense of efficacy or the kinds of civic norms that predispose individuals to be politically active. One potential group-based set of beliefs is group consciousness, a sense of kinship among group members and an awareness of their common interests. Related, but less general, are policy preferences for government activity relevant to group needs. Such beliefs would seem to be a potential resource for group mobilization. Clearly, these two group-based resources, ideology and organization, are mutually reinforcing. As we have pointed out before, common beliefs can facilitate collective organization; and organization can lead to the dissemination of group-based beliefs.

Organization as a Resource: Individual Activity

Given that the level of overall activity of the unemployed is just what would have been predicted from their demographic characteristics, our focus in probing their organizational membership is first to ascertain how much membership there is to act as a potential group-based resource. As shown in Table 10-1, the unemployed are less likely to be organization members and, correspondingly, less likely to be organization activists. This is, of course, not surprising in view of their social characteristics.

This disparity leads us to ask a question analogous to the one we asked about political activity and electoral turnout: to what degree does the participatory gap between working and jobless represent the impact of social characteristics and to what degree the impact of a syndrome of withdrawal attendant to joblessness? In light of studies of the unemployed during the 1930s, which contain convincing evidence of withdrawal from all kinds of organizations, we might expect the unemployed to drop out of the organizations of which they were formerly members.

Our evidence, however, indicates that the difference between the employed and the unemployed in terms of organizational membership and activity is largely a function of the social characteristics of the unem-

Table 10-1   Organizational involvement of the working and the unemployed.

Degree of involvement	Working	Unemployed
Member of an organization other than a union	43%	25%
Active member of an organization other than a union	30%	16%

ployed rather than the result of the direct impact of unemployment. In Figure 10-1 we relate organizational membership to occupational level for the employed and the unemployed. The data in Figure 10-1 are consistent with the well-known relationship between socioeconomic status and organizational membership. There is, nevertheless, a residual difference between the employed and the unemployed in their organizational membership. This difference diminishes when various other demographic characteristics are controlled in the multiple regression reported in Table 10-2. Unlike the situation with political activity and political involvement, when other demographic characteristics are controlled, the employed still remain somewhat more likely to be organizational members. The difference, however, is very small.

In order to test more directly the hypothesis that jobless workers withdraw from social life, we asked respondents whether they had within the past year or two left some organization of which they had been a member. Seven percent of the unemployed reported that they had done so. An identical proportion of the employed, however, report leaving some organizational affiliation. The similarity between the employed and the unemployed suggests that it is ordinary turnover in organizational membership rather than the effects of joblessness which is responsible for the slight attrition of unemployed group members.

The impact of unemployment on involvement in organizational life might be reflected, not in the frequency of membership, but in the level of activity within organizations. If unemployed individuals withdraw from social life, perhaps they do so not by the overt act of quitting, but by reducing the amount of their organizational activity. Membership in an organization represents a long-term commitment, so it is not surprising that the difference between the working and the unemployed in their organizational membership is a function of the demographic characteristics of the unemployed. If the impact of unemployment on organizational involvement were a more direct one—that is, if those who were without jobs subsequently withdrew from their involvement in volun-

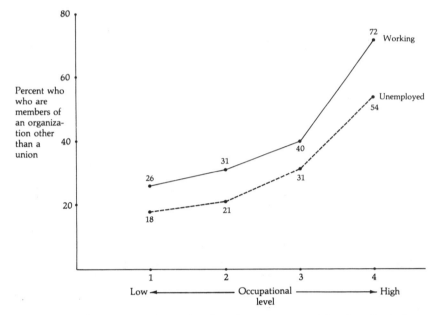

Figure 10-1   Organizational membership, by occupational level and employment status.

tary associations because of their unemployment, because they were ashamed or uncomfortable, or because they lacked the money for dues— we would expect this to be manifested less in terms of frequency of reported membership than in terms of a lowered activity rate in the organizations of which they were members.

In Figure 10-2 we compare the working and the unemployed at various occupational levels in terms of the proportion who are active organizational members—who go to meetings and participate in other group activities. At the bottom of the figure are two lines indicating the proportion of the employed and the unemployed who report that they are active organizational members. Clearly, there is a difference between the unemployed and the working at each occupational level, that difference being the greatest at the highest occupational level. However, considering the data at the top of Figure 10-2, where we present the proportion of *organizational members* who report that they are active in organizations, we find no consistent difference between the employed and the unemployed. In other words, the difference between those with and without jobs found at the bottom of Figure 10-2 reflects a difference between the two groups in the proportion who are organization members, not a difference between the employed and the unemployed in the likelihood

Table 10-2 Multivariate analysis of organizational membership.

Variable	Beta	F ratio
Education	0.19	53.1
Sex	.02	1.0
Occupational level	.23	71.5
Age	.17	122.1
Race	−.05	12.0
Employment status	.04	6.7

Multiple $r = .43$
$r^2 = .18$
Simple r, employment status and organizational membership $= .12$

that they will be active members of the organizations to which they belong.

We asked our respondents further whether their activity in organizations had changed in recent months—that is, had gone up or down—or stayed the same. If unemployment leads to withdrawal from organizational life, the unemployed would be more apt to report a decrease in activity in recent months. We would also expect that the longer an individual has been unemployed, the greater the likelihood of a decrease in activity.

Neither of these hypotheses is borne out. Figure 10-3 gives the proportion of working and unemployed respondents at each of the four occupational levels who say that their level of activity in organizations has gone down in recent months. The pattern is quite irregular. At the upper and lower end of the occupation scale the unemployed report more withdrawal; in the middle of the scale there is little difference between the unemployed and the employed. We have no ready explanation for the irregularities in these data. Our general conclusion, then, is that there is no regular relationship between unemployment and withdrawal from organizations.

We can test the withdrawal hypothesis in yet another way by considering the relationship between the length of unemployment and withdrawal from organizations. If unemployment leads to withdrawal, we should expect to find more and more withdrawal the longer the period of unemployment. However, as shown in Figure 10-4, there is no tendency for the long-term unemployed to report that they have withdrawn from organizational activity. Those who have been unemployed for a year or more are no more likely than those who have been unemployed for less than a month to say that they have reduced their level of organizational

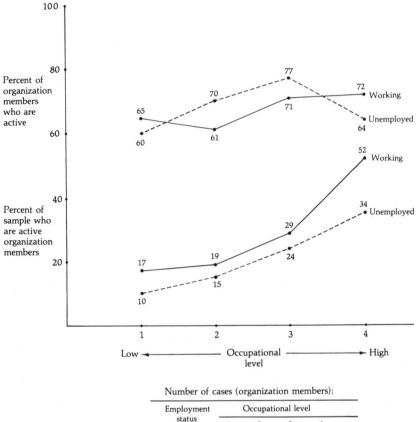

Figure 10-2 Organizational activity, by occupational level and employment status.

activity. In short, the data offer little support for the hypothesis that the experience of unemployment is accompanied by withdrawal from formal organizations.

Unemployment, then, apparently has little direct impact on the organizational involvement of individuals. However, we do have some data that show an effect on organizational participation of a particular kind, union activity. There is a sharp difference between employed and unemployed union members in the frequency with which they report a reduction in union activity. Forty-four percent of the unemployed, but only 21 percent of the employed, say that they have withdrawn some-

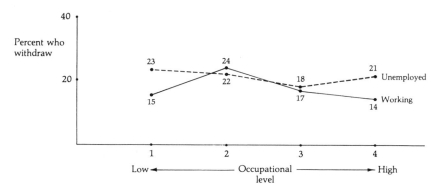

Figure 10-3 Withdrawal from organizational participation, by occupational level and employment status.

what from union activity. In Figure 10-5 we present the percentage of short-term and long-term unemployed union members who report that they have reduced their union activity in recent months. The longer the period of unemployment, the more likely is the individual to report such withdrawal. Those who have been unemployed for a month or less are very little different from the employed in terms of the frequency of reported withdrawal from union activity. Those who have been out of work for longer and longer periods of time are increasingly likely to report withdrawal.

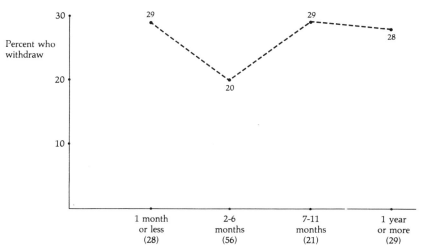

Figure 10-4 Withdrawal from organizational participation, by length of unemployment.

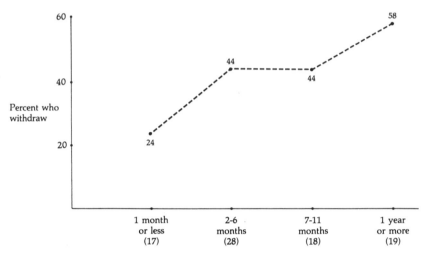

Figure 10-5   Withdrawal from union activity, by length of unemployment.

The contrast between the withdrawal of the unemployed from union activity and their stable level of participation in other organizations is perhaps surprising. However, it becomes comprehensible when viewed in terms of our other findings about the impact of unemployment. Union activity is clearly job related. Once again we find unemployment having a sharp effect that is limited in scope, an effect on personal life not generalized to those attitudes and behaviors that are less directly relevant.

Joblessness and Organization: A Further Probe

Our analysis of organizational activity confirms what we learned about overall political activity: with the crucial exception of union activity, the low level of organizational participation on the part of the unemployed stems from their social characteristics rather than from the experience of bieng out of work. So far, however, our analysis of organizational activity has been individually based. We have not really considered whether organizational membership functions as a group-based political resource for the unemployed.

Membership in organizations, even those that are not explicitly political, is associated with enhanced levels of overall participation. As shown in Figure 10-6, which presents data on the political activity of jobless workers who are and are not organization members, this is the case for the unemployed as well. At each occupational level organization members among the unemployed are more likely to be politically active. Given this clear relationship, organizational membership is a potential indirect resource for participation for the unemployed, as it has been for

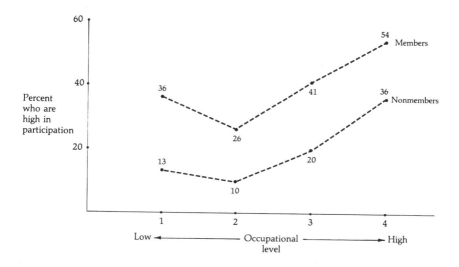

Number of cases:

Organizational status	Occupational level			
	1	2	3	4
Members	(39)	(23)	(22)	(33)
Nonmembers	(178)	(83)	(49)	(28)

Figure 10-6 Political participation, by occupational level and organizational membership (unemployed only).

other groups. However, in view of how few organization members there are among the jobless, the present effects of this potential resource are quite limited.

There is, of course, a much more direct way in which organizational activity could serve as a group-based resource: the interests of the unemployed could be represented in politics by organizations devoted to that purpose. Although the results of our inquiry based on survey data lead us to suspect that there are few such organizations, it takes far less than a total mobilization of a large group like the unemployed for a substantial and visible group effort in politics. Data collected during the era of the protest against the war in Vietnam underline this point. Certainly, it is unambiguous that there was a great deal of organized antiwar activity; yet only a very small fraction of those who opposed the war ever took part in such activities.[2] Therefore, we should not infer from the low

---

[2]See Sidney Verba and Richard Brody, "Participation, Policy Preferences and the War in Vietnam," *Public Opinion Quarterly*, 34 (Fall 1970), 325-332.

overall level of organizational participation of the unemployed that there is no group activity on behalf of their interests.

In order to get a more precise measure of the amount of organized activity by the unemployed we turned to the *New York Times Index*. Table 10-3 presents a summary of group activities representing the interests of the unemployed as listed in the *Index* for three years of high unemployment: 1974, 1975, and 1976. We include in "demonstrations" activities so labeled by the *Times,* as well as such direct acts of protest as picketing, sit-ins, and marches. "Organized acts" refer to activities undertaken through more usual channels—statements, speeches, conferences, appeals to officeholders—carried on by organizations of the unemployed or their spokespersons. The *Index* does not, of course, list all such activities; many local acts elude its coverage. But the data give some systematic indication of the volume of organized activity on the part of the unemployed. To provide a benchmark, we present parallel data on activity by blacks during the 1960s, a period of considerable civil rights activism. The contrast is striking. There was substantially more activity by blacks during the 1960s than by the unemployed a decade later. Especially when we recall that a substantial portion of the activity in the "organized acts" category is undertaken *for* the unemployed by organizations like unions rather than *by* them, it is clear that the unemployed are not a politically mobilized group.[3]

Even these data are not sufficient to justify the conclusion that the unemployed are not involved in organized activity. After all, a great deal of the most effective group activity in American politics takes place quietly through the regular interactions of government and the private sector and is shielded from media scrutiny. To enrich our understanding of the role of the unemployed in the pressure system, we conducted a series of interviews with people who are or have been involved in influencing the making of manpower policy—in Congress, the Labor Department, and private organizations such as labor unions.[4] We undertook these interviews in order to ascertain whether we were missing significant activity that might have been apparent to those involved in the policy process but invisible to outsiders.

There was virtual unanimity among those with whom we spoke that

[3]During the 1970s, although the amount of activity by blacks had diminished substantially (or, at least, had faded from the *New York Times*), blacks still tended to appear more frequently than did the unemployed. There were 4, 7, and 1 black demonstrations in 1974, 1975, and 1976 respectively and 14, 8, and 9 organized acts in those years.

[4]These interviews will be discussed more fully in the Epilogue, where we consider the policy role of organizations *for* the unemployed rather than *of* the unemployed.

Table 10-3 Organized activity by the unemployed, 1974-1976, and by blacks, 1964-1966.

Organized activity	Number of demonstrations	Number of other organized acts
By the unemployed		
1974	1	7
1975	3	9
1976	1	8
By blacks		
1964	59	8
1965	98	31
1966	70	41

SOURCE: *New York Times Index.*

our conclusion about the political quiescence of the unemployed was warranted. Regardless of the perspective of the informant—leaders of organizations involved in mobilizing the unemployed, government officials, a media observer—the situation looked the same: the unemployed are not an active force. They are, in the words of one government official, "a political zero." Perhaps the most telling indication of the lack of activity on the part of the unemployed themselves came in an interview with a Senate staff member who had been closely involved with the Humphrey-Hawkins full-employment bill, the Comprehensive Employment Training Act (CETA), and other manpower legislation. He described the groups that took part: unions, civil rights groups, and the like. With remarkable grasp of detail he expounded on the nuances of difference among the organizations and discussed the personalities involved. When asked about groups with a grass-roots unemployed membership, however, he replied that there were "not really any I can think of." He then went on to qualify the answer: "Yes, there were perhaps some groups." One was from Chicago but he could not remember the name; the other was in "Philadelphia, or maybe Jersey."

In the course of these interviews many explanations for the quiescence of the unemployed were volunteered. Most were familiar: there is no need for political activity, given the availability of unemployment compensation; many of the jobless—especially among the structurally unemployed—lack education, political skills, and resources; many of the unemployed, especially among young blacks, expect little from the government and therefore have little motivation to be politically active; the unemployed are dispersed geographically. Several of our informants focused on the difficulty of finding indigenous leadership within the unemployed: anyone with sufficient leadership skills would be devoting his talents to finding work, probably with success. One activist who had spent time trying to organize the unemployed emphasized the absence of symbols associated with joblessness. "There is prejudice against the unemployed," he said, "so you can't run a demonstration where unemployed workers get up and say 'I'm out of work and I'm proud.' " This theme was echoed by a union official who said that the unemployed are ashamed of their condition. Drawing an analogy with the gay liberation movement, he asserted that if the unemployed are to be effective, they will have to "come out of the closet." Furthermore, he continued, unemployment is debilitating. Citing the rumbles of political dissent among the unemployed during the thirties, he indicated that such political stirrings were aberrant. "There was 25 percent unemployment, but most just sat around when out of work." Things are not much different today.

Of course, there are organizations that do attempt to mobilize the unemployed. For example, some unions with a large number of members who are out of work—the United Auto Workers, a few of the construction unions—have attempted to bring jobless members to Washington to protest. However, these efforts have met with little response from the unemployed. The officials at the AFL-CIO who organized a jobs rally in the summer of 1976 and Full Employment Week the following year reported little participation by the jobless themselves. Furthermore, such efforts seem to be undertaken by a relatively small number of unions and to be one-shot affairs rather than ongoing attempts at political mobilization. By and large, union activity with respect to unemployment—which, as we shall see in the Epilogue, is indeed considerable—tends to be undertaken on behalf of rather than by the unemployed. Labor unions spend little time attempting to organize those without jobs.

Much the same can be said of the Full Employment Action Council (FEAC). It is one of few organizations whose main concern is the reduction of unemployment. It engages in such activities as lobbying for the passage of the Humphrey-Hawkins bill and tries to coordinate efforts to influence manpower policy. Its efforts to organize the unemployed have met with little success. As one of its officials told us: "This is the only movement in which I've been involved in which the victims themselves have not been involved . . . I know something about organizing and I know that organizing the unemployed has got to be the most difficult task there is." It, then, is not an organization with a grass-roots membership of the unemployed. Rather, it is an organization for the unemployed. It is a coalition of groups dedicated to full employment:

unions, civil rights groups, feminist groups, church groups, and other organizations with social welfare and social justice concerns. Each of these organizations, albeit committed to the goal of full employment, has as its main concern and priority another issue more central to its purpose.

Group Consciousness and Political Activity

It is sometimes said that organization and ideology are the weapons of the weak. We have just seen that the unemployed have few organizational weapons to use in political conflict. What about ideology—sets of political beliefs that could act as a catalyst for political activity? Although it is commonly assumed that group consciousness facilitates group mobilization, and although consciousness raising figures importantly in the strategies of those who attempt to organize the disadvantaged for politics, the proposition that consciousness begets activity has rarely been tested.[5]

Our data permit us to assess the effects of consciousness on participation. To do so, we must shift our focus once more from joblessness to social class as our measure of economic position. We do this for several reasons. First, because class disadvantage is ongoing rather than short-term, it makes more sense to expect consciousness to develop around class position than around joblessness. Furthermore, we have found no evidence of jobless consciousness among the unemployed. Perhaps it is our failing for not having measured it, but even in our follow-up inter-

[5]There are, however, some empirical assessments of this proposition. Verba and Nie test the hypothesis that group consciousness can raise activity levels beyond what would have been expected on the basis of socioeconomic status alone. They find that blacks in America—and to a lesser extent Harijans, the former untouchables in India —who are group conscious are indeed more participant that would have been predicted on the basis of their socioeconomic characteristics. Although the findings do confirm the logic of the group consciousness model, they deal with ascriptive characteristics—race and caste—rather than economic position. Verba and Nie do mention in passing (p. 253) that there is no analogous group consciousness among lower-status whites which has the mobilization effect that race consciousness has for blacks. See Verba and Nie, *Participation in America*, chap. 10; and Verba, Bashiruddin Ahmed, Anil Bhatt, *Caste, Race and Politics: A Comparison of India and the United States* (Beverly Hills, Calif.: Sage Publications, 1972), chaps. 9-10.

Arthur H. Miller, Patricia Gurin, and Gerald Gurin use data from the 1976 election survey conducted by the Center for Political Studies at the University of Michigan to assess the effects of group identification on participation. Although the relationships they uncover are quite complex (they find that ideology is related to participation for several disadvantaged groups—the poor, blacks, and women), they do not consider the question with reference to workers and working-class consciousness. See their "Electoral Implications of Group Identification and Consciousness: The Reintroduction of a Concept," paper presented at the Annual Meeting of the American Political Science Association, New York, September 1978, pp. 44-48.

views we found little evidence that the unemployed identify as such and have a politically potent sense of kinship with others who are out of work. Finally, even though we have found relatively little evidence of it, class consciousness has figured so importantly in discussions of the politics of economic position for over a century that it seems reasonable to focus upon its catalytic potential. Therefore, in looking at the impact of ideas on the mobilization of the economically disadvantaged, we focus on class position and class consciousness.

In terms of the various aspects of class consciousness delineated previously, it is plausible to expect that each of them would be positively related to political participation: that those who identify with the working class, who see the interests of workers and management as being in opposition, and who think that workers should stick together, would be more active. If one of these aspects had to be singled out for particular potency, worker solidarity would seem the logical choice. Table 10-4 presents data on the levels of political participation among blue-collar workers who are and are not class conscious. The data do not conform to these expectations in the least. In no case is there a strong positive relationship between class consciousness and political participation and in only one case, perceiving class conflict, is there even a weak positive relationship. With respect to open-ended class self-identification and believing that workers should stick together—the one variable for which the strongest positive relationship was expected—the relationship between class consciousness and participation is actually negative.[6] The

[6]The figures for closed-ended class self-identification are remarkably similar to those for open-ended class self-identification:

Activity	Self-identification as —	
	Working class	Middle class
Participation		
High	12%	15%
Medium	30	36
Low	58	49
	100%	100%
		Gamma −.17
Organizational membership		
Yes	26	32
No	74	68
	100%	100%
		Gamma −.15

Table 10-4 Political participation, by class consciousness (blue-collar workers only).

Degree of participation	Identity[a]		Conflict		Solidarity	
	Working class	Middle class	Class interests opposed	Class interests the same	Workers stick together	Get ahead on own
High	8%	15%	19%	13%	11%	17%
Medium	32	35	34	38	31	44
Low	60	50	47	49	58	39
	100%	100%	100%	100%	100%	100%
Gamma	−.20		.08		−.32	

[a]Open-ended class self-identification question.

strongest single relationship, ironically, is the negative one between solidarity and the participation scale. Those who think workers should stick
together are actually less active than those who have a more individualistic approach.

It may be that we are being too simplistic. It may be that for consciousness to have participatory effects a combination of attitudes must be
present: a subjective sense of membership in a group must be combined
with a sense that the group is in conflict with other groups and that joint
activity is necessary. That is, consciousness can have political effects
only when subjective identity is reinforced by an understanding of how
the world works.[7]

We test this proposition with reference to social class in Figure 10-7. In
Figure 10-7A we compare blue-collar workers who are class conscious—
whose working-class identification is linked to a sense that workers
should stick together—with those who are not—whose middle-class
identification is reinforced by a belief that workers should get ahead on
their own. In 10-7B we substitute for the measure of solidarity the perception of class conflict in differentiating workers who are and are not
class conscious. In the final section we compare the fully class conscious,
who identify with the working class, believe in worker solidarity, and
perceive class conflict, with their opposite numbers, those who are middle-class identifiers and neither believe in worker solidarity nor perceive
class conflict.[8] In no case are those who are class conscious more active
than those who are not. In the lower two sections of the figure we find
that conscious workers are as likely to be in the most active category and
more likely to be in the least active.[9]

We can use data from the 1976 election survey carried out by the Center for Political Studies at the University of Michigan to make an addi-

[7]We are indebted to Miller, Gurin, and Gurin for this suggestion ("Electoral Implications of Group Identification," pp. 44-48).

[8]In order to have sufficient cases for analysis, we were forced to use the closed-
ended measure of class self-identification for this figure. However, we did run the data
using responses to the open-ended question. Although in some instances there were
very few cases, the results were unchanged.

[9]We were interested to see whether class consciousness works interactively with
joblessness in influencing participation; that is, whether unemployed workers who are
class conscious are especially likely to be politically active. Although there were too
few cases of jobless workers who identify with the working class and who espouse
other class-conscious positions to do a full analysis, the results of a bivariate analysis
indicate no significant differences between the patterns of participation for working
and for jobless blue-collar workers. This analysis is confirmed by a log-linear analysis
in which employment status is controlled. The only significant effect is the negative
effect of belief in class solidarity on participation.

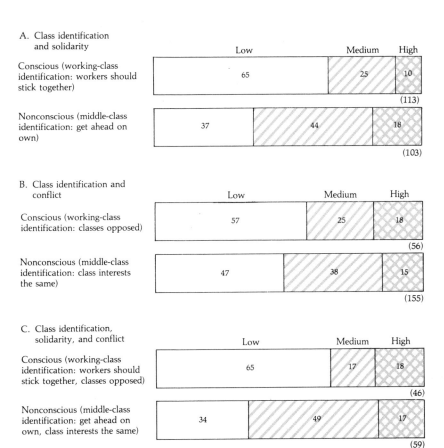

Figure 10-7 Political participation, by class consciousness (blue-collar workers).

tional test of whether class consciousness is a mobilizing force. Respondents were asked whether they felt close to members of a wide variety of groups, and then asked to select the group to which they felt closest. This measure of closeness to groups approximates the measure of class identification we have been using. It should be noted that the question is closed-ended; all respondents have some kind of identification—whether it be with a religious, age, race, sex, ideological, or class grouping. Furthermore, respondents were asked whether they felt close to "working-men" rather than to the "working class."

Figure 10-8A presents data on the average number of political activities (out of a possible seventeen national, local, and electoral activities) undertaken by blue-collar workers who identify with workingmen as op-

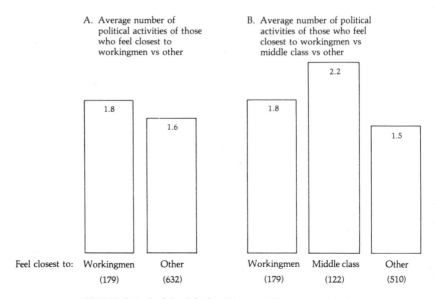

SOURCE: Center for Political Studies, University of Michigan, 1976 election survey.

Figure 10-8   Political participation, by group identity (blue-collar workers).

posed to other groups. For the first time a measure of class consciousness seems to predict political participation. Although the difference is not large, the 22 percent of blue-collar workers who feel closest to workingmen are more active than other blue-collar workers: the average score for those who feel closest to workingmen is 1.8, for other blue-collar workers 1.6.

However, when in Figure 10-8B those who feel closest to the middle class are separated out from the "other" group, the pattern changes. These individuals have an average score of 2.2 and are clearly the most active of the blue-collar groups. When this group—15 percent of all blue-collar respondents—is taken out, the participation score of blue-collar workers who identify with other groups drops to 1.5.

From our previous logic we would not expect group identity alone to have political potency. We have proposed that only when subjective identity is coupled with a sense that the group with which identification is made is somehow deprived, would consciousness have the effect of enhancing activity. In Figure 10-9 we carry our analysis one step further, combining the measure of group identification with a measure of the perceived power of various class groups. What is immediately clear is that blue-collar workers who select the middle class as the group to which they feel closest score higher on the scale of participatory acts than those

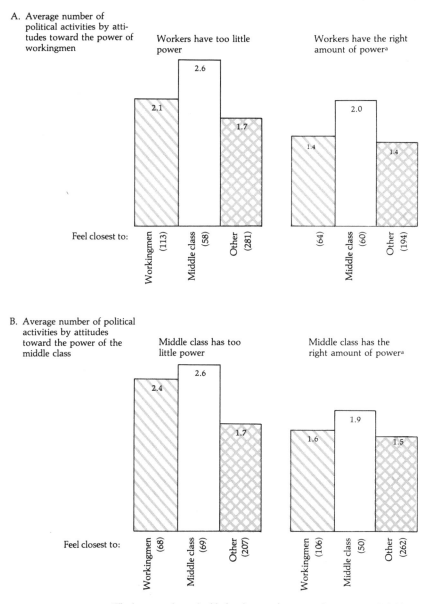

A. Average number of political activities by attitudes toward the power of workingmen

Workers have too little power

Workers have the right amount of power[a]

Feel closest to:

Workingmen (113) 2.1
Middle class (58) 2.6
Other (281) 1.7

(64) 1.4
Middle class (60) 2.0
Other (194) 1.4

B. Average number of political activities by attitudes toward the power of the middle class

Middle class has too little power

Middle class has the right amount of power[a]

Feel closest to:

Workingmen (68) 2.4
Middle class (69) 2.6
Other (207) 1.7

Workingmen (106) 1.6
Middle class (50) 1.9
Other (262) 1.5

[a]The few respondents who felt that the group has too much power are included here.

Figure 10-9 Political participation, by closeness to class groups and perception of class power (blue-collar workers).

who identify either with workingmen or with other groups—regardless of their views on the power of workingmen. It is particularly interesting to compare the fully class-conscious blue-collar workers, who feel closest to workingmen and believe that workers have too little power, with those who feel closest to the middle class and think that workingmen have the right amount or too much power. Their participation scores are nearly identical, 2.1 and 2.0 respectively.

Figure 10-9A does seem to indicate, however, that belief that working-men have too little power is associated with enhanced political activity. Within each category of group identification those who believe that workingmen have too little power are more active than those who be-lieve that workingmen have the right amount or too much power. How-ever, when in Figure 10-9B we combine group identification with beliefs about the power of the middle class, we see that blue-collar workers who believe that the middle class has too little power are more active than their counterparts who feel that the middle class has enough power. Ap-parently it is the perception that power is misallocated—that either the working class *or* the middle class has too little power—that is associated with enhanced political activity. A more class-specific sense of the politi-cally deprived state of the working class has no more impact than a sense that the middle class is politically disadvantaged.

Race Consciousness and Participation

Others who have considered the problem of the consequences for par-ticipation of group ideologies among the disadvantaged have found that group-conscious members of disadvantaged groups, especially blacks, are indeed more active.[10] Our findings seem to contradict theirs. At least insofar as blue-collar workers are concerned, we have found no evidence that the appropriate group-based ideology, class consciousness, is asso-ciated with higher levels of political activity. One possible explanation for the discrepancy is that, at least at this point in American history, the economic disadvantage associated with class position, and the attendant group-based ideology, function differently in individual citizen politics than do other kinds of disadvantage.

Although we can hardly engage in an encompassing comparison be-tween class-conscious workers and group-conscious members of other disadvantaged groups, we can make some comparisons between workers and blacks in terms of the participatory potency of their respective group-based ideologies. Table 10-5 gives data on the levels of participa-tion among race-conscious blacks, as measured by responses to two

[10]See note 5 above.

Table 10-5   Political participation, by race consciousness (blacks only).

	CONFLICT		SOLIDARITY	
Degree of participation	Racial interests opposed	Racial interests the same	Blacks stick together	Get ahead on own
High	10%	22%	15%	22%
Medium	24	28	29	15
Low	65	50	56	63
	99%	100%	100%	100%
Gamma		−.33		.06

items—discussed in Chapter 7—that are analogous to the questions about class conflict and class solidarity. The first question asks whether the interests of blacks and whites are fundamentally the same or different; the second, whether blacks who wish to get ahead should stick together with other blacks or should work on their own. It is clear from Table 10-5 that race consciousness—at least as defined by seeing the interests of the races as being fundamentally opposed and thinking that blacks should stick together—does not enhance participation among blacks. As a matter of fact, blacks who perceive race conflict are actually less active than those who do not.

We can, however, take the analysis one step further, reintroducing the proposition that it is the interaction of subjective identification and feeling of group deprivation that is potent for participation. Our questionnaire contained no open-ended question on racial identification, because such an item would have measured objective race rather than subjective closeness to blacks. Thus, for a measure of group identification among blacks we turn once again to the data from the University of Michigan 1976 election survey. Blacks who feel closest to blacks—29 percent of all black respondents—are clearly more active than those who identify with other groups. The average score on the participation scale for blacks who feel closest to other blacks is 2.3, for all other blacks 1.2. Figure 10-10 sums up the difference between race and class. We add attitudes toward group power to the sense of group identity and make comparisons between race and class consciousness. It is clear that blacks who are fully race conscious—who feel closest to blacks and who think that blacks

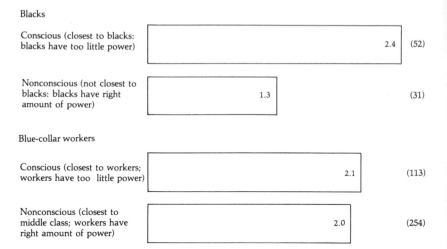

Figure 10-10 Political participation (average number of activities), by class and race consciousness.

have too little power—are considerably more active than those who are not. The average number of activities for the fully race-conscious blacks is 2.4, for those who are not race conscious—who do not feel closest to blacks and who think blacks have enough power—1.3.[11] The situation is, as we have seen, quite different for blue-collar workers. As shown at the bottom of Figure 10-10 there is virtually no difference between workers who are class conscious and those who are not.

Conclusion

Once again our expectations with respect to class and class consciousness have been confounded. Over and over in previous chapters we have found that connections we expected—between class and class consciousness, between class and attitudes, between consciousness and attitudes—are not made. To this litany we add the finding that, contrary to our expectations, class consciousness does not seem to foster participation. However, we should not casually discredit the hypothesis that group consciousness enhances participation. The comparative data for blacks make clear that, at least for blacks, the proposition that consciousness

[11]For reasons we do not understand, among blacks who do not identify with other blacks, those who think that blacks have too little power are less active than those who think that blacks have enough power. Among blacks who feel closest to other blacks, the opposite is true: those who feel that blacks have too little power are more participant than those who feel that blacks have the right amount or too much power.

begets activity seems to hold. As at so many other junctures, we find that class politics in contemporary America is somehow special.

In concluding, we should point out two different sets of contrasts. First, we can compare the politics of race with the politics of economic position with reference to the degree to which organization and ideology function as political resources for participation. Both group organization and group consciousness are more formidable resources for activity in the hands of those who are disadvantaged by their race than in the hands of those disadvantaged by their economic position. Furthermore, we can contrast organization and ideology in terms of the way in which they fail to function as resources for political activity among the economically disadvantaged. On the matter of organization as a group-based resource, organizational membership functions as we expected it to: among the unemployed, the few who are organization members are indeed more politically active; it is just that there are not very many of them. In other words, organizational membership works as predicted, but there is not very much of it. The situation is quite different with respect to ideology. There are very few class-conscious blue-collar workers, and even those few are not more politically active. Thus, not only is the level of consciousness low, but ideology does not function as predicted, at least for blue-collar workers.

The story we have told in the last several chapters is a story in which expected connections on the path to political mobilization have not been made. It is clear that neither the unemployed nor blue-collar workers are mobilized politically in the sense we originally described. However, it should not, on this basis, be assumed that economic issues are irrelevant for American politics. On the contrary, they are crucial both in the electoral system and in the pressure system. It is to the consideration of these matters that we now turn.

CHAPTER 11

Unemployment and Electoral Politics: Some Considerations

C ITIZENS IN American democracy who wish to express their political preferences have two fundamental sorts of options. They can operate within the context of the pressure system: alone, or in concert with others, they can undertake the kinds of participatory acts we have just considered and communicate their feelings and wishes directly, in the hopes that either persuasion or pressure will elicit a favorable response from political leaders. The ultimate resource of the American citizen, however, is the electoral system. It is through periodic elections that citizens are given an opportunity to translate their collective preferences into binding decisions about who shall hold office. Although when a citizen casts his ballot, he communicates little precise information about the factors that influence his decision, voting choices are critical to the process of linkage between citizens and leaders in American democracy: voting is the only political act undertaken by a majority of citizens and, with few exceptions, electoral decisions are the only binding political decisions actually made by citizens themselves.

If unemployment—or economic strain more generally—is to have an effect on the political process, we would expect it to be felt in the arena of electoral politics. The issues of American politics are constantly changing. Some—like prohibition or Freemasonry—incite brief passions and then dissolve into permanent oblivion. Others—such as relations between the races—are perennial, changing in their salience depending upon competing issues and preoccupations, but never absent for long from the political agenda. Because cycles of prosperity and recession seem endemic to American economic life and because such cycles impinge on the personal lives of so many Americans, the health of the economy is an enduring political issue. It is the common wisdom that Americans vote their pocketbooks, a wisdom to which political campaigners—ever attentive to changes in economic indicators—subscribe.[1]

In this chapter and the next we seek to test that common wisdom in a limited way, in an attempt to understand whether economic downturns have an impact upon electoral decisions and outcomes and to specify in what way the effect takes place.

Macroeconomic Performance and the Electoral Process: Evidence from Aggregate Data

We are not the first students of politics to inquire whether the performance of the economy has an impact on voting. Recently a number of scholars have attempted to measure the short-term impact of macroeconomic conditions on the vote by means of aggregate data. Our goal is somewhat different from theirs: we are interested in learning where such effects come from, rather than in giving a precise estimate over time of their size. Still, the findings of these other studies are so clearly relevant to our concerns that they deserve attention.

The focus of the aggregate studies has been on several questions: whether changes in the state of the economy affect election results; whether political incumbents are rewarded for good times or simply punished for bad ones; whether Republicans are especially susceptible to electoral punishment in times of economic downturn or whether the two major parties are equally vulnerable; and whether effects are felt in both congressional and presidential elections. The results of these studies are by no means unambiguous. Rather, they seem quite sensitive to the indicators used: whether macroeconomic performance is measured by rate of unemployment, rate of inflation, or changes in real income; whether the effects are presumed to be immediate or delayed; whether the relevant political dependent variable is voter turnout, Democratic share of the two-party vote, or presidential popularity.

Early work by Gerald Kramer appeared to show that changes in real income affected the outcome of congressional elections: an increase in income helped the incumbent party, a decline hurt. Others, however, have called these results into question. George Stigler uses a measure of

---

[1]Edward R. Tufte, in *Political Control of the Economy* (Princeton, N.J.: Princeton University Press, 1978), makes the point that those in Washington with partisan political concerns—party leaders, presidential advisers, members of the Council of Economic Advisers—make the assumption that voters respond to the economic environment when they cast their ballots.

the average economic conditions for two years before the election (rather than the single year used by Kramer) and finds little systematic effect. Arcelus and Meltzer also obtain negative results: they find that change in real income has little effect on the direction of the vote, although it has some impact on turnout.[2]

Most of the other work that has followed that of Kramer, however, supports his conclusion that economic conditions influence electoral outcomes. Bloom and Price, for example, find that voters are sensitive to changes in real income in the year preceding the election, but not to earlier economic conditions—which explains the discrepancy between Stigler's findings and those of other investigators. More important, they find a clear asymmetry. Voters are sensitive to downturns in the economy but not to improvements, punishing incumbents for sluggish times, but not rewarding them for prosperous ones. Tufte uses change in real disposable income as his indicator of economic performance: he finds that an increase in the growth of real per capita income is associated with an increase in the vote for the incumbent president as well as for the congressional candidates of the president's party.[3]

With respect to the impact on voting of the unemployment rate, the evidence is mixed. Neither Tufte nor Bloom and Price consider unemployment per se. Arcelus and Meltzer find that the rate of unemployment has little systematic effect either on turnout or on the direction of the vote. On the other hand, Lepper reports that unemployment has an anti-incumbent effect. Furthermore, Goodman and Kramer find some evidence—although it is by no means unequivocal—that the rate of unemployment has an effect on congressional voting that is favorable to the Democrats. The effect is enhanced if there is a Republican administration in office. They estimate that a 10-percent unemployment rate during a Republican administration would decrease the Republican share of the vote by about 3 percent of the votes cast.[4]

[2]Gerald H. Kramer, "Short-term Fluctuations in U.S. Voting Behavior, 1896-1964," American Political Science Review, 65 (March 1971), 131-143; George J. Stigler, "General Economic Conditions and National Elections," American Economic Review, 63 (May 1973), 160-167; Francis Arcelus and Allan H. Meltzer, "The Effect of Aggregate Economic Variables on Congressional Elections," American Political Science Review, 69 (December 1975), 1232-1269.

[3]Howard S. Bloom and H. Douglas Price, "Voter Response to Short-run Economic Conditions: The Asymmetric Effect of Prosperity and Recession," American Political Science Review, 69 (December 1975), 1240-1254; Political Control of the Economy, pp. 119, 121-122. The results presented by Tufte for presidential elections are similar to those in Ray C. Fair, "The Effect of Economic Events on Votes for President" (New Haven: Cowles Foundation, 1976).

[4]See the works cited in notes 2 and 3 above, as well as Susan J. Lepper, "Voting Behavior and Aggregate Policy Targets," Public Choice, 18 (1974), 67-81; and Saul

In summary, despite some discrepancies and ambiguities, the studies of the effects of economic conditions on congressional and presidential elections suggest that incumbents are punished for economic slowdowns, but not necessarily rewarded for prosperity, and that Republican incumbents may be more vulnerable to such electoral penalties than Democratic incumbents.[5]

It is not our purpose to give a detailed exposition and critique of the growing number of scholarly attempts to assess the political effects of macroeconomic changes, for these studies ask a somewhat different question than the one we are addressing. They aim at a more finely tuned estimate of the size of the electoral effects than we shall be able to give. But because so many of these studies are based on aggregate data, they do not permit delineation of the sources of any impact that is found. We are interested to know in particular whether it is those citizens whose lives have been directly affected by changing economic conditions who are responsible for a specific political change. If, for example, a decline in real income or an increase in the unemployment rate results in a reduction of the vote for the incumbent party, is the reduction a function of

---

Goodman and Gerald H. Kramer, "Comment on Arcelus and Meltzer, 'The Effect of Aggregate Economic Variables on Congressional Elections,' " *American Political Science Review*, 69 (December 1975), 1263.

[5]Several studies have focused on a different political dependent variable. Using the monthly public evaluation of presidential performance contained in the Gallup poll, they consider whether changing economic conditions have an effect on presidential popularity. As with the studies of voting, however, these analyses have been criticized on methodological grounds. And as with the studies of voting, there are discrepancies among the results. Mueller, for example, finds a distinct relationship between unemployment rate and presidential popularity, presidential popularity declining 3 percent for each 1-percent increase in the jobless rate over that prevailing at the beginning of the president's term. Stimson, on the other hand, finds little association between economic change and presidential popularity; he attributes decline in presidential popularity to a general pattern of disillusionment following raised expectations. In a study that takes into account the specific personal characteristics of each president as well as the depreciation of support over time, Schneider concludes that both unemployment and inflation lead to decreases in presidential popularity, the former having a somewhat larger effect. If unemployment increases by 1 percent, he estimates, popularity falls by 4 percent; a corresponding increase in inflation would result in a decline of 2 percent. See John Mueller, "Presidential Popularity from Truman to Johnson," *American Political Science Review*, 64 (1970), 18-34; James A. Stimson, "Public Support for American Presidents: A Cyclical Model," *Public Opinion Quarterly*, 40 (1976),1-21; and Friedrich Schneider, "Presidential Popularity Functions of Different Classes: A Theoretical and Empirical Approach," unpublished manuscript, undated. For a critique of the methods used in these studies, see Douglas A. Hibbs, "Economic Interest and the Politics of Macro-Economic Spending" (Cambridge, Mass.: Center for International Studies, MIT, 1975).

changes in the votes of those who have lost income or jobs, or is it a function of dissatisfaction on the part of those who are simply unhappy with the performance of the incumbents, even though they may not themselves have suffered? In addition, the aggregate studies do not allow us to isolate the role that crucial political attitudes play in mediating the effects of economic conditions on the vote: attitudes such as long-term partisan identification, evaluations of the parties or the candidates, and opinions about the proper role of the government in dealing with economic issues. Finally, the aggregate studies do not permit us to disentangle negative reactions of voters to the incumbent president from negative reactions to the incumbent party. If the public punishes those in power for economic failure, whom do they select for such punishment? Survey data on individuals are more appropriate for these questions.[6]

In the following analysis we use such data to illumine some of these questions without totally resolving them. We can look at the individual characteristics of voters in a way those who use aggregate data cannot, and we can draw conclusions about the sources of political changes; yet there are important limitations. The critical shortcoming of our particular data is that we are limited to a single election, the election of 1976. Other public opinion studies make it possible to examine the role of economic issues in other elections; however, only our 1976 study has suffi-

[6]Recent works that use survey data are Morris P. Fiorina, "Economic Retrospective Voting in American National Elections," *American Journal of Political Science,* 22 (May 1978), 427-443; M. Stephen Weatherford, "Economic Conditions and Electoral Outcomes: Class Differences in Political Response to Recession," *American Journal of Political Science,* 22 (November 1978):917-938; Donald R. Kinder and D. Roderick Kiewiet, "Economic Discontent and Political Behavior: The Role of Personal Grievances and Collective Economic Judgments in Congressional Voting," *American Journal of Political Science* (in press); and Kiewiet and Kinder, "Political Consequences of Economic Concerns," paper delivered at the Annual Meeting of the American Political Science Association, New York, September 1978.

Fiorina uses as his measure of personal economic strain a retrospective question that asks the respondent whether his economic situation has improved, stayed the same, or gotten worse in the recent past. He finds that a perception of worsening circumstances has an effect on vote both for the incumbent president and for candidates for Congress who run on the ticket with him, but no effect on congressional voting in off-year elections.

Weatherford uses the Michigan Survey Research Center's 1956-1960 panel study. He finds that changes in individual income have an effect on the vote, an effect that is greater for working-class than for middle-class respondents.

Kinder and Kiewiet consider the effects of personal experience with unemployment (measured by family exposure to unemployment or mention of unemployment as a personal problem) on congressional voting. Their results—that personal exposure to unemployment is less important in relation to voting than attitudes about unemployment—parallel our own and we shall return to them in the next chapter.

cient numbers of respondents who were out of work to permit analyzing them as a separate group.

Although our metropolitan work force survey has the advantage of an unusually large number of jobless respondents, its utility in examining the electoral effects of economic changes is severely limited. Our study was conducted in March and April of 1976, an unfortunate time from the point of view of understanding the election the following November. At that time the parade of primary contests was passing quickly and neither party had even so much as a front-runner, much less a definitive presidential nominee, and among the Democrats at least, there were still several serious contenders. Clearly, we could not expect to ask about November vote intentions, so we settled for asking respondents about the likelihood that they would vote for each of various candidates if he were nominated.

Because of these shortcomings of our data, we shall supplement them with data from the 1976 election study by the University of Michigan's Center for Political Studies (CPS). Although the relatively small number of unemployed respondents limits the extensiveness of the analysis we can undertake, the Michigan data do allow us to deal with some issues for which our own data are inadequate, especially with the voting decision itself. The fact that we have the two studies allows us to use the Michigan study more effectively, for we can check whether certain expectations about the unemployed that would be based on our somewhat larger sample are violated in the Michigan group.[7]

Before embarking on our analysis, we should pause for a brief digression into the vocabulary of voting research. For readers who are unfamiliar with the terminology and concepts involved, we provide the following brief introduction; those who are acquainted with this material may wish to move on to the next section.

A Primer of Voting Research

Students of the electoral process have developed an arsenal of terms and concepts to describe regularities in citizen behavior.[8] Among the most important of these is the notion of *partisan identification*. The majority of Americans have a long-term and relatively stable psychological

[7]The unusually large sample size of the 1976 Michigan election survey and the high unemployment rate in that year yielded 170 jobless respondents.

[8]The literature in which these concepts are defined, explored, and—more recently —criticized is vast. As an introduction, we refer the reader to the following: Angus Campbell, Philip E. Converse, Warren E. Miller, and Donald E. Stokes, *The Ameri-*

attachment to or identification with one of the two major parties. They think of themselves as Republicans or as Democrats. These partisan identifications are relatively impermeable to changes in an individual's life situation. For example, the proverbial blue-collar Democrat is relatively unlikely to change his party identification and think of himself as a Republican after realizing his dream of moving his family from the apartment in the city to the ranch house in the suburbs. Of course, in spite of the general stability of partisan identifications, there are individuals who make a change at some point in the life cycle: Republicans become Democrats and vice versa; partisans become Independents.

Students of voting behavior measure the strength and direction of these partisan attachments in public opinion surveys. The respondent is asked a question like the following: "Generally speaking, do you think of yourself as a Republican, a Democrat, an Independent, or what?" If the respondent indicates a partisan preference, he is then asked whether he is a strong or weak partisan. If he indicates that he is an Independent, he is asked whether he feels closer to the Republicans or the Democrats. On the basis of responses to these questions in the CPS election survey of November 1976, the partisan identifications of the American public can be arrayed as follows:[9]

Strong Democrats	15%
Weak Democrats	25
Independent Democrats	12
Independents	15
Independent Republicans	10
Weak Republicans	14
Strong Republicans	9
	100%

can Voter (New York: John Wiley and Sons, 1960), and their Elections and the Political Order (New York: John Wiley and Sons, 1964); Norman Nie, Sidney Verba, and John Petrocik, The Changing American Voter (Cambridge, Mass.: Harvard University Press, 1976); Richard Boyd, "Popular Control of Public Policy: A Normal Vote Analysis of the 1968 Election," American Political Science Review, 66 (June 1972), 429-449; Richard G. Niemi and Herbert F. Weisberg, eds., Controversies in American Voting Behavior (San Francisco: W. H. Freeman and Co., 1976).

[9]Only 1 percent of those contacted in the 1976 Michigan survey had difficulty accommodating their political preferences to these choices, either because they identified with another party group such as the Socialist Workers, or because they were utterly apolitical.

A citizen's underlying partisan identification predisposes him to support his party's candidates in the polling booth. In any single election, however, compelling issues and/or strong personalities can act as short-term forces influencing partisans to defect from their normal party loyalties and support candidates of the opposite party. In 1956, for example, many Democrats responded to the appeal of Eisenhower's personality and cast Republican ballots for the presidency. These Democrats did not become Republicans; they defected temporarily and returned to the partisan fold in 1960 to vote for Kennedy. Analogously, responding to issues like civil rights and Goldwater's conservatism, many habitual Republicans voted for Johnson in 1964.

From the summary figures below, it is evident that such defections are quite common, especially among weak partisans and Independent leaners. Each entry is the average proportion of voters from 1952 to 1972 who cast a presidential ballot for a candidate representing a different party from the one with which they identified:[10]

Strong Democrats	13%
Weak Democrats	34%
Independent Democrats	31%
Independent Republicans	14%
Weak Republicans	16%
Strong Republicans	3%

As a practical matter, this tendency to defect means that neither party can count on garnering all the votes of its citizen identifiers, particularly the weak identifiers and leaners. Both parties, but especially the Democrats, must appeal to their own identifiers while at the same time pursuing Independents and those attached to the opposite party.

For any group in the electorate—or for the electorate as a whole—we can calculate an expected or normal vote. This normal vote represents a probabilistic estimate of the Democratic presidential vote for a given group based on the distribution of partisan loyalties among members of that group. Built into the calculation of the normal vote are the regularities we have already observed: that strong partisans are more loyal in their voting habits than weak ones and that Republicans are somewhat more loyal than Democrats. The normal vote thus represents the baseline

[10]Arthur H. Miller and Warren E. Miller, "Partisanship and Performance: 'Rational' Choice in the 1976 Presidential Election," paper presented at the Annual Meeting of the American Political Science Association, Washington, D.C., September 1977, p. 12.

vote we would anticipate on the basis of partisan identifications alone, in the absence of short-term forces—issue and candidate factors that may cause partisan defections in any given election.

Deviations from the normal or expected vote for a group in any specific election indicate the presence of short-term issue or candidate factors. As an example let us consider the votes of a group that is normally Democratic, the Catholics. In 1952, as usual, Catholics gave a majority of their votes—52 percent—to the Democratic presidential candidate. However, on the basis of their normal vote, they would have been expected to deliver 64 percent of their votes to the Democrats. Although they were still a Democratic group, they were less Democratic than expected, probably in response to the strong short-term force of the personal appeal of the Republican candidate, Dwight D. Eisenhower. By contrast, in 1960 Catholics were even more solidly Democratic than usual in response to John F. Kennedy. Their expected or normal vote that year was 68 percent Democratic; their actual vote was 83 percent Democratic.[11]

Thus, in analyzing the electoral behavior of any specific group in any given election, we are interested not only in learning for which candidates members of that group cast their ballots, but also in understanding whether that group was more Democratic or Republican than usual. With reference to the behavior of Catholic voters in 1952, it is probably more significant that they were less Democratic than might have been expected than that they gave a majority of their votes to the Democrats. Using these tools we can calculate expected or normal votes for various groups in the electorate and measure their relative vulnerability to the impact of the short-term forces of issues and candidates that surround a specific election.

Unemployment and Electoral Behavior: Some Distinctions

Having introduced the concepts upon which our analysis will be based, we should like to make several further distinctions in order to make clear the direction of our analysis. We shall want to discuss the nature of the *magnitude* of the effects of economic conditions upon political behavior; the *aspect* of electoral behavior that is affected; and the *source* of the effects.

---

[11]The figures are taken from Arthur H. Miller and Warren E. Miller, "Issues, Candidates, and Partisan Division in the 1972 American Presidential Election," *British Journal of Political Science*, 5 (1975), 393-434.

The Magnitude of the Effects

It is important to distinguish between the effect of economic conditions upon the political behavior of the *individual* and the *aggregate* impact of such conditions on the electoral system, for effects that are significant at the individual level may be quite small at the aggregate level. Some hypothetical examples should make this clear. If, for example, a large proportion of unemployed Republicans reject the party to which they were once attached and become Independents, the magnitude of the effects of economic strain at the individual level would be considerable. If, however, there are very few jobless Republicans—either because the unemployment rate is low or because those who are out of work are disproportionately Independent or Democratic in their partisan leanings—then the effect that is so significant at the individual level will have only a negligible effect upon the aggregate distribution of partisan identifications in the electorate. Alternatively, the experience of unemployment might increase significantly the probability of an individual's voting against the incumbent candidate or party. However, if the unemployed are already predisposed by their partisan identifications to vote against the incumbent, or if they do not bother to vote at all, then the aggregate effects of this process will be slight indeed. Thus, in assessing aggregate effects we need to be sensitive both to the significance of the impact at the individual level and to the number of individuals who are available to be affected.

The Aspect of Electoral Behavior

Unemployment could potentially have an effect on any or all of several aspects of electoral behavior. At the most general—and potentially most permanent—level, it could affect *partisan identifications* either by leading partisans to switch parties or to abandon their present party affiliations altogether to become Independents, or by forging new partisan ties where none previously existed. Also, it could have an impact on *participation* by leading to changes in turnout rates. Finally, unemployment could have an effect on *voting behavior* by causing some voters to vote differently from the way they would have if the economy had been different.

We have dealt already with the impact of unemployment on electoral turnout. As we demonstrated in the previous chapter, it is slight. The turnout rate of the unemployed is below that of the employed, but this is a function of their social characteristics, not the result of their joblessness. As we shall see, the impact that the political behavior of the unemployed has on electoral outcome (through the impact of unemployment on the direction of their vote) is moderated by the low turnout rate of the jobless.

In this and the following chapter we shall look at the other two ways in which unemployment can affect the electoral process—by influencing the party affiliation of voters or by influencing the voting decision itself.

THE SOURCE OF THE ELECTORAL EFFECTS

If we find that unemployment is linked to electoral behavior, then we wish to understand whether it is those who experience the economic strain of unemployment themselves or others, not themselves under such duress, whose behavior is most likely to be affected. We are interested in learning whether the electoral behavior of the members of these two groups is differentially responsive to economic change: whether those who have experienced economic strain themselves are distinctive in either the *aspect* of electoral behavior that is affected by such changes or in the *magnitude* of such effects. This question is quite obviously relevant to one of the central concerns of our book, the process by which individual economic strain affects political attitudes and behavior. Clearly, the political behavior of both groups—those personally affected and those not directly affected by changing economic conditions—could change in response to economic conditions. Voters might respond to bad news about the economy whether or not they themselves experienced any particular hardship. However, we would expect those who are themselves personally strained to be especially sensitive to economic conditions.

The Parties and the Economy: A Dime's Worth of Difference

Those worried about economic issues—whether in response to stress in their own lives or in response to more abstract concerns—can register their views in electoral politics only if the choices they are offered are meaningful. If the alternatives offered to the electorate by the parties or their candidates are indistinguishable, then it is impossible for voters to register their discontent. However, it is hardly a secret that if the parties and their identifiers differ on anything at all, they differ most systematically on economic matters.

The Public, the Parties, and the Economy—1976

If we wish to understand the role of economic issues in voting, we must begin with the public—whether voters are concerned about the health of the economy, whether they have preferences in terms of economic policies and approaches, and whether they see differences between the parties, or the candidates they offer, in terms of these matters. As the election of 1976 approached, there was virtual unanimity of concern among voters about unemployment. All but 6 percent of those polled in the University of Michigan survey said that unemployment was an important issue, and only 11 percent felt that the government was doing a good job of handling the issue. Given this near consensus, we might have been tempted to dismiss the issue altogether as a potential factor in the 1976 election. After all, what candidate would dare defy such a trend? And besides, how could any candidate conceivably declare himself to be in favor of unemployment?

Such sentiment, nevertheless, is clearly not without potential for electoral impact. If nothing else, pervasive concern and dissatisfaction with government performance are the raw materials from which retrospective rejections of incumbents are fabricated. Furthermore, the consensus holds only at the most general level. As we saw in Chapter 8, abstract concern about jobs is nearly universal; however, the consensus on the need to end unemployment vanishes as soon as the costs of so doing—for example, having the government hire everybody who is without a job—are enumerated. The Michigan data lend confirmation to this interpretation. In spite of the nearly universal agreement on the importance of unemployment, when respondents were asked to rank its importance relative to nine other issues, a plurality (44 percent) ranked inflation as a more important issue than unemployment.[12] Since we know that policies designed to reduce unemployment may be inflationary, the higher level of concern about inflation is further confirmation of the potential of the issue of unemployment to divide Americans.

If an issue is to have an electoral impact, however, it is not just voter opinion that is necessary. Voters must perceive differences between the parties, or the candidates they offer, either in terms of their relative managerial capacities to reduce joblessness or in terms of the alternative of the economic policies they offer. In 1976 the electorate did perceive such differences. With respect to the relative abilities of the parties, Americans traditionally have seen the Democrats as more competent in handling economic matters.[13] As shown in Table 11-1, the Democrats—and their presidential candidate, Jimmy Carter—were once again viewed by the public as being more capable of handling unemployment. By a margin of nearly four to one, those who saw a difference between the parties credited the Democrats with superior ability; by a somewhat smaller margin, two and a half to one, those who saw a difference between the candidates

[12]Twenty-eight percent ranked unemployment ahead of inflation; 27 percent ranked neither among the four most important issues.

[13]Campbell et al., *The American Voter*, chap. 3. The Republicans, on the other hand, are seen as being more capable in managing foreign affairs.

Table 11-1   Public perceptions of the positions of the parties and their presidential candidates on unemployment.

Which party would do a better job of dealing with unemployment?	
Democrats	33%
No difference	50
Republicans	9
Don't know/no answer	8
Which candidate would reduce unemployment?	
Carter	34%
No difference	38
Ford	13
˙Don't know/no answer	14
Perceived position of parties on government guarantee of jobs and standard of living:	
Democrats more favorable than Republicans	35%
No difference	26
Republicans more favorable than Democrats	5
Don't know/no answer	34
Perceived position of candidates on government guarantee of jobs and standard of living:	
Carter more favorable than Ford	31%
No difference	29
Ford more favorable than Carter	7
Don't know/no answer	33

source: Center for Political Studies, University of Michigan, 1976 election survey.

saw Carter as more likely to reduce unemployment.[14] It should be noted, however, that a bare majority of those questioned saw no difference or knew too little to respond.[15]

In terms of the unemployment *policies* offered by the competing parties and their candidates, a similar number of Americans perceived differences and there was similar agreement about what these differences were. When asked to place the candidates and the parties on a seven-point scale in terms of their presumed positions on the issue of a government policy of providing jobs and a decent standard of living for all (see

[14]Respondents were asked to agree or disagree on a seven-point scale whether Ford, and then Carter, "as president, would reduce unemployment." Respondents who gave the candidates identical ratings, or ratings that differed by only one point, were considered to see no difference between the candidates.

[15]The large number of respondents who saw no difference between the parties may have resulted in part from the way the question was asked. Respondents in the Michi-

Table 11-1), about 40 percent saw differences between the positions of the parties and the candidates.[16] Once more there was general agreement on the direction of the differences: by and large, respondents who saw party or candidate differences saw the Democrats, and their candidate, as more favorable to such a policy than the Republicans and their candidate.

We can view the difference perceived by the public from another perspective as well, not from the standpoint of how many people see differences between parties or candidates but from the standpoint of how far apart they are seen to be. Respondents were asked to place the parties and candidates on eight other scales involving a variety of domestic political issues, ranging from busing to legalization of marijuana to women's rights. Only on the issue of national health insurance did the public see the parties and candidates as being farther apart than on the issue of the job guarantee. On all the other issues the parties and candidates were perceived as being closer together than on the issue of the job and standard-of-living guarantee.[17] It is interesting to note that with respect to every issue, the Republicans were viewed as being to the right of the Democrats, and Ford was viewed as being to the right of Carter; furthermore, virtually without exception, the candidates were seen as being more centrist than their parties—Ford to the left of the Republicans, Carter to the right of the Democrats.

---

gan study were given the option of indicating that there was no difference between the parties in terms of their ability to handle unemployment. In our metropolitan work force survey, we asked the same question about which party would do a better job of handling unemployment, without specifying that there might be no difference. This version elicited the following results: Democrats, 41 percent; Republicans, 10 percent; no difference, 29 percent; don't know or no answer, 20 percent. When forced to make a choice, more respondents did indicate a preference for one of the parties; and without the option of "no difference," more said that they did not know. It is interesting to note, however, that the ratio of Democratic to Republican preferences is nearly the same as that elicited by the Michigan question, about four to one.

[16]Respondents were asked to place themselves, the candidates (Ford and Carter), and the parties (Republican and Democratic) on a seven-point scale with the following anchor points: (1) the government in Washington should see to it that every person has a job and a good standard of living to (7) the government should just let each person get ahead on his own. Identical rankings, or rankings that differed by one point, were considered as indicating no difference. Respondents who were unable to place themselves on this scale were not asked about the parties or candidates. Thus the number of "don't know's" may be overstated.

[17]The differences between the average scores on these seven-point scales for parties and candidates on the nine issues are as follows: (note continued on page 292)

Party Leaders and Economic Issues

A British humorist once described American politics to his countrymen as follows: "In America, there are two political parties. There is the Republican party, which is roughly equivalent to our Conservative party. And there is the Democratic party, which is roughly equivalent to our Conservative party." The American political parties are, indeed, broad conglomerates that gather under one banner politicians of widely divergent views and that appeal to heterogeneous publics. At election time the already blurry distinction between the parties is often made even more obscure as they compete for the votes of Independents as well as wavering supporters of the opposition party.

If the parties are truly so similar, are the differences on economic matters that the public perceives merely illusory? Although party positions on many issues have been indistinct, the differences on domestic economic issues are not trivial. The depression of the 1930s and the New Deal yielded a party system based upon competition between a Democratic coalition—made up of the urban work force, blacks and other ethnic minorities, Catholics, Jews, and the South—and a Republican coalition—business interests, white northern Protestants, and rural interests. The parties offered alternatives on the fundamental economic issues of the depression: the Democratic party staked out a position in favor of more governmental intervention in the economy and greater responsibility for the economic welfare of those citizens unable to provide for

	Difference between —	
Issue	Parties	Candidates
Government medical insurance plan	1.82	1.54
Goverment guarantee of jobs[a]	1.58	1.29
Change in tax rate	1.10	1.10
Aid to minorities	1.10	0.74
Handling of urban unrest	1.07	.97
Busing	0.63	.03
Rights of accused	.53	.19
Equal rights for women	.49	.14
Legalization of marijuana	.44	.13

[a]The item about the government job guarantees was asked in both the pre-election and post-election waves of the Michigan survey. Data reported here are from the pre-election wave. When the question was asked in the post-election survey, respondents saw even larger differences between the parties and candidates.

themselves; the Republicans held to a traditional position of opposition to government intervention.

The issue of unemployment is fundamental to these party differences on economics. For one thing, the crisis of the thirties around which the new party coalitions took shape was very much an employment crisis. Furthermore, unemployment engages the economic issues that divide the parties in two basically different ways: it involves both the proper extent of government intervention in managing macroeconomic performance and the degree to which the government should take responsibility for the welfare of those in need. No matter from what perspective the parties are considered—the attitudes of the party leaders, the positions taken by the parties in their platforms, the stands taken by presidential candidates, and the voting behavior of congressional partisans—they differ substantially on the issue of unemployment. As we shall see, the differences the public perceives are real differences.

PARTY LEADERS

Issue differences between the adherents of the two parties are more substantial at the level of party leadership than at the level of rank-and-file party support. This observation, made initially by Herbert McClosky and his associates in a study comparing delegates to the 1956 presidential conventions with their partisan supporters in the mass public, has been confirmed by various studies of more recent vintage.[18]

That these differences between the leaders of the parties are particularly sharp on domestic issues is confirmed by a study of the attitudes of party leaders (members of national committees plus a sample of county chairpersons) that was conducted at roughly the same time as our study of the urban work force. As shown in Table 11-2, 73 percent of the Democratic leaders, but only 9 percent of the Republicans, indicated that the government should guarantee a job to every American. Republican and Democratic leaders were equally distinctive in terms of the priority they place on ending unemployment. When asked to rank in importance ten goals for America, Democratic leaders placed reducing unemployment first, while Republican leaders ranked it sixth. In addition, when asked specifically about the trade-off between unemployment and inflation, ten times as many Democrats as Republicans (61 vs 6 percent) indicated that the government should concentrate on fighting unemployment rather

[18]Herbert McClosky, Paul J. Hoffmann, and Rosemary O'Hara, "Issue Conflict and Consensus among Party Leaders and Followers," *American Political Science Review*, 54 (June 1960), 406-427; Jeane Kirkpatrick, "Representation in the American National Conventions: The Case of 1972," *British Journal of Political Science*, 5 (July 1975), 265-322; Nie, Verba, and Petrocik, *The Changing American Voter*, chap. 12.

Table 11-2 Differences between Democratic and Republican party leaders on unemployment-related matters.

Area of difference	Democratic leaders	Republican leaders
Percent who say the government should guarantee a job for all	73	9
Percent who say the government should stress—		
Curbing inflation	12	80
Fighting unemployment	61	6
Both, even at the risk of accomplishing neither	27	14
Ranking of top national goals	(1) Reducing unemployment	(1) Curbing inflation
	(2) Curbing inflation	(2) Reducing the role of government
	(3) Protecting freedom of speech	(3) Maintaining a strong military defense
	(4) Developing energy resources	(4) Developing energy resources
	(5) Achieving equality for blacks	(5) Reducing crime
	(6) Reducing crime	(6) Reducing unemployment
	(7) Giving people more say in government decisions	(7) Protecting freedom of speech
	(8) Achieving equality for women	(8) Giving people more say in government decisions
	(9) Maintaining a strong military defense	(9) Achieving equality for blacks
	(10) Reducing the role of government	(10) Achieving equality for women

SOURCE: Survey conducted by the Center for International Affairs, Harvard University, and the *Washington Post*, 1976. Percentages are based on a sample of party leaders. (Number of cases: Democrats, 134; Republicans, 167.)

than curbing inflation. Attitudinal differences on the subject of unemployment between Democratic and Republican party leaders are quite clear.

PARTY PLATFORMS AND CAMPAIGN PROMISES

In their quadrennial platforms the parties differ in their treatment of the unemployment issue, both in terms of the emphasis they place upon it and in terms of the positions they take. In general, Democratic platforms pay more attention to unemployment and deal with it more directly, usually suggesting both macroeconomic policies designed to stimulate the economy, and therefore to create jobs, and programs of public employment. Republican platforms devote fewer words to the subject and, in general, endorse policies of job creation through indirect stimulation of the private sector.

Although party differences on the issue of joblessness were of greatest significance during the New Deal, they antedate the depression of the thirties. In 1928, when the unemployment rate was only 4.2 percent, the incumbent Republicans mentioned unemployment in their platform only in passing. According to its platform claims, the Republican administration had defended American jobs and wages by its policies of protection against foreign competition and restriction on immigration. The Democratic platform, in contrast, devoted greater space to the whole issue and called for programs of public works if needed to create jobs.

The 1932 platforms continued these themes. The Republicans promised "to use all available means consistent with sound financial and economic principles to promote an expansion of credit to stimulate business and relieve unemployment." The Democrats had not yet committed themselves to the New Deal programs they were to espouse several years hence. Their cautious 1932 platform, however, was much more directly activist than that of the Republicans: "We advocate the extension of federal credit to the states to provide unemployment relief wherever the diminished resources of the states makes it impossible for them to provide for the needy; expansion of the federal program of necessary and useful construction effected with a public interest such as adequate flood control and waterways."[19] The Democrats called for a reduction in the work week, advance planning of public works, and unemployment and old age insurance under state laws.

These themes—the Democrats calling for direct intervention through job programs and the Republicans for an indirect attack on the problem

[19]Kirk H. Porter and Donald B. Johnson, comps., *National Party Platforms: 1840-1972* (Urbana: University of Illinois, 1974), pp. 350 and 331.

—have been repeated in party platforms down to the present. In 1968, for example, the Republicans promised increased efficiency in the federal job-training program. The Democrats, on the other hand, advocated not only job training but government job programs as well. Pledged the Democrats: "For those who cannot obtain other employment, the federal government will be the employer of last resort, either through federal assistance to state and local projects or through federally sponsored projects."[20] In 1976 the two parties continued their traditional themes, carving out positions remarkably similar to those they had advocated half a century earlier. The Republican platform devoted substantially less space to the issue than did the Democratic. The Republican strategy was to reduce unemployment by fighting inflation, encouraging business investment, and protecting the textile industry from foreign competition. The Democratic platform did not call unequivocally for a federal "job-of-last-resort" program as it had in some previous platforms, but it did appear to advocate such a program—combined with efforts in the private sector: "Every effort should be made to create jobs in the private sector. Clearly useful public jobs are far superior to welfare and unemployment payments. The federal government has the responsibility to ensure that all Americans able, willing, and seeking work are provided opportunities for useful jobs."[21]

The campaign postures of the 1976 presidential candidates reflect with reasonable accuracy the positions taken on unemployment by their respective parties, Carter talked about unemployment more often than Ford, and his comments differed in emphasis.[22] Ford made his position clear in his January 1976 State of the Union message, emphasizing that investment tax credits for plant expansion would stimulate the private sector and therefore create jobs without massive federal job programs. In vetoing a public works bill in February 1976, Ford asserted: "The best and most effective way to create new jobs is to pursue balanced economic policies that encourage the growth of the private sector without risking a new round of inflation." Consistent with this position, Ford denounced the Humphrey-Hawkins job bill—which Carter supported in April—as

[20]Ibid., p. 735.

[21]Republican Party Platform, Republican National Committee. Edward Tufte notes that the Republican 1976 platform mentions unemployment "in the context of doing something about it" only once in sixty-five pages. He counts forty-eight references to unemployment in the Democratic platform of 1976, only seven references in the Republican (Political Control, pp. 72 and 74).

[22]Using the New York Times Index to count each candidate's references to unemployment in the two months preceding the election, we found that for every three times Carter mentioned unemployment, Ford spoke about it only twice.

inflationary. Carter, on the other hand, endorsed a different set of priorities: "I'd put my emphasis on employment and take my chances on inflation."[23]

THE PARTIES IN OFFICE

This is hardly the place to engage in a detailed policy analysis of the differences between the parties in terms of their conduct in office, but a few comments seem appropriate. As of this writing, the actual policies that the Carter administration has pursued are less sharply at variance with those of his predecessor than might have been predicted from their campaign rhetoric. In general, however, the conduct of Democrats with reference to macroeconomic policies in general, and job policies in particular, has differed from that of Republicans. Tufte marshals impressive evidence that incumbent Democratic administrations are more concerned with unemployment than are Republican ones. Internal memoranda on macroeconomic policy show that economic advisers under Democratic regimes are more likely to express concern about unemployment than are their counterparts in Republican times. A similar difference is found in the public pronouncements of administrations: the *Economic Report of the President* and the *Annual Report of the Council of Economic Advisers* emphasize unemployment over inflation when the president is a Democrat, the opposite when he is a Republican.[24] One indication of the real differences between the behavior of the parties in office is congressional voting. Table 11-3, which presents the results of congressional roll-call votes over a period of several years on various unemployment-related matters, makes clear that in both houses of Congress, divisions between the parties are sharp and persistent.

We have reviewed briefly a variety of data—leadership attitudes, party platforms, campaign promises, congressional promises, congressional votes—about party differences on economic matters. Our conclusion from this survey, while hardly novel, is quite unambiguous. However heterogeneous the parties in their composition and coalitional bases, they do differ on economic issues, especially unemployment. The contrast between the parties discerned by the public is not illusory. On this set of issues the parties offer the voters real and continuing choices.

---

[23]See the *New York Times*, January 20, 1976, p. 1, for the State of the Union message. In the official Democratic rejoinder, Senator Edmund Muskie stressed the need for federal job guarantees (*New York Times*, January 22, 1976, p. 1). See also *New York Times*, February 14, 1976, p. 1, and July 14, 1976, p. 51.

[24]Tufte, *Political Control*, pp. 77-83.

Table 11-3   Congressional votes on matters relating to unemployment (percent voting yea).

	HOUSE		SENATE	
Subject of vote	Democrats	Republicans	Democrats	Republicans
1978—Full Employment and Balanced Growth Act (Humphrey-Hawkins)	85	18	93	53
1977—Public Works Jobs Program	96	53	98	62
1976—Public Works Jobs Program	96	47	95	37
1976—Unemployment compensation extension	74	33	98	83
1975—Emergency employment appropriation	91	38	93	52
1973—Public Works and Economic Development Act	95	42	98	64
1970—Manpower Training Act	80	17	86	81

SOURCE: Calculated from data in *Congressional Quarterly Almanac*, vols. 26-31 (Washington, D.C.: Congressional Quarterly).

Party Rank and File and Unemployment

Whether the cause or the result of the kinds of partisan differences we have been discussing, the citizen bases of the two parties contrast sharply with respect to these matters. What is more, the partisans can be distinguished by their experiences with unemployment as well as by their attitudes.

THE ATTITUDES OF PARTY SUPPORTERS

Although the difference between the partisans is smaller than that between the party leaders, the attitudes of the party supporters on issues related to unemployment reflect those of the leadership. Public opinion polls dating back to the years before World War II document with reassuring consistency that the opinions of Democratic voters and identifiers differ from those of their Republican counterparts on issues of welfare and the domestic economy, and that the differences are more pronounced than on any other issue.[25] As shown in Table 11-4, which sum-

[25]These studies are summarized in Everett Carll Ladd, Jr., and Charles D. Hadley,

Table 11-4   Differences between Democratic and Republican identifiers on unemployment-related issues.

Issue	Republicans	Democrats
Percent who say the govern- ment should guarantee jobs		
1956	55	69
1960	54	73
1964[a]	22	46
1968	25	46
1972	17	39
1976	17	43
Ranking of unemployment vs inflation (1976).		
Inflation more important	52	38
Unemployment more important	21	34
No ranking	26	29
	99	101

[a]In 1964 and afterward the wording of the job guarantee item was changed somewhat to include
"a decent standard of living" as well as a job. We assume that it is this change which accounts for
the decrease in the proportion of both parties who support this kind of government intervention.

SOURCE: Center for Political Studies, University of Michigan, 1976 election survey. Pre-1976 data
are from Everett Carll Ladd, Jr., and Charles D. Hadley, *Political Parties and Political Issues*
(Beverly Hills, Calif.: Sage Publications, 1973), pp. 22-23.

marizes the responses to a question asked repeatedly in the Michigan
election surveys, Democrats have been uniformly more likely than Republicans to believe that the government should guarantee jobs rather
than "stay out of it." When asked about the unemployment-inflation
trade-off in 1976, Democrats showed more concern about unemployment than did Republicans, although in this case the difference between
the groups of party supporters is neither as clear as it was between the
party leaders nor as definite as it was on the issue of the job guarantee.

PARTISANS AND THEIR EXPOSURE TO UNEMPLOYMENT

The partisan groups can be distinguished not only by their attitudes on
unemployment but also by the extensiveness of their experiences with

Political Parties and Political Issues: Patterns in Differentiation since the New Deal
(Beverly Hills, Calif.: Sage Publications, 1973), chap. 3.

joblessness. Given what we know about the vulnerability to unemployment of various groups—among others, blacks and those in lower-status occupations—and given what we know about the party coalitions—that the groups we are concerned with are heavily Democratic—the central message of Table 11-5, that unemployment touches the lives of Democrats much more directly than Republicans, is hardly surprising. The Democratic party is much more likely to find among its supporters individuals who are currently unemployed, or who have experienced past unemployment, or who are in some way exposed to unemployment. At the time of our survey of the urban work force, 15 percent of the Democratic identifiers, but only 7 percent of the Republican identifiers, were out of work.[26] What is more, the jobless Democrats were substantially more likely than their Republican counterparts to have been out of work several times in the past: 24 percent of the unemployed Democrats, as opposed to a mere 3 percent of the unemployed Republicans, have been unemployed four or more times in the past decade. Working partisans differ in an analogous way: about a third of the employed Democrats, as opposed to a fourth of the working Republicans, have been out of work at some time in the past decade.

Not only are Democratic partisans themselves more likely to have suffered from unemployment but, as shown in Table 11-5, they are more likely to live in an environment in which others around them are out of work. Respondents in the Michigan CPS study were asked whether anyone in the family had been subject to various forms of employment in-

[26]That the jobless are twice as large a share of Democratic identifiers as of Republican identifiers does not mean that there are in absolute terms twice as many jobless Democrats as jobless Republicans, simply because there are more Democrats than Republicans in the electorate. As the following figures show, this two-to-one ratio in terms of proportion of party coalition translates into a three-to-one ratio in terms of absolute numbers; that is, in 1976 among the unemployed there were more than three times as many Democrats as Republicans.

Party identification	Employment status	
	Working	Unemployed
Strong Democrat	13%	22%
Weak Democrat	24	30
Independent	40	32
Weak Republican	14	12
Strong Republican	8	4

Source: Center for Political Studies, University of Michigan, 1976 election survey.

Table 11-5   Exposure to unemployment, by party. Except where indicated, data are from the metropolitan work force survey, April 1976, and are given in percentages.

Unemployment indicator	Democrats	Republicans
Currently unemployed		
Urban work force	15	7
National work force[a]	13	7
Unemployed four or more times		
in past decade (all respondents)	10	2
Unemployed four or more times in past		
decade (unemployed only)	24	3
Unemployed in past decade (working		
respondents only)	35	26
Job-related strain on family reported[b]	33	19
Many friends out of work		
All respondents	18	6
Employed respondents	15	6
Unemployed respondents	34	11
Prospect of losing job (working respondents only)		
Very likely	6	1
Somewhat likely	16	13
Unlikely	79	86
	101	100

[a]Center for Political Studies, University of Michigan 1976 election survey.
[b]Election survey as above. A family is considered to have undergone economic strain if any family member has been subject to one or more of the following: unemployment, pay cuts, reduced hours, changed shifts, or a job below qualifications.

security—unemployment, reduced pay or hours, and the like. Only 19 percent of the Republicans, but 33 percent of the Democrats, reported that family members had suffered from one or more of these forms of job-related strain. Finally, not only are the relatives of Democrats more likely to have been exposed to such strain, their friends are too. As shown in Table 11-5, Democrats—whether employed or out of work— are far more likely than their Republican counterparts to have friends out of work. In short, from a variety of perspectives, Democratic partisans have a much wider exposure to unemployment than Republicans.[27]

[27]The importance of the unemployed as a clientele group for the Democratic party must be qualified in one way. Even though the unemployed are a larger proportion of

Conclusion

We have discussed a number of concepts that can help us in under-taking an analysis of the impact of unemployment on the electoral pro-cess, and we have reviewed a variety of kinds of evidence that can help us predict the results.

We have reviewed briefly the findings of those who have considered the effects of macroeconomic changes upon electoral outcomes. With re-spect to unemployment per se, these studies are somewhat inconclusive. But they do seem to indicate that members of the incumbent president's party suffer when the economy is sluggish. What these studies cannot do, because they are based on aggregate data, is specify the source of any alterations in electoral behavior. Our particular interest is to understand the genesis of such alterations—from those who have been directly af-fected by economic downturn or from those who, while not themselves affected, are concerned about economic conditions and policies—and to understand how attitudes intervene in the process.

---

the supporters of the Democratic party than the Republican, there is less difference than might be expected between the parties in the extent to which party activists come from the ranks of the jobless. As indicated by the following data, unemployed party identifiers, especially among Democrats, are much less likely to be active participants than are their working counterparts. Indeed, among political activists, unemployed Democrats form no larger a share of their party coalition than jobless Republicans of theirs. Of the politically active cadres of the two parties, 8 percent of the Democratic activists and 6 percent of the Republican activists were out of work as of April 1976. Thus, at the activist level, party differences in terms of exposure to unemployment are much less marked than at the level of ordinary rank-and-file support.

	Party identification	
Employment status	Democratic	Republican
Employed		
Politically active	26%	32%
Inactive	59	61
Unemployed		
Politically active	2	2
Inactive	13	5
	100%	100%
Percent of political activists who are unemployed	8	6

We have also considered several sorts of information about the positions of the two major parties on these matters. A sizable portion of the public, though indeed not a majority, perceive differences between the parties both in terms of their relative competence in dealing with the economy and in terms of the policies they pursue. The Democrats are viewed as being more capable at managing the economy and more favorable to policies aimed at reducing unemployment. We have seen also that the differences perceived by the public are grounded in reality. Attitudes of party leaders, party platforms and campaign promises, and congressional voting all indicate that the parties offer real choices on these matters. Furthermore, there are variations in the citizen bases of the parties, both in terms of attitudes and experience, which reflect the distinctions we found at the elite level: Democratic supporters are more likely than their Republican counterparts both to feel that the government should take positive steps to provide jobs and to have had personal exposure to unemployment.

All these findings lead us to conclude that analysis of the impact of unemployment on the 1976 presidential election is indeed a very complex task. We would expect Gerald Ford to have garnered relatively few votes from those concerned about unemployment. However, if this turns out to be the case, we may have difficulty in discerning whether the rejection of Ford was the rejection of an incumbent or the rejection of a Republican. Furthermore, because Democratic partisanship, direct experience with unemployment, and policy attitudes favoring government intervention to reduce joblessness all tend to be interconnected, the task of untangling the relationships is a complicated one. Among those concerned about unemployment we might expect a large vote for Carter, for a variety of reasons: because they were generally angry at the state of economic affairs; because they were Democratic partisans who normally would have voted for Carter anyway; because they thought the Democrat better able to handle the economy or preferred the economic policies traditionally offered by the Democrats; because they had been exposed to unemployment—either personally or by dint of the experiences of relatives or friends. It is to the task of unraveling these multiple associations that we now turn.

CHAPTER 12

Unemployment and Electoral Politics: Some Data

I N THE PREVIOUS chapter we introduced, perhaps too painstakingly, various conceptual tools helpful in undertaking an analysis of the impact of unemployment on the electoral process. Let us proceed to that analysis.

Unemployment and Partisanship

We begin by considering the possible links between joblessness and long-term partisan commitments. We know that the outcome of any election is in part determined by the underlying distribution of partisan identifications in the electorate. A voter's partisan identification predisposes him to support his party's candidates when casting a ballot. Any issue that alters the overall distribution of partisan identifications in the electorate has a continuing indirect effect upon electoral outcomes—even when that issue is not directly at stake in a given election. For example, the civil rights issue has certainly had such an impact on underlying partisan attachments: beginning with the New Deal, and especially since 1964, most blacks have identified as Democrats. Even in an election in which the issue of civil rights is of limited salience, it has in a sense a continuing historical impact, because the majority of blacks are predisposed to cast Democratic ballots. Of course, this predisposition is not determinative. Many partisans will respond to immediate issues and candidates and defect from their normal partisan leanings when they vote. Still, the distribution of underlying partisan loyalties is so fundamental to the framework of the electoral process that we should consider whether unemployment affects that distribution.

One way in which unemployment might have an effect is as an abstract issue. That is, citizens might use their attitudes on unemployment as a guide in choosing a party as they enter the electorate, or they might change their partisan identifications midcareer in response to their altered attitudes on unemployment. We shall not attempt to determine the degree to which attitudes about unemployment color partisan identifications. Because specific opinions often follow rather than precede partisan identifications, we cannot construe the attitudinal differences between Republican and Democratic identifiers as evidence of party switching in response to attitudes.

We shall, however, consider another possibility—that the experience of being out of work has an impact on partisan affiliation. This might happen in one of two ways. The experience of being unemployed might work against the party in power, regardless of which party it was: angry jobless partisans who identify with the incumbents might reject the incumbent party and become Independents or align themselves with the opposition party. On the other hand, the experience of unemployment might work asymmetrically to the detriment of the Republicans: jobless Independents and Republicans might find attractive the policies offered by the Democrats. In the former case, voters would be making retrospective judgments about the performance of the party in office, holding responsible for their misfortune whichever party happened to be in office. In the latter case, they would be making a more differentiated judgment of the relative merits of the parties. This situation makes greater demands upon the capacities of voters, for they must perceive differences between the parties in terms of programs offered or relative capacity to manage the economy.[1]

Although our data permit us to consider party switching between 1974 and 1976, we cannot determine whether the switching was anti-Republican or anti-incumbent since there was a Republican administration in office.[2] Ideally, one would wish to have panel data over a sufficiently long period to permit observation of the stability of partisan identification of unemployed workers in periods of both Republican and Democratic incumbency. We do not have access to such data. We can use our respondents' recollections of past changes in party attachments as a partial substitute for panel data, but such input is indeed imperfect for our

[1]We should mention a third alternative, that unemployed partisans, regardless of party, would simply abandon their party affiliation as a manifestation of general political withdrawal. After our findings about political withdrawal in Chapter 9, however, we do not consider this a convincing scenario.

[2]We shall be able to make such a distinction when we consider candidate preference because we can differentiate attitudes toward President Ford from attitudes toward other Republicans.

purposes. We asked the party identifiers whether they had always had their present partisan commitments and, if not, when they had switched —during the past two years, the past four years, in the past decade, or even before that. We concentrate our attention on those who switched within the two years preceding the interview and make comparisons between working and jobless respondents. Even with this short time span we cannot be certain of any association between party switching and employment status that may emerge. Since most unemployment is of a duration shorter than two years, it is quite conceivable that some recent party switchers who are currently working made their switch during a stint of unemployment, or that some recent party switchers who are currently out of work were employed at the time of their switch. Analogously, we have no way of knowing whether some respondents who changed their partisan identifications in the more distant past did not perhaps do so during a period of unemployment.

Table 12-1 gives data on the 1976 party identifications of 1974 partisans. We reconstruct 1974 partisanship from responses to the 1976 question—posed to party identifiers—about whether they had changed their party affiliations within the past two years; we then report, for 1974 Republicans and Democrats, the proportion who had remained loyal, who had become Independents, and who had switched to the opposite party. For the overwhelming majority of partisans, party loyalties remained stable over the two-year period. Although there seems to have been slightly more erosion among Republicans than Democrats, the overall picture is one of equilibrium rather than of change. However, among Republicans there seems to be a difference between working and jobless respondents: the share of unemployed Republicans (23 percent) who had abandoned the party is more than twice the proportion (10 percent) of working Republicans who had become Independents or Democrats. This difference between unemployed and working party supporters does not hold for the Democrats. The 1974 Democrats unemployed at the time of our study were very slightly less likely than their working counterparts to have left the party. Thus, there seems to be a difference between the parties in terms of the degree to which unemployment is associated with recent party switching: the rate of recent party abandonment among jobless Republicans is nearly four times the rate among unemployed Democrats.

There is a further difference between the unemployed partisans in terms of where they went once they left. Unemployed ex-Democrats, like employed ex-supporters of both parties, by and large became Independents. However, unemployed ex-Republicans were relatively much more likely to switch parties; 46 percent of that group identified with the Democrats by 1976 (a proportion that we can derive from Table 12-1).

Table 12-1 Employment status and party switching between 1974 and 1976; party loyalties of 1974 partisans as of 1976.[a]

	REPUBLICANS		DEMOCRATS	
Loyalty	Working	Unemployed	Working	Unemployed
Remained loyal	90%	77%	92%	94%
Became Independents	7	12	6	5
Switched parties	3	11	2	1
	100%	100%	100%	100%
	(140)	(56)	(260)	(185)

[a]Party identification in 1974 has been reconstructed from a question in 1976 on current party identification and from past history of party switching.

SOURCE: Metropolitan work force survey, 1976.

Thus we have found an association between unemployment and likelihood of having left the Republican party in the two years preceding our interviews. We should note, however, that the data are not sufficiently precise to allow us to ascertain just how many of the jobless ex-Republicans were out of work at the time they abandoned the Republican party. The relationship we have located may be a spurious one, a function of other variables such as class or age, which are related both to party switching and to unemployment.

Even if we have in fact found that unemployment enhanced the likelihood of party abandonment among Republicans during the mid-1970s, we still cannot determine whether the effect is symmetrical or asymmetrical, anti-incumbent or anti-Republican. That is, we cannot be certain whether the relatively large number of jobless Republicans who left their party did so as a rejection of the incumbent Republican administration or because they perceived the Republican party as less willing or capable of dealing with unemployment.

The individual effects we have discovered are not inconsiderable: among 1974 Republicans, 23 percent of those who were jobless—as opposed to 10 percent of those who were working—had left the party in the two years preceding the April 1976 interviews. Because the number of Republican identifiers who experience unemployment is relatively small, however, the aggregate effects are much less substantial. Indeed, in spite of the fact that the rate of party abandonment among unemployed Republicans was more than twice that for working Republicans, the unemployed contributed only 17 percent to the total Republican loss during that two-year period (a percentage also derived by manipulating the data in Table 12-1).

Table 12-2 summarizes the net effect of unemployment on party support. Of those who had considered themselves Republicans in 1974, 11 percent—of whom 9 percent were working and 2 percent were unemployed—had abandoned that identification two years later. The Democrats, on the other hand, had lost 8 percent of their 1974 supporters by 1976—7 percent drawn from the employed, 1 percent from the unemployed.[3] How would these figures have been changed had there been no difference in the behavior of the employed and the unemployed—that is, if unemployment had not been associated with a doubling of the rate of abandonment among Republican identifiers? The answer is that those net loss figures would not look much different. The Republicans, instead of losing 11 percent of their supporters through abandonment, would have lost about 10 percent. The figures would have been virtually unchanged if the behavior of working and jobless Democrats had been identical.

Thus, the association between unemployment and party abandonment for Republicans is considerable when the individual elector is considered. Yet when the aggregate impact is considered, the effect is virtually nil— a function of the small size of the group that can be affected. There just are relatively few unemployed Republicans around to engage in such disproportionate party abandonment.[4]

The 1976 Election

As is so often the case, the cast at the January 1977 presidential inauguration was quite different from what political analysts were predicting a year before. Using a strategy designed to exploit the altered institutional context in which the campaign took place—the increased number

---

[3]The figures we are citing are for party abandonment only. During the two-year period each party gained adherents, former Independents who had become partisans as well as ex-supporters of the opposite party who had changed party allegiance. The Republicans compensated for their 11-percent loss by gaining 4 percent more supporters from ex-Democrats and an unknown proportion from former Independents. The Democrats recovered 2 percent new supporters from the Republicans and an unascertained proportion from the ranks of ex-Independents. In Table 12-1 it is worth noting that the 2 percent of Democratic supporters who departed from that party became 4 percent of the smaller Republican group when they arrived.

[4]Had we been able to study these processes over a longer period, we would perhaps have found more substantial effects. If the relationship we have found holds for other periods—for times of low unemployment as well as during the relatively high unemployment we are considering, for periods when Democrats occupy the White House as well as years of Republican incumbency—then the cumulative detrimental effects on the Republicans could be more significant.

Table 12-2   Aggregate effects of party abandonment, 1974-1976 (percent).

Effect	Republicans	Democrats
Erosion of party support through abandonment	11	8
Employed component	9	7
Unemployed component	2	1
Erosion if the unemployed had behaved like the employed	10	8

SOURCE: Metropolitan work force survey, 1976.

of heats in the five-month primary marathon, the introduction of federal financing—Jimmy Carter, peanut farmer and former governor of Georgia, emerged from relative obscurity and became the second challenger in the twentieth century to defeat an incumbent president. Emphasizing a post-Watergate theme of the need to restore trust in government, moderate Carter defeated challenges by nearly a dozen Democratic hopefuls arrayed on both his left and his right. The Democratic convention was not the melee that had been anticipated, but a harmonious celebration of partisan reconciliation. Meanwhile, the nonelected incumbent president, Gerald Ford, was challenged by the attractive leader of his party's conservative wing, former California governor Ronald Reagan. It was not until an uncharacteristically conflict-ridden Republican convention that Ford emerged as his party's choice.

Although the campaign itself was not especially notable, the election of 1976 is a particularly appropriate one for considering the electoral impact of those without jobs. The unemployed were a larger portion of the electorate than at any time in over three decades, and the parties were clearly perceived as offering alternatives on economic issues.

Both because the incumbent administration was a Republican one and because the Democrats are perceived as being more competent in handling unemployment, we would expect the effect in 1976 of the unemployed as a voting bloc and of unemployment as an issue to have operated to the advantage of the Democrats. However, these effects need not have worked only by inducing Republicans and Independents who were either unemployed themselves or concerned about unemployment to give the Democrats a larger share of their votes than is normally expected. The behavior of Democratic identifiers—who, as we saw in Table 12-1, cannot always be counted on to support their party's nominees—might also have been affected. Joblessness, either as an objective fact intruding into voters' lives or as an abstract issue intruding into their consciousnesses, could have had a substantial electoral impact by cementing normal partisan commitments and inducing Demoćratic supporters not to stray.

Unemployment and Candidate Preference

We have mentioned that our metropolitan work force survey was not conducted at a particularly auspicious time from the point of view of assessing the impact of unemployment on the 1976 election, for neither party had so much as a front-runner when our data were collected. We did, however, ask respondents about the likelihood of their voting for each of several candidates—Republicans Gerald Ford and Ronald Reagan, Democrats Morris Udall and Henry Jackson.

The preferences for these candidates, shown in Figure 12-1, give an indication of the electoral potential of the unemployed. Among Democrats there is virtually no difference between working and jobless respondents in terms of their willingness to support their party's candidate. When it comes to their likelihood of voting for a candidate of the Republican party, however, we find a small difference between the working and the unemployed. The unemployed were a little less likely to say that they would vote for any of the Republican candidates. Among Republicans the unemployed show a slight tendency to reject their own party, a tendency particularly noticeable in the proportion reporting they would be likely to vote for one of their own party's candidates. Seventy-two percent of the working Republicans had at least one Republican candidate for whom they indicated likely support if that candidate were nominated, while only 62 percent of the unemployed Republicans had such a favored Republican candidate. The data on the willingness of Republican adherents to support Democratic candidates show a less clear pattern. There is virtually no difference between working and unemployed Republicans in terms of reporting that there was a Democratic candidate for whom they might vote; but on the more difficult question of whether there was a candidate for whom they would be *likely* to vote, it turns out that working Republicans were somewhat more likely than jobless Republicans to have such a favored Democratic candidate.

Thus, in terms of candidate preferences early in the 1976 campaign, we find some very slight differences between working and jobless party supporters. Unemployment does not seem to have moved Democrats away from their own party, but it does seem to have made them a bit less supportive of Republican candidates. Among Republicans there was some movement away from candidates of their own party, but not much evidence for a positive movement in the direction of the Democrats.

The clearest distinction in Figure 12-1, however, is not between working and unemployed, but between Republican and Democrat. A much

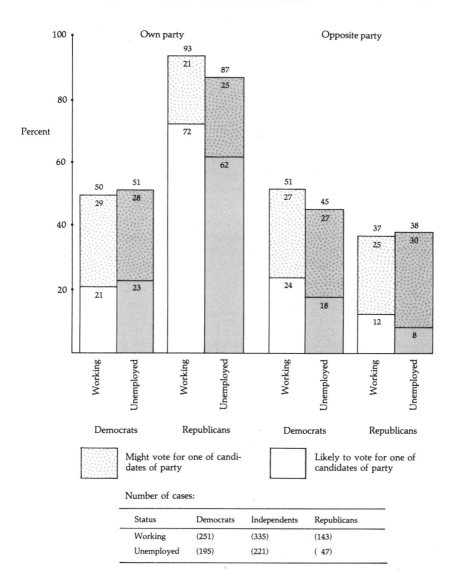

Figure 12-1 Candidate preference, by partisanship and employment status.

higher proportion of Republican than Democratic identifiers indicated a propensity to support the candidates of their own party and to reject the candidates of the opposition. This is not an appropriate place for extensive analysis of this striking difference, but it could reflect a variety of tendencies. First, while the options of Ford and Reagan exhausted the viable Republican alternatives at the time, the choices of Udall and Jackson barely scratched the surface of the Democratic alternatives. Democrats at the time were divided among supporters of more than half a dozen candidates, of whom Udall and Jackson were only two. It is not surprising that virtually all the Republicans, but a much smaller share of the Democrats, indicated a willingness to vote for one of the two candidates mentioned from their party. Furthermore, as we saw in Chapter 11, when compared to their Democratic counterparts, Republican identifiers are somewhat more loyal to their own party's candidates in voting.

Anti-Republican or Anti-Incumbent?

We can investigate further the slight anti-Republican tendency that emerged from Figure 12-1 by distinguishing between preferences for the two Republican candidates, the incumbent president, Gerald Ford, and his Republican challenger, Ronald Reagan. The data in Figure 12-2 can help us decide if the effect of unemployment was anti-Ford or anti-Republican. Among Republicans, whose preferences on this matter obviously are central, there is quite a sharp difference between the working and the unemployed in terms of the number who said they would be likely to vote for Ford. Sixty-two percent of the working Republicans, but only 37 percent of their jobless fellow partisans, reported being likely to vote for Ford. A similar, though less striking, pattern is found among the Democrats and Independents. When it comes to preferences for Ronald Reagan, there is little variation between the working and the unemployed in any of the partisan groups.

It is not that the unemployed were more favorable to Reagan than to Ford. It is rather that, unlike their working fellow partisans (who were more kindly disposed toward Ford than toward Reagan), the unemployed expressed similar levels of potential support for the two Republican contenders. The relative rejection of Ford by the unemployed when compared to their working fellow partisans is perhaps puzzling. We might expect the unemployed to be especially sensitive to the views of candidates on issues pertaining to the economy and to be more likely than their working partisan counterparts to reject candidates who stress fiscal conservatism and limitation of government efforts on behalf of those in need. On this basis we would expect a relative rejection of Reagan, who was widely considered to be more conservative than Ford.

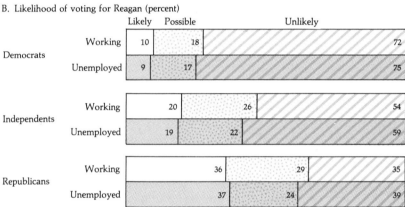

A. Likelihood of voting for Ford (percent)

B. Likelihood of voting for Reagan (percent)

Figure 12-2 Preference for incumbent vs nonincumbent, by partisanship and employment status.

Reagan had received a good deal of press and television coverage for his plan, announced during the New Hampshire primary in February, to shift support for social security from the federal government to the states, a plan which many considered a serious challenge to the social security system and which Ford attacked during the Florida primary.[5] In

[5]Furthermore, survey data shortly before our study indicate that the public saw Reagan as more conservative in economic matters than Ford. When asked whether various candidates preferred a balanced budget or spending for services, 78 percent saw Reagan as on the conservative side, 65 percent saw Ford there (*New York Times/ CBS* poll, February 1976).

view of the policy differences between the two Republicans, we interpret the relative tendency of the unemployed to reject Ford as the expression of a generalized anti-incumbent effect rather than a more selective response to the Republican party on the basis of policy differences between the parties.[6]

In 1976 the two forces of anti-incumbency and belief that Democrats would do a better job of ending unemployment operated in the same direction to produce a noticeable reduction in preference for Gerald Ford at the individual level. Still, even when these forces work together, the aggregate result is quite insignificant. The reason is simple. Even in periods of fairly high unemployment, the jobless are a small portion of the electorate. In addition, although the unemployed in each partisan group were undeniably less enthusiastic about Ford than their working counterparts, the group that was most distinctive is indeed a very small one— unemployed Republicans.[7] Thus it is not surprising that the net effect is negligible. To be more specific, 29 percent of our respondents—31 percent of those with jobs and 17 percent of those without—declared themselves likely to vote for Gerald Ford. If, however, the unemployed had been as favorable to Ford as their employed fellow-partisans, then 30 percent of our sample would have expressed support for Ford, an increase of a mere 1 percent.[8]

Job Insecurity and Anti-Incumbency

By focusing on the candidate preferences of the unemployed, we may have understated the impact of joblessness. Unemployment can have an oblique effect on the personal economic situation of those who remain employed by making them somewhat less secure in their employment, and this anxiety can affect their political attitudes or behavior. It seems reasonable, therefore, to delve into the effects of job insecurity.

---

[6]We do not know if there would have been an equivalent anti-incumbent effect if the incumbent had been a Democrat. The effect in that case might have been tempered by the widespread belief, particularly among Democrats, that the Democratic party is more competent in handling unemployment.

[7]Also, as we have seen, the unemployed are less likely to be voters. The analogue to this finding in our candidate preference data is that the unemployed are more likely to have no candidate preferences at all.

[8]Because of the differences in the partisan composition of the working and the unemployed groups, the overall level of support for Ford would still be somewhat lower among the jobless than among the working if the unemployed supported Ford to the same extent as their working partisan counterparts. That is why, under these hypothetical conditions, aggregate support for Ford reaches only 30 percent, not the 31 percent of the working respondents taken alone.

Figure 12-3 compares working people at various levels of job security in terms of their expressed likelihood of voting for Ford. Our measure of job security is the one we have used before, a scale that includes length of present employment, history of unemployment, and fear of job loss. The data show that job insecurity among the working is related to anti-incumbent feelings among Republicans. The less secure workers fall in between the workers with high job security and the unemployed in their loyalty to President Ford. Among Democrats and Independents, job insecurity among the working has no systematic relationship to likelihood of voting for Ford.

In sum, it is among the Republicans that we find unemployment—either as actual joblessness or as job insecurity—to have the strongest association with anti-incumbent sentiments. Among Democrats and Independents, the fact of joblessness has a weaker effect on attitudes toward the incumbent and job insecurity almost no effect at all.

Unemployment and the Vote

In order to assess the impact of unemployment on the vote, we turn to the 1976 Michigan election survey, which is particularly useful because respondents were contacted just before and just after the election. Its unfortunate drawback from our point of view is that the sample contains fewer unemployed respondents than one would wish.

Table 12-3 presents the basic data on the 1976 voting behavior of the working and unemployed members of each of the partisan groups. Given what we already know about differences between the parties, both in terms of the policies they offer and the representation of the unemployed among their supporters, it should not be surprising that those who were out of work were more likely than those with jobs to support Carter. Sixty-two percent of the jobless voters, as opposed to 50 percent of the working ones, voted for the Georgia governor. Two other points emerge clearly from these data. The first is the highly partisan nature of the voting patterns: the partisans give the bulk of their votes to their respective party's candidates; the Independents split their support. A second immediately evident finding is that the unemployed were less likely to have voted at all. Thirty-seven percent of the unemployed, as opposed to 25 percent of the working respondents, did not go to the polls.

We can clarify the relationship between employment status and the vote by using normal vote analysis. (This is the technique that compares the actual vote of a group with the vote that would have been expected on the basis of the partisan composition of that group.) Table 12-4 presents the results of such an analysis for our employment groups. In item A we compare working and unemployed work force members in terms of

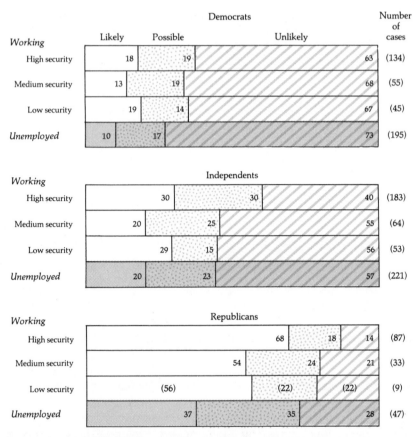

Figure 12-3 Likelihood of voting for Ford, by party and job security.

their expected and actual 1976 presidential votes. The unemployed have a higher expected Democratic vote, a reflection of the disproportionate number of Democratic identifiers among the jobless. Their actual vote was just about what would have been expected on the basis of their underlying partisan commitments. This might tempt us to conclude that the large Democratic vote among the unemployed was in no way unusual, that it reflected party loyalties alone and not any special effects of unemployment. In the context of the 1976 election, however, this conclusion is not justified. As shown at the top of Table 12-4, the electorate as a whole was 4 percent less Democratic than normal, indicating the presence of short-term forces advantageous to the Republicans. Like the electorate as a whole, working voters were 4 percent more Republican than would have been predicted on the basis of partisanship alone. Thus,

Table 12-3 Vote in 1976, by party identification and employment status.

Vote	WORKING				UNEMPLOYED			
	Total	Democratic	Independent	Republican	Total	Democratic	Independent	Republican
Percent of the electorate								
Carter	38	63	31	11	39	49	34	15
Ford	35	15	34	70	22	9	31	46
Other	2	1	3	2	2	4	0	0
Did not vote	25	22	33	16	37	38	34	39
	100	101	101	99	100	100	99	100
Percent of voters								
Carter	50	80	46	14	62	79	53	27
Ford	47	19	50	84	35	14	47	73
Other	2	1	4	2	4	7	0	0
	99	100	100	100	101	100	100	100
Number of cases:	(1,272)	(460)	(515)	(297)	(133)	(67)	(45)	(21)

SOURCE: Center for Political Studies, University of Michigan, 1976 election survey.

Table 12-4   Normal vote analysis[a], 1976, by amount of exposure to unemployment.

Exposure to unemployment	Democratic vote (percent)			
	Expected	Actual	Deviation from expected	
All voters	54.2	50.2	−4.0	
Current employment status:				
A. Working respondents	53.8	50.2	−3.6	(956)
Unemployed respondents	62.2	61.5	−0.7	(85)
B. Neither respondent nor head of household unemployed	53.7	49.0	−4.7	(1559)
Respondent and/or head of household unemployed	61.4	62.5	+1.1	(112)
History of unemployment:				
C. Respondent working and not unemployed in past year	52.6	47.0	−5.6	(787)
Respondent unemployed currently or in past year	59.0	61.9	+2.9	(230)
D. Neither respondent nor head of household unemployed currently or in past year	53.2	47.7	−5.5	(1414)
Respondent and/or head of household unemployed currently or in past year	58.9	62.3	+3.4	(257)

[a]Computation of the normal vote is based on the method suggested in Philip E. Converse, "The Concept of the Normal Vote," in Angus Campbell, Philip E. Converse, Warren E. Miller, and Donald E. Stokes, *Elections and the Political Order* (New York: John Wiley and Sons, 1964), pp. 9-39. The specific parameters used derive from recent work by Arthur H. Miller and reflect electoral changes since the original parameters were calculated. See Miller, "Normal Vote Analysis: Sensitivity to Change over Time," *American Journal of Political Science,* 23 (May 1979), 406-425.

SOURCE: Center for Political Studies, University of Michigan, 1976 election survey.

the fact that the unemployed match the long-term prediction obscures the fact that, in relative terms, they were unexpectedly Democratic in their votes. While the electorate as a whole—and working voters as well— were 4 percent more Republican than usual, the unemployed, in resisting the effects of the Republican short-term forces, actually tilted in the Democratic direction.

The unemployed are not the only ones to feel the impact of unemployment. Those in families where the main breadwinner is unemployed or who have experienced unemployment in the past might also have their vote influenced by that experience. In that way the impact of unemployment in the election might be expanded. In Table 12-4 we present several other normal vote analyses that take as our comparison groups respondents who are unemployed or who live in households where the household head is unemployed and respondents who have been exposed to unemployment in the past year. Section B of Table 12-4 shows the normal vote comparison of those undergoing current family experience with unemployment (where the respondent or the household head is jobless) and those with no such family unemployment. The data are similar to those in A: being unemployed oneself or being in a household where the head is unemployed has a similar effect on the vote, causing those exposed to unemployment to deviate slightly in a Democratic direction from their expected vote.

The bottom two portions of Table 12-4 contain normal vote analyses based on comparisons between those who had not been exposed to unemployment in the previous year and those who had. The comparison in C is between respondents who have a recent history of unemployment and those who do not, while in D it is between those with a *family* history of unemployment and those without such a history. Interestingly, although the basic pattern is the same, the effect is somewhat stronger for these measures than for the measure of current experience of unemployment. Those who had experienced unemployment in the past year deviate 3 percent in a Democratic direction; those who had not deviate 6 percent in the opposite direction. Those with a family history of unemployment deviate 3 percent toward the Democrats; those without a family history deviate 5 percent in a Republican direction. It is somewhat puzzling, however, that past experience with unemployment appears to have had a stronger effect on the vote than the current unemployment status of the individual. We have no idea why this should be the case.

FEAR OF UNEMPLOYMENT

Unemployment might have an impact on the vote through the *fear* of unemployment. Those who anticipate that they might lose their jobs would deviate from their normal vote. In this way a high unemployment rate would have its major effect, not on the unemployed themselves, but on those who are made anxious. As we have seen, for instance, job insecurity has an effect on candidate preference. Unfortunately there was no question about felt job insecurity on the 1976 election study, so we cannot relate it to the vote. There was, however, a question on expectations for the future. Respondents were asked if they expected their own economic situation to deteriorate, remain the same, or improve.

The normal vote analysis presented in Table 12-5 indicates that there is some relationship among working respondents between expectations for the future and their vote. Those who expected their economic situation to improve or stay the same were more likely to vote for Ford; those who expected deterioration, to vote for Carter. A parallel comparison for the unemployed shows that such expectations make little difference. (In this instance we group those who believe that their situation will remain the same or deteriorate into our more pessimistic category. This makes substantive sense and in any case is necessary, since few unemployed expect their situation to worsen.) The data are consistent with an argument we make below, that the electoral impact of unemployment is felt via the employed rather than the unemployed.[9]

The Aggregate Effect of Unemployment

We must add a caveat that we have interjected before. The deviation of the unemployed in favor of Carter as revealed by a normal vote analysis is not a measure of the aggregate impact of unemployment on the division of the vote. In order to measure the impact of differential support for the Democrats by the unemployed, we need to consider not only the way they cast their ballots but the size of the group of unemployed voters, a function in turn of both the rate of unemployment and the rate of turnout among those out of work. Even when a relatively small group is very distinctive in its voting behavior—as, for example, blacks are, but the unemployed are not—the aggregate effect of that group upon the

[9]We should note in passing that there is a certain ambiguity about the meaning of a respondent's future expectations. Is the respondent making a purely personal assessment? If so, then the measure is a measure of economic strain in personal life analogous to unemployment or job insecurity. Or is the respondent making, as well, an implicit political judgment? For example, is he a Republican who assumes that the Democrats are going to win the election and that his personal economic circumstances therefore will suffer? If so, there is no reason to expect this personal pessimism to tilt his vote in a Democratic direction. Because we do not have information on the respondent's expectations about which party will win or on his assessment of the meaning of that party's victory for his personal economic circumstances, we urge that these data be interpreted with caution.

Table 12-5 Normal vote analysis, 1976, of attitudes on one's economic future for unemployed and working respondents.

Expectation for future economic condition	DEMOCRATIC VOTE (PERCENT)		
	Expected	Actual	Deviation from expected
If working, things will—			
Get better	52	42	−10 (360)
Stay the same	54	52	−2 (405)
Get worse	57	62	+5 (116)
If unemployed, things will—			
Get better	65	66	+1 (34)
Stay the same or get worse	62	60	−2 (47)

overall partisan division of the vote will be quite small. It seems appropriate, therefore, to assess the impact of unemployment on the vote not only at the individual level but at the aggregate level as well.

Our analysis so far has shown the unemployed to have been distinctive in their voting habits in two ways: they were more likely to cast Democratic presidential ballots and they were less likely to go to the polls. These two tendencies of the unemployed work in opposite directions: their distinctive voting patterns augmented Carter's vote; their propensity not to vote diminished it. Each of these characteristics, we should add, potentially entails both a long-term predisposition and an unemployment-related component. With respect to voting patterns the long-term component is partisanship, the fact that the unemployed are a relatively Democratic group. The unemployment component is the additional Democratic tilt, above what is explained by distinctive partisanship. With respect to turnout, the long-term factor is demographic, the fact that the unemployed are drawn selectively from the ranks of lower socioeconomic groups, which are relatively inactive. As we saw in the analysis of the 1972 census data, there is no short-term component associated with unemployment. Differences in turnout between jobless and working groups are a function of characteristics independent of the experience of being out of work.

Table 12-6 analyzes the net impact of unemployment on the vote. Because we are interested in gauging its effects on the electorate in its entirety, rather than solely on that part of the electorate which is in the work force, we use a measure of employment status based on family experience. We compare respondents who are themselves out of work, or whose head of household is out of work, with respondents who are not themselves unemployed and whose household heads are not out of work.[10] In previous analyses we have compared the unemployed with the working members of the work force, omitting those not in the work force. Such a comparison highlights the effects of economic position. Including the employment status of the head of household makes possible a better picture of the impact of unemployment on the electorate taken as a whole.

Let us begin by considering the effect of differential turnout rates on the overall division of the vote. As shown in Table 12-6, those who were either out of work themselves or whose head of household was out of work—for the sake of simplicity we shall call this group "unemployed"—were less likely to vote than those who were not unemployed and whose head of household was not unemployed. Suppose the unemployed had voted as they did, but had turned out at the rate at which the employed did; that is, suppose the unemployed had cast 62.5 percent of their presidential ballots for the Democrats, but 71.5 percent of them had gone to the polls instead of the 64.7 percent who actually did.[11] How would Carter's vote have been altered? Under these hypothetical conditions, Carter would have won 50.4 percent of the vote instead of the 50.2 percent he actually received. In other words, the differential turnout of the unemployed depressed Carter's vote by two-tenths of one percent.

We can make similar calculations of the overall impact on the division of the vote of the tendency of the unemployed to vote disproportionately for the Democratic candidate. Had they voted as everybody else did—that is, had they cast 49.0 percent of their votes for Carter—then Carter's share of the vote would have been diminished by 1.2 percent, from its actual level of 50.2 percent to 49.0 percent.

It is misleading, however, to state as even a hypothetical alternative that the unemployed would vote like the employed, because their underlying partisan commitments are different. What we wish to do is isolate the impact of unemployment per se in the election result. We do this by

[10]In the metropolitan work force survey, we asked about "main wage earner"; the investigators in the Michigan survey inquired about "head of household."

[11]We realize that a change in the turnout of the unemployed is unlikely, based as it is on the social characteristics of the jobless rather than on unemployment per se.

The turnout rates reported in the Michigan study are higher than those in the actual election. There are a number of reasons, including a tendency of respondents to inflate their turnout and the likelihood that the sample of reinterviews is skewed somewhat in the direction of segments of the population with high turnout.

Table 12-6   Net impact of unemployment in household on vote for Carter in 1976.

		DEMOCRATIC VOTE OF INDIVIDUALS (PERCENT)		
Unemployment factor	Turnout	Expected	Actual	Deviation from expected
All voters	70.6	54.2	50.2	−4.0
Respondent and/or head of household unemployed	64.7	61.4	62.5	+1.1
Neither respondent nor head of household unemployed	71.5	53.7	49.0	−4.7
				5.8

	DEMOCRATIC VOTE IN AGGREGATE (PERCENT)		
	Expected	Actual	Deviation from expected
Hypothetical cases			
If the unemployed had voted as they did, but turned out at rate of the employed	50.4	50.2	−0.2
If the unemployed had voted as the employed	49.0	50.2	+1.2
If the unemployed had voted as their fellow partisans	49.7	50.2	+0.5

SOURCE: Center for Political Studies, University of Michigan, 1976 election survey.

comparing the actual two-party vote with what that vote would have been if the unemployed had deviated in their vote from the electorate as a whole only to the extent that would be predicted by their partisanship and not to the additional extent resulting from their unemployed status. We return to the technique of a normal vote analysis to separate the long-term voting deviation of the unemployed based on partisanship from the short-term based on unemployment.

At the top of Table 12-6 we show the results of such an analysis. As we have seen, the two groups did not respond equivalently to the package of

short-term forces surrounding the election: the unemployed were 1.1 percent more Democratic in their votes than would have been predicted on
the basis of partisanship alone, the employed 4.7 percent less Democratic
than predicted. What if the unemployed had reacted to the election as the
employed—if they, like the employed, had been 4.7 percent less Democratic than expected? Had the unemployed deviated from the employed
only by the amount that derives from their long-term partisanship (the
7.7 percent difference between their expected Democratic votes) with no
additional impact from unemployment, they would have cast 56.7 percent (61.4 percent expected − 4.7 percent deviation) of their ballots for
Carter rather than the 62.5 percent they did. Under these circumstances
Carter's share of the vote would have been 49.7 percent instead of the
50.2 percent he actually received. Thus, Carter gained one-half of one
percent from the unemployed that was not related to their partisanship.[12]

We were tempted to calculate a final figure that would include the effects of both differential turnout and differential vote patterns, but decided that it would be inconsistent with the preceding logic. On the
assumption that there was no reason to expect the unemployed, whose
partisan commitments differ from those of the employed, to vote like the
employed, we ignored the increment in the vote that accrued to Carter
from the underlying partisanship of the jobless and considered only the
residual increment that could not be attributed to partisanship in considering the effects of differential vote patterns.

We can make an analogous argument with respect to turnout. There is
no reason to expect the unemployed to turn out at rates equivalent to the
employed, because they differ in terms of their underlying demographic
characteristics. As we have seen, the experience of being out of work
does not contribute to the differential in turnout between working and
jobless voters. If it is the short-term effects of unemployment per se that
we wish to measure, then we should ignore the differential in turnout
because that differential is a function of long-term demographic factors
alone.

Given the severity of the economic situation in 1976 and the fairly substantial number of unemployed in the electorate—and the number exposed to unemployment in their families—the overall impact of the unemployed appears quite muted, less than half of one percent. Our analysis has uncovered several reasons why this is so. First of all, although
unemployment has a noticeable effect upon voting at the individual level,
that effect is relatively small; for the unemployed are not as distinctive in

---

[12]For two reasons these figures should be interpreted with some caution. First, the
differences are based on relatively small numbers of cases. Furthermore, it is sometimes argued that normal vote analysis may not remove all the long-term effects from
the vote. Demographic characteristics may influence the vote as well.

their voting behavior as many other groups. In addition, the potential impact of their distinctive bias toward the Democrats is diminished by the relatively low turnout rate characteristic of the unemployed. Furthermore, the aggregate impact of the jobless was quite small in 1976 because even in a period of high unemployment they were a small proportion of the electorate. (Yet we may be underestimating the contribution of the unemployed to Carter's vote. In considering the relationship of employment status to changes in party affiliation, we noted a slight tendency for jobless Republicans to leave the party. If this effect has been a continuing one, then partisanship is not merely an underlying characteristic but reflects experiences with unemployment as well.)

Although a 0.5-percent increment seems very small, we should not ignore it altogether. In a close election, as many presidential contests indeed are, shifts of even this size can be decisive. In 1960, for example, a nationwide shift of 0.5 percent would have given the plurality of votes to Nixon rather than to Kennedy. And a shift of only that magnitude would have deprived Nixon of his victory in California or Kennedy of his in Illinois.

Furthermore, as we have mentioned numerous times, the impact of unemployment may not be limited to those who are unemployed at the time of the election. Those who have experienced unemployment or those who are concerned about unemployment in the future may also deviate in their votes. While we cannot calculate the impact on the vote of fear of future unemployment, we can repeat the analysis in Table 12-6 for the larger group of those currently or recently exposed to unemployment: those who themselves or whose heads of household either were out of work at the time of the election or had been out of work during the preceding year. This group is three times the size of the group unemployed at the time of the election and for reasons that are unclear to us, was even more distinctive in its voting behavior, voting 3.4 percent more Democratic than expected. Referring to the figures contained in Table 12-4D, we repeat our previous calculations. If those exposed to unemployment in the past year through their own joblessness or that of the household head had, like those with no exposure to unemployment, voted 5.5 percent less Democratic than expected on the basis of partisanship alone, then Carter's vote would have been diminished by 1.7 percent, a not insignificant figure in a close election.

Attitudes, Economic Strain, and the Vote

Considering the high rate of unemployment in 1976, the concern about pocketbook issues expressed by the electorate, and the evident differences in the positions of the parties—differences that the public apparently perceived—the resultant impact of the unemployed on the division of the vote is surprisingly small. These data, however, neglect an important alternative way in which unemployment can affect electoral outcomes. Unemployment can have an impact on the vote if voters who are not themselves unemployed nevertheless vote on the basis of a concern about joblessness or on the basis of preferences with respect to economic policies. Clearly, a voter does not have to suffer from job insecurity himself to consider unemployment a major problem and have it influence his vote. As a matter of fact, we have already seen that it is the leaders of the two parties, who are relatively less likely to have been unemployed themselves, whose views on the subject are most polarized.

Presumably, attitude toward unemployment and economic issues can operate independently of employment status or in tandem with the experience of joblessness. It is our expectation that opinions on these matters would have a special salience for the unemployed. That is, we expect that the combination of an objective condition, unemployment, and subjective attitudes would be a particularly potent influence on voting.

In Table 12-7 we present a normal vote analysis of the voting behavior of respondents who take various positions on issues relating to unemployment: whether inflation or unemployment is considered a more important national problem; whether the government should see to it that every person has a job and a decent standard of living or should let each person get ahead on his own; whether the problem of unemployment would be handled better by the Republicans or the Democrats; and whether Ford or Carter would be more likely to reduce unemployment. There are distinct deviations from the expected vote in the various categories of the attitude questions. Those who considered unemployment more important as a problem than inflation; those who believed that the government has an obligation to provide jobs; those who believed that the Democratic party would deal with the problem more effectively; and those who deemed Carter more likely to reduce unemployment—all voted Democratic in numbers substantially beyond what would have been expected on the basis of their partisanship alone. Those who took the opposite positions voted Republican beyond what would have been predicted on the basis of party loyalties.

When we refer back to Table 12-4, it is obvious that these deviations are greater than those found in relation to unemployment as an objective circumstance. In each case the spread in Democratic vote between the attitude groups is larger than that which separated the employed from the jobless. Although the gap is noticeable with respect to considering unemployment a problem and advocating a government policy of providing jobs, it is especially prominent when it comes to which party or candidate would do a better job on the unemployment issue. In each case the difference between the attitude groups—both in actual vote and

Table 12-7   Normal vote analysis, 1976, of attitudes toward unemployment.

| Attitude | DEMOCRATIC VOTE (PERCENT) | | |
	Expected	Actual	Deviation from expected
Which is a more important national problem?			
Inflation	50	42	−8 (858)
Unemployment	60	67	+7 (499)
Should the government provide jobs and a decent standard of living?			
No	47	38	−9 (366)
Mixed	53	49	−4 (313)
Yes	65	73	+8 (722)
Which party would handle unemployment better?			
Republican	25	4	−21 (174)
No difference	49	39	−10 (897)
Democrats	70	79	+9 (593)
Which candidate would reduce unemployment?			
Ford	36	11	−25 (238)
No difference	48	33	−15 (668)
Carter	69	86	+17 (602)

SOURCE: Center for Political Studies, University of Michigan, 1976 election survey.

in vote when adjusted for partisanship—is larger than that between the working and unemployed. It seems that subjective views on unemployment issues play a more significant role in relation to the vote than does the objective status of being on the job or out of work.

What we have not yet confronted is the possible interaction of objective employment status and subjective attitudes. It seems reasonable to predict that subjective views about unemployment would have a greater effect on the behavior of the unemployed than on the employed—that is, that the unemployed who considered unemployment to be a problem or felt that the government was responsible for dealing with unemployment or who saw a difference between the parties or the candidates in their ability to deal with the problem of unemployment—would be especially likely to vote on the basis of these beliefs rather than simply on the basis of their long-term partisan commitments.

The data in Table 12-8 indicate that there is no such interaction effect. In the table we replicate the preceding normal vote analysis, but present the data separately for the employed and the unemployed. In only one case, seeing unemployment as a more important problem than inflation, is the deviation from the expected vote more substantial for the unemployed than for the employed. With respect to which candidate or which

Table 12-8 Normal vote analysis, 1976, of attitudes toward unemployment of working and unemployed respondents.

	Democratic vote (percent)		
Attitude	Expected	Actual	Deviation from expected
Which is a more important national problem?			
Working			
Inflation	50	44	−6 (492)
Unemployment	58	67	+9 (281)
Unemployed			
Inflation	59	43	−16 (38)
Unemployment	65	80	+15 (36)
Should the government provide jobs and a decent standard of living?			
Working			
No or mixed	51	43	−8 (626)
Yes	64	70	+6 (197)
Unemployed			
No or mixed	55	55	0 (45)
Yes	69	69	0 (32)
Which party would handle unemployment better?			
Working			
Republican	28	6	−22 (106)
No difference	49	39	−10 (497)
Democrats	69	80	+11 (350)
Unemployed			
Republican	[Too few cases]		
No difference	53	47	−6 (37)
Democrats	72	78	+6 (45)
Which candidate would reduce unemployment?			
Working			
Ford	39	16	−23 (155)
No difference	47	34	−13 (401)
Carter	68	86	+18 (340)
Unemployed			
Ford	[Too few cases]		
No difference	57	47	−10 (29)
Carter	72	82	+10 (42)

source: Center for Political Studies, University of Michigan, 1976 election survey.

party would be more competent in handling unemployment, working respondents, if anything, deviate slightly more from the expected vote than do the unemployed. Finally, attitudes toward the issue of the government's responsibility in providing jobs and a decent standard of living seem to be more strongly related to voting among the working than among those out of work. Why this should be the case—in contrast to the other attitudes where the effect of the attitude on the vote is substantial for both the working and the unemployed—is unclear.[13]

We should add one last note. Although attitudes about unemployment appear to have a stronger effect on the way an individual casts his ballot than does the experience of being out of work, the net impact of attitudes on the overall division of the vote is somewhat ambiguous. After all, attitudes about unemployment work in both directions at once. That is, those who deemed Carter or the Democrats more competent in handling unemployment voted very solidly Democratic, more Democratic even than would have been predicted on the basis of their already Democratic partisanship; those who took the opposite position voted Republican, more Republican than would have been predicted on the basis of their

[13]One possible explanation is that the unemployed, being somewhat less educated, are not so likely to make connections among their personal economic circumstances, general attitudes on whether the government should see to it that all citizens have jobs, and their votes. To make such links demands an awareness that the parties take different positions and an ability to connect the right party with its stand. The unemployed may not recognize this as readily as the employed.

The comparison in Table 12-8 between the employed and the unemployed was repeated using the alternative definitions of exposure to unemployment given in Table 12-4, to see whether those who experienced unemployment in the family or who had a history of exposure to unemployment were more likely to adjust their vote to match their attitudes. The results are no different from those reported on Table 12-8; there is no interaction between objective exposure to unemployment and subjective attitudes.

In order to confirm our analysis of the relative importance of objective employment status and subjective views, we carried out a multivariate analysis of the vote, using multiple classification analysis. The dependent variable was a dichotomy: whether the respondent voted Democratic or Republican. The independent variables were attitudes toward unemployment plus a measure of the individual's own employment status. Party identification was entered into the analysis as a covariate, a procedure that removes the impact of long-term partisan identification from the vote. When objective employment status was put into the analysis along with a measure of the perception that unemployment is a national problem and a measure of attitudes toward the government's responsibility for unemployment, the positive relationship between objective employment status and the vote disappeared. When two more attitudes—the beliefs that Carter would do a better job than Ford and that the Democrats would do a better job than the Republicans—were added to the analysis, the relationship between objective employment status and the vote reversed; in other words, when these attitudes were held constant, the employed were more likely to vote Democratic than those out of work.

party ties. One might be tempted, on this basis, to surmise that the effect of unemployment as an issue was nil, since opposing attitudes were associated with opposing votes. However, the effects did not cancel each other out. As shown by Table 12-7, a clear plurality of voters considered Carter and the Democrats more capable of contending with unemployment. Even though Ford collected votes from those who considered the Republicans and their candidate more competent, such voters were far less numerous than those who held the opposite point of view. Thus, the effect of such attitudes was clearly to benefit the Democrats.

Conclusion

There were more people out of work and the unemployment rate was at a higher level in 1976 than in any presidential election year since the depression. Many in the electorate had been exposed to unemployment—either personally or by virtue of the joblessness of those around them, family or friends. The political parties, which have for over a generation taken opposing positions on the unemployment issue, presented candidates who differentiated themselves from each other in the tradition of their respective parties. As a result, 1976 was a good time to investigate the role of unemployment in electoral politics.

Our analysis, however, indicates that the unemployed as a group contributed less significantly to the electoral outcome in 1976 than the common wisdom would have suggested. The limited impact of the unemployed on the election was in part a function of the fact that not only were they a relatively small portion of the electorate, but a disproportionate number of jobless voters never even bothered to vote. Thus, no matter how distinctive their behavior might have been, the impact of the unemployed was necessarily limited by the small number of jobless voters. And their behavior was not all that distinctive. With respect to pre-election candidate preferences, the working and the unemployed expressed quite similar views—except for unemployed Republicans, who were in April considerably less likely than their working fellow partisans to report willingness to support Gerald Ford. When it came to the actual casting of ballots, 62 percent of the unemployed voted for Carter. This is a solid Democratic majority—equivalent to the share of the vote won by Carter in that traditionally Democratic bloc, unionized workers, but considerably less than the share of the vote he won among Jews, or among blacks and other racial minorities. Thus, not only were the unemployed only a small fraction of the electorate, but they did not act as an especially cohesive group in voting.

How do we reconcile our finding of the limited contribution made by the unemployed to the electoral outcome in 1976 with the findings of some of the studies based on aggregate data, that poor macroeconomic performance is associated with electoral punishment of incumbents and, perhaps, of Republicans? Our analysis suggests two potential answers. First, personal exposure to unemployment is not confined to those who are out of work at the time of an election. When we added to those unemployed at the time of the 1976 election those who had been out of work during the past year as well as those whose heads of household had experienced unemployment, the net effect on Carter's votes tripled, rising from 0.5 percent to 1.7 percent.

Additional insight emerges from our data on attitudes. Although we cannot measure with any precision the magnitude of that impact, the data presented indicate clearly a relationship between attitudes toward unemployment and the vote. We found, moreover, not only that attitudes are more potent in predicting votes than objective employment status, but that the relationship between attitudes and votes holds for both the employed and the jobless. As a matter of fact, working respondents—for reasons we cannot explain—actually seem somewhat more likely than the unemployed to convert these attitudes into votes. Thus, our findings are consistent with the hypothesis that unemployment has potential for influencing national electoral outcomes, but that the effect comes, not from the unemployed themselves, but from others who vote in accordance with their opinions on unemployment as an issue.[14]

With respect to our fundamental concern with the relationship between personal economic strain and microlevel political behavior, our findings reinforce our previous conclusion that the impact of unemployment seems to be quite contained. In the 1976 election the unemployed as a group behaved quite similarly to others in the electorate who share their social backgrounds and partisan preferences. With respect to turnout, they were less likely to vote than the employed. However, their propensity not to vote reflects their demographic characteristics more than unemployment-induced withdrawal. When it came to voting, the unemployed were a rather Democratic group. However, their tendency to support Carter at the polls was more a function of their long-term partisan

[14]This conclusion is consistent with Kinder and Kiewiet's analysis of congressional elections. They find that unemployment as a problem in one's personal life has only a small impact on congressional voting. In contrast, attitudes toward unemployment as a national problem play an important role in the voting choice. See Donald R. Kinder and D. Roderick Kiewiet, "Economic Discontent and Political Behavior: The Role of Personal Grievances and Collective Economic Judgments in Congressional Voting," *American Journal of Political Science* (in press), and their "Political Consequences of Economic Concerns," paper delivered at the Annual Meeting of the American Political Science Association, New York, September 1978.

commitments than of their jobless condition. As shown by our normal vote analysis, the unemployed do deviate in a Democratic direction, beyond what would have been expected on the basis of their party ties, but this deviation is not as great as that associated with beliefs about unemployment among working and unemployed alike.

The data on the 1976 election thus are consistent with the pattern we have found relative to other aspects of the political beliefs and behavior of the unemployed. The lack of a job creates a severe personal strain on the individual, but that strain is not translated into politically meaningful activity. Political activity is more a function of beliefs about politics than of specific personal experiences; political beliefs, in turn, are more a function of general social beliefs than of personal experiences. Once again, the severe economic strain of job loss has little direct impact on political life. However, under certain circumstances what is clearly a weak effect at the individual level can have a noticeable impact if the group is large. The unemployed and those who have experienced unemployment are not a small group and they do show a tilt against the incumbent. And when the impact of beliefs about unemployment is added to the impact of the experience of joblessness, the size of the effect grows to the point where it could be of significance in a close election.[15]

[15]Unemployment may have a more long-term impact on electoral outcomes, an impact not apparent at any one election. Consider our data on party switching, where we observed some tendency for jobless Republicans to change to the Democratic party. If unemployment has had a continuing anti-Republican effect on party identification, then some of the propensity of the unemployed to vote Democratic, which we attributed to their underlying partisanship, may in fact be related to joblessness, past or present.

Epilogue

Participation, Policy, and Pluralism

WRITING DURING THE 1930s, John Maynard Keynes solved an old economic riddle: how to explain the existence of idled workers and silent machines in the midst of crushing human needs. He pointed out that there is nothing self-regulating about an economy in recession, for there can be economic equilibrium at less than full utilization of economic resources. With respect to the idled workers themselves, Robert Heilbroner summarizes Keynes's theory: "The unemployed are little more than economic zeros; they might as well be on the moon for all the economic influence they exert on the market place."[1] We need not label them political ciphers to see that the unemployed have an analogous position with respect to the polity. We have found little evidence of political action by the jobless to influence political outcomes. What we have been describing, then, is a situation of political equilibrium at less than full mobilization of political interests.

We have confirmed the antipluralist observation that the representation of politically relevant needs in the political process is by no means automatic. But just because the unemployed are not active and clamorous on their own behalf, it would be erroneous to conclude that their problems are entirely overlooked. Unlike, for example, the issue of equality for women (which had no place on the political agenda until the activity of those who had long endured but only recently recognized their deprivation placed it there), unemployment is a political issue: polls report that people are concerned about it; the media pay attention to it; candidates talk about it; government policies try to reduce it or contain

[1] *The Worldly Philosophers*, rev. ed. (New York: Simon and Schuster, 1961), p. 236.

its effects. As a matter of fact, during the period of our study two major pieces of legislation dealing with unemployment were enacted: the Humphrey-Hawkins Full Employment and Balanced Growth Act, and the Comprehensive Employment and Training Act (CETA). Unemployment unambiguously has a place on the political agenda, but that position has not been achieved through the efforts of the unemployed themselves.

Given that the problem of unemployment engages the attention of political leaders, is the political quiescence of those who are out of work, then, irrelevant? If the government was already worrying about them and acting on their behalf, would it have made any difference if they had been more articulate in making demands? Would the policies designed to aid them have been pursued more vigorously if the jobless had been vocal and organized? If what did not happen had indeed taken place, would the unemployed have been better off?

In order to arrive at a tentative answer to these questions we mined the work of scholars who have studied the making of employment policy, perused the record of recent congressional actions in the *Congressional Quarterly*, and considered the testimony given in recent congressional hearings. We supplemented what we learned by talking with people who are involved in making policy—congressional staff, Labor Department officials, lobbyists from unions and other organizations—as well as informed observers from universities, research organizations, and the press. It was not our purpose to undertake a full-scale analysis of the making of employment policy. Even if we had done so, however, our final assessment of the political impact of the inactivity of the unemployed would have been speculative.

Public Policy and Unemployment

Virtually any policy that deals with the state of the economy has consequences for the unemployed. It is convenient, however, to group the policy instruments used to aid the jobless into three categories. First are those designed to provide income to those out of work, either by giving them money directly through unemployment compensation or general welfare programs or by providing work relief (short-term employment in the public sector at low wages) until permanent work becomes available. Short-term job-creation programs are often coupled with a second kind of effort designed to aid those out of work: programs to provide job skills, training, counseling, and placement so that the unemployed can reenter the labor market on a competitive basis. A third group of measures—fiscal and monetary policies, tax policies, area redevelopment, and expanded public works—is intended to increase the overall demand for labor and thereby create jobs for the unemployed.

A remarkably consistent pattern emerges from the various studies of the making of such policies. All of these are policies that redistribute wealth across broad social categories of have's and have-not's; in general, the politics of such policies involves conflict between inclusive, ideologically based coalitions of liberals and conservatives.[2] Unlike the coalitions often said to be characteristic of American politics—issue-specific, short-lived associations between narrow interests that may find themselves in opposition on subsequent issues—these are ongoing alliances among peak associations that speak for broad constituencies. Furthermore, these issues hew to the lines of party cleavage and divide Republicans from Democrats.[3] By and large, then, these issues mobilize the activist, liberal coalition that formed under the Democrats during the New Deal—based on labor, urban groups, racial minorities, the disadvantaged, and liberal intellectuals—a coalition that tends to be resurrected when economic issues are at stake. Of course, there are exceptions to such a pattern of conflict between frozen coalitions: for example, many business leaders broke with their tradition of fiscal orthodoxy and supported John F. Kennedy's 1963 tax cut.[4]

An additional element is introduced into the politics of manpower programs in which jobs are created or job training is given, especially those in which federal funds are funneled to state and local governments. The characteristic conflict between liberals and conservatives remains present. But because manpower programs are distributive in character— that is, they can be targeted to provide certain kinds of programs for certain kinds of workers in certain specific locales—there is also intense pressure from potential beneficiaries. In addition to groups like the AFL-CIO and the Chamber of Commerce, whose interest is broadly ideologi-

[2]See, for example, Stephen K. Bailey, Congress Makes a Law (New York: Columbia University Press, 1950); Eveline M. Burns, "The Determinants of Policy," in Joseph M. Becker, ed., In Aid of the Unemployed (Baltimore: Johns Hopkins Press, 1965), pp. 275-289; James L. Sundquist, Politics and Policy: The Eisenhower, Kennedy and Johnson Years (Washington, D.C.: Brookings Institution, 1968), chaps. 2, 3; Herbert Stein, The Fiscal Revolution in America (Chicago: University of Chicago Press, 1969); Arthur Okun, The Political Economy of Prosperity (Washington, D.C.: Brookings Institution, 1970); Lawrence C. Pierce, The Politics of Fiscal Policy Formation (Pacific Palisades, Calif.: Goodyear Publishing Co., 1971); Roger Davidson, The Politics of Comprehensive Manpower Legislation (Baltimore: Johns Hopkins University Press, 1972); Gary Orfield, Congressional Power: Congress and Social Change (New York: Harcourt, Brace, Jovanovich, 1975), chaps. 10, 11.

[3]As we saw in Chapter 11, there is a sharp and consistent difference between the parties in terms of their economic priorities: Republicans at all levels are more concerned about inflation, Democrats about unemployment. See also Edward R. Tufte, Political Control of the Economy (Princeton, N.J.: Princeton University Press, 1978), chap. 4.

[4]Sundquist, Politics and Policy, p. 47.

cal, narrowly self-interested groups like the U.S. Conference of Mayors, the American Federation of State, County, and Municipal Employees, the American Vocational Association, and spokesmen for special target groups such as veterans or the elderly are heard from. As is so often the case when government subsidies are at stake, the path of least political resistance is to satisfy all of these intensely interested potential recipients by providing something for each:

> One inexperienced Nixon appointee had warned [Senate subcommittee chairman Gaylord] Nelson's staff director not to report out a [manpower] bill with so many categorical programs. "You'll be the laughing stock of everyone," the administration aide protested. "Why, there is something for everybody in that bill!" The remark occasioned much laughter around Nelson's office, for of course that was the very reason for the bill's attractiveness.[5]

Whatever the nuances in the individual descriptions of the politics of the making of various policies, one thing is invariable. The unemployed themselves figure not at all. With one exception—in 1958 a special Senate subcommittee under the chairmanship of freshman Sen. Eugene McCarthy met and talked directly with the unemployed and generated nine volumes of quite moving testimony[6]—the jobless are not part of the process. Unlike other beneficiaries of the programs (the municipal officials who would administer them, the federal bureaucrats in whose agencies they would be lodged, the social workers who would staff them), the unemployed do not press their case spontaneously. Nor are they consulted.

Policy in the 1970s: Humphrey-Hawkins and CETA

In order to answer the difficult question of whether it would have made any difference if the unemployed had indeed been more active on their own behalf, we looked more closely at the policy process during the mid-1970s. During the period contemporaneous to our study, a number

[5]Davidson, *Politics of Manpower Legislation*, p. 37. Orfield makes a similar point. He reports that consensus for manpower legislation was built by "including everyone's special concern—from Indians to aerospace workers—in the bill, with little effort to sort out priorities" (*Congressional Power*, p. 242).

Our description of the general patterns of conflict that are characteristic of redistributive and distributive issues follows the outlines set forth by Theodore J. Lowi in "American Business, Public Policy, Case Studies, and Political Theory," *World Politics*, 16 (July 1964), 677-715. Also relevant is James Q. Wilson's typology, which categorizes policies according to whether the costs and benefits are concentrated or distributed. See his *Political Organizations* (New York: Basic Books, 1973), chap. 16.

[6]Sundquist, *Politics and Policy*, p. 80.

of measures relevant to employment were enacted at the federal level. Included among these were various public-works bills and modifications of unemployment compensation. In our attempt to understand the implications of the silence of the unemployed we focused on the two measures that seemed to generate the most controversy and attract the most attention from the media, the Humphrey-Hawkins Bill and the renewal of CETA.

As introduced in 1976 by Rep. Augustus Hawkins and Sen. Hubert Humphrey, the Full Employment and Balanced Growth Act was an ambitious bill designed to implement the general principle embodied in the Full Employment Act of 1946. According to the bill as introduced, the federal government would guarantee jobs to everyone able and willing to work. Federal employment services were to be extended and a standby job corps established to place those who could not find other employment into temporary public-service jobs. The president would be required to submit a "full employment and national purpose" budget each year outlining a plan to achieve 3-percent unemployment. An appropriation of $15 billion was recommended for the first year.

A quite different bill was passed by Congress in the fall of 1978. It barely resembled the original proposal. The operative parts of the program had been excised, leaving a symbolic full-employment policy, now defined as 4-percent unemployment. Even the symbolism was diluted by the concurrent articulation of an inflation goal—3 percent in the short run, 0 percent in the long run. Each goal individually was somewhat unrealistic, and combining the two was still more so. Yet most proponents of the bill considered its passage a victory. As several of its advocates told us, even a weak bill sets a precedent for more effective legislation in the future.[7] In its final attenuated form, Humphrey-Hawkins was broadly—if symbolically—redistributive in intent and offered no specific benefits to particular groups.

The Comprehensive Employment and Training Act differs from Humphrey-Hawkins in its distributive aspects: specific benefits become available to particular groups. Following the pattern outlined, the politics of CETA involved intense competition among contenders for these resources—not simply among advocates for various groups of jobless workers who might be singled out for categorical mention, but more im-

---

[7]It might be claimed that these advocates were being naive. Murray Edelman argues that policy makers often take symbolic steps in order to defuse public pressure. Having satisfied popular demands for action, they are able to avoid making tangible concessions. See *The Symbolic Uses of Politics* (Urbana: University of Illinois Press, 1964), chap. 2. The Full Employment Act of 1946 illustrates Edelman's contention perfectly: a symbolic gesture was made and was not followed up by real benefits.

portantly among the officials of the public and private agencies that manage the jobs programs.

Since its passage in 1973, CETA has been controversial in several respects.[8] There are, first of all, conflicts over whom the program should assist. Successive versions of the program have varied in terms of their emphasis upon aiding the cyclically unemployed (those out of work because of economic slowdown) by stimulating the economy, or aiding the structurally unemployed (those whose skills or location are out of phase with the needs of the labor market). Title VI, added in 1976, was clearly countercyclical; it allowed the hiring of workers who had been out of work only fifteen days at reasonably generous wages. Title VI came under fire, in part for benefiting skilled workers and failing to reach the structurally unemployed. It was revised in 1978 to limit eligibility to those who had fairly low incomes and who had been out of work at least fifteen weeks. A related matter has been the controversy over what is called "creaming." Under pressure to produce an impressive success rate, CETA programs have sometimes skimmed off the most skilled among the unemployed, ignoring the poor and the hard-core jobless. Critics argue that CETA jobs should be targeted to help those who are most in need.

Another area of disagreement is how much autonomy to give the local units that administer the programs. The arguments are familiar ones, typical of many federal programs that depend on local implementation: local prime sponsors complain of burdensome paper work and of insufficient independence to meet local needs; critics of local autonomy complain of disregard of overall program objectives and inefficiency, favoritism, and sometimes outright corruption in the use of funds. A related problem is "fiscal substitution." The accusation is made that local governments are using CETA as a federal subsidy not to hire new workers, but to pay workers whose salaries once came from local taxes. In many cities a quarter of all workers, and in many counties a third, are paid by CETA funds. The rejoinder is made that without CETA these people would have to be fired; in essence, then, jobs are being created.

Who Speaks for the Unemployed?

The configuration of political forces on these two employment-related policies was remarkably similar to that depicted in the literature on the making of economic policy. With reference to Humphrey-Hawkins, the array of contending groups is little changed from the one described by

[8]For a discussion of the controversies surrounding CETA, see Harrison H. Donnelly, "CETA: Successful Jobs Program or Subsidy to Local Governments?" *Congressional Quarterly Weekly Report* (April 1, 1978), 799-806.

Stephen K. Bailey for the Full Employment Act of 1946.[9] What he calls the "lib-lab" coalition which supported that act was coordinated by the Union for Democratic Action, an umbrella group for various other organizations (the AFL and the CIO, the National Farmers' Union, the National Catholic Welfare Conference, the NAACP, the YWCA, the American Veterans' Committee, and other religious, labor, and civil rights groups). A generation later the liberal coalition that emerged to support Humphrey-Hawkins under the loose leadership of the Full Employment Action Council included virtually the same groups: the AFL-CIO and numerous operating unions, civil rights groups such as the Urban League and the NAACP, religious groups like the National Council of Churches, women's organizations, and public-interest organizations. The principal differences are that the farmers seem to have disappeared, and trained economists seem to have acquired a significant role.[10] As in 1946 the measure was sponsored by Democrats and involved a relatively high level of conflict between the parties. And, as before, the unemployed were nowhere to be found in the process.[11]

Chaired jointly by civil rights leader Coretta King and union leader Murray Finley, president of the Amalgamated Clothing and Textile Workers of America, the Full Employment Action Council (FEAC) speaks for the unemployed, but its members are not jobless workers. Although FEAC has made sporadic—and largely unsuccessful—attempts to organize the unemployed, it is basically a consortium of organizations. The board comprises representatives of member organizations, not people who are out of work. Furthermore, none of the member groups is an organization of the unemployed. Although civil rights groups—and, to a lesser extent, women's groups and unions—organize constituencies that suffer from relatively high levels of unemployment, in no case is a group constituted solely of the unemployed. It is clear, furthermore, that in no

[9]*Congress Makes a Law*, chaps. 5, 7.

[10]The growing influence of professional economists in the making of macroeconomic policy has been a major change in the policy process. These technical experts are housed in the goverment—in agencies like the Office of Management and Budget, the Council of Economic Advisers, and the Commerce, Labor, and Treasury Departments—as well as in private institutions such as research centers and universities. It should be noted that these specialists often give conflicting advice. On the role of economists see Pierce, *Politics of Policy Formation*, and Okun, *Political Economy of Prosperity*.

[11]To say that they were nowhere to be found is a slight overstatement. Among the 173 witnesses whose testimony we reviewed, there was one unemployed person.

As mentioned in Chapter 10, we asked our informants whether there had been political activity on the part of the unemployed that we had missed. They confirmed that there had not.

case is support for full employment a response to membership pressure. The position taken by organization leaders on employment matters has reflected ideological commitment to social justice rather than a desire to meet the particular needs, or to respond to the expressed wishes, of the rank and file. With respect to unions, for example, a number of our informants differentiated between the sentiments of union rank and file, most of whom have jobs, and the ideological commitments of those at the top. Described by one as "the usual do-gooder bunch," union leaders have on "their social-service caps" when they lobby for full employment. This helps to explain why advocacy of full employment has often been stronger within the AFL-CIO, a peak association with a broader constituency, than within the operating unions.[12]

Because the groups in the full-employment coalition were all organized for other purposes and serve constituencies of people who are, for the most part, not unemployed, employment policy for them is a matter of sincere, but not paramount, concern. What this means is that each has an agenda of priorities reflecting the parochial needs of its members; employment policy is only one item on that agenda. According to an FEAC staff member, all the members of the coalition had "other fish to fry" at the time Humphrey-Hawkins was being considered. The women's groups were giving their highest priority to extension of the Equal Rights Amendment deadline; the civil rights groups were preoccupied with affirmative action; and the labor unions were giving precedence to two measures with serious implications for the welfare of unions as organizations, the common-situs picketing bill and the Labor Law Reform Act.[13] Even though in each case the commitment to full employment was sincere, these anterior concerns diminished the resources available to press

[12]Some of the operating unions, for example, the Amalgamated Clothing Workers, United Automobile Workers, International Union of Operating Engineers, and International Association of Machinists, take a strong stand. Others, however, offer only token support. Derek C. Bok and John T. Dunlop point out that among operative unions, commitment to broad goals of social justice is a function of both the philosophy of the leadership and the needs of members. See their *Labor and the American Community* (New York: Simon and Schuster, 1970), p. 385.

Civil rights seems to be an area in which the liberalism of the unions' position is particularly a reflection of the ideology of leadership rather than pressure from rank and file. See *Labor and the American Community*, pp. 134 and 460, and J. David Greenstone, *Labor in American Politics* (New York: Alfred A. Knopf, 1969), p. 343.

[13]The Labor Law Reform Act, killed in a Senate fillibuster in the summer of 1978, would have modified the 1935 National Labor Relations (Wagner) Act in order to make it easier for unions to organize nonunion firms. Because it would have affected the ability of the unions to build up membership, it was vital to their organizational maintenance needs. The common-situs picketing act would have permitted picketing

for full employment. This was particularly obvious in the case of labor. One observer estimated the relative effort devoted to labor law reform as opposed to Humphrey-Hawkins at 100 to 1, an assessment confirmed by others. The leading AFL-CIO lobbyist described to us the time he had spent on Humphrey-Hawkins: full-time, intense work when the bill was drafted, when it was on the House floor, and at other crucial junctions. However, when the bill was in the Senate Banking Committee, where the crippling inflation amendment was added, he was "tied up with other things" and able to do almost nothing. For other groups the pattern was the same. Thus, although the support by coalition members was well-meaning and sincere, it hardly entailed all-out effort.

The politics of CETA are somewhat different, conforming to the distributive pattern described for manpower programs. Because CETA, unlike Humphrey-Hawkins, provides concentrated benefits to identifiable groups, it was the target of intense lobbying by groups motivated by considerations of narrow self-interest rather than broad ideology. Some of those who lobbied represented the interests of special categories within the eligible population, such as municipal workers, veterans, or the handicapped. However, much more common than activity on behalf of the ultimate recipients of CETA assistance were efforts by those who would administer CETA programs. A great deal of pressure was exerted by local government officials, who had in the past used CETA funds as a form of revenue sharing to pay workers who would otherwise have been a drain on local budgets. Even after the 1978 version of CETA made it more difficult to use funds for budget relief, local officials, recognizing the potential usefulness of CETA funds as a political resource, continued to be in-

---

of an entire construction site in disputes involving only one subcontractor and therefore was critical to the organizational enhancement of construction unions. Common situs was passed in 1975, but vetoed by President Ford and defeated when it was brought up again in 1977. On the politics of the Labor Reform Act, see Harrison H. Donnelly, "Labor Law Revision: Senate Fight Looms," *Congressional Quarterly Weekly Report* (February 11, 1978), 330-331, and "Labor Bill Recommitted after Sixth Cloture Failure," *Congressional Quarterly Weekly Report* (June 24, 1978), 1599. On common situs, see Norman J. Ornstein and Shirley Elder, *Interest Groups, Lobbying and Policymaking* (Washington, D.C.: Congressional Quarterly Press, 1978), chap. 5.

James Q. Wilson argues that unions consider matters of organizational maintenance a priority because they need a high proportion of workers in their field to succeed. Once organizational needs are met, union leaders have considerable autonomy: "One consequence of the growth and institutionalization of union security arrangements is that much of the political activity of unions can be directed towards ends that large numbers of union members either do not share or actively oppose. These political activities . . . reflect in all probability more the interests of professional staff members and key union leaders" (*Political Organizations*, p. 136).

volved with CETA and sought control over the distribution of funds. Parallel concern was evidenced by leaders of community-based organizations that would sponsor programs and the social-service professionals who would staff them. All had an interest in aiding the hard-core jobless in their locales as well as a self-interested stake in cornering as large a share of available resources as possible.[14]

The position of organized labor with reference to CETA was less unambiguous than in the case of Humphrey-Hawkins, because CETA provides benefits to certain categories of organized workers while simultaneously threatening others. Once again, organized labor joined with other members of the liberal coalition to support CETA for reasons of altruistic commitment to social justice. However, the most intense pressure came from unions having a more specific stake. Municipal workers' unions supported provisions that funded local government jobs—especially the remunerative jobs held by their members. Other unions supported CETA training programs in order to raise the skill level of union members. Opposition came from unions that wished to keep CETA workers from providing competition at reduced wages.

A systematic examination of the testimony given in congressional hearings substantiates our informants' descriptions of the contrasting patterns of support for the two measures. In Table E-1 we categorize the statements of those who testified on each bill in terms of the degree of support. Several interesting differences emerge. First, those who testified on Humphrey-Hawkins were more likely to indicate unequivocal support or opposition than those who testified on CETA, the overwhelming majority of whom made specific suggestions for changes. Furthermore, with respect to Humphrey-Hawkins, the support of the Lib-Lab coalition is arrayed against the opposition of business. With respect to CETA, however, there is no such clear pattern of conflict between groups. Interestingly, on the latter bill, no union representatives expressed unambiguous support and no business representatives expressed unambiguous opposition. As a matter of fact, the pattern for business and labor is remarkably similar; two-thirds of the spokesmen from each group suggested major changes in CETA. It is not surprising that, when specific benefits are being distributed, interested parties pay close attention to details and suggest many revisions. This pattern is quite different from that for

[14]According to Martha Derthick, the federal social-service programs of the 1960s begat a host of organized pressures in Washington. Social-service professionals, community action leaders, mayors, county officials, and governors all have increased their Washington representation and have become skilled in grantsmanship. See *Uncontrollable Spending for Social Services* (Washington, D.C.: Brookings Institution, 1975), pp. 75-76.

Table E-1 Analysis of testimony on employment measures by various groups (number of appearances and position taken).

Group	HUMPHREY-HAWKINS				CETA			
	Unequivocal support	Minor changes suggested	Major changes suggested	Unequivocal opposition	Unequivocal support	Minor changes suggested	Major changes suggested	Unequivocal opposition
Lib-Lab coalition								
Unions	15	4	0	0	0	10	22	1
Other (civil rights, women's, church, etc.)	22	8	1	1	9	18	55	4
Businesses[a]	4	0	12	10	1	6	12	0
State and local officials and employees[b]	3	7	0	0	18	97	103	3
Economists, academics	15	6	16	4	0	5	17	2

[a]Individual businessmen and representatives of organizations such as the U.S. Chamber of Commerce or the Rubber Manufacturers Association.

[b]Individual officials and representatives of organizations such as the Interstate Conference of Employment Security Agencies or the National Governors' Conference.

SOURCE: Congressional Information Service, Inc., Washington, D.C., *Abstracts of Congressional Publications and Legislative Histories*, 1970, 1972, 1974-1978.

the symbolically redistributive Humphrey-Hawkins bill, which polarized liberals and conservatives and pitted old antagonists against one another.

We might also note the dominance of the state and local officials and employees in testimony on CETA. Although they did show an interest in Humphrey-Hawkins, they far outnumbered representatives of any other interest in testifying on CETA, eclipsing the economists, the Lib-Lab coalition, and business. As a matter of fact, our categorization actually underestimates the importance of public employees, for more than half of the union representatives came from unions that organize public-service workers—teachers, fire fighters, police officers, and other government employees. It is also interesting that these advocates rarely expressed unequivocal support or opposition to the measure. Because of their concern with particular provisions, they frequently called for specific changes.[15]

Political parties played a less distinctive role with respect to CETA than Humphrey-Hawkins. As one would expect, CETA enjoys more support from Democrats than Republicans. Still, much of the dispute about it has crossed party lines as legislators and interest groups concentrate on the specific benefits available. As is so often the case with pork-barrel policies, the competition for resources engages officials of state and local government and community organizations without regard to party. Political concerns of some members of the House—who feared that CETA sponsors would become political rivals in their districts—were similarly nonpartisan in character.

With CETA, then, unlike Humphrey-Hawkins, a large number of those who supported policies designed to reduce unemployment had personal interests at stake. These interests, however, were organizational. Once again, those who pressed for CETA were not unemployed people looking for jobs. They were not even representatives of organizations of jobless workers. Although there were advocates for certain eligible populations such as urban teenagers or Native Americans, the unemployed themselves were not part of the process.

Would It Have Made Any Difference?

In our discussions we posed the "What if . . . ?" question to those involved in the policy process, inquiring whether it would have made any difference if the unemployed had been more vocal. The question was

[15]The role played by the economists and other academics deserves mention. Among the groups listed, they constituted the largest group of witnesses testifying on Humphrey-Hawkins, an issue on which they split in their opinions. With reference to CETA, an issue that did not polarize them, they were greatly outnumbered by representatives of other groups.

greeted with unanimous assent. Most felt that the problem would have been perceived as being more urgent if the unemployed had dramatized their own plight. A number of our informants felt that activity on the part of the unemployed would have been particularly effective in attracting the attention of the younger northern Democrats in Congress, who tend to be more liberal on social issues than on the economic issues that have united Democrats since the New Deal:

> "The freshman Democrat today is likely to be an upper-income type," said the AFL-CIO's [lobbyist Kenneth] Young, "and that causes some problems with economic issues. It's not that they don't vote what they perceive to be working-class concerns, but I think a lot of them are more concerned about inflation than unemployment."[16]

Activity by the unemployed might well have aroused sympathy in such quarters.

Another point made by our informants is that the surrogates who act on behalf of the jobless tend to be, at least with respect to unemployment, foul-weather friends. When the news on the unemployment front is bad, the attention of the full-employment advocates is engaged. However, when unemployment is steady or falling, although the absolute level of joblessness may still be high, their attention may wane. Similarly, when unemployment is upstaged by more pressing concerns, including high rates of inflation, the spokesmen may be diverted. As a matter of fact, a number of the people to whom we spoke blamed persistent inflation and the decline in the unemployment rate from its 1975-1976 peak for the diminishing attention given to Humphrey-Hawkins and the dilution of that bill with an anti-inflation proviso. Analogously, the growing criticism of CETA that preceded changes in the program was attributed to the erosion of concern with unemployment among members of Congress.[17] Had the unemployed been consistent in their attentiveness, as the surrogates on their behalf were not—so the logic goes—they would have fared better.

If the policy makers to whom we spoke were unanimous in agreeing that the unemployed would have been better off if they had been more insistent, they had more trouble in specifying just what might have been

[16]"The AFL-CIO: How Much Clout in Congress?" *Congressional Quarterly Weekly Report* (July 19, 1975), 1532, quoted in Ornstein and Elder, *Interest Groups*, p. 143. The distinctiveness of the younger northern Democrats is examined in William Schneider and Gregory Schell, "The New Democrats," *Public Opinion*, 1 (November/December 1978), 7-13.

[17]See *Congressional Quarterly Weekly Report* (August 12, 1978), 2106.

different. Several pointed to the obvious enfeeblement of Humphrey-Hawkins. Some alluded to the ways that CETA funds have been diverted from the structurally to the cyclically unemployed. Others discussed the implications of specific sets of pressures, such as the intense lobbying by construction unions for public-works programs. The general belief, however, was that the silence of the unemployed left the field to those groups with more specific interests.

Our short excursion into the politics of employment policy suggests—although it hardly proves—that the quiescence of the unemployed makes a difference. It is not that they are ill served by the surrogates who lobby so articulately on their behalf. Their advocates in the full-employment coalition work diligently and sincerely. Even in relation to CETA, a program with many specific benefits to offer, voices were heard speaking for social welfare and the plight of the jobless. Nevertheless, our informants all agreed—and it does appear plausible—that more consistent and insistent pressure by the jobless would have impressed those engaged in making policy with the gravity of the situation and with the seriousness of their needs. It is a case that they could make most compellingly on their own behalf. Thus, our tentative answer to the question "What if . . . ?" is that the absence of direct pressure from the unemployed does have ramifications for government policy.

Unemployment, Class, and Political Response: A Summary

We began our investigation by proposing a series of hypothetical steps that link stress in personal life to government action. We suggested that those disadvantaged economically by their joblessness or their low socioeconomic position would perceive their objective deprivation subjectively, would consider government activity relevant to the alleviation of their problems, would develop a sense of group consciousness and a concomitant set of policy preferences as a prelude to mobilization, electoral, and pressure activity aimed at securing favorable treatment from the government. What we have found is quite different. The ends of the chain are there, but in between are no couplings to join the separate links that we thought would connect them.

Let us summarize briefly our findings. Objective economic disadvantage—especially that associated with joblessness, less so that associated with holding a job that commands little pay, demands little skill, and carries little prestige—produces strain. Of the two variants of economic disadvantage, the short-term one associated with unemployment seems to be accompanied by special stress. When compared to their counterparts who have jobs, the unemployed are much less satisfied both with their income and with their accomplishments in life. We considered the varied characteristics that are alleged to make the "new unemployment" less burdensome—the fact that many of the unemployed are job leavers, new entrants, or reentrants, rather than job losers; that many of them are secondary earners; that much employment is short term; and that many of the unemployed are covered by public and private unemployment-compensation schemes. We found that some of these factors did indeed diminish the strain of unemployment. However, these factors were much less important than we had anticipated. The unemployed—regardless of the reason for their unemployment, the length of their joblessness, their family responsibilities, or their access to benefits—are less satisfied than those with jobs. Furthermore, though our unemployed respondents made strenuous efforts to cope on their own, their efforts did not seem to reduce significantly the economic or psychological strain of joblessness. The fact that unemployment hurts was supported by the data from our structured interviews and confirmed by the intensity of response in our follow-up interviews. That fact is crucial to our argument. The material condition of an individual can be considered a source of strain with possible political implications only when the individual feels the strain.

Having established the reality of the subjective strains, we began to look for the forward links from the strain associated with economic disadvantage to social and political ideology. We considered two aspects of social ideology: class consciousness and belief in an American Dream of individual opportunity for success. In the main, our data supported the stereotyped version of American social ideology—relative commitment to the American Dream and relatively limited evidence of class consciousness. In addition, comparative data from the 1930s showed that although levels of class consciousness were not particularly high even then, they have diminished substantially during the ensuing decades. Furthermore, we found a link between the two components of social ideology: belief in the American Dream is associated with a diminution of class consciousness.

Although the components of social ideology seemed to have a certain internal coherence, it was in relation to social ideology that we found the first major gap in linkages of our model. There appeared to be little connection between personal economic condition and social ideology. This was seen most strikingly in the absence of a link between the severe personal strain of unemployment and cynicism about the American Dream or heightened class consciousness. But other measures of personal experience, such as the individual's own experience with social mobility or his belief about the fairness of his wages, also have little association with social ideology. We did find some connection between low-status occupation and social ideology, but the link is surprisingly weak and, ironically, is weakest in relation to measures of class consciousness. It was remarkable how little relationship there is between objective class and subjective sense of class consciousness.

Social ideology, we believed, would be a crucial connecting link between personal economic strain and political views—views about the responsibilities of the individual for dealing with economic strain as well as preferences for policies to relieve it. We approached the question of whom the unemployed hold responsible for their joblessness with contrary expectations. Given the commitment to the American Dream we had uncovered, it seemed reasonable to anticipate that joblessness would be construed in individualistic terms and therefore that the problem would not be politicized: that is, that the individual would take the blame for his or her joblessness and would take full responsibility for dealing with its consequences; that the unhappiness concomitant to being out of work would not be generalized to political attitudes; and the government would be left out. Given the tendency for the modern state to expand its activities into realms once considered private, and given the tendency in the last decade or two for those who feel themselves aggrieved to look to the government for solutions to their problems, an alternative scenario seemed equally plausible: that the individual would blame the system for his joblessness and hold the government responsible for helping him to cope with the hardships attendant to being out of work.

Neither scenario turned out to be wholly accurate. What we found was an interesting amalgam of views. The unemployed did not blame themselves for their joblessness. We found little of the personal guilt about joblessness said to be characteristic of the 1930s. The unemployed, however, did not deny personal responsibility; most individuals took it upon themselves to cope with unemployment by finding new jobs and making efforts to manage better financially. This is not to say, on the other hand, that the government was absolved of all responsibility. Almost unanimously our jobless respondents agreed not only that the government should be responsible for creating jobs and helping those in economic need, but also that the government is not doing enough in this regard. And, in general, they saw this intervention as their right, not as a matter of governmental beneficence. Our respondents do not seem to have lost their belief in the individual's responsibility to take care of himself, but they couple it with an equally insistent belief that the government has a responsibility also.

With respect to preferences for specific economic policies, we found the relationships between economic deprivation and attitudes to be surprisingly weak. When it came to moderate policies directly relevant to the alleviation of their economic problems—government intervention to provide jobs or benefits for those in need—the unemployed were more likely than their working counterparts to be favorably inclined. However, when it was a matter of policies more drastic in their effects or less directly relevant to the problems of the unemployed, we found little association with joblessness. Nor did other measures of economic insecurity—length of unemployment and pessimism about finding work among the unemployed, job insecurity among the working, exposure to unemployment in the community—have any consistent relationship to views on such matters. With respect to the long-term economic deprivation associated with low socioeconomic position, we found virtually no relationship between social class and economic policy preferences. We also looked into the impact on attitudes of general beliefs about the social order. We had assumed that, if present, class-conscious views would have the potency ascribed to them by Marx. What we found was contrary to this expectation: in the infrequent cases in which class-conscious attitudes appeared, they had a weak and inconsistent association with preferences for policies of economic change. Interestingly, this has not always been the case. When we introduced comparative data from the late 1930s, we found that objective circumstances, social class, unemployment, and subjective class consciousness had a far more substantial relationship to attitudes at that time.

Quite consistently we have found the long-term economic deprivation associated with social class to have weak effects; the impact of the short-term deprivation concomitant to joblessness is far more severe, but is contained. It is associated with real personal unhappiness and with preferences for certain policies designed to ameliorate the situation, but not with general disenchantment with American life, wholesale changes in social ideology, or adoption of radical policy positions.

When we moved from the realm of social ideology and attitudes to the realm of political behavior, we found a continuation of these patterns. Any direct effects of the economic strain of joblessness were targeted, narrowly focused upon aspects of behavior quite relevant to the joblessness itself. Dealing first with political participation, we found—as have many before us—a strong association between political activity and social class. Those who are out of work consistently participate less than their working counterparts, regardless of whether the measure of participation is political interest, voting, or other political activity.

However, this lower level of participation appeared to be the result of the social characteristics of the unemployed—their selective recruitment from social groups that are ordinarily not active—rather than of the experience of unemployment per se. With one exception we found no evidence that the experience of joblessness is accompanied by a withdrawal from political or organizational life. That single exception bears mention: the unemployed seem to withdraw from union activity. The seeming discrepancy between union activity and other forms of political and social activity becomes comprehensible when seen in terms of our overall findings about the effects of joblessness. Union activity is clearly job related in a way that other forms of political and social activity are not. Thus, once again, unemployment seems to have a sharp impact that is nonetheless contained, an effect on that which is proximate but not generalized to attitudes and behaviors less immediately relevant.

We considered two ways in which the economically disadvantaged might be mobilized to higher levels of political activity than one would ordinarily expect from a group with their social characteristics: through organization or through a sense of group consciousness. We found that organizational affiliation among the unemployed is associated with heightened political activity—as is the case among the employed as well —but we also found the unemployed to be relatively unorganized. Consonant with their social characteristics, the unemployed were less likely to be in any organization than were the employed. Furthermore, when we looked beyond our survey data for evidence of organizations specifically aimed at mobilizing the unemployed, we could find none. When we considered the possibility that class consciousness might engender political activity among the economically deprived—as we and others have found race consciousness to do among blacks—we found no evidence that class-conscious workers were more active. If anything, those workers who hold to what can only be considered middle-class identification and beliefs are more active. Thus, just as we found policy preferences to have no moorings in class consciousness, we found political participation among the economically deprived not to be tied to class-conscious beliefs.

Our findings on the direction of the vote were more or less parallel to those with respect to participation. The behavior of the unemployed was a function not of their joblessness, but of their long-term characteristics, in this case their partisanship. Considering presidential voting in the 1976 election—an election in which many voters deemed unemployment an important issue and perceived differences between the parties and their candidates—we found the unemployed to be distinctive in their voting behavior. In casting their ballots, they were much more solidly Democratic than the electorate as a whole. Once again, however, their distinctiveness was in large part a function of a long-term attribute—their partisan commitments—rather than a result of their jobless condition. In this case there is evidence that unemployment per se has a small impact on behavior; the unemployed were slightly more Democratic in their electoral choices than would have been predicted on the basis of their partisanship alone. However, voter evaluations of the relative competence of the competing parties and candidates to handle unemployment and voter attitudes about policies relevant to unemployment turn out to be much better predictors of votes than employment status. What was especially noteworthy was that the relationship between attitudes and votes holds for both working and jobless voters. As a matter of fact, employed voters actually seemed more likely to convert their beliefs about unemployment into electoral choices.

Thus, our data told a consistent story: the effects of unemployment are severe but narrowly focused, manifest in ways that are proximate to the joblessness itself. Many of the connections we had originally expected between unemployment and political beliefs and conduct simply were not made. However, we did find islands of coherence: material condition was related to personal dissatisfaction but not much else; aspects of social ideology were related to one another, but neither backward to material conditions nor forward to political attitudes; political attitudes were related to political behavior as manifested in the voting choice, but they were linked strongly neither to general social ideology nor to material conditions.

The Multiple Solutions to the Puzzle

When we initially posed the puzzle of why nothing happens when injury is added to insult, we remarked that the helpful kibitzers to whom we described our enterprise had provided us with too many solutions. At least one of the suggested solutions to the riddle has turned out to be quite wrong. Each of the others has been a partial key, helpful in unlocking the puzzle but insufficient on its own.

The argument that the unemployed do not *need* to be politically active —because they have limited family responsibilities, because they are out of work for only short periods of time, because they are jobless by choice, because they are protected by financial benefits—was found to be wanting.

The contention that it is *irrational* for the jobless to be politically active because they can contribute more substantially to solving their problems by devoting their limited resources of time and skills to finding work was found to be more persuasive. When questioned, the unemployed themselves recognized the costs of collective political activity and deemed self-help strategies more cost effective. What this interpretation fails to explain is the degree to which the effects of unemployment are contained: the failure of the experience of joblessness to have a substantial impact on social ideology, policy preferences, or direction of the vote once at the polls. Thus, the rationality argument does not explain the failure of unemployment to have effects where the effects are associated with little cost.

A third argument—that the unemployed do not *want* to be politically active because they are committed to an individualistic American Dream and are not class conscious—was similarly a partial key. We indeed found strong evidence of these ideological commitments and saw that the unemployed assume the main burden of coping with the strains of joblessness to be individual. Contrary to this interpretation, however, the jobless do expect the government to assist them. Furthermore, the absence of class consciousness does not seem to be responsible for the lack of activity; even when present, class consciousness seems to have no mobilizing impact.

Finally, the argument that the unemployed *could* not be active because they lack the political resources and skills that more advantaged groups command was found to be correct, but insufficient. Our finding that the unemployed are not a politically active group—for reasons that derive from their socioeconomic status rather than from their jobless condition—is consonant with this interpretation. However, the explanation remains partial because it does not allude to the prior connections that were left unmade. The unemployed are kept out of the political arena not only—and perhaps not primarily—by their lack of political resources, but also by their failure to politicize fully the stresses they undergo.

Pluralism and the Politics of Belief

In spite of serious differences in their assessment of the permeability of the political process, the equality of political resources, and the justice of political outcomes, pluralist analysts of American politics and their anti-pluralist critics have tended to concur in characterizing American politics in terms of conflicts among the self-interested. Pluralists are agnostic in arguing for no particular definition of interest: a citizen's primary interest —be it money, power, clean air, or peace of mind—is whatever he deems it to be. However, of the array of possible politically relevant interests, the pluralists reserve a special place for the pursuit of economic interests in American politics. American politics is about many things, they say, but first and foremost it is about competition among groups activated by their pocketbook interests.

What we have found departs significantly from this characterization. We have found, not a politics of economic self-interest, but a politics of political beliefs—beliefs that are coherent and potent in terms of their effects on behavior, but only weakly rooted in the personal experience of the individual. We have seen that beliefs are not inevitably a mask for self-interest, and we have seen that self-interest—narrowly conceived—does not always supersede political belief as a mainspring for political action. Of course, we do not want to overstate our claim. We do not in the least wish to imply that American politics is not principally a politics of self-interest. Even in our discussion of the politics of full-employment policy, a number of groups emerged—governors or social-welfare professionals, for example—that were motivated by narrow self-interest. However, it is significant that American politics is not *wholly* a politics of self-interest.

As we investigated the politics of economic disadvantage, these themes emerged consistently. We found political and social attitudes to be somewhat autonomous from both the particular life circumstances of the individual and the larger economic collectivities to which he belongs. Although neither the short-term stress associated with unemployment nor the long-term disadvantage associated with class was strongly related to attitudes, political beliefs seem to have a coherence of their own and firm connections to political behavior. We saw that beliefs about government responsibility for providing jobs or about the relative importance of inflation and unemployment were more potent in predicting 1976 presidential ballots than the fact of being out of work. Interestingly, attitudes toward these issues seemed to have more effect upon the votes of working than unemployed people. It is often said that the electoral threat in a recession comes not from the jobless themselves, but from working people who are fearful of losing their jobs. We found this formulation to be only partially accurate. In 1976, aggregate electoral threat was indeed derived from voters with jobs. However, in casting their ballots these voters were responding to their beliefs about economic matters more than to job insecurity in their own lives.

Curiously, what emerged from our brief investigation of the politics of employment policy parallels these themes. Many of the individuals most active in shaping manpower policy have direct interests at stake: city officials seeking budget relief or patronage resources, or construction unions concerned about jobs on public-works projects, seek manpower policies that will yield selective benefits to themselves and their immediate constituencies. However, the support of most of the members of the broad liberal coalition that represents the interests of the unemployed cannot be explained in terms of narrow self-interest. In order to understand the position taken by those who act as surrogates for the unemployed, we must look beyond self-interest to beliefs, ideological commitments that do not merely reflect and do not always yield to self-interest in politics. Perhaps it is not altogether surprising that the leaders of organizations like the National Council of Churches are motivated by broad commitments to social justice when they fight for full-employment policies. After all, such organizations are self-consciously dedicated to humanitarian purposes. However, even the union leaders appear to be motivated by broad ideological concerns, rather than narrow self-interest, when they support the full-employment coalition. We realize that it is tricky to assess and impute interests. Sometimes even those who contest most vigorously—for example, the doctors who fought Medicare only to discover, when defeated, that the long-opposed program was a windfall—have interests that are by no means unambiguous.[18] Labor unions operate in a particularly complicated context: in terms of their narrow self-interest on issues of redistributive policy, the assessments vary. On the one hand, it can be argued that it is self-interested for unions to support such policies, because their interests are so intimately joined to the fortunes of the Democratic party that whatever expands and strengthens the Democrats' electoral base benefits the unions. On the other hand, it is plausible to reason that self-interested unions would cultivate membership by monopolizing control of welfare, retirement, and jobless benefits and would therefore oppose government policies in these areas.[19]

In spite of the complexities and ambiguities in ascertaining labor's true interests, it seems clear that leaders of the AFL-CIO, UAW, and others who support the unemployed are not motivated by specific narrow interests analogous to those of, say, the mayors who seek CETA funds.[20] They are not responding to membership pressures or to the needs and interests of their direct constituents. Nor are there obvious payoffs in terms of organizational maintenance to be derived from their support for policies to aid the jobless. Rather, their role as advocates for the unemployed derives from ideals of social justice. Even for members of the full-employment coalition who are in most contexts committed to and adept at self-interested political action, support of the unemployed is in large part a matter of social belief.

[18]On the difficulty of appraising self-interest in politics, see Raymond A. Bauer, Ithiel de Sola Pool, and Lewis Anthony Dexter, *American Business and Public Policy*, 2nd ed. (Chicago: Aldine Publishing Co., 1972), pp. 472-475 and passim. The specific example of the American Medical Association and Medicare is taken from Theodore R. Marmor, *The Politics of Medicare* (Chicago: Aldine Publishing Co., 1973), p. 123.

[19]The former position is taken by Greenstone in *Labor in American Politics* (chap. 10), the latter by Martha Derthick, unpublished manuscript on social security, Brookings Institution.

[20]Here, of course, we except certain operative unions whose narrow self-interest in manpower policies has been discussed.

If it seems unorthodox to think of American politics in terms of a politics of belief rather than a politics of interest, we should add that our findings parallel those of other investigators. Studies exploring realms as diverse as personal experiences with the war in Vietnam and busing confirm the disjunction between personal circumstance and political attitude, and the gap between private problems and public behavior.[21] Furthermore, all of these studies that demonstrate the attenuation of the links between personal experience and political belief show, as we do, substantial connections between such beliefs and political behavior.

With respect to another theme iterated here, we echo the comments of those who note the degree to which political controversy in American politics is no longer anchored in conflict between broad economic classes. Whether what is found is an individuation in which traditional demographic cleavages no longer hold, or a class inversion in which upper-status groups lose their distinctive conservative ideological coloration and Republican partisanship, the evidence points to the conclusion that political conflict in American politics no longer cleaves to the fault lines of economic class.[22]

[21]Bruce Russett and Elizabeth C. Hansen, in *Ideologies and Interest: The Foreign Policy Beliefs of American Businessmen* (San Francisco: W. H. Freeman and Co., 1975), pp. 110-130, show that international attitudes of businessmen could not be predicted from the specific interests of their firms in defense contracts or foreign trade. Richard R. Lau, Thad A. Brown, and David O. Sears, in "Self-Interests and Civilians' Attitudes toward the War in Vietnam" (*Public Opinion Quarterly*, 42 [Winter 1978], 464-483), indicate that attitudes on the war in Vietnam do not seem to have been grounded in personal involvement, such as having relatives or friends there. David O. Sears, C. P. Hensles, and L. K. Speer, in "Opposition to Busing: Self-Interest or Symbolic Racism" (*American Political Science Review*, in press), find that attitudes on racial matters cannot be predicted from the impact of racial policies in personal life.

In terms of actual political behavior, D. Roderick Kiewiet and Donald R. Kinder, in "Political Consequences of Economic Concerns: Personal and Collective," a paper prepared for the 1978 Annual Meeting of the American Political Science Association, find that those who consider unemployment an important personal problem were not distinctive in their 1976 presidential ballots. More generally, Richard A. Brody and Paul M. Sniderman find the impact on voting of having a personal problem for which the government is held responsible to be weak and inconsistent. See "From Life Space to Polling Place," *British Journal of Political Science*, 7 (July 1977), 337-360, and "Coping: The Ethic of Self-Reliance," *American Journal of Political Science*, 21 (August 1977), 501-522.

[22]On these themes see, for example, Richard E. Dawson, *Public Opinion and Contemporary Disarray* (New York: Harper and Row, 1973), chap. 4; Gerald Pomper, *Voter's Choice* (New York: Dodd, Mead and Co., 1975), chap. 3; Everett Carll Ladd, Jr., with Charles D. Hadley, *Transformations of the American Party System*, 2nd ed. (New York: W. W. Norton, 1978). Also relevant is Ronald Ingelhardt, *The Silent Revolution* (Princeton, N.J.: Princeton University Press, 1977).

This reduction in the degree to which class divisions structure our politics fulfills the expectations of those who predicted an end to ideology. However, it has not been accompanied by the end of politics that they foresaw. American politics has not, in an age of absolute affluence and relative deprivation, become devoid of conflict. Rather, it is replete with contention, and the economic matters that have traditionally divided class groupings retain undiminished salience. Furthermore, we have not witnessed the emasculation of ideas in American politics. On the contrary, in recent years citizen political attitudes have grown in internal consistency and become more potent.[23]

In terms of the ultimate question of politics—"Who gets what?"—the meaning of all this for the unemployed is perhaps ambiguous. Although the jobless are not active on their own behalf, their needs are represented more vigorously and more articulately than the antipluralists might have predicted. Having left the field to others, their interests are served by the activity of two kinds of surrogates. First are those who themselves stand to benefit from certain manpower policies; advocacy of the unemployed is a by-product of the pursuit of specific interests. Second are those whose support for full employment derives from their commitment to social justice. For such spokesmen full employment is only one entry on a list of priorities. Sincere and dedicated as they may be, they cannot focus undivided attention or lavish unlimited resources on the issue. Furthermore, they cannot bring to their advocacy the sense of personal urgency and intensity that emerged so clearly when we talked to the unemployed. Thus, our admittedly speculative response to the question of whether policies to aid the unemployed would have been pursued more vigorously if those involved had been more articulate is that the silence of a group so large and so vitally interested in government policy does indeed make a difference.

[23]On these issues see, among others, Herbert Asher, *Presidential Elections and American Politics* (Homewood, Ill.: Dorsey Press, 1976), chap. 4, and Norman H. Nie, Sidney Verba, and John Petrocik, *The Changing American Voter* (Cambridge, Mass.: Harvard University Press, 1976). See also the essays and additional references contained in Richard G. Niemi and Herbert F. Weisberg, eds., *Controversies in American Voting Behavior* (San Francisco: W. H. Freeman and Co., 1976), pts. 2 and 3.

Appendixes
Index

Appendix A
Sample Design

The purpose of our study was to assess the impact of joblessness on individual citizens. It was necessary, therefore, to have a sample containing a sufficient number of cases of unemployed workers to allow reliable comparisons with employed members of the work force and to allow analysis of variations among types of unemployed. As we have indicated, an ordinary sample of the adult population would contain too few cases of workers without jobs for extensive analysis. One approach would have been to seek unemployed respondents at places where they congregate; in particular, at centers where unemployment compensation checks are picked up. We decided against that approach, since not all of those who are out of work are eligible for unemployment compensation and those who are eligible are by no means a representative sample of the unemployed. (See the discussion in Chapter 3.) Furthermore, we wanted to compare the attitudes and behavior of the unemployed who received such compensation with the attitudes and behavior of those who did not.

We decided to attempt to obtain a representative sample of the unemployed in the work force as a whole. This required drawing a much larger sample, which was then screened to locate unemployed respondents to be interviewed. The most efficient method proved to be a telephone survey that used a random-digit dialing technique. We approached telephone interviewing with some trepidation—in terms of both the accuracy of the sample and the reliability and validity of the responses. Our experience, shored up by a growing number of systematic studies of sample accuracy and response bias, has convinced us that the technique provides results of accuracy comparable to in-person surveys for a study such as ours—and the approach is extremely cost efficient.[1]

[1] See William R. Klecka and Alfred J. Tuchfarber, "Random Digit Dialing: A Comparison to Personal Surveys," *Public Opinion Quarterly*, 42 (Spring 1978), 105-114, as well as the literature cited therein.

We also reduced costs by limiting the universe of our sample. It was defined as the labor force eighteen years of age and older living in the 150 largest metropolitan areas. These areas range in size from New York on the one hand to Altoona, Pennsylvania, on the other. Membership in the labor force was defined as being presently employed or seeking employment. The retired, the disabled, those at home, and students (including working students whose jobs were secondary to their education) were excluded.

In order to obtain enough unemployed respondents, two samples were selected, a "regular" sample of the work force and a special sample of the unemployed.

(a) *The regular sample.* For this sample the size of the labor force was determined for the leading 150 metropolitan areas. A sample of 60 primary sampling units (PSUs) was selected from the universe, proportionate to the size of the labor force in each of the 150 areas; 51 of the areas were included in the sample.

All telephone directories pertaining to a given PSU were secured. If the PSU encompassed more than one telephone directory, then one directory was selected with a probability proportionate to the number of resident listings it contained in relation to the total number of residential listings within the PSU.

The final stage was a sequential selection (one in every fifth) across the entire selected directory; then the last two digits of the selected telephone number were dropped and two final digits were randomly generated. The use of this "digit-dropping" technique increased the efficiency of the telephone survey by reducing the number of inoperative numbers dialed, without creating the bias that would exist if numbers were selected directly from directories.

Within the designated households a random selection procedure was used to choose the respondent to be interviewed from those who fell into the universe by being in the work force. Eligible persons were identified through the following question: "How many people living in your household are 18 years of age or older and are either working, have a job but are temporarily not working, or are not working and are looking for a job?" Callbacks were used if necessary to complete the interview.

This sample produced 912 completed interviews, of which 799 were with employed and 113 with unemployed respondents.

(b) *The unemployment sample.* This sample followed the same basic procedure, except that the initial stage involved the selection of 30 PSUs from among the 51 metropolitan areas included in the labor force sample. A similar technique was used to choose the telephone numbers.

Within the designated household a screening question similar to the one above was used to locate members of the work force, who were then further screened to locate unemployed respondents who "either have a job but are temporarily not working, or are not working and are looking for a job." The result was a selection of 3,694 members of the work force, of whom 3,236 were employed and 458 were unemployed. The former were not interviewed; the latter were. (The equivalence of the two samples is reflected, we believe, in the fact that an equal share of the members of the work force were unemployed in both cases.) For our analyses the two samples were merged and weighted so as to reflect the proportion represented by the unemployed in the work force as a whole.

The definition of an unemployed person is more complicated than is indicated by the screening questions we used to locate work force members and unemployed persons. It would be possible, for instance, for someone not at work because of temporary illness to appear to be unemployed on the basis of our screening question, and yet that person would not be unemployed. The distinction of whether or not an individual was unemployed for the purposes of our analysis is not based on the screening question but on responses to the full set of employment-status items used in our questionnaire—questions that largely replicate those used by the Census Bureau to distinguish working from unemployed respondents.

The interviews in most cases were thirty to forty minutes in length. The refusal rate was 28 percent.

Follow-up interviews: In addition to the telephone interviews, we conducted another 60 follow-up interviews with unemployed respondents. These were less structured and generally were conducted in person. They ran a good deal longer than the initial interviews and were intended to probe more deeply into some of the subjects dealt with earlier. The respondents for these interviews were selected from a limited number of cities. A deliberate attempt was made to select a range of types of unemployed workers.

Appendix B
Number of Cases

The tables that follow contain the number of cases in the cells of the most common categories in this book. Using these tables, the reader should be able to reconstruct the actual number of cases on which percentages are based in the text tables and figures. In many instances the actual number of cases for a particular table or figure differs slightly from the numbers given below because of missing data on other variables in the analysis. These discrepancies are quite small.

Employment status	
Working	799
Unemployed	571

	Occupational level			
	1	2	3	4
Working	177	191	182	201
Unemployed	223	111	73	61

		Employment status	
		Working	Unemployed
White collar	794	543	251
Blue collar	469	236	233

	Occupational level			
Race	1	2	3	4
White	261	251	219	227
Black	115	41	26	23

	Race	
	White	Black
Working	670	82
Unemployed	365	159

Length of unemployment	
1 month or less	112
2-6 months	235
7-11 months	73
1 year or more	125

	Party identification		
	Republican	Independent	Democrat
Working	143	335	251
Unemployed	47	221	195

	Occupational level			
Age	1	2	3	4
18-29	155	147	97	76
30-39	74	52	67	76
40-54	76	68	52	71
55 and over	33	34	37	36

Appendix C
Metropolitan Work Force
Survey Questionnaire

GEORGE FINE RESEARCH, INC.
55 WEST 42nd STREET
NEW YORK, NEW YORK 10036

NATIONAL EMPLOYMENT STUDY
JOB NO. 31901

1. Last week, were you working, going to school, keeping house, unemployed, looking for a job, or what?

    ☐1 Working → Skip to Q.19   (5)
    ☐2 With a job, but not at work
    ☐3 Unemployed, looking for work
    ☐ Retired, in school, keeping house, unable to work (because of disability, etc.) → Terminate - Do not use questionnaire

2. Did you have a job from which you were temporarily absent or on layoff last week?

    ☐1 Yes   (6)
    ☐2 No → Skip to Q.6

    ☐9 Don't know/No answer

3. Why were you absent from work last week -- were you sick, on vacation, laid off, or what?

    ☐1 Sick . . . .⎫   (7)
    ☐2 On vacation . . . . . . ⎬Skip to Q.19
    ☐3 On strike . . . . ⎪
    ☐4 Waiting to start new job ⎭
    ☐5 Laid off → Continue with Q.4

    ☐9 Don't know/No answer

4. When were you laid off? (Record month and year.) _____ (8-11)

    ☐99 Don't know/No answer

5. Do you have a callback date?

    ☐1 Yes → Skip to Q.19   (12)
    ☐2 No

    ☐9 Don't know/No answer

6. Have you been looking for work at any time during the last three months?

    ☐1 Yes   (13)
    ☐2 No → Skip to Q.9

    ☐9 Don't know/No answer → Skip to Q.9

7. How long have you been looking for work? (Record number of months.) _____

    ☐99 Don't know/No Answer   (14-15)

8. What do you think your chances are that you will find an acceptable job in the near future -- do you have a good chance, some chance, or very little chance of finding a job?

    ☐1   Good chance   (16)
    ☐2   Some chance
    ☐3   Very little chance   }   Skip to Q.11

    ☐9   Don't know/No answer

9. Do you intend to look for work within the next year?

    ☐1   Yes   (17)
    ☐2   No → Skip to Q.11

    ☐9   Don't know/No answer → Skip to Q.11

10. What do you think your chances are that you will find an acceptable job within a reasonable time when you do start looking -- do you have a good chance, some chance, or very little chance of finding a job?

    ☐1   Good chance   (18)
    ☐2   Some chance
    ☐3   Very little chance

    ☐9   Don't know/No answer

11. When was the last time that you worked for six consecutive months or more at a full time job or business? _____ (Record month and year.)

    ☐00 Never has worked six months or more → Skip to Q.30   (19-20)

    ☐99 Don't know/No answer

12. Why did you leave your last job?   (DO NOT READ LIST)

    ☐1   Lost job - Fired   (21)
    ☐2   Lost job - Permanently laid off; plant closed
    ☐3   Lost job - Other reason or no reason given
    ☐4   Quit to return to housekeeping or because pregnant
    ☐5   Quit to return to school
    ☐6   Quit - Disliked job
    ☐7   Quit - Other or no reason given

    ☐9   Other; Don't know; No answer

13. What kind of work did you do? That is, what was your job called?

_____

(If not already answered)→What did you actually do in that job?
Tell me, what were some of your main duties?

_____

What kind of place did you work for? (If not already answered)
What did they make/do?

_____

(If not already answered) Were you self-employed or did you work
for somebody else?

_____

(If not already answered) Were you a direct employee of the
government -- whether national, state or local?

_____

```
-------------------------------------------------
|              FOR OFFICE USE ONLY              |
| Occupational Code:_____   (24-28)  |
| ☐ 99898  Inappropriate                        |
| ☐ 99999  Don't Know/No Answer                 |
|                                               |
| Self Employment Code:                         |
|     ☐1 Worked for self            (29)        |
|     ☐2 Did not work for self                  |
|     ☐8 Inappropriate                          |
|     ☐9 Don't Know/No Answer                   |
|                                               |
| Government Employment Code:                    |
|     ☐1 Worked directly for government  (30)   |
|     ☐2 Did not work directly for government   |
|          (Include employees working under     |
|           govt. contract for private firms)   |
|     ☐8 Inappropriate                          |
|     ☐9 Don't Know/No Answer                   |
-------------------------------------------------
```

14. How long did you hold that job?

☐1 Less than 6 months   (31)
☐2 6 months, but less than 1 year
☐3 1 year, but less than 2 years
☐4 2 years, but less than 3 years
☐5 3 years, but less than 5 years
☐6 5 years or more

☐9 Don't Know/No Answer

-3-

15. (Ask only if not self-employed) Would you like to go into any kind
     of business for yourself?

     ☐1 Yes   (32)
     ☐2 No

     ☐9 Don't know/No answer

16. How much formal education does somebody need to get the kind of job
     you had -- no special formal education, a high school diploma, college
     education, or what?

     ☐1 No special formal education   (33)
     ☐2 High school diploma
     ☐3 Technical school after high school, but not college education
     ☐4 Undergraduate education in the liberal arts or a profession,
             but no graduate training
     ☐5 Graduate training

     ☐9 Don't know/No answer

17. How long does a person have to spend in training on the job to be
     able to handle a job like yours?

     ☐1 No time at all   (34)
     ☐2 1 day - less than 1 month
     ☐3 1 month - less than 3 months
     ☐4 3 months - less than 1 year
     ☐5 1 year or more

     ☐9 Don't know/No answer

18. Thinking about your earnings on that job, would you say that you
     were paid less than you deserved, about what you deserved, or more
     than you deserved?

     ☐1 Less than deserved ⎫   (35)
     ☐2 About what deserved ⎬
     ☐3 More than deserved   ⎱ Skip to Q.29
                               ⎰
     ☐9 Don't know/No answer ⎭

┌───┐
│ FOR THOSE WITH JOBS -- CONTINUE HERE   │
└───┘

19. Is yours a part-time or a full-time job?

     ☐1 Part-time   (22)
     ☐2 Full-time → Skip to Q.21

     ☐9 Don't know/No answer → Skip to Q.21

-4-

20. Would you prefer to have a full-time job?

☐1 Yes   (23)
☐2 No

☐9 Don't know/No answer

21. What kind of work do you do? That is, what is your job called?

_____

(If not answered) What do you actually do in that job? Tell me,
what are some of your main duties?

_____

What kind of place do you work for?

_____

(If not answered) What do they make/do?

_____

(If not answered) Are you self-employed or do you work for
somebody else?

_____

(If not answered) Are you a direct employee of the government -
whether national, state, or local?

_____

```
-----------------------------------------------------------
           FOR OFFICE USE ONLY
Occupational code: _____                    (24-28)
    ☐ 99898   Inappropriate
    ☐ 99999   Don't Know/No Answer

Self Employment Code:
    ☐1 Works for self            ☐8 Inappropriate      (29)
    ☐2 Does not work for self    ☐9 Don't Know/No Answer

Government Employment Code:
    ☐1 Works for government       ☐8 Inappropriate      (30)
    ☐2 Does not work directly     ☐9 Don't Know/No Answer
         for government
-----------------------------------------------------------
```

22. How long have you had this job?

☐1 Less than 6 months   (31)
☐2 6 months, but less than 1 year
☐3 1 year, but less than 2 years
☐4 2 years, but less than 3 years
☐5 3 years, but less than 5 years
☐6 5 years or more

☐9 Don't Know/No Answer

23. (Ask only if not self-employed): Would you like to go into any
    kind of business for yourself?

☐1 Yes   (32)
☐2 No

☐9 Don't Know/No Answer

24. How much formal education does somebody need to do a job like yours --
    no special formal education, a high school diploma, college education,
    or what?

☐1 No special formal education   (33)
☐2 High School diploma
☐3 Technical school after high school but not college education
☐4 Undergraduate education in the liberal arts or a profession,
     but no graduate training
☐5 Graduate training

☐9 Don't Know/No Answer

25. How long does a person have to spend in training on the job to be
    able to handle a job like yours?

☐1 No time at all   (34)
☐2 1 day - less than 1 month
☐3 1 month - less than 3 months
☐4 3 months - less than 1 year
☐5 1 year or more

☐9 Don't Know/No Answer

26. Thinking about your earnings, do you feel that you are paid less than
    you deserve, about what you deserve, or more than you deserve?

☐1 Less than deserve   (35)
☐2 About what deserve
☐3 More than deserve

☐9 Don't Know/No Answer

27. Do you think that there is any chance that you may lose your job over
    the next year or so? Would you say that it is very likely; somewhat
    likely; or very unlikely that you will lose your job?

☐1 Very likely   ☐3 Very unlikely   (36)
☐2 Somewhat likely   ☐9 Don't Know/No Answer

-6-

28. In the past year have you been laid off or unemployed and looking for work?

    ☐1 Yes   (37)
    ☐2 No

    ☐9 Don't Know/No Answer

29. About how many times in the past ten years have you been unemployed or laid off for a month or more?

    ☐1 Never   (38)
    ☐2 Once
    ☐3 2 to 3 times
    ☐4 More than 3 times

    ☐9 Don't Know/No Answer

30. Among people whom you know, are many of them out of work, a few of them out of work, or do most of the people whom you know have jobs?

    ☐1 Many are out of work   (39)
    ☐2 A few are out of work
    ☐3 Most have jobs

    ☐9 Don't Know/No Answer

31. Who is usually the main wage earner for this household?
(Probe for relationship to respondent if unclear.)

    ☐1 Respondent → Skip to Q.41   (40)
    ☐2 Husband
    ☐3 Wife
    ☐4 Mother
    ☐5 Father
    ☐6 Daughter
    ☐7 Son
    ☐8 Other

    ☐9 Don't Know/No Answer → Skip to Q.41

32. Last week, was he/she working, going to school, keeping house, unemployed, looking for work, or what?

    ☐1 Working → Skip to Q.40   (41)
    ☐2 With a job, but not at work ⎱ Continue with Q.33
    ☐3 Unemployed, looking for work ⎰
    ☐4 Retired, in school, keeping house — Skip to Q.39

    ☐9 Don't Know/No Answer → Skip to Q.41

33. Did he/she have a job from which he/she was temporarily absent or on layoff last week?

    ☐1 Yes → Continue with Q.34   (42)
    ☐2 No → Skip to Q.37

    ☐9 No answer/Don't know → Skip to Q.41

34. Why was he/she absent from work last week -- was he/she sick, on vacation, laid off, or what?

    ☐1 Sick . . . . ⎫   (43)
    ☐2 On vacation . . . . ⎪
    ☐3 On strike . . . . ⎬ Skip to Q.40
    ☐4 Waiting to start new job . ⎭
    ☐5 Laid off → Continue with Q.35

    ☐9 Don't know/No answer → Skip to Q.40

35. When was he/she laid off? _____ (44-45)
    (Record month and year.)

    ☐99 Don't know/No answer

36. Does he/she have a callback date?

    ☐1 Yes → Skip to Q.40   (46)
    ☐2 No

    ☐9 Don't know/No answer

37. Has he/she been looking for work at any time during the last three months?

    ☐1 Yes   (47)
    ☐2 No → Skip to Q.39

    ☐9 Don't know/No answer

38. How long has he/she been looking for work? _____ (48-49)
    (Record number of months.)

    ☐99 Don't know/No answer

39. When was the last time that he/she worked for six consecutive months or more at a full-time job or business? _____
    (Record month and year. If never, Skip to Q.41.)

    ☐00 Never has worked six months or more   (50-51)

    ☐99 Don't know/No answer

40. What kind of work did he/she do? That is, what was his/her job called?

_____

_____

(If not already answered) What did he/she actually do in that job? Tell me, what were some of his/her main duties?

_____

_____

What kind of place did he/she work for? (If not already answered) What did they make/do?

_____

_____

```
┌─────────────────────────────────────────┐
│  FOR OFFICE USE ONLY                     │
│  Occupational Code: _____ (52-56)      │
│  ☐ 99898  Inappropriate                  │
│  ☐ 99999  Don't Know/No Answer           │
└─────────────────────────────────────────┘
```

[ASK EVERYONE]

41. How do you think the economy has been doing recently -- has it been improving, staying the same or getting worse?

    ☐1 Improving   (57)
    ☐2 Staying the same
    ☐3 Getting worse
    ☐9 Don't know/No answer

42. What about your own personal economic situation, in recent months has it been improving, staying the same, or getting worse?

    ☐1 Improving   (58)
    ☐2 Staying the same
    ☐3 Getting worse
    ☐4 Don't know/No answer

43. In these times many people have been feeling a financial pinch. In your household have any of the following actions been necessary in order to make ends meet?

	YES	NO	DON'T KNOW/ NO ANSWER	
Has somebody who wasn't working taken a job?	☐1	☐2	☐9	(59)
Have you dipped into savings?	☐1	☐2	☐9	(60)
Have you gotten financial help from family or friends?	☐1	☐2	☐9	(61)
Have you taken out any loans?	☐1	☐2	☐9	(62)
Has somebody who was already working taken a second job?	☐1	☐2	☐9	(63)
Has anyone in the household collected unemployment compensation?	☐1	☐2	☐9	(64)
Has anyone in the household received food stamps or welfare?	☐1	☐2	☐9	(65)
Has anyone in the household received unemployment benefits from a company or union?	☐1	☐2	☐9	(66)

44. In recent months have the members of your household had to cut back on what they spend in order to make ends meet? Have you had to cut back substantially? Somewhat? Not at all?

    ☐1 Substantially   (67)
    ☐2 Somewhat
    ☐3 Not at all
    ☐9 Don't know/No Answer

45. As you look ahead to the next few months, do you think your own economic situation will improve, stay the same, or get worse?

    ☐1 Improve   (68)
    ☐2 Stay the same
    ☐3 Get worse
    ☐9 Don't know/No Answer

46. Do you think that the government should be making considerable efforts to end unemployment?

    ☐1 Yes   (69)
    ☐2 No → Skip to Q.48
    ☐9 Don't know/No Answer

47. Here are some suggestions as to how we might end unemployment. Some people find these solutions too drastic. Others think that unemployment is such an important problem that drastic measures are in order.

    a. Would you still favor ending   ☐1 Yes   (70)
        unemployment even if it meant   ☐2 No
        that the government would have
        to hire everybody who was   ☐9 Don't Know/No Answer
        without a job?

    b. Would you still favor ending   ☐1 Yes   (71)
        unemployment even if it meant   ☐2 No
        that the government would have
        to tell workers where and what   ☐9 Don't Know/Nc Answer
        they must work at -- to assign
        them to their jobs?

    c. Would you still favor ending   ☐1 Yes   (72)
        unemployment even if it meant   ☐2 No
        the end of the capitalist
        system?   ☐9 Don't Know/No Answer

48. Which political party -- the Republicans or the Democrats -- would be more likely to end unemployment?

    ☐1 Republicans   (73)
    ☐2 Democrats
    ☐3 No difference
    ☐9 Don't know/No answer

49. I am going to read you a list of statements. After I read each one, tell me if you agree or disagree.

	AGREE	DISAGREE	DON'T KNOW/ NO ANSWER
- The government is run by a few big interests looking out for themselves and not for the benefit of all the people.	☐1	☐2	☐9 (74)
- Almost all those who are unemployed could find decent jobs if only they would look hard enough.	☐1	☐2	☐9 (75)
- The government should see that every family has enough money to have a decent standard of living.	☐1	☐2	☐9 (76)
- The government should reduce taxes on big business.	☐1	☐2	☐9 (77)
- The government should tax the rich heavily in order to redistribute wealth.	☐1	☐2	☐9 (78)
- The government should limit the amount of money any individual is allowed to earn in a year.	☐1	☐2	☐9 (79)
- The size of the government should be reduced even if it means cutting back on government services in areas such as health and education.	☐1	☐2	80-1 ☐9 (5)

50. Do you think that the interests of management and workers are basically opposed or are their interests basically the same?

    ☐1 Basically opposed   (6)
    ☐2 Basically the same
    ☐3 Mixed: Depends; some interests conflict, others don't
    ☐9 Don't know/No answer

51. Do you think that the interests of blacks and whites are basically opposed, or are their interests basically the same?

    ☐1 Basically opposed   (7)
    ☐2 Basically the same
    ☐3 Mixed: Depends; some interests conflict, others don't
    ☐9 Don't know/No answer

52. Some people think that American workers would be better off if they
     stuck together and worked to solve their common problems. Others feel
     that the average worker would be better off if he made greater efforts
     to get ahead on his own. Which do you think -- should workers stick
     together or should they try harder to get ahead on their own?

     ☐1 Should stick together   (8)
     ☐2 Should try harder to get ahead on their own
     ☐3 Depends
     ☐9 Don't know/No answer

53. Would you say that, in general, factory workers are paid more than they
     deserve, about what they deserve, or less than they deserve?

     ☐1 More than they deserve   (9)
     ☐2 About what they deserve
     ☐3 Less than they deserve
     ☐9 Don't know/No answer

54. What about business executives? Are they generally paid more than
     they deserve, about what they deserve, or less than they deserve?

     ☐1 More than they deserve   (10)
     ☐2 About what they deserve
     ☐3 Less than they deserve
     ☐9 Don't know/No answer

55. How much chance does the child of a factory worker have to become
     a business executive or a professional -- a good chance, some chance,
     a slight chance, or no chance at all?

     ☐1 A good chance   (11)
     ☐2 Some chance
     ☐3 A slight chance
     ☐4 No chance at all
     ☐9 Don't know/No answer

56. Do you think that the child of a factory worker has about the same
     chance to get ahead as the child of a business executive, has somewhat
     less chance to get ahead, or much less chance to get ahead than the
     child of a business executive?

     ☐1 About the same chance → Skip to Q.58   (12)
     ☐2 Somewhat less chance ⎫ Ask Q.57
     ☐3 Much less chance   ⎭
     ☐9 Don't know/No answer → Skip to Q.58

57. Do you think that's fair?

     ☐1 Yes   (13)
     ☐2 No

     ☐9 Don't know/No answer

-12-

58. Comparing blacks and whites, who has a better chance to get the good jobs -- blacks, whites, or is there no difference?

　□1 Blacks　　　　　　　　　　　　　　　　　　　　　　(14)
　□2 Whites
　□3 No Difference → Skip to Q.60

　□9 Don't Know/No Answer → Skip to Q.60

59. Do you think that's fair?

　□1 Yes　　　　　　　　　　　　　　　　　　　　　　　(15)
　□2 No

　□9 Don't Know/No Answer

60. How would you compare the opportunities to succeed in your parents' lives with those in your life -- were your parents' opportunities better, not as good, about the same?

　□1 Better　　　　　　　　　　　　　　　　　　　　　(16)
　□2 About the same
　□3 Not as good

　□9 Don't Know/No Answer

61. How many children do you have?

　□1 One　　　　□4 Four　　　　□7 Seven or More　　　(17)
　□2 Two　　　　□5 Five　　　　□9 Don't Know/No Answer
　□3 Three　　　□6 Six　　　　□0 None

62. (If has children): How many of your children are dependent on you for support?

　□1 One　　　　□4 Four　　　　□7 Seven or More　　　(18)
　□2 Two　　　　□5 Five　　　　□9 Don't Know/No Answer
　□3 Three　　　□6 Six　　　　□0 None are dependent for
　　　　　　　　　　　　　　　　　　support

63. (If children) How would you compare your children's opportunities to succeed with those in your own life -- do you consider their opportunities better, not as good, about the same? (ANSWER BELOW)

(If no children) If you had children, would you expect their opportunities to succeed to be better, not as good, or about the same as yours?

　□1 Better　　　　　　　　　　　　　　　　　　　　　(19)
　□2 About the same
　□3 Not as good
　□9 Don't Know/No Answer

64. If you had to choose: Which of these things is most important
    in determining who gets ahead in America -- luck, hard work, or
    family background?

    ☐1 Luck   (20)
    ☐2 Hard work
    ☐3 Family background
    ☐9 Don't know/No answer

65. If it were necessary to solve our nation's problems, would you be
    in favor of the following changes?

	YES	NO	DON'T KNOW/ NO ANSWER
Limiting the right of citizens to speak against government policies	☐1	☐2	☐9 (21)
Limiting the right of labor unions to strike	☐1	☐2	☐9 (22)
Limiting criticisms of the government in the press	☐1	☐2	☐9 (23)
Limiting the right of businesses to make whatever profits they can	☐1	☐2	☐9 (24)

66. Do you think that you can believe the things that government leaders
    say just about all the time, most of the time, only some of the time,
    or none of the time?

    ☐1 Just about all the time   (25)
    ☐2 Most of the time
    ☐3 Only some of the time
    ☐4 None of the time
    ☐9 Don't know/No answer

67. Suppose you took a problem to a government official, would you expect
    the official to pay serious attention, pay some attention, or pay no
    attention at all?

    ☐1 Pay serious attention   (26)
    ☐2 Pay some attention
    ☐3 Pay no attention at all
    ☐4 Don't know/No answer

-14-

68. Some people say the government does more than it should for certain groups and less than it should for others.

	MORE	LESS	ABOUT RIGHT	DON'T KNOW/ NO ANSWER	
- Thinking about businessmen, do you think the government does more than it should for businessmen, less than it should, or about what it should for them?	☐1	☐2	☐3	☐9	(27)
- What about black people? Does the government do more than it should, less than it should or about what it should for them?	☐1	☐2	☐3	☐9	(28)
- What about people on welfare? Does the government do more than it should, less than it should or about what it should for them?	☐1	☐2	☐3	☐9	(29)
- What about people like you? Does the government do more than it should, less than it should or about what it should for them?	☐1	☐2	☐3	☐9	(30)

69. Of all the people who have been mentioned in connection with the 1976 Presidential election, is there anyone whom you would especially like to see become President?
(If yes)→Who is that? (DO NOT READ LIST)

(31-32)

☐ 01 Birch Bayh
☐ 02 Jimmy Carter
☐ 03 Gerald Ford
☐ 04 Fred Harris
☐ 05 Hubert Humphrey
☐ 06 Henry Jackson
☐ 07 Teddy Kennedy

☐ 08 Ronald Reagan
☐ 09 Nelson Rockefeller
☐ 10 Sargent Shriver
☐ 11 Mo Udall
☐ 12 George Wallace
☐ 13 Other _____ (Specify)

☐ 98 No particular candidate
☐ 99 Don't Know/ No answer

70. Here are some men who have been mentioned in connection with the 1976 Presidential election. After I read each one tell me if you would be likely to vote for that candidate if he were nominated, if you might vote for that candidate depending upon whom he was running against, or if you would be unlikely to vote for him.

	LIKELY	MIGHT	UNLIKELY	DON'T KNOW/ NO ANSWER	
Gerald Ford	☐1	☐2	☐3	☐9	(33)
George Wallace	☐1	☐2	☐3	☐9	(34)
Ronald Reagan	☐1	☐2	☐3	☐9	(35)
Henry Jackson	☐1	☐2	☐3	☐9	(36)
Morris Udall.	☐1	☐2	☐3	☐9	(37)

71. How interested are you in politics and national affairs -- very
interested, somewhat interested, only slightly interested, or not
at all interested?

   ☐1 Very interested   (38)
   ☐2 Somewhat interested
   ☐3 Only slightly interested
   ☐4 Not at all interested
   ☐9 Don't know/No answer

72. About how often do you read a newspaper -- every day, once or twice
a week, less than once a week, almost never?

   ☐1 Every day   (39)
   ☐2 Once or twice a week
   ☐3 Less than once a week
   ☐4 Almost never
   ☐9 Don't know/No answer

73. About how often do you watch the national news on television -- every
day, once or twice a week, less than once a week, almost never?

   ☐1 Every day   (40)
   ☐2 Once or twice a week
   ☐3 Less than once a week
   ☐4 Almost never
   ☐9 Don't know/No answer

74. Could you tell me if you've ever done any of the following: Have
you ever contributed money or done work for a candidate in a political
campaign? (If yes) Have you done that in one election campaign or
more than one?

   ☐1 Never   (41)
   ☐2 Once
   ☐3 More than once
   ☐9 Don't know/No answer

75. Have you ever contacted or written a letter to a public official,
somebody like a Congressman or Senator or a state or local official?
(If yes) Was that once or more than once?

   ☐1 Never   (42)
   ☐2 Once
   ☐3 More than once
   ☐9 Don't know/No answer

76. Have you ever picketed or taken part in a demonstration on some
political issue?
(If yes) Was that once or more than once?

   ☐1 Never   (43)
   ☐2 Once
   ☐3 More than once
   ☐9 Don't know/No answer

77. Are you a member of a labor union?

☐1 Yes   (44)
☐2 No → Skip to Q.80
☐9 Don't know/No answer → Skip to Q.80

78. Are you an active union member -- that is, do you go to meetings or take part in other union activities?

☐1 Yes   (45)
☐2 No

☐9 Don't know/No answer

79. Would you say that your union activity has changed in recent months -- has it gone up, gone down, or stayed the same?

☐1 Gone up   (46)
☐2 Stayed the same
☐3 Gone down   } Skip to Q.81

☐9 Don't know/No answer

80. Is anyone in your household a union member?

☐1 Yes   (47)
☐2 No
☐9 Don't know/No answer

81. Aside from a labor union, are you a member of any other group or organization -- a fraternal or service organization, a veterans' group, a school service organization like the PTA, a business or professional organization?

☐1 Yes   (48)
☐2 No → Skip to Q.84
☐9 Don't know/No answer → Skip to Q.85

82. Are you an active group member -- that is, do you attend meetings or participate in other activities?

☐1 Yes   (49)
☐2 No

☐9 Don't know/No answer

83. Has your activity in these kinds of organizations in any way changed in recent months -- has it gone up, gone down, or stayed the same?

☐1 Gone up   (50)
☐2 Stayed the same
☐3 Gone down   } Skip to Q.85

☐9 Don't know/No answer

-17-

84. In the past year or two, were you a member of such a group which
    you left for one reason or another?

    ☐1 Yes   (51)
    ☐2 No

    ☐9 Don't know/No Answer

	VERY SATIS-FIED	SOMEWHAT SATIS-FIED	SOMEWHAT DISSAT-ISFIED	VERY DISSAT-ISFIED	DON'T KNOW/ NO ANSWER	
85.						
a. Thinking about your life as a whole, would you say that you are very satis- fied, somewhat satisfied, somewhat dissatisfied, or very dissatisfied?	☐1	☐2	☐3	☐4	☐9	(52)
b. What about your family life? Are you	☐1	☐2	☐3	☐4	☐9	(53)
c. What about your income?	☐1	☐2	☐3	☐4	☐9	(54)
d. What about what you are accomplishing in life?	☐1	☐2	☐3	☐4	☐9	(55)
e. What about how much you are admired and respected by other people?	☐1	☐2	☐3	☐4	☐9	(56)

86. About how many hours a day do you watch television?

    ☐ _____(HOURS PER DAY)   (57-59)

    ☐000 Never Watches TV

    ☐999 Don't Know/No Answer

┌─────────────────────────────────────┐
│ FOR THOSE WITH A JOB, SKIP TO Q.89   │
└─────────────────────────────────────┘

87. [ASK ONLY OF UNEMPLOYED] : Many people who have been out of work have
    found that when they were around the house more, there was more family
    tension. Since you have been unemployed, has there been more family
    tension, less tension, or hasn't it made any difference?

    ☐1 More tension   (60)
    ☐2 Less tension
    ☐3 No difference

    ☐9 Don't Know/No Answer

-18-

88. **ASK ONLY OF THE UNEMPLOYED** When you think about the fact that other people have jobs and you are out of work, do you get angry, or do you think that that is just how life is sometimes?

 ☐1 Gets angry   (61)
 ☐2 Thinks that's just how life is

 ☐9 Don't know/No Answer

89. **ASK EVERYONE** If you had to describe the class you belong to, what word would you use? (INTERVIEWER -- RECORD RESPONSE VERBATIM)

_____

90. (IF RESPONDENT SAYS ANYTHING BUT "WORKING CLASS" OR "MIDDLE CLASS", ASK THE FOLLOWING): If you had to choose, which term would you use to describe the class you belong to -- middle class or working class?

 ☐1 Middle class in response to this question   (62)
 ☐2 Working class in response to this question
 ☐3 Inappropriate; respondent said "middle class" on Q.89
 ☐4 Inappropriate; respondent said "working class" on Q.89
 ☐9 Don't know/No answer

91. Generally speaking, do you usually think of yourself as a Republican, a Democrat, an Independent, or what?

 ☐1 Republican   (63)
 ☐2 Democrat
 ☐3 Independent
 ☐4 Other →Skip to Q.93
 ☐9 Don't know/No answer →Skip to Q.93

(IF REPUBLICAN OR DEMOCRAT) Would you call yourself a strong (PARTY CHOSEN) or a not very strong (PARTY CHOSEN)?

 ☐1 Strong   (64)
 ☐2 Not very strong
 ☐9 Can't decide how strong/No answer

(IF INDEPENDENT) Do you think of yourself as closer to the Republican or to the Democratic party?

 ☐1 Closer to the Republicans   (65)
 ☐2 Closer to the Democrats
 ☐3 Neither/Can't decide
 ☐9 No answer

92. (If DEMOCRAT ask): Have you ever considered yourself a Republican?

    (If REPUBLICAN ask): Have you ever considered yourself a Democrat?

    (If INDEPENDENT ask): Have you ever considered yourself
                           a Democrat or a Republican?

    ☐1 Formerly Democrat   } Ask Q.92a below   (66)
    ☐2 Formerly Republican }
    ☐3 Never considered self other party/Never changed

    ☐9 Don't Know/No Answer

a. (If formerly DEMOCRAT or REPUBLICAN, ask): When did you switch
    from being a . . . . (FORMER PARTY) to a . . . . (PRESENT PARTY OR
    INDEPENDENT) -- was it within the last two years, the last four years,
    the last ten years, or longer ago than that?

    ☐1 Last two years   (67)
    ☐2 Last four years
    ☐3 Last ten years
    ☐4 Before that

    ☐9 Don't Know/No Answer

93. What was the last grade of school you attended? (DO NOT READ LIST)

    ☐1 Eighth Grade or Less   (68)
    ☐2 Some High School
    ☐3 High School Graduate
    ☐4 Some College -- does not include technical or vocational school
    ☐5 College Graduate
    ☐6 Graduate School

    ☐9 No Answer

94. Are you currently married, widowed, divorced, separated, or single?

    ☐1 Married   (69)
    ☐2 Widowed
    ☐3 Divorced
    ☐4 Separated
    ☐5 Single

    ☐9 No Answer

95. What is your religious preference? Is it Protestant, Catholic,
    Jewish, some other religion, or no religion?

    ☐1 Protestant   (70)
    ☐2 Catholic
    ☐3 Jewish
    ☐4 Other
    ☐5 No Religion

    ☐9 No Answer

96. In what year were you born? _____ (71-72)

☐77 Refused/No Answer

97. Sex: ☐1 Male ☐2 Female ☐9 No Answer (73)

98. Do you own your own home?

☐1 Yes ☐2 No ☐9 No Answer (74)

99. Was your total family income last year before taxes over or under $11,000?

(If under $11,000): Is it over or under $6,000

(If over $11,000): Is it over or under $16,000?

☐ Under $11,000 →☐1 Under $6,000 (75)
  →☐2 Over $6,000

OR,

☐ Over $11,000 →☐3 Under $16,000
  →☐4 Over $16,000

☐9 Refused/No Answer

100. What race do you consider yourself?

☐1 White (76)
☐2 Black
☐3 Other:_____(Specify)
☐9 No Answer

101. (Ask only if Black): Some people think that American blacks would be better off if they stuck together and worked to solve their common problems. Others feel that the average black would be better off if he made greater efforts to get ahead on his own. Which do you think -- should blacks stick together or should they try harder to get ahead on their own?

☐1 Should stick together (77)
☐2 Should try harder to get ahead on their own
☐3 Depends
☐9 Don't Know/No Answer

Thank you very much. Your answers have been very helpful.

Interviewer:
```
Record from Computer Dialing Sheet:
   Time Net #: _____                    (78-79)
   Sample Page #: _____
```

80-2

-21-

Index